The *Data*
Coach's Guide
to Improving Learning
for All Students

To Our Families

The *Data Coach's Guide*

to Improving Learning
for All Students

*Unleashing the Power
of Collaborative Inquiry*

Nancy Love • Katherine E. Stiles
Susan Mundry • Kathryn DiRanna
Foreword by Ruth Johnson

A JOINT PUBLICATION

CORWIN PRESS
A SAGE Company
Thousand Oaks, CA 91320

T E R C

RBT

WestEd

This material is based on work supported by the National Science Foundation under Grant No. ESI-0221415. Any opinions, findings, and conclusions or recommendations expressed in this material are those of the author(s) and do not necessarily reflect the views of the National Science Foundation.

For information:

Corwin Press
A SAGE Company
2455 Teller Road
Thousand Oaks, California 91320
www.corwinpress.com

SAGE India Pvt. Ltd.
B 1/I 1 Mohan Cooperative Industrial Area
Mathura Road, New Delhi 110 044
India

SAGE Ltd.
1 Oliver's Yard
55 City Road
London EC1Y 1SP
United Kingdom

SAGE Asia-Pacific Pte. Ltd.
33 Pekin Street #02–01
Far East Square
Singapore 048763

Printed in the United States of America.

Library of Congress Cataloging-in-Publication Data

The data coach's guide to improving learning for all students: unleashing the power of collaborative inquiry/by Nancy Love . . . [et al.].
    p. cm.
Includes bibliographical references and index.
ISBN 978-1-4129-5000-8 (cloth w/cd)
ISBN 978-1-4129-5001-5 (paper w/cd)
  1. Educational statistics. 2. Academic achievement—Data processing. 3. Curriculum planning—Data processing. 4. School improvement programs—Data processing. I. Love, Nancy.

LB2846.D318 2008
370.2'1—dc22   2007029949

This book is printed on acid-free paper.

08 09 10 11 10 9 8 7 6 5 4 3 2

Acquisitions Editor:	Rachel Livsey
Managing Editor:	Dan Alpert
Editorial Assistants:	Phyllis Cappello, Tatiana Richards
Production Editor:	Cassandra Margaret Seibel
Copy Editor:	Teresa Wilson
Typesetter:	C&M Digitals (P) Ltd.
Proofreader:	Taryn Bigelow
Indexer:	Sheila Bodell
Cover Designer:	Scott Van Atta

Contents

Book

Contents

CD-ROM

Foreword

Unleashing the Power of Collaborative Inquiry

Ruth Johnson

This book offers a compelling message of hope and resolve. Love, Stiles, Mundry, and DiRanna's three-year journey in a multiplicity of diverse, underperforming, high-poverty schools across the nation has resulted in a treasure chest of knowledge and experiences about how to professionally develop Data Coaches in ways that benefit some of our most underserved students.

Data analyses and use in schools and districts is generally limited to test scores. Teachers and principals rarely use data to understand the complexity of issues related to underachievement. The authors of *The Data Coach's Guide to Improving Learning for All Students: Unleashing the Power of Collaborative Inquiry* recognize that simply telling busy school professionals that data helps to solve complex problems is insufficient and shortsighted. From the outset, the authors make clear that achievement gaps are not inevitable or immutable, and then they proceed to set forth data strategies that promise to close achievement gaps. They challenge the notion that underachievement rests only on the backs of students and their families. In its place, they have crafted a book that provides a model for professional development that counters notions of *blame the victim*. The text offers ways to assist schools to build cultures of inquiry that focus on equitable outcomes for students through the use of Data Coaches. The focus of the book is on preparing Data Coaches to work in diverse settings in a variety of our nation's schools.

During the three-year grant period of the Using Data Project, the authors gained valuable insights on how to prepare Data Coaches to facilitate school inquiries. The work was based in project schools that served many African American, Latino/a, Native American, and students living in poverty. Through these field experiences, they learned critical lessons about leveraging data to raise student achievement, and they share an enormous amount of information. This book's strategy of professionally developing Data Coaches is rooted in a goal of building institutional knowledge about conducting equitable inquiries. Educators who desire broad-scale improvement in student outcomes must embark on a challenging process of changing whole systems—and the cultures within them. The barriers to change—and the conditions that must be created to allow for change to take hold—are significant. But what must give us hope is that many schools have risen and continue to rise to these challenges, using data inquiries at every stage to inform their direction.

Collaborative inquiry is an approach that has the potential to authentically embrace and use the voices of the school community for improvement. This requires coaches to have skills for using data and, more important, the skills and dispositions to implement an equity agenda through the school communities' use of data. The authors understand the power of data and how it leads to deeper levels of discovery—to see familiar things as you have never seen them before—and then to move to the next step when warranted, using the information to challenge and transform the status quo. This book aims to prepare Data Coaches who can work along with others to uncover practices that disenfranchise children and to use this information to change practice. These coaches must be ones who have the need to know about information that can be used for positive change.

The facilitation process set forth in this book engages potential Data Coaches in conducting culturally responsive inquiries. The authors discuss the critical issues that schools must surmount in order to turn around low-performing schools. This requires that coaches have an understanding of the processes needed to engage professionals in sensitive conversations and to raise issues about information that is often not uncovered and often not spoken about in schools. It requires coaches to have the skills to facilitate uncomfortable situations. It requires coaches who know how to deal with confrontations and disparate belief systems. This book provides many of the tools that coaches will need in these situations. The authors provide background literature, rich real-life case studies, and templates to guide activities. A very useful CD-ROM accompanies the text. This provides users with protocols, templates, PowerPoint slides, handouts, and a comprehensive Toolkit.

The Data Coach's Guide to Improving Learning for All Students: Unleashing the Power of Collaborative Inquiry provides information for a wide range of audiences. It offers a variety of templates, literature, and processes for professional development. In the end, we know that this book in and of itself cannot create equitable schools. Merely learning to manipulate information and being trained in how to facilitate collaborative inquiry can result in a series of symbolic events if one does not bring the vision, passion, and a belief about what is possible for all children. What this book can do is provide powerful resources to those who have the belief, passion, and desire for rich resources for implementing collaborative data inquiries in schools and districts.

Acknowledgments

At times our own light goes out and is rekindled by a spark from another person. Each of us has cause to think with deep gratitude of those who have lighted the flame within us.

—Albert Einstein

The authors are deeply grateful for the many people who have kindled and rekindled the flame within us to create this book. First, we want to acknowledge the dedicated educators who brought the ideas in this book to life in their Data Teams, schools, and classrooms and joined us in cocreating the Using Data Process of Collaborative Inquiry. Nothing is more inspiring than to see our theory of action actually improving results for students. For that, we have the administrators and teachers in schools participating in the Using Data Project to thank and the following collaborators, who worked at our side to unleash the power of collaborative inquiry in these schools: the Arizona Rural Systemic Initiative at the American Indian Programs at Arizona State University Polytechnic in Mesa, including Program Manager Karen Brighton, Project Director Dorthea Litson, and field staff and consultants Eileen Armelin, Yvonne Billingsley, Rebecca Bogert, Linda Fulmore, Rea Goklish, Laura Laughran, Nelson Letts, Brownie Lindner, Kristen Moorhead, Pam Patina, Virgil Prokopich, Nora Ramirez, and LaVonne Riggs; the Clark County School District, Las Vegas, Nevada, and the Local Systemic Change Initiative, the Mathematics and Science Enhancement (MASE), K–5 Using Technology Project, including coordinator of K–5 mathematics and science Thelma Davis, director of K–12 mathematics, science, and instructional technology Kristy Falba, and project facilitators Abby Burke, Lori Fulton, Laura MacDonald, Steve Piccininni, and Linda Role; the Stark County Mathematics and Science Partnership, Canton, Ohio, including Principal Investigator Mike Bayer, Co-PIs Melissa Marconi, Dr. Jane Dessecker, and Richard Dinko, and Teacher Coaches Leslie Austin, Nancy Baker Cazan, Pam Bernabei-Rorrer, Bill Carli, Patty Carmola, Mike Conkle, Dale Gallucci, Amy Gasser, Sharon Kessler, JoMarie Kutscher, Chad Merritt, Amy Miller, Debbie Poland, Mary Beth Stefanko, Ann Wacker, Kristy Welsh, and Wendy Williams; Johnson County Schools, Tennessee, Director of Instruction Dr. David Timbs; and the K–12 Science Curriculum Dissemination Center at EDC with Barbara Berns, Director. Many of the vignettes and examples in this book come directly from our experiences working with these schools and projects over the last four years.

Many collaborators brought their own light to this book by contributing to its writing: Jennifer Unger, codeveloper of the Using Data Online Course, wrote several of the data literacy tools, helped to shape Task 5, worked on the glossary, and created many of the data examples. Lori Fulton, Thelma Davis, Janet Dukes, Greg Gusmerotti, and Joan Lombard documented their own collaborative inquiry in the Clark County case study. WestEd's K–12 Alliance Regional Directors Diane Carnahan, Karen Cerwin, Kathryn Schulz, Jody Skidmore Sherriff, Rita Starnes, and Jo Topps helped to write the Toolkit. Finally, we are grateful to Pam Bernabei-Rorrer and Kristy Welsh, who provided us with images of collaborative inquiry in action through the stories and examples they wrote.

Developing this work has opened our eyes to issues of race, class, and culture and the importance of cultural proficiency to the Using Data Process, thanks to the generosity, humanity, and wisdom of our special advisers, Ruth Johnson, Brenda CampbellJones, Franklin CampbellJones, and Kimberly Kinsler. John Zuman and Madga Raupp of the Intercultural Center for Research in Education, as external evaluators, helped us to draw rich lessons from our experiences and to use data ourselves to monitor our own results, as did our formative evaluator, Elizabeth Rowe of TERC.

We also want to thank our national field-test group members, who gave us the gift of their candid feedback and ignited the Using Data Process in many schools across the country: Dona Apple, Angelicque Tucker Blackmon, Carol Blunt-White, Deb Chittenden, Aileen Dickey, Karen Falkenberg, Limmie Flowers, Marla Gardner, Catherine Hill, Carolyn Karatzas, Terry Lashley, Virginia Love, Gary Money, Linda Mooney, Diane Naghi, Stacy Poor, Judith Powers, Yvette Barnes Robinson, Carol Ross, Aminata Umoja, Colleen Wallace, Jackie Walsh, and Helen Weingart. Special thanks also to Sue Card, our former Using Data colleague, and Jeanette Millard, project consultant, for their early contributions to this work. For advice on statistics, we thank William Finzer, Harold McWilliams, Andee Rubin, and Richard Schaefer. For help with mathematics and science content, we extend our appreciation to Myriam Steinback and Page Keeley.

We are filled with gratitude to a few individuals who did the arduous and painstaking work of turning our words-on-a-page into a coherent, beautifully formatted, and publishable manuscript. Peggy Liversidge pored over every word, figure, table, graph, and chart, and scrubbed our inordinately complicated manuscript clean. Much more than a copy editor, she is the best partner to the finish line any authors could wish for. In record time, our graphic designer, Valerie Martin, graced our book with her artistry and did so with infinite patience and good spirits. Early on, Bryce Flynn and Jim Caruso contributed to the PowerPoint slides. Deanna Maier acquired the multitude of permissions needed for this book with the competence and efficiency that are her trademark. Maya Lagu provided able and enthusiastic assistance in production.

Dennis Bartels, Mark Kaufman, and Diana Nunnaley at TERC sparked us with their faith in this work, going back more than 10 years, and sustained us with their ongoing support. The National Science Foundation and Program Officer Janice Earle made this book possible with their financial support. We are also grateful to our publisher, Corwin Press, and our supportive, patient, and flexible acquisitions editors Rachel Livsey and Dan Alpert. Thanks to Corwin Press's reviewers. Nancy also wishes to acknowledge her coach, Bill Rentz, of Breakthrough Enterprises. All of us thank our families and colleagues, who continue to support us through the impossible demands so that we can do the work we love. Finally, we honor the memory of Susan Loucks-Horsley, to whom we owe the greatest debt of gratitude for letting us know we had the spark inside us all along.

PUBLISHER'S ACKNOWLEDGMENTS

Corwin Press would like to acknowledge the following reviewers:

Brenda CampbellJones, PhD
CampbellJones & Associates
Laurel, MD

Franklin CampbellJones, EdD
CampbellJones & Associates
Laurel, MD

Mike Greenwood
Windsor Public Schools
Windsor, CT

Lori L. Grossman
Instructional Coordinator
Houston Independent School District
Houston, TX

Bill Nave, EdD
Research and Evaluation Consultant
Winthrop, ME

Aminata Umoja
Founder, Umoja Consulting LLC
Atlanta, GA

About the Authors

 **Nancy Love** is director of program development at Research for Better Teaching in Acton, Massachusetts, where she leads this education consulting group's research and development. She is the former director of the Using Data Project, a collaboration between TERC and WestEd, where she led the development of a comprehensive professional development program to improve teaching and learning through effective and collaborative use of school data. This program has produced significant gains in student achievement as well as increased collaboration and data use in schools across the country. Love has authored several books and articles on data use, including *Using Data/Getting Results: A Practical Guide to School Improvement in Mathematics and Science* (2002) and *Global Perspectives for Local Action: Using TIMSS to Improve U.S. Mathematics and Science Education* (2001) with Susan Mundry. She is also well known for her work in professional development as a seasoned and highly engaging presenter and author of articles and books, including *Designing Professional Development for Teachers of Science and Mathematics* (2nd ed., 2003) with Susan Loucks-Horsley, Katherine E. Stiles, Susan Mundry, and Peter Hewson. In 2006, she was awarded the prestigious Susan Loucks-Horsley Award from the National Staff Development Council in recognition of her significant national contribution to the field of staff development and to the efficacy of others.

 **Katherine E. Stiles** is a project director and senior program associate at WestEd. She is codirector of WestEd's National Academy for Science and Mathematics Education Leadership and several other projects designed to enhance the knowledge and skills of leaders. She is coauthor of books and articles focused on professional development and leadership, including *Designing Professional Development for Teachers of Science and Mathematics* (2003) and *Leading Every Day: 124 Actions for Effective Leadership* (2005), which received the National Staff Development Council's 2003 Outstanding Book of the Year Award for its first edition (2002). She is also the lead author of the *Facilitator's Guide to Leading Every Day* (2006). In 2002, Katherine was awarded the Paul D. Hood Award for Distinguished Contribution to the Field from WestEd. As a senior staff member on the Using Data Project, a collaboration between TERC and WestEd, she codeveloped the professional development program and provided technical assistance to participating schools in Ohio and Arizona as they engaged in collaborative inquiry into data. Katherine has more than 10 years of experience evaluating science education and professional development programs, including NSF-funded Local Systemic Change projects and State

Systemic Initiatives, California-funded MSP projects, technology-based science education programs, and science curriculum development projects. Prior to joining WestEd in 1995, Katherine worked at the National Science Resources Center in Washington DC as a science curriculum developer and authored four curriculum units for the *Science and Technology for Children* program. With degrees in psychology, special education, and education, and teaching experience in elementary programs, she brings 20 years of experience to her current work in science and mathematics education and professional development.

Susan Mundry is associate director of mathematics, science, and technology programs at WestEd. She directs national projects focused on developing leadership in education and improving professional development programs. Susan codirects the National Academy for Science and Mathematics Education Leadership and is principal investigator for a National Science Foundation project developing instructional materials for leaders in education. She has contributed to numerous publications on leadership and teacher development. She coauthored the best-selling book *Designing Effective Professional Development for Teachers of Science and Mathematics*, as well as *Working Toward a Continuum of Professional Learning Experiences for Teachers of Science and Mathematics: Designing Successful Professional Meetings and Conferences in Education* and *Global Perspectives for Local Action: Using TIMSS to Improve U.S. Mathematics and Science*. Susan coauthored the toolkit *Teachers as Learners*, a videotape collection of 18 professional development programs, a guidebook, and Web site activities that illustrate diverse strategies for teacher learning.

Susan coauthored the award-winning book *Leading Every Day*, which was named the National Staff Development Council's 2003 Book of the Year. Prior to joining WestEd, she served in many roles, from staff developer to associate director, at The NETWORK, Inc., a research and development organization focused on organizational change and dissemination of effective practice. There, she developed two popular simulation games on organizational change: *Making Change for School Improvement* and *Systems Thinking/Systems Changing*. Susan was the recipient of the National Staff Development Council's annual Susan Loucks-Horsley Award for her distinguished contribution to the field of professional development. She also was recognized with WestEd's Paul D. Hood Award for her contributions to the field of education in 2002 and again in 2006. Susan is a graduate of the University of Massachusetts–Amherst and Boston University and lives in Newburyport, Massachusetts.

Kathryn DiRanna is the statewide director of WestEd's K–12 Alliance, which focuses on school- and department-wide change by providing programs that address content, instructional strategies, assessment, and leadership. She has served as a principal investigator or project director for several NSF-funded projects, including the California Systemic Initiative, the Center for the Assessment and Evaluation of Student Learning (CAESL), and Science Partnerships for Articulation and Networking (SPAN). For the past 20 years, Kathryn has helped shape California's science education programs by creating strategic alliances between educational institutions and programs, as well as between business and education. On the national level, Kathryn served as the mentor coordinator for the National Academy of Science and Mathematics Education Leadership, the co–project director for the BSCS/WestEd National Academy for Curriculum Leadership, and a senior staff member and codeveloper of the Using Data Project's professional development program, a collaboration between TERC and WestEd. She has been a featured speaker at state and national conferences and served as the program coordinator for NSTA's 2006 national convention. Kathryn received the California Science Teachers Association's Margaret Nicholson Award for Distinguished Service to Science Education and the Paul D. Hood Award from WestEd for distinguished service to the field.

Introduction

Despite endless pessimistic messages about the state of public education, the authors of this book find much to celebrate. As staff of the National Science Foundation–supported Using Data Project, we have worked with schools that are serving children who are among the poorest in this country—students from Native American reservations in Arizona, the mountains of Appalachia in Tennessee, and large and mid-size urban centers in the Midwest and West. A few years ago, some of these students were simply passing time in school with "word search" puzzles or other time fillers; some were permanently tracked in an educational system that doled out uninspired, repetitive curriculum. Some of the schools in which we worked had not one single student pass the state test, and the vast majority were performing at the lowest proficiency level.

Today, students in these schools have a more rigorous curriculum, and they are reaching proficiency on assessments in record numbers. Schools implementing the Using Data Process narrowed the achievement gaps between students with exceptional needs and general education students in all content areas and grade levels; tripled the percentage of African Americans proficient in middle school mathematics; demonstrated significant and steady gains in mathematics in elementary, middle, and high schools; and cut the failure rate of Native American children in half. These schools are not only experiencing significant and continuous gains in local and state assessments in mathematics, science, and reading, but also changing their culture. Our project evaluators documented increased collaboration and reflection on practice among teachers; frequent and in-depth use of multiple data sources, including high-stakes, formative, and benchmark assessments as well as data about practice; and instructional improvement (Zuman, 2006).

CATCH THE SPIRIT OF SUCCESS

These and other improving schools give us hope. They dispel the myth that some students cannot learn; they inspire us to even greater levels of commitment and action to take on the biggest problems that schools face: cultures rife with resignation, isolation, stagnation, and mistrust; racist and classist attitudes and practices that result in failure to see and serve students who do not look or act like members of the dominant culture; outdated and inexcusable instructional practices; teachers who are not as well prepared as they need to be to teach to rigorous content standards; and ineffective and dangerous uses of student data. With our collective decades of work in school improvement, the authors do not underestimate the grip these problems have on schools' and educators' spirits. Yet we have witnessed every one of these seemingly insurmountable barriers begin to fall away when school teams learn to work together and use data and research to identify and tackle the causes of student

1

failure. We know it can be done. We wrote this book to make the tools and the process these improving schools used available to every school seeking to enhance learning and build professional culture. We hope their success will inspire you to use collaborative inquiry to achieve similar or even greater success in your own schools.

HOW THIS BOOK CAME ABOUT

Beginning in 2003, the Using Data Project, a collaboration between TERC and WestEd, set out to develop, pilot, and field-test a program to provide educators with the skills, knowledge, and dispositions to put school data to work to improve teaching and learning and close achievement gaps. The goal of the project was to prepare education professionals to serve as Data Coaches to lead a process of collaborative inquiry with school-based teams and to influence the culture of schools to be one in which data are used continuously, collaboratively, and effectively to improve teaching and learning. The project had education partners who were instrumental in influencing and shaping the Using Data Process, including Clark County School District (Las Vegas, Nevada) in collaboration with their Local Systemic Change Initiative, Mathematics and Science Education (MASE); several schools serving primarily Native American children on reservations in Arizona in collaboration with the Arizona Rural Systemic Initiative, based at the American Indian Programs at Arizona State University Polytechnic in Mesa, Arizona; and the Stark County Mathematics and Science Partnership, where we focused on seven urban school districts in the Canton, Ohio, area.

In addition, the project conducted two national field tests, one in collaboration with the Education Development Center's K–12 Science Curriculum Dissemination Center. Field-testers gave us immediate feedback on the materials and the professional development and, in several cases, took the materials and implemented them in schools in which they were working, including schools in Los Angeles, California; Johnson County, Tennessee; and Colorado Springs, Colorado. Although our effort focused on mathematics and science improvement, schools quickly applied the process to all other content areas, demonstrating that the Using Data Process is generic and broadly applicable.

Through the rich experiences and work with our partner schools, the project gleaned a wealth of technical and practical knowledge about how to prepare Data Coaches to work with Data Teams in diverse settings, from large urban areas to mid-size cities to small rural schools. This book is the product of that work. It provides the knowledge and tools produced by the Using Data Project, including how to

- design, implement, and sustain a districtwide (or projectwide) program of continuous improvement in diverse settings;
- prepare Data Coaches to lead Data Teams in collaborative inquiry and high-capacity uses of data;
- keep the focus on equity and closing achievement gaps;
- increase the power, focus, and effectiveness of professional communities;
- use data as a catalyst to powerful conversations about race/ethnicity, class, educational status, gender, and language differences;
- get staff excited about using data regularly and collaboratively;
- apply robust tools for making sense of data; and
- connect data use to instructional improvement and learning results.

PURPOSE OF THE BOOK

Our first driving purpose for this book is to contribute to dramatic and permanent improvement in the way schools go about their business so that they make a greater positive difference in students' lives. Through a combination of information (skill building and knowledge) and inspiration (will building), we intend for this book to guide educational leaders in unleashing the power of collaborative inquiry to improve schools.

What ignites the Using Data Process is *will*—the appetite, passion, choice, and determination to serve every child as if he or she were our own, a mindfulness of the awesome influence we have in the students' lives that we touch, and a commitment to use that influence to produce the best possible results for every one of them. So a second purpose of this book is to strengthen your resolve and the resolve of others with whom you work to do whatever it takes to educate every student to the peak of his or her capacities. We provide tools and processes for opening up dialogue about the assumptions that underlie interpretations of the data, gaining clarity about the Data Team's vision and purpose, shifting conversations away from blame and toward possibility, and staying focused on what is most important—the actions we can take to improve students' learning and the quality of their lives.

Author and cultural proficiency expert Franklin CampbellJones says, "Get ethical before you get technical" (personal communication, December 10, 2005). This book intends to do both. "School improvement" without will and moral purpose—without a genuine commitment to all students—is an empty exercise in compliance that, in our experience, can do more harm than good. The authors have seen educators use data to "more accurately" track students, further widening the opportunity-to-learn gap. In response to achievement gaps, one school mandated lunchtime tutoring for all African American students—regardless of whether or not they failed the state test (Confrey & Makar, 2005). Avoiding these and other data-based disasters is not a technical matter. It is an ethical matter that begins with will, passion, and determination.

Our third purpose is to "get technical"—to build skills and knowledge about how to lead a process of collaborative inquiry with school-based Data Teams and to influence the culture of schools to be one in which data are used continuously, collaboratively, and effectively to improve teaching and learning. In the last few years, educators have been called upon to do work they have never done before and were, in most cases, never prepared to do, including

- work productively in professional learning communities,
- apply principles of cultural proficiency to data use and school improvement,
- understand and draw sound inferences from a variety of different kinds of data,
- accurately identify root causes of problems the data surface,
- implement research-based instructional improvements linked to goals, and
- monitor interim and long-term progress toward goals.

This book addresses this capacity crisis by providing you with detailed and technical guidance in how to engage in systematic and continuous improvement. You will learn how to move schools away from unproductive data practices and toward high-capacity uses of data that are built on a strong foundation of data literacy and collaborative inquiry knowledge, skills, and dispositions as well as a spiritual and moral commitment to serve each and every student.

AUDIENCE

This book is for anyone who wants to make and sustain change in schools. It is, of course, primarily for those who will serve as Data Coaches with responsibility for facilitating Data Teams. The book is also for school and district administrators, educational improvement project staff, education service center staff, foundations concerned with education, state department of education personnel, parent and community organizations, and others who are concerned about building capacity and systems for sustaining improvement in student learning. Finally, it is for all teachers, who can use the process and tools themselves and provide leadership in their buildings to enhance results for students.

ASSUMPTIONS

The Using Data Process places a major emphasis on surfacing and engaging in dialogue about assumptions. Therefore, an introduction to this book would not be complete without a discussion of the assumptions the authors held as we developed the entire Using Data Process. Please use these as a catalyst to clarify your thinking as well as for dialogue with your Data Teams.

Assumption 1: Making significant progress in improving student learning and closing achievement gaps is a moral responsibility and a real possibility in a relatively short amount of time—two to five years. It is not children's poverty or race or ethnic background that stands in the way of achievement; it is school practices and policies and the beliefs that underlie them that pose the biggest obstacles.

Federal and state policies will come and go. But one moral imperative is abiding. As Michael Fullan (1993) reminds us, "You can't mandate what matters" (p. 21). And what matters is educators' deep responsibility for the learning of every child. This assumption implies a shift from a compliance mentality—a sense of external accountability, something someone is making us do—to a sense of internal and collective responsibility. It also reflects the authors' belief that it is impossible to use data as a lever for change without talking about race, class, and culture and our beliefs about the capabilities of children. It is the silence about these issues that has kept us from confronting problems and taking action.

The potential to dramatically improve the learning of traditionally underserved students has been demonstrated time and again. The Using Data Project schools serving African American, Latino/a, Native American, and poor students significantly improved student achievement within three years (Zuman, 2006). The Education Trust database Dispelling the Myth contains the data on thousands of schools that are serving students living in poverty and from diverse racial and ethnic backgrounds, yet are achieving at high levels (Education Trust, 2003). Glenn Singleton and Curtis Linton (2006), in their book *Courageous Conversations About Race*, report on the Del Roble Elementary School in Oak Grove, California, which dramatically accelerated the progress toward mastery of standards of African American and Latino/a students in a year's time by "acknowledging that racial biases existed in their own work and that these biases made it difficult for some student of color groups to succeed" and then taking corrective action (p. 36).

Improvement strategies such as aligning curriculum to rigorous standards, frequently monitoring student progress, organizing schools to engage in short cycles of collaborative inquiry, providing professional development linked to student goals, and offering immediate extra help for students who need it—many of which can happen quickly—were implemented in the Using Data field-test sites and paid off with increased student-learning gains.

> *To examine one's assumptions and beliefs about educating children—in particular, given the history of our country, African American children—is crucial to becoming a successful teacher of Black children.*
>
> —CampbellJones and
> CampbellJones, 2002, p. 136

Assumption 2: Data have no meaning. Meaning is imposed through interpretation. Frames of reference, the way we see the world, influence the meaning we derive from data. Effective data users become aware of and critically examine their frames of reference and assumptions (Wellman & Lipton, 2004, pp. ix–xi). Conversely, data themselves can also be a catalyst to questioning assumptions and changing practices based on new ways of thinking.

This assumption is closely related to the first and is why we place so much emphasis on surfacing assumptions, particularly assumptions about children and their capabilities and beliefs about teaching and learning. If one holds the view that whether students learn is the student's responsibility and not that of the teacher, one might then look at a student's poor performance on assessments and conclude that it is entirely the student's fault. There is nothing to be done to improve teaching. If one believes that African American students are not as capable as White students, then data that reveal an achievement gap between these groups does nothing but confirm that belief. The reaction is complacency or resignation. Beliefs about teaching also profoundly influence data interpretation. For example, one teacher believes that students learn best when they are actively constructing their own meaning. Another believes that skill building and practice and teacher talk are how students learn. When examining student work that reveals a student's confusion, these two teachers will react very differently.

On the other hand, when one is open to critically examining assumptions, data can be a catalyst to discarding old frames of reference and embracing new ones. We have seen educators in our project look at disaggregated student-learning data and become outraged by inequities that they had not been aware of before. Simply examining data about schools that were closing achievement gaps has caused others to question their belief that these gaps are inevitable. When teachers observed that teaching in a new way actually reached more students, they changed their assumptions about teaching and learning. Through their collaborative inquiry, many Data Team members threw out unproductive, blame-the-victim explanations of students' poor performance and shifted the focus to instruction.

Assumption 3: Collaborative inquiry—a process where teachers construct their understanding of student-learning problems and invent and test out solutions together through rigorous and frequent use of data and reflective dialogue—unleashes the resourcefulness and creativity to continuously improve instruction and student learning.

Teachers possess tremendous knowledge, skill, and experience. Collaborative inquiry creates a structure for them to share that expertise with each other, discover what they are doing that is working and do more of it, and confront what isn't working and change it. When teachers generate their own questions, engage in dialogue, and make sense of data, they develop a much deeper understanding of what is going on relative to student learning. They develop ownership of the problems that surface, seek out research and information on best practices, and adopt or invent and implement the solutions they generate. The research base on the link between collaborative, reflective practice of teachers and student learning is well established (Little, 1990; Louis, Kruse, & Marks, 1996; McLaughlin & Talbert, 2001). When teachers engage in ongoing collaborative inquiry focused on teaching and learning and making effective use of data, they improve results for students.

Assumption 4: A school culture characterized by collective responsibility for student learning, commitment to equity, and trust is the foundation for collaborative inquiry. In the absence of such a culture, schools may be unable to respond effectively to the data they have.

This assumption is based on a dual meaning of the word responsibility. As in our first assumption, responsibility implies the moral imperative. But it also holds another meaning, which is, quite literally, the ability to respond: "response-ability" (Wellman & Lipton, 2004). Long before state tests, plenty of data were available to let us know some students were not learning—students slumping down in their seats; going through day after day of school without being engaged; having poor grades, poor attendance and high dropout rates. However, in the absence of a collaborative culture where everyone takes responsibility and is committed to improving student learning, educators literally could not respond to the data. Schools that have "response-ability" do not leave student learning to chance. As Rick DuFour and his colleagues (2004) describe it, "They create a schoolwide system of interventions that provides all students with additional time and support when they experience initial difficulty in their learning" (p. 7). Collaborative schools are organized in grade-level or course- or subject-based teams where this response-ability is enacted as part of the daily work of teachers.

A hallmark of such a high-performing culture is a commitment to equity. Singleton and Linton (2006) define educational equity as "raising the achievement of all students while narrowing the gap between the highest- and lowest-performing students and eliminating the racial predictability and disproportionality of which student groups occupy the highest and lowest achievement categories" (p. 46). Equity does not mean that all students receive an equal level of resources and support, but that those of the greatest need receive the level of support they need to succeed.

A collaborative community committed to equity requires a high level of trust. In high-functioning cultures, educators trust each other enough to discuss "undiscussables" such as race, reveal their own practice and mistakes, root for one another, and face together the brutal facts that data often reveal (Barth, 2006). For all of these reasons, districts that make the most of their investment into data management systems place an equal or greater priority in strengthening school cultures and the ability to respond to the data.

Assumption 5: Using data itself does not improve teaching. Improved teaching comes about when teachers implement sound teaching practices grounded in cultural proficiency—understanding and respect for their students' cultures—and a thorough understanding of the subject matter and how to teach it, including understanding student thinking and ways of making content accessible to all students.

It is easy to get swept away in the data-driven mania provoked by federal and state education accountability policies, where data can sometimes seem to be an end in themselves. But test results, lists of "failing" schools, bar graphs, tables, proficiency levels, even student work do nothing by themselves to improve teaching unless they spark powerful dialogue and changes in practice. For example, it doesn't take hours of data analysis to discover that students struggle with solving nonroutine mathematics problems or reading informational text. But talking about and learning more and more about what to *do* about those problems does take time and is where teams gain momentum for instructional improvement.

Questions like the following merit as much time in Data Team meetings as does the actual data analysis:

Who among us is having success and what are they doing?

What does research say about how students learn this content or what typical misconceptions they struggle with?

What have other schools done to solve this problem?

What would a culturally proficient approach to this content look like? What content knowledge and pedagogical content knowledge will strengthen our ability to teach this content? What does the research base on effective teaching tell us?

What kind of professional development will help us learn these skills and knowledge?

The data are just the tip of the iceberg, alerting us to problem areas and reminding us that what lies beneath is what counts—the curriculum, instruction, assessment, and professional development practices that will improve student learning. Data use is not a substitute for the hard work of improving instruction. Throughout the Using Data Process, Data Teams are guided to draw on and add to the rich knowledge base about teaching and learning.

> *Leaders matter. Therefore significant change in organizations begins with significant changes to what leaders think (depth of understanding and beliefs), say (the speech forms we use and the content of our speech), and do (a continuous flow of powerful actions within a culture of interpersonal accountability).*
>
> —Sparks, 2005, p. xii

Assumption 6: Every member of a collaborative school community can act as a leader, dramatically impacting the quality of relationships, the school culture, and student learning.

The Using Data Process supports and promotes distributed leadership, where all staff members take full responsibility and do their parts to get the job—academic success for all students—done. Marzano, Waters, and McNulty (2005) identified 21 leadership behaviors correlated with student academic achievement. Virtually all of these 21 responsibilities, which include celebrating accomplishments, challenging the status quo, fostering shared beliefs and community, staying focused on goals, communicating ideas and beliefs, actively engaging others in decision making and instructional improvement, and fostering strong relationships, are functions of Data Coaches and Data Team members as well as of school and district administrators. In particular, data use is no longer a specialty of the assessment or central office or the principal. Everyone in the school understands and uses data in ways that contribute to instructional improvement.

Becoming a Data Coach and building Data Teams is all about developing the ability to think, speak, and act differently—to act as courageous leaders. Educators we work with often ask us, "How do we deal with resignation in our schools?" or "How do we get more people to believe that all students can learn?" One answer is to be full of possibility yourself, to frequently, succinctly, and clearly articulate what you believe, and to consistently act on those beliefs. We have seen Data Teams shift their direction completely when one team member took a clear stand against tracking students and provided evidence of its damaging effects. In Johnson County, Tennessee, the former superintendent, Mrs. Minnie Miller, and other district leaders consistently communicated two messages: "the little engine that could" and "what is *is.*" Virtually everyone in the district knew what they meant: "All kids can, do, and will learn," and "stop focusing on what we have no control over." When asked to what they attributed their dramatic success—virtually closing the gap between students with exceptional needs and general education students in one year, in all grade levels and every content area—teachers and principals consistently reported that they were inspired by those two messages.

A WORD ABOUT OUR LANGUAGE

> *The historic legacy of education in America is rooted in acts of separation and inequality, and these attributes currently operate in the lexicon of the education profession.*
>
> —CampbellJones and
> CampbellJones, 2002, p. 135

In this book we avoid the terms "minority," "economically disadvantaged," and "culturally disadvantaged" because they reflect and reinforce stereotypes of those who are not White and middle class as "different" or "less than" (CampbellJones & CampbellJones, 2002; Lindsey, Nuri Robins, & Terrell, 2003). Even a seemingly benign term like "subgroup" connotes "less than" or "under." The term "achievement gap" communicates that African American, Latino/a, or Native American students do not achieve as well as White or Asian students, but ignores the legacy of racist practices that underlie this outcome. The achievement gap might better be called a "testing gap" or a "racial teaching gap." The very fact that we struggled as authors to find language that is both respectful and acknowledges the reality of race testifies to the grip that the language of oppression has on our vocabulary.

In this book, we use "groups" or "student populations" instead of "subgroups" to refer to the disaggregation of the total student population into groups based on race/ethnicity, language, economic status, gender, mobility (students moving from school to school), and educational status (students with exceptional needs and the general education population). We use the terms African American, Native American, Latino/a or Hispanic, and Asian, which, though imprecise, are used commonly in the equity literature and are generally, although not universally, preferred by members of those groups (Lindsey, Nuri Robins, & Terrell, 2003). (For more on identifying student groups, see Chapter 3, Task 2.) Although we are ambivalent about the term achievement gap for the reasons stated earlier, we use it to name the current reality with the caveat that it is important to examine what is in the gap—a long history of institutional racism in society as a whole, low expectations, overt and covert discrimination, and biased testing, to name just a few causes of the gap.

HOW TO USE THIS BOOK

Organization of the Book

This book is a guide to leading Data Teams. It provides step-by-step notes and tested tools for setting up and working with Data Teams. The print portion of this book is organized into seven chapters as outlined below.

Chapter 1: "The Power of Collaborative Inquiry" explains the rationale and theory of action that underlie the authors' approach to collaborative inquiry, summarizes results achieved, and introduces the Using Data Process of Collaborative Inquiry framework. Readers can use this chapter with parents, community, school boards, faculty, and Data Teams to build understanding and support for implementing collaborative inquiry.

Chapter 2: "Getting Organized for Collaborative Inquiry" provides guidance on how to establish the conditions needed for collaborative inquiry and to prepare Data Coaches. It describes the coach's role, knowledge, and skills. It also draws out lessons the authors have learned from implementing the Using Data Process in many sites. This chapter is especially relevant for district and school leaders who are planning for and supporting implementation of collaborative inquiry as well as for Data Coaches at the school, district, or multidistrict level.

Chapters 3, 4, 5, 6, and 7: These five chapters describe in detail how Data Coaches facilitate each of the components of collaborative inquiry. Each component is covered in one of the chapters and is broken down into a sequence of tasks as illustrated in the table below. Tasks are further broken down into a set of activities that Data Coaches carry out with their Data Teams. At the beginning of each task, you will find a Task-at-a-Glance table, summarizing the purposes and activities within that task. This is followed by Background Information for Data Coaches; directions for preparing for the task, including materials and data preparation; illustrative data for varied content areas and grade levels; and Data Coach Notes, detailed step-by-step procedures for conducting each activity in the task with a Data Team. Data Coach Notes embed directions for incorporating tools from the Toolkit into the task, so the reader does not have to jump to the Toolkit on the CD-ROM to follow the task (see CD-ROM Toolkit description below). You will also find short vignettes with examples of real or illustrative Data Teams and longer, real-life examples of Data Teams in action, often contributed by Data Coaches working in schools.

The table "Navigating Chapters 3–7" briefly describes the purpose of each of these chapters, the tasks included, and the types of data and research used.

Navigating Chapters 3–7

Chapter	Purpose
Chapter 3: "Building the Foundation," Tasks 1–4	Establish Data Teams; build commitment to the Using Data Process; use demographic data to learn about students, faculty, and the community; raise awareness of cultural proficiency; envision the school of our dreams

(Continued)

Navigating Chapters 3–7 (Continued)

Chapter	Purpose
Chapter 4: "Identifying a Student-Learning Problem," Tasks 5–12	Drill down into student-learning data, using multiple levels of state CRT data, student work, and local common assessments to pinpoint a student-learning problem and goal
Chapter 5: "Verifying Causes," Tasks 13–14	Use local data about practice, such as surveys, observations, and interview data, and relevant research to verify causes of an identified student-learning problem
Chapter 6: "Generating Solutions," Tasks 15–17	Use a logic-model process to identify outcomes aligned with strategies and monitoring plans to address the student-learning goal
Chapter 7: "Implementing, Monitoring, and Achieving Results," Tasks 18–19	Implement improvement plans and gather and monitor data on implementation and results; celebrate successes

Chapter 8: "Clark County, Nevada: Collaborative Inquiry in Action," written by practitioners, provides the reader with a vivid picture of how the process unfolded in one district and school—the challenges they faced and how they surmounted them. Learn how a district leader organized for collaborative inquiry at the district level. Then follow the Katz Elementary School Data Team as they build their foundation, identify a student-learning problem, verify causes, generate solutions, and achieve results in mathematics problem solving. While short vignettes are woven throughout the book, this is the one place you can go to see the whole process in action over three years, including commentary from the Data Coach (called a Project Facilitator in this case) and principal involved.

The **CD-ROM Toolkit Guide** is a directory to the 29 tools in the Toolkit located on the CD-ROM, including their purposes and the tasks in the Using Data Process in which they are used. An example of one tool, Introducing the Logic Model, is illustrated to show you what you will find on the CD-ROM. Use this guide to help you select tools from the CD-ROM Toolkit to fit your needs.

CD-ROM

Materials for the 19 Tasks of the Using Data Process found on the CD-ROM include data examples and Excel templates for your own data, handouts, PowerPoint slides, resources, and sample goals and agendas for your use in facilitating the 19 tasks with Data Teams. How and when to use these materials are explained in the write-up about each task in the print version of the book. The CD-ROM is organized with links for each chapter and task, so all the material you need is readily accessible for printing, copying, or presenting. Also included in each task's link, for your convenience, are materials that pertain to tools in the Toolkit, when required for use in a task. You will find these same materials in the Toolkit, though they are numbered differently.

The CD-ROM Toolkit contains 29 discrete tools used in the Using Data Process. Some are protocols for engaging in data-driven or equity dialogues. Others are group process tools for establishing norms or roles. Still others are tools for analyzing data or templates or forms to organize or document the work of Data Teams. Most tools are for use with an individual Data Team, but some are primarily for engaging with larger groups, such as an entire faculty, community or parent groups, or multiple Data Teams. In the Toolkit, readers will find detailed instructions along with ancillary materials such as PowerPoint slides or handouts. The Toolkit provides easy access to the individual tools, which are organized alphabetically. You will also find toolkit directions embedded within the procedures for tasks when they are a core part of that task.

A Using Data Glossary of Statistical Terminology on the CD-ROM defines 29 terms used in data analysis. Many have graphic representations.

Icon Guide

A focus on equity is embedded as a central theme throughout the Using Data Process. The Equity Lens icon prompts the Data Coach and the Data Team at particularly important junctures to view their work through an Equity Lens. When readers see the Equity Lens icon, it is a reminder to include the voices of diverse staff, students, and parents in their data collection and dialogue or to consider interpretations and responses to data that reflect a commitment to equity.

It is also the duty of the Data Teams to ensure a productive school culture in which everyone takes consistent action to serve all students. Periodically, throughout the Using Data Process, the coach will prompt the team to review its vision and core values or reassess the strength of its collaborative culture. These opportunities are highlighted with the School Culture Review icon.

Finally, the Caution icon is a reminder to pay attention to potential abuses or misinterpretations of data that may arise with a particular type or level of data.

Multiple Entry Points:
It's Not as Linear as It Looks!

For all readers, we recommend starting with Chapters 1 and 2 to become familiar with the Using Data Process and learn about the role of the Data Coach. From then on, there are multiple pathways through the book. The authors created a comprehensive, sequential, and structured process because the Data Coaches we worked with found it valuable. But every context is different. Use this book with your context in mind and find the best fit between your purpose and our product. For most people, this will not be a sit-down-and-read cover-to-cover book.

For example, if you are taking on the role of Data Coach and want to follow the entire process, here is a possible course: After reading Chapters 1 and 2, scan Chapters 3–7, reviewing the components of the Using Data Process and the procedures for implementing the 19 tasks and the associated activities. Then consult the

CD-ROM for other materials relevant to the tasks. As you prepare to implement each task, it will be important to read all of the material related to that task in detail. For the first time through, we suggest working through the tasks in order. It is not necessary or even recommended, however, to conduct all activities for all tasks for every Data Team. Instead, customize the process by considering the knowledge, skills, beliefs, and experiences of your Data Team and the time and data available. The guide includes a variety of assessments of data literacy and school practices that will help you tailor your own approach to these materials.

Another pathway through the book is for readers who already have an established continuous improvement process in place in their schools. You can use this guide to strengthen that process by implementing specific components of the Using Data Process. For example, your Data Teams may want to go directly to the "Verifying Causes" chapter (Chapter 5) if that is a stage you have been overlooking. Other readers may be looking for ways to bring equity issues to the forefront of school improvement work. For this, Chapter 3 ("Building the Foundation") is a good place to start, especially Task 3 (Raise Awareness of Cultural Proficiency). Then you can use the Equity Lens icons to follow how cultural proficiency and equity are woven throughout the process.

For those who prefer to see the whole picture before getting into the details, consider starting off by reading Chapter 8, the case study about Clark County, Nevada. Finally, some readers may want to go directly to the Toolkit on the CD-ROM and scan for specific tools to use with their Data Teams or faculty. Whatever pathway you take, please use this guide to inspire your own creativity and to unleash the power of collaborative inquiry to make a better future for each and every student.

1

The Power of Collaborative Inquiry

What the best and wisest parent wants for his own child, that must the community want for all of our children.

—John Dewey

Lea is a spunky fourth grader who loves geography, expressive writing, gymnastics, and her friends, but homework is a constant struggle for her.

Bethany loves gymnastics and is highly kinesthetic. She is catching up on her reading and, after some difficulty, is expected to be at grade level by the end of this year.

Brianna's strength is her intelligence about nature; she can name and give great details about all the fauna and flora in the neighborhood. A seventh grader, she struggles in school and now attends a school for students with exceptional needs.

Jared is going into second grade. His strength is his sense of identity and what it means to be Navajo. He loves to draw; his challenge is reading. This past school year he had to work very hard on his reading skills.

Chinua just graduated from high school and received a full scholarship to Morehouse College. He is extremely bright and loves science and mathematics. He gets bored easily if he is not challenged.

Figure 1.1

Reprinted with permission.

We begin this book with images of children we know because they inspire us to do the work we do (see Figure 1.1). It could be so easy to get lost in the numbers—student identification numbers, scale scores, proficiency cut points (see Figure 1.2)—and forget that the numbers represent the hope and future of real children with strengths as well as challenges, each deserving the kind of education we want for our very own children (see Figure 1.3).

> *When asked what they would want for their own children, most educators inevitably say they expect the highest levels of education. Do other people's children deserve any less?*
>
> —Johnson, 2002, p. 320

Figure 1.2

173364814

4375643853

567238467

1832444323

Figure 1.3

Thanks to Chris Demers for contributing this idea.

We care about data because we care about children learning and succeeding. Data can sound the alarm when someone is not learning and activate an immediate response. The data give us a powerful entrée into dialogue about the toughest issues, such as confronting how well our schools are working for all children and the inequitable practices that persist. They challenge and help us rethink basic assumptions. They hold a mirror up to instructional practice to pinpoint what is and is not working. Data help to set the right goals for action and, once changes are implemented, they provide constant feedback to guide mid-course corrections and monitor results.

Data also give us cause for celebration and opportunity to recognize teachers and students for a job well done. Using data to guide action is the most powerful lever we have to improve our schools; and yet, despite the increasing quantity now available, data are woefully underutilized as a force for change.

Schools are gathering more and more data, but having data available does not mean that data are used to guide instructional improvement. Many schools lack the process to connect the data that they have with the results they must produce.

—Love, 2004, p. 23

BRIDGING THE DATA GAP

Increasing the effective use of data to improve learning is the problem the authors set out to solve. Imagine two shores with an ocean in between (see Figure 1.4). On one shore are data—the myriad data now inundating schools: state test data sliced and diced every which way, local assessments, demographic data, dropout rates, graduation rates, course-taking patterns, attendance data, survey data, and on and on. On the distant shore are the desire, intention, moral commitment, and mandate to improve student learning and close persistent achievement gaps. But often there is no bridge between the shores and a wide ocean in between. Sadly, it is children who are drowning in the data gap, particularly children of color, English Language Learners, children living in poverty, and those with exceptional needs.

Why is there such a wide data gap? Although there are many contributing factors, the authors of this book agree with Richard Elmore that the data gap is primarily a problem of capacity:

With increased accountability, American schools and those who work in them are being asked to do something new—to engage in systematic, continuous improvement in the quality of the educational experience of students and to subject themselves to the discipline of measuring their success by the metric of students' academic performance. Most people who currently work in public schools weren't hired to do this work, nor have they been adequately prepared to do it either by their professional education or by their prior experience in schools. (Elmore, 2002, p. 5)

When you combine lack of adequate preparation with intense accountability pressures, poor use and even abuses of data abound. For example, if educators do

Figure 1.4   The data gap.

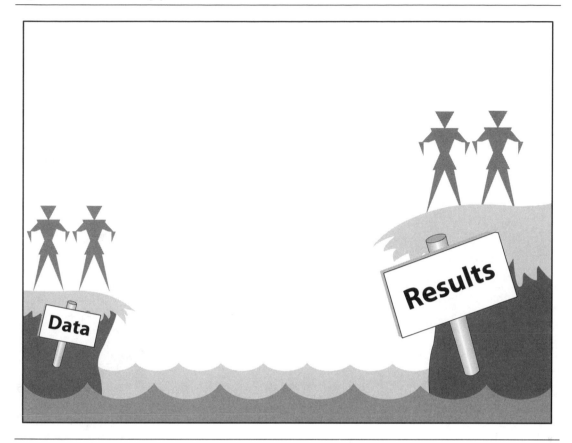

not thoroughly understand their content and how to teach it, they can incorrectly diagnose student-learning problems and resort to drilling students on test items or tutoring "bubble" students—those who just missed a proficiency-level cut point—just to pass the test (Abrams & Madaus, 2003; Love, 2003). On the other hand, as Ann Lewis asserts, "There is plenty of evidence around that, when teachers know their content and know how to teach it at high levels to all students, 'teaching to the test' fades into the background of everyday instruction and learning" (as quoted in Sparks, 2005, p. 90).

If educators do not believe in all children's capacity to reach challenging standards, they can react with complacency or resignation when they see achievement gaps among racial/ethnic and economic groups; or even worse, they can choose to institute practices such as tracking, which further limit opportunities to learn (Jerald, 2005; Love, 2003; Zuman, 2006). If they do not know how to interpret data and student work accurately, they can jump to flawed and even damaging conclusions (Confrey & Makar, 2005; Love, 2004). And without a systematic improvement process, schools, particularly those serving underserved students, languish in chronic underperformance—no matter what the pressures of accountability. As Elmore (2003) warns, "when we bear down on testing without the reciprocal supply of capacity . . . we exacerbate the problem we are trying to fix" (p. 6).

Figure 1.5   Connecting data to results.

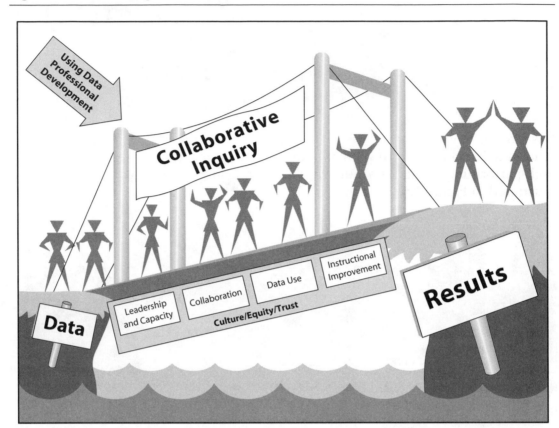

COLLABORATIVE INQUIRY IS THE BRIDGE

Schools know that they *have to* improve. But they often do not know *how* to improve. Collaborative inquiry is the how. It is a systematic improvement process where teachers work in Data Teams to construct their understanding of student-learning problems and generate and test out solutions through rigorous and frequent use of data and reflective dialogue. When engaged in collaborative inquiry, Data Teams investigate the current status of student learning and instructional practice and search for successes to celebrate and amplify. Their ongoing investigation into how to continuously improve student learning is guided by these simple questions:

How are we doing?

What are we doing well? How can we amplify our successes?

Who isn't learning? Who aren't we serving? What aren't they learning?

What in our practice could be causing that? How can we be sure?

What can we do to improve?

How do we know if it worked?

What do we do if the students don't learn?

Collaborative inquiry is the relentless pursuit of excellence and equity subjected to the rigor of evidence and results. Although it is a process, not a destination, collaborative inquiry does not roam aimlessly. Data Teams turn problems into quantifiable goals to be achieved and move purposefully toward them, one at a time, sometimes in small steps, sometimes with big leaps. Schools in which staff master this process know how to get better and better. As collaborative inquiry grows, schools shift away from traditional data practices and toward those that build a high-performing Using Data Culture. These shifts are summarized in Table 1.1 and illustrated in Figure 1.5.

Table 1.1   Moving Toward a High-Performing Using Data Culture

Element	Less emphasis on	More emphasis on
Leadership and capacity	Individual charismatic leaders; data literacy as a specialty area for a few staff	Learning communities with many change agents; widespread data literacy among all staff
Collaboration	Teacher isolation; top-down, data-driven decision making; no time or structure provided for collaboration	Shared norms and values; ongoing Data-Driven Dialogue and collaborative inquiry; time and structure for collaboration
Data use	Used to punish or reward schools and sort students; rarely used by the school community to inform action	Used as feedback for continuous improvement and to serve students; frequent and in-depth use by entire school community
Instructional improvement	Individually determined curriculum, instruction, and assessment; learning left to chance	Aligned learning goals, instruction, and assessment; widespread application of research and best practice; systems in place to prevent failure
Culture	External accountability as driving force; focus on opportunities to learn for some	Internal responsibility as driving force; focus on opportunities to learn for all
Equity	Belief that only the "brightest" can achieve at high levels; talk about race and class is taboo; culturally destructive or color-blind responses to diversity	Belief that all children are capable of high levels of achievement; ongoing dialogue about race, class, and privilege; culturally proficient responses to diversity
Trust	Relationships based on mistrust and avoidance of important discussions	Relationships based on trust, candid talk, and openness

OUR THEORY OF ACTION: BUILDING THE BRIDGE BETWEEN DATA AND RESULTS

Through our work as staff of the Using Data Project, the authors of this book set out to build the bridge between data and results and help to bring about the shifts in culture described earlier. The theory of action that guided us is illustrated in Figure 1.5. Our intervention, represented by the arrow pointing to the bridge, was the Using Data professional development program. The program addresses the critical capacity crisis described earlier by building the knowledge and skills of Data Coaches—education leaders especially trained to guide the use of data—to lead Data Teams in collaborative inquiry (see definitions in the sidebar). Data Teams become vital and productive centers of collaboration, meeting weekly to engage in Data-Driven Dialogue, using multiple data sources, including common and formative assessments (see Task 5 for detailed information on what kind of data to use and how often). Staff collaborate in their use of data to make critical and research-based instructional improvements. These improvements are the final and necessary step to reach the shore of improved results for students. The bridge is supported by a foundation of a collaborative school culture, a commitment to equity, and a climate of trust.

After four years of field-testing our approach in diverse schools across the country, schools putting this theory into action are building bridges between data and results: Student learning is improving; achievement gaps are narrowing; teachers are working together, making effective uses of data, and improving instruction; and their school cultures are shifting toward greater shared responsibility for all students' learning, trust, and commitment to equity (see "Student Learning Improves in Schools Implementing the Using Data Process" later in this chapter and Handout H1.3 on the CD-ROM for Task 1). The key to their success rests on their implementation of a model for collaborative inquiry we call the Using Data Process.

Data Coaches are education leaders (teacher-leaders, instructional coaches, building administrators, or district staff) who guide Data Teams through the process of collaborative inquiry and influence the culture of schools to be ones in which data are used continuously, collaboratively, and effectively to improve teaching and learning. Their role is to engage others in making sense of and responding to data in ways that improve learning for all students. They facilitate the work of Data Teams, build capacity to use data well, and sustain the improvement process.

Data Teams in this book refers to teams of four to eight teachers, other school faculty, and, ideally, their building administrator who work together to use data and improve student learning. At an elementary school, Data Teams can be grade-level teams or representatives of different grade levels and focused on a particular content area, such as mathematics, or on school improvement in general. In a middle school or junior high and high school, Data Teams are often organized by department, content area, or common courses taught.

Collaborative inquiry is the process by which Data Coaches and the Data Teams use data to develop their understanding of a student-learning problem and test out solutions together through rigorous use of data and constructive dialogue.

THE USING DATA PROCESS: A FRAMEWORK FOR COLLABORATIVE INQUIRY

The Using Data Process of Collaborative Inquiry (Using Data Process) offers Data Coaches and Data Teams a structured process for ongoing investigation of data with the goal of improving teaching and learning. The approach incorporates multiple safeguards to prevent data disasters and keep the team focused on each step across the bridge. In this book, Data Coaches are provided with the materials and guidance to lead Data Teams through this process.

Figure 1.6   The Using Data Process components and tasks.

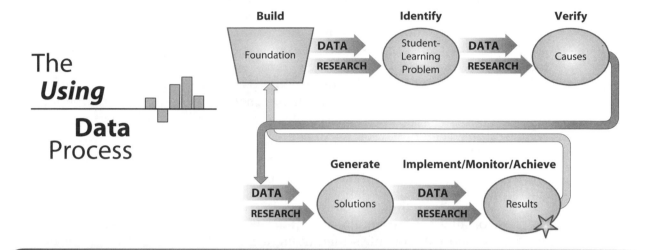

BUILDING THE FOUNDATION

Task 1: Launch the Data Team
Task 2: Reflect on Our School
Task 3: Raise Awareness of Cultural Proficiency
Task 4: Commit to Shared Values, Standards, and Vision

IDENTIFYING A STUDENT-LEARNING PROBLEM

Task 5: Build Data Literacy
Task 6: Drill Down Into State CRT Data: Aggregate-Level Analysis
Task 7: Drill Down Into State CRT Data: Disaggregate-Level Analysis
Task 8: Drill Down Into State CRT Data: Strand-Level Analysis
Task 9: Drill Down Into State CRT Data: Item-Level Analysis
Task 10: Examine Student Work
Task 11: Drill Down Into Common Assessments and Other Local Student-Learning Data Sources
Task 12: Identify a Student-Learning Problem and Goal

VERIFYING CAUSES

Task 13: Conduct Cause-and-Effect Analysis
Task 14: Verify Causes Through Research and Local Data

GENERATING SOLUTIONS

Task 15: Build Your Logic Model
Task 16: Refine Outcomes and Strategies
Task 17: Develop a Monitoring Plan

IMPLEMENTING, MONITORING, AND ACHIEVING RESULTS

Task 18: Take Action and Monitor Results
Task 19: Celebrate Success and Renew Collaborative Inquiry

As depicted in Figure 1.6, the Using Data Process is made up of five components. Within each component is a sequence of tasks that Data Coaches carry out with Data Teams. The first component is Building the Foundation; it includes Tasks 1–4. Here, Data Coaches lay important groundwork with the Data Teams to get them off to a good start. The team focuses on establishing the culture and commitment to equity that will serve as the foundation of the bridge of collaborative inquiry. They establish their purpose as a team, learn about the Using Data Process, and make commitments to each other. They reflect on their school by examining demographic data and assessing where their school is on the road to creating a high-performing Using Data Culture. They raise their awareness of cultural proficiency and begin a process of open dialogue about issues of race/ethnicity, class, culture, gender, and diversity. Finally, they envision a desired future for their school and plan for moving toward it. The themes that are introduced in this component—norms of collaboration, Data-Driven Dialogue (Wellman & Lipton, 2004), cultural proficiency, vision, values, and high-performing culture—are recurrent throughout the Using Data Process.

The second component is Identifying a Student-Learning Problem; it includes Tasks 5–12. Guided by the Data Coach, the team members develop data literacy and examine multiple sources of student-learning data. They learn to use tools to make sense of the data and surface assumptions and frames of reference. The outcome of this component is a clearly articulated student-learning problem that can be supported with evidence from multiple data sources, including student work.

The third component, Verifying Causes, includes Tasks 13 and 14. This component is critical because it is the one often omitted in other improvement processes. Here the team members look carefully at the possible causes of their student-learning problems and examine data about their own practices as well as relevant research before drawing conclusions. The goal here is to make sure that the causes that are being acted upon are supported in research and focused on policies, practices, and beliefs that are within educators' control to act upon—not on blaming students or their circumstances.

Generating Solutions, the fourth component, includes Tasks 15–17. Here, Data Teams apply logic-model thinking to generate valid solutions to improve results. They draw on best practices in their own school and nationally as well as on research to create action plans that are clearly linked to improved student learning. They also identify the evidence that they will use to monitor implementation of new practices and measure impact on student learning.

Finally, in the fifth component, Implementing, Monitoring, and Achieving Results (Tasks 18 and 19), the Data Team implements new practices to solve the student-learning problem. The team gathers data to monitor implementation and results and identifies any mid-course corrections needed. As evidence is produced that the school is achieving or progressing toward the goal, Data Teams organize celebrations to recognize the people and practices that are making a difference for students.

WHAT'S UNIQUE ABOUT THE USING DATA PROCESS?

The Using Data Process was designed with several unique features that are essential to its success.

Building Leadership and Capacity

Figure 1.7   Core competencies for high-capacity data use.

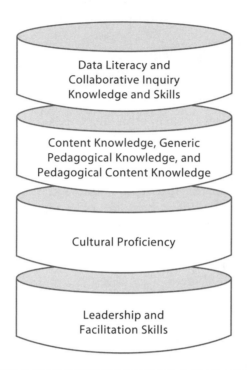

First is the focus on building leadership and capacity that Richard Elmore calls for—the first and critical step across the bridge from data to results. By leadership, we mean teachers and administrators with the knowledge and skills to use multiple data sources effectively and collaboratively to improve teaching and learning. The assumption that underlies the essential shift in leadership and capacity is that in a high-performing school, all members of the school community, and especially teachers, act as leaders, impacting the quality of relationships, the school culture, and student learning. When such leadership is widespread and institutionalized, with built-in mechanisms to sustain it, the result is organizational capacity. Michael Fullan (2005) describes capacity building as "developing the collective ability—dispositions, skills, knowledge, motivation, and resources—to act together to bring about positive change" (p. 4). That is what is called for to sustain continuous improvement and what the Using Data Project set out to develop among Data Coaches, who in turn spread this knowledge to others.

If collaborative inquiry were easy, lots of schools would be doing it. It is not. It does not occur magically when data management systems are put in place to provide teachers with timely and accurate data. It does not happen just by giving teachers data and asking them to do something about them. It does not automatically result when schools are organized into professional learning communities and teachers are provided with time to work together. Although time for collaboration and access to timely, accurate data are necessary for collaborative inquiry, much more is required. Effective data users draw on four core competencies, illustrated in Figure 1.7, that are the basis for high-capacity uses of data—those that translate into sustained and significant improvements in instruction and learning and act as the antidote to the abuses of data discussed earlier. They are:

• Apply data literacy and collaborative inquiry knowledge and skills to collect, accurately interpret, and analyze multiple data sources and research to identify student-learning problems, verify causes and generate solutions, test hypotheses, and improve results.

• Apply content knowledge, generic pedagogical knowledge, and pedagogical content knowledge (how to teach a particular body of content based on understanding of student thinking, key ideas that compose the discipline, and ways of making content accessible to students) to generate uses and responses to data that result in effective interventions and improved teaching and learning.

• Apply cultural proficiency (the ability to interact knowledgeably and respectfully with diverse cultures) to view achievement gaps as solvable problems, not inevitable consequences of students' backgrounds; generate solutions that reflect an understanding of diverse students' strengths, values, and perspectives; and handle cultural conflict effectively.

• Apply leadership and facilitation skills to create high-functioning teams, facilitate productive dialogue focused on teaching and learning, foster commitment to rigorous standards for all students, build collegial relationships based on trust and respect, and sustain collaborative inquiry.

Learning From Experience

Although our program espoused a strong commitment to equity from the outset, we quickly learned that that was not enough. On the second day of our national field test, participants were engaged in dialogue about demographic data. Suddenly, and to our great surprise, conflict erupted in the group between a White participant and an African American participant. The staff was not equipped to handle it. At the same time, we realized that this kind of conflict is not unexpected and, in fact, likely when groups first start talking about race. We were missing an important opportunity if we did not prepare Data Coaches to handle these conversations productively. We were fortunate to have the help of four leading equity experts, who led us to strengthen the program. We added a focus on deepening Data Coaches' understanding of cultural proficiency and skill building in facilitating dialogue around issues of race, class, culture, gender, and other differences that inevitably arise from examining data. These themes of cultural proficiency are now incorporated throughout the program.

In this book, Data Coaches learn to apply and spread these core competencies as they facilitate the Using Data Process tasks with Data Teams. (For more on developing Data Coach knowledge and skills see the vignette, "Organizing for Collaborative Inquiry—The Data Coach's Role" in Chapter 2 and Task 5.)

Emphasis on Cultural Proficiency and Equity

Diversity is a reality in all schools. The question is not *if* Data Teams deal with diversity. The question is *how*. Examining data (especially demographic, achievement, and disaggregated data) frequently surfaces negative assumptions about what children of color, students with exceptional needs, or students living in poverty are capable of learning and achieving. Educators using data can disintegrate into destructive conflict around these issues or engage in constructive dialogue.

The Using Data Process incorporates several features to help Data Teams and the Data Coach address diversity constructively and maintain a focus on equity. In Task 3, the Data Team studies principles of cultural proficiency and a framework for understanding a range of responses to diversity. In subsequent tasks, we provide guidance on how to facilitate constructive dialogue about diversity issues that will likely surface in the specific tasks.

Throughout the process, the Data Coach and the team are reminded to view data through an Equity Lens, seeking diverse voices and perspectives and keeping their eye on the goal of serving all students equitably.

Focus on Building a Data Culture and Collaborative Relationships

Some approaches to using data focus only on data collection and analysis. Others focus only on building school culture. The Using Data Process combines both. Data Coaches learn how to lead Data Teams to collect and analyze data using a tool called Data-Driven Dialogue (Wellman & Lipton, 2004). They establish group norms and attend to the group process as well as to the tasks and products. Data Teams learn not just how to look at data; they learn how to talk about them together.

In addition, Data Coaches do more than facilitate data use and dialogue; they play a role in influencing school culture and strengthening relationships of trust and shared commitments. Data Teams build a foundation for a strong collaborative culture in the early tasks by anchoring the Data Team's work in shared values, vision, and a goal of creating a high-performing, data-using school culture. The Data Coach guides the team to keep the values and vision alive and to periodically assess the team's progress in achieving their larger goal of creating a data culture. In addition, the Data Team and Coach continually strategize about how to reach out to other initiatives in the school and/or district, engage the faculty and community in Data-Driven Dialogue, and broaden the impact of the Data Team on the entire school.

Long-Term and Short-Cycle Improvement

The Using Data Process accommodates both long- and short-cycle improvements. The 19 tasks can unfold over a 1- to 1½-year implementation cycle and can operate as the school's ongoing school improvement system. The team goes through a rigorous process of examining multiple data sources, identifies a problem, uses other data sources to verify the causes of the problem, and builds a logic model to link school improvement strategies to desired outcomes. They carefully plan implementation and monitor results. They think systemically and develop plans to improve several aspects of their system, such as their policies, grouping practices, and instructional materials.

But a Data Team can also move much more quickly through the Using Data Process, even in a week or a month. For example, the Data Team examines quarterly benchmark assessment data one day and discovers a student-learning problem related to specific content. They immediately generate possible solutions, which are tested out in the classroom that week, gathering data to assess whether the solution improved student understanding of the specific content. Within the longer-term improvement process, the Data Team is continually improving instruction by regularly monitoring student learning, implementing new practices, and collecting evidence of effectiveness. In this way, the Using Data Process combines the rigor of a long-term improvement process with the immediacy of short-cycle changes.

Look Before You Leap

During our work with schools, we observed Data Teams that were quite proficient at using data to identify problems, but, initially, they did not do the best job of verifying the causes. Often they would leap to assigning cause without checking out their theories. For example, as you can read in the Clark County, Nevada, case study in Chapter 8, one of the Data Teams accurately identified that their students had difficulty solving nonroutine mathematics problems. They concluded that the cause was that students were not persisting and that they were unable to read the problems. It wasn't until they actually observed 40 students engaged in problem solving that they saw their theory didn't hold water. Students were persisting. And even when the problem was read aloud to the students, they still weren't able to solve it. Through their observations and by consulting research, the team came to the conclusion that the cause of the problem was that students lacked problem-solving strategies, not persistence. This led to a very different course of action. The Using Data Process builds in checks and balances to guide teams to verify the causes of problems with data and research. Another place the process can break down is in generating solutions. Data Teams would seize upon a strategy such as implementing a professional development workshop. But they wouldn't think through exactly what that workshop would accomplish that would get them closer to their student-learning goal. This led us to incorporate logic-model thinking to increase the accuracy of Data Teams' action planning.

STUDENT LEARNING IMPROVES IN SCHOOLS IMPLEMENTING THE USING DATA PROCESS

When our middle school mathematics Data Team received their most recent state achievement test results, they broke into cheers and tears. That's ownership!

—Pam Bernabei-Rorrer,
Mathematics and Data Coach, Canton City, Ohio

The true power of collaborative inquiry is its potential to improve student learning. In Canton City, Ohio, all four middle schools, comprising 66–82 percent poor students and 30–45 percent African American students, increased the percentage of students scoring proficient or above on the Ohio Proficiency Test in mathematics between 2002–03 and 2004–05. One school doubled the percentage while another more than doubled it. The percentage of African American students passing the Sixth Grade Ohio Proficiency Test in mathematics almost tripled from 2002–03 to 2004–05 (Ohio Department of Education, 2005). (For more details on these and other results, see Handout H1.3 on the CD-ROM for Task 1.)

On the Ohio Seventh and Eighth Grade Achievement Tests, all student groups, including all racial groups, students with special needs, those receiving free and reduced lunch, and males and females, made gains. The percentage of high school students earning proficient or above on the Ohio Graduation Test increased by 25 percentage points from 2004 to 2006. As in the seventh and eighth grade, all student groups made progress (Ohio Department of Education, 2006).

In Clark County School District, Nevada, the Wendell Williams Elementary School (with 100 percent of students eligible for free and reduced lunch, 75 percent African American and 19 percent Hispanic) saw improved student performance in third- and fifth-grade reading and mathematics on the Nevada criterion-referenced test (CRT) in one year. The percentage of students scoring proficient or above in fifth-grade mathematics jumped from 18 percent to 42 percent (Nevada Department of Education, 2005). Similar results were achieved in other participating schools.

In Johnson County, Tennessee, a poor, rural area with 70 percent of students on free or reduced lunch, the schools exceeded the growth rates of some of the wealthiest and highest-performing districts on the state assessment. Most impressive were gains for students with disabilities. In Grades 3, 5, and 8 mathematics, the percentage of students with disabilities proficient in mathematics increased from 36 to 74 percent from 2004 to 2006. In reading for the same grade levels, the percentage proficient increased from 54 to 70 percent (Tennessee Department of Education, 2005, 2006).

Several of the schools participating in the Arizona Rural Systemic Initiative in Mesa, Arizona, serving a high percentage of Native American children, made gains in student achievement on the Arizona State Assessment. For example, San Carlos Junior High School in San Carlos, Arizona, cut the percentage of students in the Falls Far Below category from 95 percent in 2001 to 45 percent in 2005 in eighth-grade mathematics and met Adequate Yearly Progress (Arizona Department of Education, 2005; Eileen Armelin, personal communication, September 29, 2005).

SCHOOLS BUILD HIGH-PERFORMING USING DATA CULTURES

Equally exciting are changes in school culture, instructional improvement, data use, collaboration, and leadership. The evaluation provided evidence that the shifts toward high-performing Using Data cultures are taking hold in schools that participated in the Using Data Project. "As a result of UDP participation, many teachers have reported a significant shift in their culture of using external factors to explain lack of student achievement. Many acknowledged that the process of discussing student test data has made them more accountable for the results and more mindful that teachers are in a position to influence gains in student outcome" (Zuman, 2006, p. 2).

I don't think we can ever go back. Using Data has become a part of our culture.

—Mary Ann Wood, Data Coach,
Salt River Elementary School, Mesa, Arizona

The next chapters will walk you through the steps you can take to unleash the power of collaborative inquiry.

2

Getting Organized for Collaborative Inquiry

This chapter discusses how school districts and individual schools lay the groundwork for successful implementation of the Using Data Process. It answers basic questions about what to consider as you get organized for implementation and how to get started: How can collaborative inquiry be integrated into your existing improvement efforts and with other initiatives? How do you build support among key people? Organize Data Teams? Select and prepare Data Coaches? Create time for collaboration? Ensure timely access to robust local data? Based on lessons learned through the Using Data Project, these are the conditions that can make or break the success of collaborative inquiry. The chapter is written for the people responsible for initiating the local Using Data effort, including individual Data Coaches or leaders who are preparing Data Coaches. The following vignette highlights some of the key actions Data Coaches take to get started with collaborative inquiry.

Vignette: Organizing for Collaborative Inquiry—The Data Coach's Role

The Nevazoh Data Coach generated interest in the Using Data Process when she talked with several key staff and made a short presentation at a faculty meeting in their middle school. The teachers were really intrigued by the process of looking at the school's demographic data and discussing it. The Data Coach's sense was that the teachers could have spent at least another hour talking about what they saw. She promised them more opportunities in the future if they wanted them.

She worked out ahead of time that the principal would announce that the Data Coach had support to convene a Data Team from the school to begin planning an effort to use data to improve mathematics teaching and learning and to ask the staff to consider how they would like to be involved. The principal pointed out there would be a Data Team that would meet weekly to collect and analyze data and ultimately make recommendations for action and that all of the staff could be involved in other ways such as attending sessions to gain data literacy skills and analyze data together.

After the meeting, the Data Coach followed up with several of the mathematics and special education teachers and other faculty who seemed enthusiastic about the Using Data Process during the faculty meeting. In one-on-one chats, she asked them what they thought of the idea, what their concerns were, and if they would like to be involved. She took careful note of their questions and concerns, especially when they raised the issue of data usually being used to point fingers at teachers. She realized that the Data Team would need to demonstrate quickly that this was not how it would operate. These conversations, along with a discussion with the principal and mathematics chair, helped the Data Coach think through the possible membership for the Data Team. She was careful to select a manageable group size of 5–10 people representative of the school and diverse in terms of perspective and culture. She invited the following people to form the team:

- The school principal
- Three of the six mathematics teachers, one from each of the three grade levels
- Three of the nine special education teachers, each with a special education inclusion class at one of the three grade levels
- One of the five Title I teachers who was designated for sixth-grade mathematics and had a keen interest in closing the achievement gap in the school

After numerous conversations with each team member and several meetings with the principal, the district mathematics coordinator, and the county educational center's mathematics leader, the Data Coach helped craft a written agreement that outlined the specific roles and responsibilities for the team as a whole as well as for each individual team member. Everyone involved agreed that the Mathematics Improvement Data Team would have the authority to recommend and lead the implementation of schoolwide changes in the mathematics program, including changes in curriculum, instruction, and local assessment. These recommendations would be made after the Data Team had analyzed a variety of student learning and other data and examined the research to develop an appropriate action plan with clear specifications for ongoing data collection and analysis and monitoring of the action plan's impact on student learning. The rest of the mathematics faculty would be informed at critical junctures and their input solicited. The district mathematics coordinator, the principal, and the county educational center's mathematics leader each clarified how and when they would be available for support, and the Data Team was ready to be launched.

As you begin to consider implementing the Using Data Process in your own setting, your biggest question might be "Where can I start?" This chapter discusses seven steps you will take to establish collaborative inquiry within your school(s). They are

1. Make collaborative inquiry an integral part of your school operation and improvement initiatives.

2. Build stakeholder support.

3. Assess and take steps to strengthen a collaborative culture.

4. Select, prepare, and empower Data Coaches.

5. Organize Data Teams.

6. Create time for collaboration.

7. Ensure timely access to robust data sources.

MAKE COLLABORATIVE INQUIRY AN INTEGRAL PART OF THE SCHOOL OPERATION AND IMPROVEMENT INITIATIVES

Often teachers and administrators are engaged in a variety of new programs and activities. Too often these initiatives are disconnected and incoherent. The Using Data Process attempts to remedy this by making the implementation of collaborative inquiry in participating schools and districts central to the staff's ongoing work—not an add-on. "If you don't look at the data, everything else is just a guess," explained Mike Bayer, principal investigator of the Stark County Math and Science Partnership and Using Data collaborator from Stark County, Ohio. "The data give us direction on where to focus to raise achievement." For any school improvement effort, using data is the foundation. Consider how to embed the use of data in your existing school operation. What happens now when teachers get student-learning data? Does the district's data management system suggest ways to use data to enhance results? Do grade-level teams look at student results together? The Using Data Process of examining data can be applied in any of these contexts. Are you engaged in school improvement initiatives such as implementing new curriculum, technology, or learning communities? If so, using data in an ongoing way will help to ensure that your improvement initiatives are focused on the areas that are most critical for improving student learning and will help you measure your progress and results.

Before implementing collaborative inquiry, consider your school's procedures related to data use as well as all the school improvement initiatives currently under way in the school(s) or district. Talk to the people involved with data use, and explore ideas for linking the Using Data Process with current school procedures. Also think about how the existing initiatives might support each other and share rather than compete for resources, including staff time, energy, and commitment. Coordinate with leaders of other initiatives to develop a plan for communicating with them about your actions and progress. Coordination is especially important with other data initiatives, such as the implementation of data management systems. (See Chapter 2: Resource 1 on the CD-ROM for a tool to guide your planning.)

Resource R2.1

Chapter 2: Resource 1
Standard School Procedures Related to Data Use
and Current Initiatives Under Way on Site

1a. What are the school's standard procedures involving the use of data? (e.g, How do teacher's grade-level teams and principals use student-learning data?)

For example, the Clark County School District in Nevada instituted a systemwide data management system a year after 15 of their schools began to implement the Using Data Process. Some participants saw the two initiatives as competing, whereas others saw the new data management system as replacing the Using Data Process. Other schools, however, understood that the two initiatives could be complementary. The data management system provided the timely access to data, and the Using Data Process of Collaborative Inquiry gave teachers the tools to put those data to work to improve their instruction. The schools that were clear about the synergy between the two initiatives were able to adapt both to better meet the needs of their students (see the Clark County, Nevada, case study in Chapter 8; Zuman, 2006).

BUILD STAKEHOLDER SUPPORT

The success or failure of collaborative inquiry rests on the commitment and support of key stakeholders. Karen Brighton, project director of a systemic reform initiative in Arizona, put it this way: "Stakeholder support is foundational. This is serious work and requires serious conversations. We went to the people in the districts and had multiple conversations. We went to the school boards. When the superintendents changed, we went back and retraced our steps. You need to stay the course to build real commitment, not just a signature."

Table 2.1 lists the audiences involved in launching this work and provides suggestions for how to work with them to build interest and engagement. In this book, take advantage of materials in Chapter 3, Task 1, including PowerPoint slides and handouts on the CD-ROM, to raise awareness and build support for the Using Data Process. The third column of the table describes each audience's role in sustaining collaborative inquiry. Ultimately, the program's success hinges on each of these stakeholders helping to create a system within the district that supports continuous improvement. You can use this column to guide your conversations with stakeholders, make requests, and as the basis for cooperative agreements that each stakeholder signs. The vignette on page 33 illustrates how one district leader went about building stakeholder support for the Using Data Process.

Table 2.1   Building Stakeholder Support

Audience	How to engage (see Task 1, Handouts H1.1–H1.3 and PowerPoint slides for Using Data Process overview)	Their role in sustaining collaborative inquiry
District administrators	Meet with district administrators to provide an overview and share results other districts have had with the Using Data Process; ask for their support and provide examples of the specific ways they can help	Communicate vision clearly and often Require alignment of curriculum, standards, and assessments Commit to developing Data Coaches and Data Teams Provide professional development to support collaborative inquiry Require participation of principals Create a safe environment for data use Provide teachers with timely access to data and time to meet Support the development and use of common benchmark assessments

(Continued)

Table 2.1 (Continued)

Audience	How to engage (see Task 1, Handouts H1.1–H1.3 and PowerPoint slides for Using Data Process overview)	Their role in sustaining collaborative inquiry
School administrators	Meet with building administrators to review the goals and process for collaborative inquiry and plan how to communicate with the entire school community	Communicate vision clearly and often Be a strong supporter of the Data Team and of data use Create a safe environment for data use Actively participate as a member of a Data Team Delegate Data Team leadership to a Data Coach Empower teachers to make instructional decisions based on data Help the team access resources, e.g., research or curriculum materials Model the practice of using data Provide teachers with timely access to data and time to meet
School faculty	Lead a presentation on the Using Data Process for all faculty; plan to give regular updates on the Data Team's work to all faculty	Actively participate on Data Teams or sessions led by Data Teams Use data to improve teaching Keep informed of Data Team's work if not on a team Take collective responsibility for improving student learning
Department chairs, opinion leaders, union representatives, instructional coaches, and specialists	Check in with key people to see if they need more information about the process and to address any concerns	Be a strong supporter of the Data Team and of data use Actively participate as a member of a Data Team Provide guidance and resources for Data Teams Model using data in their own practice Provide teachers with timely access to data and time to meet Advocate for collaborative inquiry among faculty
Potential Data Team members	Conduct an informational meeting and/or one-on-one conversations about what is entailed in serving as a Data Team member and the benefits	(See list later in this chapter.)
School board members	Conduct a short presentation at a board meeting to explain what you are doing and why	Support policies that provide time and resources for Data Coaches and Data Teams' work
School improvement team	Attend school improvement team meetings to discuss how the Using Data Process can support that team's work	Coordinate efforts with Data Teams Model the practice of using data to inform school improvement decisions
Parents	Introduce parents to the Using Data Process, including data on results through the newsletter or Listserv; provide overview at parent's night or PTO meeting	Keep informed of Data Team's work Participate in Data Team—sponsored events for parents Respond promptly to requests for data, such as parent surveys
Data or assessment coordinators	Meet with the staff responsible for assessment and data to inform them of your plans and to learn how to work together to access district data	Provide systems for timely access to local data Stay in communication with Data Coach

---

**Vignette: Clark County, Nevada, Builds Stakeholder
Support at the District and Building Levels**

In Clark County, the Mathematics and Science Enhancement (MASE), K–5 Using Technology project director and coordinator of K–5 mathematics and science, Thelma Davis, built stakeholder support for implementing collaborative inquiry in a variety of ways. She showed district leaders how using collaborative inquiry was closely aligned with the district's goals to increase data use, improve student achievement, and meet accountability requirements. She communicated to leaders of the MASE project how this collaborative approach to using data furthered the work of the project, which focused on implementing inquiry-based approaches to teaching and learning in collaborative settings. She made sure that MASE schools were included among participants. She met with regional superintendents and codeveloped an implementation plan with them. The plan included three participating schools in each of the district's regions, helping to build the regional superintendent's support, and also required that principals, as well as teacher-leaders, participate fully in training and implementation. Finally, she recognized that keeping stakeholders committed to the project required ongoing communication. She invited key district and building leaders to events and stayed in regular communication with them about the project and its progress (see Clark County, Nevada, case study in Chapter 8).

As indicated in Table 2.1, there are several strategies suggested for different audiences to build their understanding of the Using Data Process and collaborative inquiry. Think carefully about who needs to be involved in your local sites and how much time they can be involved, and make choices accordingly. For example, the principal, curriculum directors, teachers, and other key stakeholders must reach agreement on the parameters of the project. How are you going to facilitate this agreement? Set up a time to talk with them one on one, and invite them to participate in an outreach session.

Who are the formal and informal leaders in the school or district? Have a conversation with them to find out about their interest and ask who else they think should be involved. Collaborative inquiry is intended as an inclusive process, so even though you may only have a half-dozen people on a Data Team, the rest of the faculty need to value the process enough to respect the conclusions, results, and recommendations of the Data Team. To help develop awareness and "buy-in," provide them with information and clarify expectations about the process. Anticipate the concerns about innovation overload—"we can't do one more thing"—and be ready to explain why this initiative is important and complementary to other initiatives. Use Chapter 2: Resource 2 on the CD-ROM to develop your own outreach plan.

As you conduct your outreach, monitor how you are doing at reaching your key audiences. For example, are there new people involved who need to be briefed on the process? After launching the work with the Data Team (see Task 1), routinely ask the members to identify other people to reach out to about the Using Data Project and collaborative inquiry. A good rule of thumb is to ask everyone on the Data Team to talk with at least one other person every week to share what you are doing and how it will enhance the school's success. You can also send out regular (e.g., weekly or monthly) e-mail updates on your progress to everyone in the school

Resource R2.2

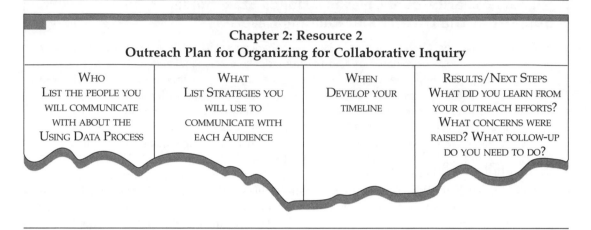

Chapter 2: Resource 2
Outreach Plan for Organizing for Collaborative Inquiry

WHO LIST THE PEOPLE YOU WILL COMMUNICATE WITH ABOUT THE USING DATA PROCESS	WHAT LIST STRATEGIES YOU WILL USE TO COMMUNICATE WITH EACH AUDIENCE	WHEN DEVELOP YOUR TIMELINE	RESULTS/NEXT STEPS WHAT DID YOU LEARN FROM YOUR OUTREACH EFFORTS? WHAT CONCERNS WERE RAISED? WHAT FOLLOW-UP DO YOU NEED TO DO?

community to keep them informed of activities of the Data Team. As you build stakeholder support, keep the following outcomes in mind:

- All key stakeholders understand what the Using Data Process is and how it will be used to enhance student learning.
- There is a process in place for ongoing communication about the project.
- You have a list of people who may be interested in serving on the Data Team(s).
- The building principal and/or a key administrator such as a curriculum coordinator or department chair agree to be actively involved in the process.
- The assessment or data coordinator understands the project and is lined up to assist with access to data.

ASSESS AND TAKE STEPS TO STRENGTHEN A COLLABORATIVE CULTURE

The Using Data Process both builds and benefits from a collaborative culture. If your school and district is new to collaboration, you will need to spend more time up front helping team members learn to work together; build a shared vision and the knowledge, skills, and habits of collaboration; and tackle school or district structures that get in the way of collaboration. There are several tools in this book for helping you assess your culture, including the Program Elements Matrix (PEM) for a Using Data Culture and the Consensogram (see Toolkit). If your setting does not have a history of collaboration focused on improving practice, you will probably spend much of the first six to nine months working to build that culture. The tasks in Chapter 3 are a good place to start. If, on the other hand, there is already a strong norm for working together, examining student work and data, and examining practice, you can move faster, but you will still want to make sure everyone is clear and comfortable with the Using Data Process, so use the tasks in Chapter 3 to strengthen skills of collaborative inquiry.

SELECT, PREPARE, AND EMPOWER DATA COACHES

Effective [Data Coaches] are key to the long-term sustainability of the Using Data Process.

—Zuman, 2006, p. 12

Chances are there is no one at your school or the schools you work with right now who is officially known as a Data Coach. This is a new role that is emerging as schools become more focused on using their data effectively to improve results. One of the most important findings from the four years of implementing the Using Data Process in schools across the country is that Data Coaches are the linchpin of successful collaborative inquiry. Without them, participating schools would not have achieved the gains in student learning, the increase in collaboration and data use, the instructional improvement, or the changes in the school culture.

Data Coach: An education leader who guides Data Teams through the process of collaborative inquiry and influences the culture of schools to be one in which data are used continuously, collaboratively, and effectively to improve teaching and learning.

The Data Coach Role

If you want to take control and make it run your way, just do it yourself. If you want to build a team, you have to let that team evolve—with some parameters. Make it clear that we are not going to complain about kids or make excuses. The only thing we can work on is what we have control over.

—Ann Wacker, Mathematics and Data Coach,
Plain Local Schools, Canton, Ohio

You may have a clear picture in your mind of different kinds of coaches—instructional coaches or sports coaches. But what does a Data Coach do? As defined by the Using Data Project, the Data Coach plays three major roles in collaborative inquiry. As illustrated in Figure 2.1, in the inner circle, the Data Coach's central role is modeling and spreading *data literacy* among all members of the Data Team. Data literacy is the ability to interpret and use multiple data sources effectively to improve teaching and learning. (See Task 5 for details on the knowledge and skills involved in data literacy and where in the book Data Coaches learn more about them.) Coaches are instrumental in gathering data for Data Teams, but they do not do the data analysis themselves. They lead the Data Team through the process of digging into the data to see what can be learned from it. Like a football or soccer coach, they are often on the sidelines while the Data Team is in the game, making their own sense of the data and using it to improve performance. But the Data Coach makes sure that the team has the resources—the data, the skills, the tools, and the practice—to get the job done well.

The next ring in the circle illustrates the Data Coach's role as *facilitator*. Data Coaches convene the Data Teams, plan team meetings, facilitate the process of Data-Driven Dialogue, and guide the team through collaborative inquiry. While Data Coaches play the role of facilitator, they are not always neutral. They take a stand for promoting equity and effective learning for all students. They speak their truth and challenge assumptions and practices that get in the way of providing all students with a high-quality education. At the same time, they create an environment on the team where each member feels safe saying what he or she thinks.

Figure 2.1 The Data Coach role.

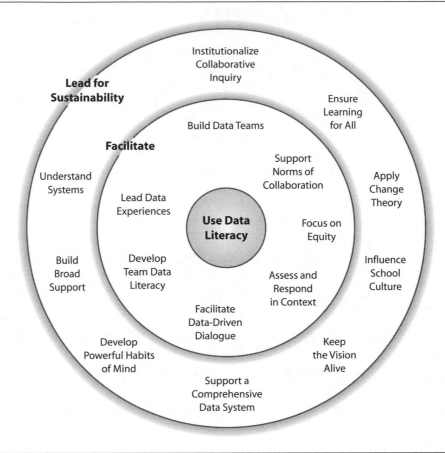

This book provides step-by-step guidance for Data Coaches to facilitate Data Teams as they implement the Using Data Process. As facilitator, your role includes the following:

• Focus on equity: Be a champion for ensuring equity. Take a stand for all students and against racism and other forms of bias; encourage the team to do the same.

• Support norms of collaboration: Guide teams to commit to, apply, and become skilled at group norms.

• Build Data Teams: Create high-functioning teams that talk about difficult issues and take effective action together.

• Lead data experiences: Guide Data Teams through the sequence of tasks and activities in the Using Data Process.

• Develop team data literacy as well as their other knowledge and skills for high-capacity data use (uses that lead to improved teaching and learning), including:
  o Data literacy and collaborative inquiry: Build the capacity of others to engage with data productively.
  o Cultural proficiency: Encourage the team to better understand and interact respectfully with diverse cultures and respond to data in respectful ways.

  o Content knowledge, pedagogical content knowledge, and generic pedagogical knowledge: Keep the focus on improving instruction; guide the team to deepen their own knowledge of content, pedagogy, and pedagogical content knowledge as they analyze data and implement solutions.
  o Leadership and facilitation skills: Develop others' leadership and facilitation skills; grow more Data Coaches!

• Facilitate Data-Driven Dialogue: Help the team separate observation from inference and examine assumptions (see Toolkit).

• Assess and respond to context: Use data about the team, students, and school to tailor the Using Data Process to local realities. Shift as the context shifts.

The third major area of responsibility for Data Coaches is to provide leadership for sustainability of the practice of collaborative inquiry to continuously enhance student learning. Specifically, Data Coaches

• Institutionalize collaborative inquiry: Data Coaches pay attention to what it takes to sustain the use of collaborative inquiry, including involving key people and leaders; building the culture to support the practice; working to infuse collaborative inquiry into ongoing structures such as faculty meetings, curriculum and other committees, and policy decisions; and making the use of student data to inform action an expectation for all staff.

• Ensure learning for all: Data Coaches use their influence to convince people of the importance of intervening when data show low levels of learning for any students. They have the ability to shift conversations away from blame and toward collective responsibility for closing achievement gaps.

• Apply change theory: Data Coaches understand that their role is to build awareness and support among all key players in the schools and districts. They provide ample opportunities for people to clarify what collaborative inquiry is and why it is beneficial for the school. They help as many staff as possible to develop data literacy skills, and they encourage administrators to sanction the use of collaborative inquiry and provide structures such as time to support its use.

• Influence school culture: Data Coaches model the cultural shifts needed, such as use of data, dialogue, and collaboration. They engage Data Teams and other key stakeholders in building a vision of the culture they want to create for their school.

• Keep the vision alive: Data Coaches look for opportunities to celebrate successes. They support the Data Team, administrators, and other key stakeholders to share the success stories and document how collaborative inquiry is helping to solve student-learning problems.

• Support a comprehensive data system: Data Coaches know what a huge task it is to make data immediately available and useable. That is why they work with the Data Team, administrators, and others to support the school and district to use a comprehensive data system that provides timely and accurate information on student learning and other important outcomes.

Table 2.2   Habits of Mind Shifts

From	To
Resignation, complaints, and resistance	Possibility, self-determination, and commitment
Unclear values, purpose, and goals	Clear, focused goals; clarified purpose and values
Single conversation	Sustained, persistent interaction
Unclear points of view	Clear, succinct, data-driven, powerfully expressed points of view
Superficial attending	Committed listening
Your truth as the truth	Reliance on data to support conclusions

SOURCE Adapted from Dennis Sparks, *Leading for Results* (2nd ed.), 2007. Thousand Oaks, CA: Corwin Press. Used with permission.

- Develop powerful habits of mind: Data Coaches walk the talk by demonstrating powerful habits of mind such as those illustrated in Table 2.2. For example, they are skilled at shifting conversations from resignation, complaints, and resistance to possibility. Subtle language shifts away from saying "I should" and "I must" toward "I can" and "I will" can be very powerful in moving teams from feeling victimized by mandates and high-stakes testing to making commitments and taking action (Ellis, 2002; Sparks, 2007). Data Coaches lead by their example. They ask others in the school to act on these habits of mind and build a shared vision for collaborative inquiry in the school.

- Build broad support: Data Coaches know that school improvement happens in the broader context of the school district. They meet with central office administrators to explain what collaborative inquiry is and why it is an essential tool for the district. They regularly update key administrators on what is being accomplished and what has to happen next. They make presentations at parent and teacher meetings to raise awareness of the use of collaborative inquiry.

- Understand systems: Building on all of the actions listed earlier, the Data Coach understands that the school and district operate as a system that is also part of a broader community and state system. As such, the school is affected by policies and practices in the broader system. Data Coaches think about how to leverage state policies such as requirements for data reporting and student achievement to encourage the school to build a culture for data use and ongoing improvement. They know their context well and think strategically about how to build on strengths and diminish weaknesses.

To assess your own strengths related to the three dimensions of the role of Data Coach and set goals for growth, see Chapter 2: Resource 3 on the CD-ROM. Use this book as one source for your growth and development along with the experience you will gain as you act as a Data Coach. Monitor your growth periodically, using the self-assessment, and celebrate your progress.

Resource R2.3

Chapter 2: Resource 3
Data Coach Self-Assessment and Goal-Setting

Data Coaches can use this self-assessment to reflect on their current knowledge and set learning goals.

Data Literacy and Collaborative Inquiry Knowledge and Skills

Use demographic data to accurately identify characteristics of students, teachers, and community (see Chapter 3, Task 2)	
Degree to which I know this area:	Degree to which I want to learn more:

Criteria for Selecting Data Coaches

Interpersonal communication is key. If you develop a relationship with people, they will work with you. You've also got to be very comfortable with the data.

—Ann Wacker, Mathematics and Data Coach
Plain Local Schools, Canton, Ohio

Few people come with the full complement of knowledge and skills that are desirable for Data Coaches. Data Coaches are made, not born. They will develop over time through training and experience. In selecting Data Coaches, look for someone

- with the sanction or authority of the district or school administration to play the coach role and to lead Data Teams: Data Coaches can only operate if their role is officially sanctioned and they have the authority, time, and legitimacy to convene and lead Data Teams. Often instructional, assessment, school improvement coaches or coordinators, principals or assistant principals, or team leaders become Data Coaches.
- who demonstrates leadership in instructional improvement—either as an effective and collaborative teacher, an instructional coach, or an administrator who garners the respect of others and is an instructional leader.
- who has a moral commitment to ensuring equity and learning for all students: The role calls for people who are passionate about equity, willing to stand up for their beliefs, and committed to strengthening their own cultural proficiency.
- who is a skilled collaborator and team facilitator.
- who has basic knowledge of school data and assessments: Data Coaches do not need to be experts in statistics or complex data management systems, but they should know the basics of interpreting results and not be afraid of data. Basic knowledge of Excel is a plus.
- who has a willingness to take risks, make mistakes, and continuously learn.

Developing Data Coaches

This book is designed to prepare Data Coaches to carry out their role. It provides step-by-step directions for conducting the 19 Using Data tasks with Data Teams. Individual Data Coaches can prepare themselves for their role by studying the background information and following the detailed procedures in this book and on the CD-ROM. If you are a leader who will be preparing a group of Data Coaches to assume their role, we suggest that you form a study group for the coaches focused on learning the material in this book. The Data Coaches can learn and practice using the tasks with each other in their study group and then use them with Data Teams. After Data Team meetings, the Data Coaches can come back together, debrief their experiences, and prepare for the next set of tasks.

Besides preparation and time to get to know the materials in this book, Data Coaches need time to meet with teams, full access to data, and administrative support. How much time? Some Data Coaches in the Using Data Project worked full-time leading Data Teams in just one school. These Data Coaches gathered and prepared common assessment data and facilitated the process for all the grade-level teams in every content area in their buildings. In most of the elementary and middle schools in Clark County, Nevada, three Data Coaches (a principal and two full-time teachers) shared the role. In Canton City, Ohio, two full-time Data Coaches served four middle schools, one in mathematics and one in science, and two more full-time Data Coaches, one focused on mathematics and one on science, served the district's two major high schools.

ORGANIZE DATA TEAMS

A Data Team is a group of teachers and ideally their building administrator, typically from four to eight members, who work together to use data and improve student learning at the school level. Data Teams can take many different forms. At an elementary school, they often are composed of representatives of different grade levels and focused on a particular content area, such as mathematics. Or they can be a school improvement team or leadership team looking at all content areas and grade levels. In some elementary schools, there is a schoolwide Data Team with representatives from each grade level, who in turn lead grade-level Data Teams. In a middle school or junior and high school, Data Teams are generally organized by department or content area. In some cases, all the members of the department constitute the Data Team. In others, the Data Team is a smaller representative group from the department. In high schools, teachers who teach the same course may form a Data Team. In schools organized as professional learning communities with all teachers participating in teams, those teams function as Data Teams. In the Using Data Project, many schools started out with just one Data Team, but later expanded to every teacher being a member of a Data Team.

As you consider whom to invite onto the Data Team, keep the purpose of your Data Team in mind and use that as a criterion for membership. For example, if the purpose is to use collaborative inquiry in a particular subject area such as language arts or mathematics, your team should include teachers and other staff who have responsibilities in this area, such as members of the district's curriculum committee and staff who have been involved in other related initiatives (e.g., textbook selection and professional development planning in these subjects). If the purpose is to use the Using Data Process to look across all subject areas, you will want to balance the representation to include members from across the different curriculum areas. Other equally important considerations are racial/ethnic diversity and inclusion of specialists such as teachers of English Language Learners or of students with exceptional needs.

There may be a group already in place that you can tap for the Data Team. For example, you may have a group of teacher-leaders who are responsible for mentoring other teachers or a school improvement committee. Look for people who are opinion leaders and reflect different perspectives and can be ambassadors to others for the project. While membership on Data Teams is usually on a volunteer basis, work with others at your site to encourage people who might not volunteer right away to consider being a part of the team. Relying on the "usual suspects" who volunteer for everything can sometimes result in a team of people with too many competing demands on their time and/or who are not representative of the diversity in your school. You may want to consider tapping individuals who are even somewhat skeptical of the process. These individuals can be particularly helpful in identifying roadblocks and concerns that others may be thinking, but not comfortable voicing.

What Do Data Teams Do?

Typical responsibilities for Data Team members might include

- collecting and analyzing a variety of types of school data
- developing or adapting common assessment instruments
- commiting to norms of collaboration and to examining data from an equity perspective
- using the processes and tools in this guide to identify student-learning problems, verify causes, generate solutions, and monitor and achieve results for students
- consulting research to investigate problems, causes, and best practice
- developing data-supported action plans
- communicating with staff and key stakeholders about the findings and the plans
- overseeing the implementation of the plan (schoolwide or vertically) and/or implementing instructional improvement in their own classrooms (grade, course, or subject teams)
- sharing successes and challenges from their own classrooms and/or at the school level
- engaging a broader group of stakeholders to gain their input, involvement, and commitment
- coordinating with other school or district initiatives and leaders
- developing their knowledge and skills in data literacy and collaborative inquiry; content knowledge, pedagogical content knowledge, and generic pedagogical knowledge; cultural proficiency; and leadership and facilitation

Clarifying Roles and Responsibilities

With new structures such as Data Teams and new roles such as Data Coaches, it is important to clarify roles and responsibilities. (Review the checklist of roles and responsibilities in Table 2.3.) As you plan to launch Data Teams, meet with your district and building administrators to clarify the role of the team and its decision-making authority. For example, can the team decide to implement interventions to address student-learning problems, or are they responsible for recommendations to someone else who makes that decision? What ongoing feedback should be provided and to whom about the Data Team's findings? What resources are needed, and how will they be provided? The following checklist can guide you in clarifying roles and responsibilities of Data Teams.

Table 2.3   Checklist for Clarifying Roles and Responsibilities

___ Have you come to agreement with building and district leadership on the roles of the Data Team?

___ Have you documented the decisions that the Data Team has the authority to make and those that are outside of the team's scope? Have you shared that information with the appropriate administrators and potential Data Team members?

___ Have you clarified when and how to involve more of the staff, key stakeholders, and decision makers in the process?

___ Have you identified what you will need in terms of resources for yourself and the Data Team, such as a time and place to meet, a budget for supplies, and resource materials?

___ Have you identified a school or district leader who will be responsible for supporting the effort and on whom you can call when you need help?

CREATE TIME FOR COLLABORATION

Teaching is a three-part act—planning, doing, and reflecting. Unfortunately, school schedules often reflect the assumption that if teachers are not in the classroom in front of students, they are not doing their job. The school day typically has provided time for teaching, but not for the equally important functions of planning and reflecting. Stigler and Hiebert (1999) create an image of a teacher's day that is not unlike a college professor's, with time for teaching and research, collaborative planning and reflecting with colleagues, and "office hours" with individual students. Although this vision may not become a reality in schools in the near future, changing the school schedule somewhat to create time for teacher collaboration is a requirement for collaborative inquiry. A growing body of research linking teacher collaboration with student achievement (Darling-Hammond, 2004; Little, 1990; Louis, Kruse, & Marks, 1996; McLaughlin & Talbert, 2001) makes this conclusion inescapable and urgent: Time for teacher collaboration is not a luxury—it is a necessity for schools that want to improve.

How much time? Along with other school improvement experts, we recommend a minimum of 45 minutes per week of uninterrupted, protected time for collaboration. Many schools participating in the Using Data Project were able to carve out weekly or even daily time for teachers to work together by creative use of specialists, block scheduling, or reallocation of teacher contract time. Others convened the Data Team quarterly for a full release-day of analyzing common benchmark assessment results, along with two- to three-day data retreats in the summer. The growing number of schools across the country that now schedule time for teacher collaboration during the school day prove that finding time is a solvable problem when the will is present to do so.

ENSURE TIMELY ACCESS TO ROBUST DATA SOURCES: THE DEMOCRATIZATION OF DATA

By the end of the 2004–2005 school year most grade levels had given some common assessments and had tried to compile the data. We did this using Math-and-Science Partnership project time during the school day. This was a long process because we had to compile the data by hand. We had no time left to actually dive into it and discover what we needed to change in terms of instructional strategies. All that changed with the purchase of the Principia software package. Now we are able to use that same time to make data-driven decisions.

—Ann Wacker, Mathematics and Data Coach
Plain Local Schools, Canton, Ohio

In the early days of the Using Data Project, staff confronted a confounding obstacle: The very people who could make the best use of student-learning data—the teachers—had the least access to the data. Test data were "under lock and key" and were the "private property" of the research, assessment, or other district office. Teachers often did not receive assessment data at all, or received them so long after the tests were administered that they were not even teaching the same children. Project staff and district and school-based collaborators had to advocate strongly to "democratize the data," giving teachers access to their students' results. Thankfully, times are changing as more districts put timely data systems into place that make a variety of school data readily available to teachers.

However, even with the best data management systems, data access can still be problematic. For example, many states do not report data at the item level or release test items for teachers to analyze. Yet item-level data (see Task 9), when used in conjunction with the actual test items, are among the most useful data teachers have to improve their instruction.

One way around this problem is for schools to make or buy their own assessments and assure that teachers have just-in-time access to both the item-level results and the items themselves. This is one reason why common benchmark assessments are so important to improvement. Because they lend themselves to item analysis, are administered periodically throughout the school year, and align with local standards and curriculum, they can fuel collaborative inquiry.

But the data access problem may not yet be solved. The next challenge is to get results from common assessments to teachers fast, within a few days—in time for them to actually *do* something about them. Fortunately, this problem has a simple technological solution: inexpensive software programs and scanners, which can scan about 200 tests per hour, placed in easy access of the Data Coach. When put in place in participating Using Data schools, these machines removed the data bottleneck and got collaborative inquiry moving.

The good news is that much of the data that fuels collaborative inquiry is not dependent on expensive data management systems. Simple scanners will do the job of churning out the item-level data on local assessments. Some of the most robust data sources, formative classroom assessments and common assessments such as student work, mathematics problems of the week, and science journals, require no data management system at all—just teachers collecting their students' work and sharing it with colleagues. While data management systems facilitate data access, they are not a prerequisite for collaborative inquiry.

SUMMARY

As you lay the groundwork for implementing collaborative inquiry in a school, district, or educational improvement project, remember the adage "Go slow to go fast." It is well worth the time to create the conditions for success: an effort that is aligned and integrated with other initiatives and data management; buy-in from key stakeholders; well-prepared Data Coaches with authority and time to carry out their role; Data Teams of teachers and administrators established at the school, grade, department, and/or course level; a minimum of 45 minutes weekly for Data Teams to work together; and the mechanisms for giving teachers timely access (within days of the assessment) to student-learning data, especially at the item level.

Building the Foundation

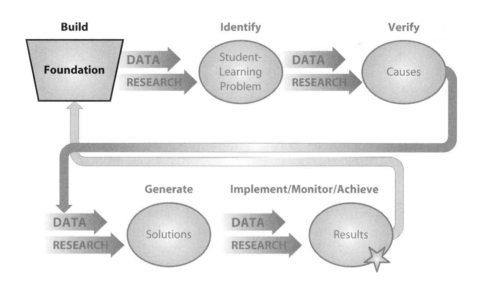

Blaming students for poor test scores is actually a part of the status quo. In this country, no matter what our color, we are all bombarded with information that is racist, classist, and sexist. Data Coaches have to spend significant time on building the foundation or we carry harmful ideas into the data dialogue with us. This became apparent during a training I conducted. A quarter of the participants missed the Building the Foundation component of the program. The difference between the participants who experienced Building the Foundation and those that did not was huge. When we got into looking at the data, the participants without

the foundational tasks did not have the same awareness about equity issues. They jumped to inferences about the limitations of certain students rather than questioning instructional practices. If you skip Building the Foundation you will put our children at risk. We have to attack harmful beliefs head-on.

—Aminata Umoja, Using Data Trainer and
Independent Consultant, Atlanta, Georgia

What really attracted me to the Using Data Process was the foundational pieces—finding out what the context is, getting that commitment, asking, "Do we want to go in the same direction? Build collaborative leadership? Have the same goals?" If I have one piece of advice for others, it is to do more about laying the groundwork.

—Karen Brighton, Program Manager
Arizona Rural Systemic Initiative

We start this chapter with a request: Please do not skip over these activities! The tasks in Building the Foundation set the Using Data Process apart from other approaches to using data. In these tasks, the Data Team builds a rock-solid foundation of commitments to each other, to all students, and to the Using Data Process of Collaborative Inquiry. These commitments will help keep the Data Team standing strong and able to fulfill their larger purpose—improving teaching and learning and closing achievement gaps.

In Task 1, the team members learn about the Using Data Process and clarify their purpose, decision-making authority, and roles and responsibilities. In Task 2, they study their own context so that they understand the diversity of students whom they serve and consider the changes in culture, equity, data use, collaboration, and results that they will help to bring about in their school. In Task 3, they learn to view their work through the lens of cultural proficiency—continually strengthening their own understanding and respect for diverse cultures so that data are truly a catalyst for closing achievement gaps. Finally, in Task 4, they openly explore their own values about student learning and equity, "getting ethical before they get technical" (F. CampbellJones, personal communication, December 10, 2005). They identify what they want students to learn and how they will know when students learn it. And they vividly create a vision of the school of their dreams.

Like a strong building foundation, these tasks help the Data Team stand up to the pressures, conflicts, and challenges they will inevitably face. For example, when they begin their analysis of student-learning data, if comments reflect a lack of understanding and respect for African American students, the team will have language and tools for challenging assumptions. If they grow discouraged by low test scores, they will have a compelling vision to keep them motivated. If conflict erupts in the group, they have established collaborative norms to negotiate difficult conversations.

The work the Data Team does in the four tasks in this chapter is pertinent to every subsequent task in the Using Data Process. They establish the parameters, understandings, values, and vision that will guide the Data Team throughout the Using Data Process. Throughout this book, the authors will prompt the Data Coach to refer back to the understandings and products of these early tasks to inform, inspire, and guide the Data Team as they analyze data and plan for and take action. These tasks and the outcomes for Data Teams are summarized in the Table 3.1 below.

Table 3.1   Building the Foundation Tasks and Data Team Outcomes

Building the foundation tasks	Data Team outcomes: The Data Team . . .
Task 1: Launch the Data Team	• Can describe the Using Data Process and collaborative inquiry. • Is clear about their purpose, membership, roles and responsibilities, decision-making authority, relationships with other initiatives and staff, and agreements about working together.
Task 2: Reflect on Our School	• Can identify trends over time in student enrollment and teacher and community characteristics through analysis of demographic data. • Can compare dialogue and discussion. • Can distinguish between observation and inference. • Can define the cultural changes in their school that they are working toward. • Can identify where their school is now in the process of creating a high-performing Using Data culture.
Task 3: Raise Awareness of Cultural Proficiency	• Can explain the relevance of cultural proficiency to their work as a Data Team. • Understands the five cultural proficiency principles. • Can apply the Cultural Proficiency Continuum to assess their own as well as their team's cultural proficiency and to set growth goals.
Task 4: Commit to Shared Values, Standards, and Vision	• Embraces a shared vision for their school. • Can answer the questions: what they want students to know and be able to do, how they will know if students don't know, and what they will do if students don't learn. • Agrees on core values about student learning and equity.

FOUNDATIONAL TOOLS

The Building the Foundation component of the Using Data Process is foundational in another way. During this part of the process, the team is introduced to six tools that are at the core of the work and are used in most other Using Data Process tasks. Descriptions of these six tools follow:

Collaborative Norms (for example, the Seven Norms of Collaboration, from Garmston & Wellman, 1999; see Toolkit). Collaborative norms are agreements about how team members will interact—agreements that will help them work together effectively. Collaborative norms are introduced in Task 1 and used throughout the Using Data Process. (See Task 1 section, "Background Information for Data Coaches," for more on norms.)

Data-Driven Dialogue (adapted from Wellman & Lipton, 2004; see Toolkit). At the heart of the Using Data Process is a structured approach that enables a Data Team to explore predictions and observation of data before offering explanations or solutions. It includes four phases: (1) predict, (2) go visual, (3) observe, and (4) infer/question. In all the tasks that involve data analysis, Data-Driven Dialogue is the process used for exploring assumptions and making sense of data.

Go Visual (based on the work of Grinder, 1997; see Toolkit). Data Teams create large, visually vibrant, simple, and colorful displays of data and other products of the Using Data Process to facilitate team engagement and learning. This concept can be applied to virtually every task in the Using Data Process. Data Teams can generate visual displays of their vision, the Cultural Proficiency Continuum, and their self-assessment of their data culture in Building the Foundation. They display their data in color-coded graphs in Identifying the Student-Learning Problem and Verifying Causes. Finally, they go visual with their cause-and-effect analysis (Verifying Causes) and their Logic Model (Generating Solutions). Visuals anchor the team's work and can be shared with other audiences.

The Program Elements Matrix (PEM) of a Using Data School Culture (see Toolkit). Data Teams use this reflection and planning tool for assessing and moving toward the major shifts in school culture, data use, equity, instruction, collaboration, and student learning that they desire. The team does the self-assessment and planning in the Building the Foundation component and periodically reassesses their progress throughout the Using Data Process.

The Cultural Proficiency Continuum (Cross, 1989; Lindsey, Nuri Robins, & Terrell, 2003; see Toolkit). This framework describes a range of responses to diversity from cultural destructiveness to cultural proficiency. In Building the Foundation, the team members learn about the concepts that underlie the continuum and explore each of its dimensions. Periodically they will revisit the continuum to assess the extent to which their dialogue, causes, and solutions reflect understanding and respect for diverse cultures.

School of Our Dreams (see Task 4). This is a visioning activity in which the team constructs a visual representation of the ideal school. They envision what student learning, curriculum, instruction, equity, and critical supports such as professional development, school culture, and leadership will be in their ideal school. The School of Our Dreams guides the team throughout the Using Data Process and acts as a touchstone to assure that actions the team takes align with their vision and values and move them closer to their dream school. Periodically, the Data Team is asked to check for alignment and to see if and how their vision has evolved.

STANDARD PROCEDURES FOR DATA TEAM MEETINGS

The tasks described in this and subsequent chapters are carried out in Data Team meetings. The instructions for the tasks include time estimates for how long each activity will take. Some tasks may be completed in a single 45-minute meeting; others will span several meetings. While each task has its own unique set of directions, there are some standard procedures you will use for every Data Team meeting, no matter which task you are doing. These include

Preparing for Data Team Meetings: Processes

• Prior to each Data Team session, read through the procedure for the task in the book, including Background Information for Data Coaches, and in the relevant task link on the CD-ROM.

• Schedule the meeting well in advance, create an agenda for the session (see "Sample Goals and Agenda" on the CD-ROM), and distribute it to all Data Team members prior to convening. Confirm attendance one to two days prior to the session.

• Prepare your handouts and other materials as noted. All procedures and material-preparation steps are based on facilitating the process with one Data Team that consists of four to eight members. If your Data Team is larger or smaller, adapt the directions accordingly.

• Each time you convene the Data Team, it is important to consider the room arrangement. Ideally, have the Data Team work together at large oval, round, or rectangular tables. Provide wall space for posting charts and graphs from each task as part of the Data Wall, a display of the data that the team analyzes along with their observations and inferences about the data (see Toolkit: Data Wall). Typically, each task requires three to five sheets of chart paper. The more wall space the better, since you will be adding more chart paper to your Data Wall as you analyze new data sources (see Tasks 6–12). A complete Data Wall requires space for two rows and six or more columns of chart paper.

• The team will be documenting its history through the products it generates. Many Data Coaches have used large artist portfolio cases to store and transport the Data Wall and other important visual products of the Data Team meetings. Save important artifacts of the team's work and bring them to each meeting. This is a responsibility that can be assigned to the person who takes on the role of materials manager (see Task 6 and Toolkit: Group Roles). To help manage the Data Wall, the materials manager can remove and store prediction charts after each task involving Data-Driven Dialogue for possible later reference.

Preparing for Data Team Meetings: Materials

For each task, the Data Team will require a variety of supplies. Most require several sheets of chart paper, a flip chart stand, several different colored marking pens, and masking tape. You should also have available one or two sets of highlighters (red, green, and yellow), Post-its, graphing chart paper, card stock (heavy-duty paper), one package of ¾-inch round color-coding labels, scissors, a timer, and a computer and an LCD projector for displaying PowerPoint slides. For Tasks 6–12, you will also need sentence strips (strips of heavy-duty paper that are about 3" × 24" in size); they can be bought or you can cut your own. We recommend putting together a toolbox that includes all of these items. It is a good idea to purchase several pads of chart paper and keep them in a secure place. The person who takes on the role of materials manager (see Task 6 and Toolkit: Group Roles) should be asked to restock the supplies prior to each meeting.

• Create a poster-size version showing the five components of the Using Data Process of Collaborative Inquiry to post on the wall (see PowerPoint Slide S1.2 in the Task 1 CD-ROM link). If possible, laminate it since you will bring it to each team meeting. Use a Post-it in the shape of an arrow to mark where the team is in the process at any given time.

• Your collaborative norms will be used in each task. Make a large poster of these norms to tape to the wall or make several regular-size copies, laminate them, and put them on the table each time the Data Team convenes. You are prompted to help the Data Team reflect on and process their use of the norms at the beginning and end of each Data Team meeting. The "Seven Norms of Collaboration" (see Toolkit) provides suggestions for processing of collaborative norms.

• In addition to the collaborative norms, your Data Team will be introduced to group roles in Task 6 and will practice these roles in all subsequent tasks. Directions are provided in Task 6 for preparing group role table-tent cards. Make sure these cards are available to the team during Tasks 6 through 19.

• Two charts that you and the Data Team create in Building the Foundation— Cultural Proficiency Continuum (Task 3) and School of Our Dreams (Task 4)—will be referenced in numerous tasks. Make sure that these two charts are posted in the room during each Data Team meeting. Also, keep your Program Elements Matrix (PEM) of a Using Data School Culture charts (Task 2) for possible reference in later tasks.

In summary, you will want to have the following materials available for Data Team meetings:

Agenda with goals

Toolbox of materials

Using Data Process of Collaborative Inquiry poster

Collaborative norms poster

An established process for reflection on the collaborative norms

Group role table-tent cards

Cultural Proficiency Continuum chart

School of Our Dreams chart

Program Elements Matrix (PEM) of a Using Data School Culture charts

Task 1: Launch the Data Team

Task-at-a-Glance

Purpose	To introduce the Data Team to the Using Data Process and clarify the team's purpose, roles, and norms and procedures for working together
Data	None
Questions to ask	What is the purpose of the Data Team? What is the Using Data Process of Collaborative Inquiry? What are the roles and responsibilities of the Data Team and Data Coach? How will we interact with other teams, initiatives, or stakeholders? How will we work together?
Concepts	Using Data Process of Collaborative Inquiry Data Team Group norms Seven Norms of Collaboration Four Agreements of Courageous Conversations Discussing "undiscussables"
Activities	Activity 1.1: Connect as a Team Activity 1.2: Introduce the Using Data Process of Collaborative Inquiry Activity 1.3: Clarify the Data Team's Purpose and Roles and Responsibilities Activity 1.4: Establish Collaborative Norms

Vignette: Why Take Time to Launch the Data Team?

One Latino member of a Data Team points out that the Latino/a students believe that advanced courses are for White students. Other team members argue that there is no racial bias in the school and that all students are treated the same. "Why do we have to talk about race? Why can't we just talk about students?" The subject of race never comes up again, closing down the opportunity for the team to tackle a serious barrier to student learning in their school.

The Data Team finds out after the fact that it can only recommend, not decide. Members are frustrated and angry that all their hard work has led to naught.

No one on the team feels comfortable or safe enough to share the results of their classroom assessments with others.

As the science department chair and someone who has been in most of the science teachers' classrooms, Yolanda has some insightful ideas about what really happens in classrooms and how teachers are teaching. However, the rest of the team rarely pauses long enough for Yolanda to get a word in edgewise. Her frustration grows since she is unable to contribute in a meaningful way to identify some of the potential causes of low student achievement in science.

WHAT IS TASK 1?

A team is a small number of people with complementary skills who are committed to a common purpose, performance goals, and approach for which they hold themselves mutually accountable.

—Katzenbach and Smith, 1994, p. 45

High-functioning teams are clear about their purpose, work interdependently to achieve shared goals, and are accountable to each other. The purpose of Task 1 is to get the Data Team off to a strong start on its way to becoming a high-functioning team. In this task, you will guide the Data Team to answer the following questions: (1) Who are we as a team? (2) What are we doing? (3) Why are we doing it? (4) How will we work together to achieve results?

This task includes a team-building activity to help members get to know each other, especially if they are a new team. Also in this task, the Data Coach introduces the Using Data Process and helps the team establish its purpose—that is, to improve student learning and close achievement gaps through collaborative inquiry. Building on the advance preparation you have done organizing for collaborative inquiry (e.g., building stakeholder support and clarifying roles and responsibilities, as described in Chapter 2), you will now help clarify the Data Coach's and the team's roles, responsibilities, and decision-making authority and plan for how the team will interact with other teams and initiatives. Finally, you will assist the team in establishing agreements about how the team members will work with each other. The product for this task will be a completed Launching the Data Team Planning Template (see Handout H1.4, as well as illustrations in the Data Coach Notes, Activities 1.3 and 1.4).

As the vignettes on page 52 illustrate, being part of a dysfunctional team is a frustrating experience. We've all been there—on teams that meander aimlessly or devote their time to discussing trivial matters because they don't have a focus on student learning, teams that step around the elephant in the living room rather than talk about tough issues like race or poor teaching, or teams that avoid conflict or implode through destructive or unresolved conflict. Task 1 is preventive medicine. It lays the foundation for teams to function well and make a difference by establishing the basic skills and processes of good teamwork.

BACKGROUND INFORMATION FOR DATA COACHES

What Are the Basics of Successful Data Teams?

Successful Data Teams commit themselves to a common, compelling purpose—in this case, to improve results for all students. When the road gets rough, they go back to their purpose as a touchstone and motivator. This is your opportunity to get the team excited about the Using Data Process, to tap into their commitment to improve the lives of students, and to enlist them in continuous improvement of student learning. This task will prepare them for the challenges that lie ahead, remind them why they are poring over so much data, and guide them as they set student-learning goals and take action to achieve them.

A second "basic" of successful Data Teams is that they have clearly defined roles, responsibilities, and decision-making authority, and the teams organize themselves to do their work. High-functioning teams share leadership and the workload. Each member takes on a key role in helping the team be successful and achieve its goals. In your Data Team, you will play the role of Data Coach. The roles of the Data Coach and of the Data Team members are described in Chapter 2. As the team progresses, members will take on specialized roles such as facilitator, recorder, materials manager, dialogue monitor, and timekeeper—these roles are described in Group Roles (see Toolkit) and are introduced to the team in Task 6. Finally, effective teams are organized to do their work. Such teams establish regular meeting times, structures for meetings, and agendas. They work on one task and usually one kind of data at a time and learn the processes and skills of collaborative inquiry.

Third, successful Data Teams have agreements about how they will work with each other, are mutually accountable, and discuss the "undiscussables." The effectiveness of the team is in direct proportion to the interpersonal skills of team members. High-functioning team members are skilled at interpersonal communication, conflict resolution, and collaborative norms. They speak candidly, listen intently, make commitments to each other and acknowledge when they break a commitment, and cheer for and celebrate each other's successes while openly sharing their own weaknesses. Team members aren't born this way. They develop these skills through commitment, practice, and ongoing monitoring and reflection.

How Do Data Teams Establish Collaborative Norms?

We are always working on the norms in our team of field staff and Data Coaches. We individually choose a norm to focus on, pair up to coach each other, and collect data to debrief. This has made a huge difference in including everyone's voice and embracing the diversity of our team, which includes Native Americans and Whites, males and females.

—Karen Brighton, Program Manager
Arizona Rural Systemic Initiative

An important dimension of your role as Data Coach is to guide the group in agreeing on a set of collaborative norms for the team. We recommend that Data Teams study group norms already developed, such as the Seven Norms of Collaboration (adapted from Garmston & Wellman, 1999) or the Four Agreements for Courageous Conversations (Singleton & Linton, 2006), which have been useful to a variety of school teams. Each is described briefly below. Then Data Teams can decide to (1) adopt one, the other, or both, (2) adapt one or both to better suit the team's needs, or (3) generate their own new set of norms for working together.

The Seven Norms of Collaboration

The Seven Norms of Collaboration (see Toolkit) are drawn from the work of Robert Garmston and Bruce Wellman (1999) and others. They are

1. Pausing: Pausing before responding or asking a question allows time for thinking and enhances dialogue.

2. Paraphrasing: Using a paraphrase of another team member's statements allows members of the group to hear and understand each other better as they consider ideas and formulate decisions.

3. Probing for specificity: Using gentle, open-ended probes or inquiries, such as "I'm curious about . . ." or "I'd like to hear more about . . . ," increases the clarity and precision of the group's thinking.

4. Putting ideas on the table and pulling them off: Ideas are the heart of a meaningful dialogue. Label the intention of your comments by saying, for example, "One thought I have is . . ." or "Here is a possible approach. . . ." It is equally important to know when an idea may be blocking dialogue or "derailing" the process and therefore should be taken off the table.

5. Paying attention to self and others: Meaningful dialogue is facilitated when each group member is conscious of self and of others and is aware not only of what he or she is saying but of how it is said and how others are responding.

6. Presuming positive intentions: Assuming that others' intentions are positive promotes and facilitates meaningful dialogue and eliminates unintentional put-downs. Using positive presuppositions in your speech is one manifestation of this norm.

7. Pursuing a balance between advocacy and inquiry: Pursuing and maintaining a balance between advocating for a position and inquiring about the positions held by others helps create a genuine learning community.

Although these norms have been widely used in the Using Data work, cognitive coaching, and other school contexts, they also have been criticized for not being culturally sensitive and may not be appropriate for all groups. For example, during the development of the Using Data work, some African Americans and Latinos/as participating in a group with White members found it difficult to embrace "positive intentions" given the long history of racism in schools and society. Until White team members clearly demonstrated a commitment to work on their own racism, the African Americans and Latinos/as did not feel that they could authentically commit to this norm without putting themselves in emotional jeopardy. On the other hand, Native Americans who participated in our project appreciated the norm of pausing, as it is commonly practiced in their culture and allows time for the constant translation they make between their language and culture and the dominant White culture. We recommend asking the team if there are any norms that any member cannot live with and eliminating those from the list or revisiting them later in the team's work.

Four Agreements of Courageous Conversations[1]

Glenn Singleton and Curtis Linton, in their book *Courageous Conversations About Race* (2006), offer another approach to collaborative norms that is especially relevant to talking about race. Their Four Agreements of Courageous Conversations are

1. Stay engaged: Staying engaged means "remaining morally, emotionally, intellectually, and socially involved in the dialogue" (p. 59).

---

1. SOURCE *Courageous Conversations About Race: A Field Guide for Achieving Equity in Schools*, by Glenn E. Singleton and Curtis Linton, 2006, Thousand Oaks, CA: Corwin Press. Reprinted with permission.

2. Experience discomfort: This norm acknowledges that discomfort is inevitable, especially in dialogue about race, and that participants make a commitment to bring issues into the open. It is not talking about these issues that creates divisiveness. The divisiveness already exists in the society and in our schools. It is through dialogue, even when uncomfortable, that healing and change begin.

3. Speak your truth: This means being open about thoughts and feelings and not just saying what you think others want to hear.

4. Expect and accept nonclosure: This agreement asks participants to "hang out in uncertainty" and not rush to quick solutions, especially in relation to racial understanding, which requires ongoing dialogue (pp. 58–65).

A third option is for the groups to simply generate their own group norms by brainstorming together and eliminating any norms that any team member cannot live with. Whichever approach the team chooses, it is important to make sure that Data Team members are clear about the norms. Then, at virtually every meeting, ask members to focus on a specific norm for that meeting, practice it, and reflect on their effectiveness afterwards. This keeps the group focused on improving their group process at the same time that they are accomplishing the tasks. Changes can be made at any time if a norm is no longer serving the group or the group sees that a new one needs to be added.

Regardless of which approach to collaborative norms you choose, teams are more productive when members are mutually accountable for keeping the agreements that they make. One of the authors, while working with cooperative learning groups in the classroom, recalls a student who, though chronically absent, made sure he showed up to present the team's project. He felt accountable to the team. That's the sense of commitment you want your team members to develop. We make promises to each other—to bring our student work, to prepare for meetings, to be candid, to practice the collaborative norms—and we keep our word. As Data Coach, you play an important role in modeling these behaviors and developing them in team members.

Finally, effective teams discuss "undiscussables," defined by Roland Barth (2006) as "important matters that, as a profession, we seldom openly discuss" (p. 9) except in parking lots or behind closed doors, such as race and racism, class and classism, underperforming teachers and administrators, and the nature of relationships among the adults within the school. Topics of discussion that researchers have found to be associated with high-functioning teacher teams in particular are high frequency of talking to each other precisely and concretely about the practice of teaching (Little, 1982) and asking for and providing one another with assistance (Rosenholtz, 1991). You may want to ask the Data Team how willing they are to take on these and other topics that may not typically be talked about in their school. Data open the door to the undiscussables, but we found Data Teams faced difficulty in entering because they lacked experience and norms for having these hard discussions. Your job as Data Coach is to help the team walk through the door safely in the Data Team meeting, not in the parking lot afterwards. This guide will provide you with dialogue tools to help.

What Is the Using Data Process of Collaborative Inquiry?

This task also introduces the Data Team to the Using Data Process of Collaborative Inquiry, a process where teachers and administrators work together to construct their understanding of student-learning problems and embrace and test out solutions through rigorous use of multiple data sources and reflective dialogue. As discussed in Chapter 1, the Using Data Process is a structured approach to collaborative inquiry represented by the Using Data Process model and the 19 tasks that form the core of this book (see Figure 1.6).

What Are the Challenges and Pitfalls Inherent in This Task?

Unresolved Personal and Informational Concerns

When beginning a new program, participants typically have personal and informational concerns (Hall & Hord, 2006). Personal concerns pertain to the self: "How will this affect me? Will data be used against teachers? Can I do what is expected of me? I'm not all that comfortable with data. How much time will it take? Is this going to be another one of those start-ups that fizzle after a year?" Informational concerns include questions such as "How long is the time commitment? What resources will be available? What are the goals of the program? What will be expected of me?" Resolving these concerns helps participants move ahead. Failure to resolve them can derail you.

Early in the process, encourage these personal and informational concerns to surface and directly address them. Provide clear and accurate information about process in a variety of ways—in writing, presentations, and video. Be enthusiastic. Include, if possible, people who have used the process elsewhere with success. Help the team understand how this will help them better serve students and do their work (Hall & Hord, 2006). Keep the introduction to the program at what Hall and Hord refer to as "awareness level." Don't jump into implementation until these concerns are dealt with. Make sure that information is provided both about the program and about the resources and support available to assure its effectiveness. Also be aware that personal and informational concerns are likely to surface again later in the Using Data Process as new tasks are encountered. Be prepared to address these as they arise. (See Toolkit: Stages of Concern and Levels of Use for more information.)

The Data Team Has Not Clarified Its Relationship With Other Initiatives

Often, schools have multiple initiatives in place, leaving teachers and administrators feeling overwhelmed and overburdened. Their attention, motivation, and commitment levels are strained. In one school the authors worked with, the Data Team identified 22 separate mathematics and science initiatives, only a few of which had been in place for more than two years.

Set aside time in Activity 1.1 below to list all of the important initiatives under way in the school. Help the Data Team explore ways in which the initiatives might support each other and share rather than compete for resources, including staff's time, energy, and commitment. Coordinate with leaders of those initiatives, and develop a plan for staying in communication with them about your actions and progress.

Data Team Members Are Impatient With the Process and Want to Get Right to the Data

Assure the team that Task 2 will get them into data. Provide the rationale for "going slow to go fast"—establishing a solid process so that the team can be efficient and effective in doing its work with data.

RESOURCES

Cozemius, A., & O'Neill, J. (1999). *The handbook for SMART school teams.* Bloomington, IN: National Educational Service.

Garmston, R. J., & Wellman, B. M. (1999). *The adaptive school: A sourcebook for developing collaborative groups.* Norwood, MA: Christopher-Gordon.

Katzenbach, J. R., & Smith, D. K. (1994). *The wisdom of teams: Creating the high-performance organization.* New York: HarperBusiness.

Singleton, G. E., & Linton, C. (2006). *Courageous conversations about race: A field guide for achieving equity in schools.* Thousand Oaks, CA: Corwin Press.

MAJOR ACTIVITIES FOR TASK 1

Task-at-a-Glance

Activity	*Time required*	*CD-ROM materials: Task 1 link*	*CD-ROM Toolkit: Relevant tools*
Activity 1.1: Connect as a Team	20 minutes		Synectics
Activity 1.2: Introduce the Using Data Process of Collaborative Inquiry	60 minutes	PowerPoint slides S1.1–S1.18 Handout H1.1: Using Data Process Overview Handout H1.2: The Using Data Process Components and Tasks Handout H1.3: Using Data Gets Results	Key Concepts/ Key Words
Activity 1.3: Clarify the Data Team's Purpose and Roles and Responsibilities	30 minutes	Handout H1.4: Launching the Data Team Planning Template Handout H1.5: Data Team Responsibilities	
Activity 1.4: Establish Collaborative Norms	45 minutes	Handout H1.4: Launching the Data Team Planning Template Handout H1.6: Norms of Collaboration	Seven Norms of Collaboration

PREPARING FOR THE TASK

- Read "Background Information for Data Coaches"; see the CD-ROM: Task 1 for handouts, PowerPoint slides, and sample goals and agenda; and review "Standard Procedures for Data Team Meetings" (see the introduction to Chapter 3 in this book and on CD-ROM). Although tool directions are embedded in the Data Coach Notes below, you can also reference in-depth descriptions of relevant Toolkit entries on the CD-ROM.

- Read Chapters 1 and 2 of this book. Make sure the advance work of organizing Data Teams and determining team membership, described in Chapter 2, has been completed.

- Determine if you can conduct all Task 1 activities during one Data Team meeting or if these activities should span two meetings. One possible way to split the activities into two meetings is to do Activities 1.1 and 1.2 in one meeting and 1.3 and 1.4 at a subsequent meeting (see "Sample Goals and Agenda" on CD-ROM).

- Make sure you have clarified with building and district leadership what the roles and responsibilities of the Data Team will be, including the authority the team has to make decisions and take action and other responsibilities the team will carry out.

MATERIALS PREPARATION

- Print Handouts H1.1–H1.6 from the CD-ROM, and make one copy for each team member (note, however, that H1.3 is optional—it's for those who desire more detailed evaluation results about the Using Data Process). In addition, print H1.2 in color if possible. Provide the team with Handouts H1.1 and H1.2 in advance of the meeting, and ask them to read the material and bring the handouts to the meeting. You might want to make a few extra copies in case someone forgets to bring them.

- For the Synectics activity, collect a variety of postcards (two to three cards per person) so that each person or group of people has a selection to choose from. Good choices are ones that show a variety of people or animals in funny or serious predicaments. Remember to consider diversity in your selection of cards by including people of varied racial and ethnic groups and both genders.

- Have available chart paper and a flip chart stand, marking pens, and one highlighter per Data Team member.

- Prepare to show the PowerPoint slides, an overview of the Using Data Process. Read over the Notes Pages for each slide. See Chapter 1 for additional background information.

DATA COACH NOTES

 ### Activity 1.1: Connect as a Team

1. Welcome the team, and review the purpose of this task and the goals and agenda of the meeting.

2. Introduce the Data Team to the purpose of Synectics, a strategy developed by William Gordon (1961), which is to break the ice, hear each team member's voice, use their creativity, and start them thinking about the work of the Data Team in a light and engaging way.

> **Facilitation Note:** Although there are thousands of icebreaker activities to choose from, the authors have had success and fun with Synectics, a creative brainstorming strategy for connecting two completely dissimilar ideas, such as "How is a challenge you face with using data like a truck loaded down with bundles and no driver?"

3. Pose a question that will elicit the group's experience with data, such as "How often do you use data, and for what purpose do you use that data?" Ask each person to select a postcard that reflects his or her experience with using data. If necessary, prompt with additional questions, such as "How have you used data? What challenges or struggles do you face when looking at or using data?" For example, when looking at a picture of a truck loaded with bundles but with no driver, someone might say, "We are loaded down with data, but lack a clear direction in how to use them."

4. Distribute the postcards. After everyone has selected a card, ask each person to describe the image on the card and to share why he or she selected the card.

5. Record the comments on chart paper.

6. Synthesize the learning from the activity by pointing out the key points of what was shared.

7. Build on the team's comments by making the point that the Using Data Process of Collaborative Inquiry is a way to meet some of the challenges they identified in Synectics. Throughout the Using Data Process they will emphasize the positive aspects of data use while deemphasizing the more negative aspects identified.

 ### Activity 1.2: Introduce the Using Data Process of Collaborative Inquiry

1. Introduce the Data Team to the purpose of this activity—to explore the main components and overarching goals of their work together in the Using Data Process.

2. Do a brief presentation of the PowerPoint slides to orient the team to the program (see the notes for each slide in the View: Notes Page on the CD-ROM).

3. Ask Data Team members to take out Handout H1.1 (which they received in advance of the meeting, along with Handout H1.2), and distribute highlighters to each Data Team member. (Have a few extra copies of the handouts available in case anyone forgot to bring them.)

> **Facilitation Note:** For those who are interested in more details about the impact of the Using Data Process on student learning and school culture, share Handout H1.3.

4. Introduce the Key Concepts/Key Words strategy (adapted from Wellman & Lipton, 2004; used with permission). Explain to the Data Team that they will read the selection and use the highlighters to mark key concepts or key words that they think convey the meaning of the reading.

5. Provide appropriate time for the reading.

6. Have team members find a partner. Ask them to share with each other what they highlighted and why.

7. Debrief the reading and the process with the entire team. Note which concepts or words were most frequently highlighted. Did these convey the meaning of the reading? What concepts or words did only a few people highlight? How did their highlighting add to the group's understanding of the reading?

8. Use the reading as a springboard for the task the team is addressing. How will the reading inform their work? What did the team learn that they want to apply to their work?

9. Engage the whole Data Team in a discussion of the ideas in the reading. Here are some prompting questions to use:
- How is the Using Data Process similar to and different from other approaches to using data?
- What are the core values that underlie the work? How do these align with the team members' core values?
- What has been the impact of the Using Data Process in other schools? What results would we most like to see in our school?
- What is your reaction to the idea of making shifts toward a higher-performing Using Data School Culture? To what extent are we already making these shifts in our school? Where could we put more emphasis?
- What questions do you have now?

10. Once the team has a basic understanding of the Using Data Process, team members may want to know that the district or project is committed to the effort, that resources such as time and data will be provided, that principals and key district administrators support the effort, and that the Using Data Process will be well coordinated and integrated with other initiatives. Share the plan to date that has emerged from your work in coordinating with other initiatives and building stakeholder support (on CD-ROM, see Chapter 2: Resources R2.1 and R2.2). Ask for questions. Let the team know that the groundwork has been laid, and the team will plan further in the next activities how they will engage stakeholders and coordinate with other initiatives.

Activity 1.3: Clarify the Data Team's Purpose and Roles and Responsibilities

1. Distribute Handout H1.4, and let the team know that you will be recording responses to the questions on the Planning Template on chart paper.

2. Ask the Data Team to review the purpose of collaborative inquiry and Data Teams outlined in Handout H1.1. Then direct their attention to the statement at the end of the first paragraph, which sums up the purpose of the Using Data Process and indicates that Data Teams engage in collaborative inquiry and influence the culture of schools by using data collaboratively, continuously, and effectively to improve student learning and close achievement gaps. Engage the team in a dialogue about the purpose for their team. Do they agree with this purpose as stated? How do they want to modify it? Once the team agrees on a purpose statement, record it on the Launching the Data Team Planning Template (Question 1).

Handout H1.4 page 1

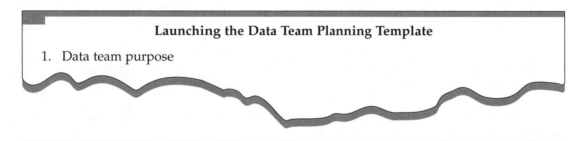

Launching the Data Team Planning Template

1. Data team purpose

Sample Timeline for a Mathematics Data Team

2e) The timeline for the team's work is

April–June: Build our foundation (Tasks 1–4).

August data retreat: Implement Tasks 5–12 with state CRT data and district high school mathematics data, develop common benchmark assessments for all mathematics courses.

October: Analyze first common assessment; begin short-cycle improvements.

November: Collect and analyze local assessment data and research to verify causes (Tasks 13–14); share with key stakeholders.

December–January: Analyze second common assessment and continue short-cycle improvement.

February–March: Analyze third common assessment and continue short-cycle improvements; finalize long-term action and monitoring plans (Tasks 15–17); share plans with key stakeholders.

April–June: Implement action plans; analyze fourth common assessment and continue short-cycle improvements; examine monitoring data (Task 18).

3. Distribute Handout H1.5, and give the team time to look over the list of typical Data Team responsibilities (see Chapter 2). Ask them to adapt the list as relevant in their setting, and record it on the Planning Template (Question 2a). Then review your role as Data Coach with the Data Team (see Chapter 2). Answer any questions participants have, and record the role in Question 2b.

4. Based on the work you have done in advance to clarify decision making (see Chapter 2), discuss Questions 2c–2f with the Data Team, and record the agreements on the Planning Template (see example of a sample timeline, Question 2e, in sidebar).

5. Remind the team that an important part of their role is communicating with others about their findings and plans and coordinating with other school or district initiatives and teams (see Chapter 2). Using the first table in Question 3 of the Planning Template, guide the team to list all of the initiatives, teams, and stakeholders that they will communicate with, how and when, and what results they expect. A key stakeholder group will be the faculty. Ask them to consider how they will keep the entire faculty informed about and engaged in the work of the Data Team.

6. Ask the team whom it would be important to talk with about what they have just learned about the Using Data Process. Ask each team member to write a one-minute "elevator speech" summarizing what to say to convey the essence of the Using Data Process. Have them practice their speeches in pairs.

August retreat: Review progress, celebrate success, and plan for next steps (Task 19); implement Tasks 5–12 with new state CRT, district, and common assessment data; modify and plan for continuing implementation of long-term action plan.

Handout H1.4 page 2

PLAN FOR ONGOING COMMUNICATION/COORDINATION WITH OTHER INITIATIVES, TEAMS, FACULTY, AND STAKEHOLDERS				
OTHER INITIATIVES, TEAMS, FACULTY, AND STAKEHOLDERS	WHAT IS THEIR PURPOSE? HOW DOES THEIR WORK RELATE TO OURS?	HOW WILL WE INTERACT/SHARE RESOURCES AND COMMUNICATE WITH THESE INITIATIVES?	WHEN?	RESULTS/ NEXT STEPS
Initiatives:				

Facilitation Note: An "elevator speech" is a short speech—one that takes about the time an elevator ride does—in which one communicates an idea succinctly and clearly. Here is an example:

"The Using Data Process is a way for us to work together in teams to use data to improve student learning. We will learn a continuous improvement process that will help us use multiple data sources to identify a student-learning problem to focus on, verify causes of that problem, generate solutions that will achieve our goal, and regularly monitor progress toward our goal. The process includes lots of tools for understanding, talking about, visualizing, and responding to data. It also helps us stay focused on meeting the learning needs of all of our students. In all, I think it will help us answer the question, 'How can we make the best use of data to improve our instruction and close achievement gaps?'"

7. Using the second table in Question 3 on the Planning Template, ask the team to consider the people they want to support their efforts as well as the specific types of support they will want from these people so that the team can carry out its responsibilities and achieve its goals (see Table 2.1 in Chapter 2 for suggestions). Guide the team to decide how these requests for support will be communicated and negotiated with the relevant parties.

Handout H1.4 page 3

SUPPORT NEEDED FROM OTHER STAKEHOLDERS	
WHO	WHAT SUPPORT WE WANT
Building principal	
Department chair(s)	

 ### Activity 1.4: Establish Collaborative Norms

Vignette: Collaborative Norms

Establishing norms for collaborative work can often provide benefits that we may not even be aware of. For the Arizona Using Data Project leaders who formed their own Data Team, the concept of "go visual" ended up becoming one of their group norms. Two of the team members are of Native American heritage and often found themselves processing in two languages: English and their native languages. They explained the process as one in which they first heard the discussions in English, mentally translated into their native language, processed and thought about the ideas in their language, and then translated back into English to share their thoughts verbally with the rest of the team. Unfortunately, by the time they were ready to share their thoughts, the conversation had usually moved on to another topic, and they often had "headaches from too much mental processing." In fact, when one of the authors works with this Data Team, she always checks in with these two women, seeking input on "headache levels" as a form of feedback on how well the group norms are working and whether the group has gotten "too mental" and not enough "visual."

The Data Team learned that going visual provided a much-needed process to alleviate headaches and, in fact, led to fewer misunderstandings among all team members. They quickly adopted "go visual" as a collaborative norm to enhance all Data Team members' learning, thinking, and sharing.

---

1. Let the Data Team know that the purpose of this activity is to arrive at clear agreements about norms for working together, which they will add to the Planning Template.

2. Ask the team to think about a "working group" at their school site, in their community, or in other social groups. Whip around the room and share the challenges of working within these groups. Document the comments on a sheet of chart paper.

3. Emphasize the importance of groups having tools and processes to help them communicate more effectively and work together more productively. Distribute Handout H1.6, and give the team time to read over the descriptions of the Seven Norms of Collaboration and the Four Agreements. Then facilitate a discussion about what norms they wish to adopt to govern their work together. Explain that these could be one or the other of the sets on the handout, an adaptation of one or both of

these, or other norms that the group generates. If you decide to use the Seven Norms of Collaboration, follow the directions in the Toolkit. Note that if anyone in the group cannot live with a particular norm that has been suggested, do not include it, and let them know that the norms they choose now can be adjusted as the team evolves in its work together. Once the team has agreed to a set of norms, write them on the Planning Template (Question 4a).

Seven Norms of Collaboration

1. Pausing
2. Paraphrasing
3. Probing for specificity
4. Putting ideas on the table and pulling them off
5. Paying attention to self and others
6. Presuming positive intentions
7. Pursuing a balance between advocacy and inquiry

SOURCE From Garmston & Wellman, 1999. Reprinted with permission.

Four Agreements of Courageous Conversations

1. Stay engaged.
2. Experience discomfort.
3. Speak your truth.
4. Expect and accept nonclosure.

SOURCE From Singleton & Linton, 2006, pp. 58–65. Reprinted with permission.

---

4. Explain that these norms will be practiced and monitored throughout the work of the Data Team. Earlier we suggested that you enlarge and laminate your norms and post them at each meeting. Throughout the book, this is referred to as your Norms of Collaboration poster.

Handout H1.4 page 4

---

4. Agreements about working together as a team

   a. Collaborative norms:

5. Introduce the idea of "undiscussables." Ask the team what the undiscussables are in their school. Prompt them with some examples (e.g., race and racism, poor teaching, incompetent administrators, individual classroom teachers' results). List the undiscussables the team generates on the Planning Template (Question 4b).

6. Ask the team what might make it safe for their team to discuss these issues. Refer back to the collaborative norms they have just established. How will these help them discuss the undiscussables? Do they want to add any norms to the list that will facilitate tough discussions? If so, add to your list of norms.

7. Ask the team if there are other agreements they want to make, such as being on time to meetings or doing advance preparation. Add these to the Planning Template (Question 4c).

8. Summarize any agreed-upon next steps and who is responsible for completing them. Close the session by letting the team know that they will be focusing on and strengthening their own group process and level of trust through their work. Ask the team members to each reflect on and write down one thing they found useful in launching the work of the Data Team and one wish or suggestion they have for future meetings. If time permits, they can share these aloud. If not, collect them and summarize them in a follow-up e-mail or at the start of the next meeting.

Task 2: Reflect on Our School

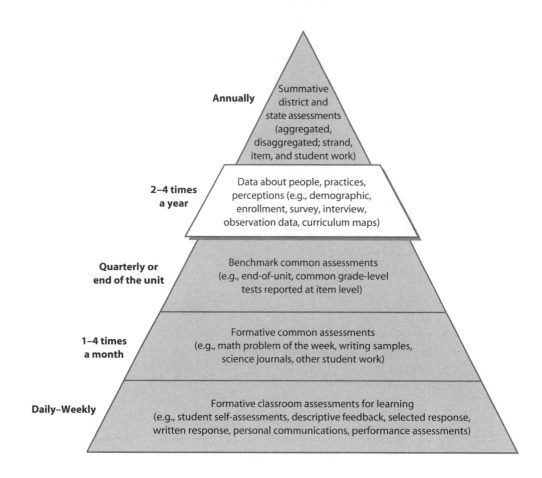

Annually — Summative district and state assessments (aggregated, disaggregated; strand, item, and student work)

2–4 times a year — Data about people, practices, perceptions (e.g., demographic, enrollment, survey, interview, observation data, curriculum maps)

Quarterly or end of the unit — Benchmark common assessments (e.g., end-of-unit, common grade-level tests reported at item level)

1–4 times a month — Formative common assessments (e.g., math problem of the week, writing samples, science journals, other student work)

Daily–Weekly — Formative classroom assessments for learning (e.g., student self-assessments, descriptive feedback, selected response, written response, personal communications, performance assessments)

Task-at-a-Glance

Purpose	To better understand the students, staff, and community that the school serves through engagement with demographic data; to understand the elements of a high-performing Using Data Culture and assess the school's progress toward that vision; to practice Data-Driven Dialogue
Data	Three to five years of student enrollment data disaggregated by race/ethnicity, gender, economic status, language, mobility, and educational status for the school and district
	One year of demographic data about teachers disaggregated by race/ethnicity and gender
	Additional facts about teachers, e.g., years of experience, percentage certified, percentage teaching out of field
	One to five years of dropout, retention, attendance, and discipline rates (optional)
	Features of the community, e.g., per capita income, employment rates, poverty rates, mobility (optional)

(Continued)

Task-at-a-Glance (Continued)

Questions to ask	Who are our students?
	Who are our teachers?
	What is the makeup of our community?
	Is our student population and our community changing over time? How?
	Does our teacher population reflect our student population? If not, what might the impact be for our students?
	What equity issues might be surfacing, such as which students are assigned to special education?
	Where are we in the process of creating a high-performing Using Data School Culture?
	What actions will we take as a result of what we have learned?
Concepts	Demographic data
	Race/ethnicity
	Economic status
	Educational status
	Language
	Mobility
	Dialogue versus discussion
	Data-Driven Dialogue
Activities	Activity 2.1: Create the Body of Our School
	Activity 2.2: Engage in Data-Driven Dialogue With Demographic Data
	Activity 2.3: Reflect on Program Elements Matrix of a Using Data School Culture
	Activity 2.4: Synthesize Learning

WHAT IS TASK 2?

An important part of building the foundation is understanding the context in which the team is operating so that they can both work effectively within it and begin to shape it in positive ways. They will engage with demographic data to gain a deeper awareness of who their students are, how the population might be changing, and how students can be better served. They will also look at data about the staff, the district, and the community. While examining these data, the team will experience Data-Driven Dialogue and learn about principles for using data effectively and collaboratively. In addition, the Data Team will reflect on where their school is on the road to creating a high-performing Using Data School Culture in relation to five dimensions that the Using Data Process seeks to strengthen: collaborative communities, data use, teaching and learning, equity, and leadership and capacity to sustain continuous improvement.

BACKGROUND INFORMATION FOR DATA COACHES

What Are Demographic Data and What Can You Learn From Them?

Demographic data include total student enrollment data and enrollment data disaggregated by grade levels, race/ethnicity, language, gender, economic status, mobility, and educational status. Looking at these data over three to five years (preferably five if available) is helpful in identifying trends in how the student population might be changing over time. If the Data Team discovers that there is an increasing frequency of mobility among students and their families, they can begin to consider programs to help those students be successful. If the Latino/a population is increasing, the implication might be that teachers need to learn more about the diverse cultures these students represent, reach out to their families, alter their curriculum to be more inclusive of Latino/a culture, and use knowledge of Latino/a discourse patterns and culture to vary their instructional approaches. If they discover a disproportional percentage of African American boys in special education, a national pattern, they can begin to examine and change practices and prejudices that produced this inequity.

Don't teachers already know who their students are? Perhaps. But really examining the demographics can be eye opening. For example, one team in rural Maine was not aware of the extent of their Native American population until they looked at their demographic data. They had quite literally made these students invisible. The data raised their awareness about the inclusion of these students in their school and stimulated their thinking about how to better serve them. In other cases, staff may not be aware of how student populations are changing over time.

Demographic data can also begin to answer questions about the faculty, such as "What is our racial/ethnic diversity? How reflective is the faculty's race/ethnicity of our student population?" Many schools serving a majority of students of color have mostly White faculties. Research suggests that this racial/ethnic difference between students and teachers can impact teacher expectations, relationships with students and their parents, and teaching and learning (Delpit, 2006). One important reason to examine demographic data is to consider what the impact of this difference might be on students and ways in which the faculty and the school's programs could be more responsive to their students.

Other important demographic information about teachers includes their years of experience and the percentage of teachers who are certified in their field. Again, these data can raise important equity issues (Johnson, 2002). Low-income schools have many of their teachers teaching out of field, especially in mathematics (40 percent) and science (20 percent) (Education Trust, 2001). Other schools assign the least experienced teachers to the students who need the most help. Examining demographic data can raise important questions that will inform later deliberations about causes and solutions to identified student-learning problems and achievement gaps. For example, one school in New York City that one of the authors worked with discovered that most of their fourth-grade teachers were brand new. This information helped them later in the process to generate solutions to their student-learning problem by providing new teachers with mentoring.

What Do We Mean by Race/Ethnicity, Economic Status, Educational Status, Language, and Mobility?

Race/Ethnicity

Education researchers and practitioners argue endlessly about how to define and describe race and ethnicity. Lindsey and colleagues (2003) define race as large groups of people distinguished from one another by physical appearance. Many researchers on race and ethnicity object to racial categorizations because they were created to affirm the superiority of Caucasians and are inaccurate, disrespectful, and inadequate descriptors of the many cultural communities to which individuals belong (Lee, 2002). With widespread migration and intermarriage, racial groups are themselves mixed and diverse and define themselves in many different ways. Researcher Carol D. Lee (2002) highlights the complexity of racial and ethnic identities by revealing her own background. She identifies as African American but also has Native American and Irish ancestors. On the other hand, antiracist activists such as Glenn Singleton and Curtis Linton (2006) argue that because of a history of institutional oppression based on race, it is important to talk about race explicitly and use the terms Black, White, and Brown to "put racial identity on par with ethnic identity such as Asian American and African American" (p. 9).

Ethnicity describes groups of people with shared history, ancestry, geographic and language origin, and physical type. Carol Lee (2002) argues that ethnicity has greater explanatory power than race for people of African descent living in the United States. Whenever possible, Lindsey et al. (2003) recommend using the names for various racially defined ethnic groups preferred by members of that group: African American, Asian, Pacific Islander, European American, Hispanic or Latino/a, American Indian or Native American or People of the First Nations. These terms, however, are not without their problems. No ethnic group is monolithic or homogeneous. Whenever possible and relevant, we recommend further disaggregating broad groups such as Asian, which can be extremely diverse and include Cambodians, Chinese, Hmong, Indians, Japanese, Koreans, Laotians, and Vietnamese. Other important variations within ethnic groups relate to the duration of time individuals have been in the United States. For example, one school in Boston disaggregated its Puerto Rican population by first- and second-generation immigrants and learned that second-generation immigrants can have greater difficulties learning English than first-generation immigrants. Native American tribal cultures also vary greatly; disaggregating these populations by their First Nation can help educators better understand their students.

As the team begins to analyze demographic data, help them understand both the value and the limitations of the demographic categories and to stay mindful of the nuances and complexities of individuals' identities. For the purposes of this book, the authors will use the term "race/ethnicity" together to honor this complexity and use African American, Asian, Latino/a or Hispanic, Native American, and White for the major racial/ethnic groups represented in U.S schools.

Economic Status

Economic status is important to examine in demographic data because schools have a history of poorly serving students living in poverty. Poverty is typically defined in schools by students eligible for free and reduced lunch. While imperfect, this indicator is probably the best available for identifying students living in poverty. Other terms used to identify students living in poverty are "low income," "low SES" (social economic status), and "economically disadvantaged" (not preferred by the authors).

Educational Status

This term refers to a generic way of describing different groups of students according to their designation in the educational system, including students who are gifted, those in general education, and those with a variety of learning and behavioral differences. Increasingly, demographic data that are disaggregated by educational status are reported as students in "general education" and "students with exceptional needs," but you may also find the terms "students with special needs," "students with disabilities," and "regular education students." The Data Team may find it useful to further disaggregate data about educational status according to the state's disability categories, which might include autism, deaf and hard of hearing, blind and low vision, and emotional disability. In addition, because of a well-documented practice of disproportionately assigning African American boys to special education and other inequities in assignments, it will be important to disaggregate students with exceptional needs by race/ethnicity (Holtzman, 2006).

Language

Students speak a diversity of languages. This category identifies students for whom English is a second language. The term *English Language Learner* is frequently used to designate these students, but it is a diverse category that can include many different native language speakers. If this is the case in your school, it will be useful for the Data Team to further disaggregate English Language Learners by their native language and length of time in the United States.

Mobility

Students move from one school to another for a variety of reasons, including promotion and changes in family jobs and residences. The 2000 U.S. census data indicate that 15–18 percent of school-age children moved in the previous year (Schachter, 2001). The mobility rate for a school is generally calculated by the total of new student entries and withdrawals during the year divided by the total opening day official enrollment. Schools with high mobility rates can benefit from further disaggregating their mobility data to determine how many times students move within a school year.

Other

In some cases, the "other" category may refer to a combination of numerous racial groups, which, by themselves, constitute less than 10 percent of the student population. For example, the "other" category might consist of Asian and Native American students in a school with a small population of both racial/ethnic groups. However, the "other" category may simply refer to how students and their families indicate their racial or ethnic background: A student or the student's family may select the "other" category if the child is of mixed heritage and does not strongly identify with one race or cultural heritage over another.

How Accurate Are Demographic Data?

The complexity of race and ethnicity described earlier suggests that demographic data are rough sketches rather than fully detailed and accurate drawings of the diversity of students and staff. As most demographic data are based on self-reporting, they reflect how people identify themselves. The free and reduced lunch indicator of economic status is often underreported since it is dependent on families applying for this benefit. And mobility and homelessness are very challenging for school districts to track.

What Do I Do If the Data Team Veers Into Culturally Destructive or Blind Conversations?

At a later stage in the process, demographic data can inform analysis of student learning data. But be careful! There is the danger when first examining demographic data about student populations that the Data Team may use demographics as an excuse for poor student performance. Of course, demographics alone are not a predictor of student achievement or an excuse for students' not learning. There are many examples of high-performing schools with a majority of students living in poverty, with high mobility rates, and with a high percentage of students of color (see Introduction, Assumption 1). But there is a widely held and false belief that schools with a high percentage of students of color or students living in poverty are doomed to perform poorly. Demographic data can trigger culturally destructive comments such as "No wonder we don't make AYP. If only we didn't have so many [fill in the blank] students." Or some staff may be resistant to looking at demographic data because "We just see kids as kids. Why do we have to look at all these groups? Doesn't this just make things worse?" As Data Coach, you will want to be prepared for such comments.

In Task 3, the Data Team is introduced to the Cultural Proficiency Continuum, which describes a range of responses to students' culture from culturally destructive to culturally proficient. We recommend that you read ahead in Task 3 about the continuum so that you can begin now to monitor your team's dialogue for comments that reflect both cultural proficiency as well as lack of respect and understanding for students' cultures. If you are hearing comments in the cultural destructiveness, cultural incapacity, or cultural blindness dimensions of the continuum, here are some possible approaches:

• Reflect those comments back to the team. Ask them to consider how consistent these comments are with the purpose of the Data Team established in Task 1. Invite a respectful and safe dialogue based on your agreed-upon collaborative norms.

• Take a stand that cultural destructiveness will not be tolerated on this team. Open a dialogue about the team's commitment to respond knowledgably and respectfully to diverse cultures. Ask them how they want to handle this kind of conflict on the team. Make sure the team's collaborative norms are being followed.

• Stop the process. Move to Task 3: Raise Awareness of Cultural Proficiency. This is exactly what happened at the Using Data national field test, where we shifted the agenda when it became apparent that participants needed a common language and safety for talking about issues of race, class, and culture.

- Explain the purpose and value of examining demographic data—not to assign blame to any group, but to figure out how we can best meet the educational needs of all student groups.

What Is Dialogue Versus Discussion? How Will We Use These Two Ways of Talking on Our Data Team?

Skillful teams use two different modes of conversation: dialogue and discussion. Each of these ways of talking has different purposes (see Handout H2.1: Dialogue Versus Discussion). In the Using Data Process, the Data Team will frequently be engaged in dialogue, a process of developing shared meaning and understanding through open sharing and deep listening. The team will use dialogue when making sense of data together, surfacing their assumptions about the data or about students, teaching, and learning, dealing with conflict, or exploring equity issues. When it is time for a decision, the team shifts into discussion mode, which is characterized by advocating for a point of view. An important dimension of the role of Data Coach is to make explicit which way of talking best suits the team's purpose and to provide a safe environment for each (see the Task 5 section, "What Are Some Data 'Safety Regulations' to Guide the Use of Data?").

What Is Data-Driven Dialogue?

Until teachers started talking deeply about the data, they would create plans that never got implemented. The best thing about UDP [the Using Data Process] is that it creates a structured framework for deep discussion of data.

—Richard Dinko, former co–principal investigator
Stark County Mathematics and Science Partnership

Figure 3.1 Data-Driven Dialogue.

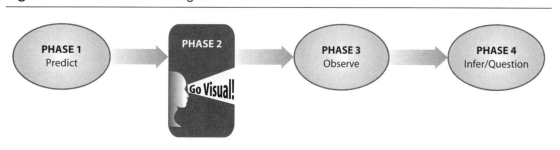

SOURCE Adapted from Lipton, L. & Wellman, B. (2003). *Data-Driven Dialogue: A Facilitator's Guide to Collaborative Inquiry.* Sherman, CT: Mira Via, LLC. Used with permission. For additional information go to www.miravia.com.

This task introduces the four-phase process of Data-Driven Dialogue (see Figure 3.1), a core dialogue tool that will be used throughout the Using Data Process (see Toolkit: Data-Driven Dialogue). Adapted from a model developed by Bruce Wellman and Laura Lipton, Data-Driven Dialogue is "steeped in current understandings about how we learn" (2004, p. 43). It applies what is known about how learners make sense of new knowledge through activating prior knowledge, using vibrant visual displays, opening up extended opportunities for exploration and discovering, and engaging in dialogue about assumptions. The learners in this case are the Data Team members, and the source of their new knowledge is the data they will be examining.

We learned not to skip the predict phase. It was so important in getting our team excited about and ready to learn from the data.

—Data Coach, Stark County, Ohio

Phase 1: Predict

Since the best predictor of new knowledge is access to prior knowledge, Data-Driven Dialogue begins with a prediction phase, where participants in the dialogue activate their prior knowledge and surface the assumptions that they bring to the data. This, of course, occurs before team members ever see the data. This first phase of predicting accomplishes several purposes. First, it gets the participants in the dialogue ready to learn by activating their ideas and assumptions; their predictions help them navigate the new information they are about to get—comparing the data to their predictions. It also raises participants' awareness about the assumptions they have that influence their interpretations of the data. By articulating these assumptions, they can more easily set them aside and examine the data more objectively. For example, in making predictions about the demographic data, the team might predict that they have had an increase in student mobility. They will be looking at the data to see if this is so and may be surprised to learn later that the mobility rate was constant. Or a team member might assume that there has been an increase at their school in the percentage of students living in poverty. They will use this assumption to filter the data later when they have a chance to make observations.

Phase 2: Go Visual

The next phase in the dialogue is to "go visual," a principle developed by non-verbal communications expert Michael Grinder (1997) and based also on the work of Edward Tufte (1983). Grinder and Tufte revealed the power of large, visually vibrant, color-coded displays of data in fostering group ownership, sense making, and engagement. Simple, large, and colorful data displays that four to six people can look at together at once are a hallmark of the Using Data Process. The authors have been amazed at how this one minor change in how data are typically displayed increases ownership of the data among team members. We have also seen positive results from Data Team members hand-drawing their own graphs (see the Task 6 section, "Background Information for Data Coaches"). Because this task has several graphs, Data Coaches may want to create these charts themselves—either electronically or by hand, but then enlarge them to poster size (18" × 24" is recommended) and in color if possible. See Figure 3.2 for examples of "going visual." (Note that Go Visual is a tool in itself and can be used for other tasks that do not involve Data-Driven Dialogue. See Toolkit: Go Visual.)

Figure 3.2 Go visual examples.

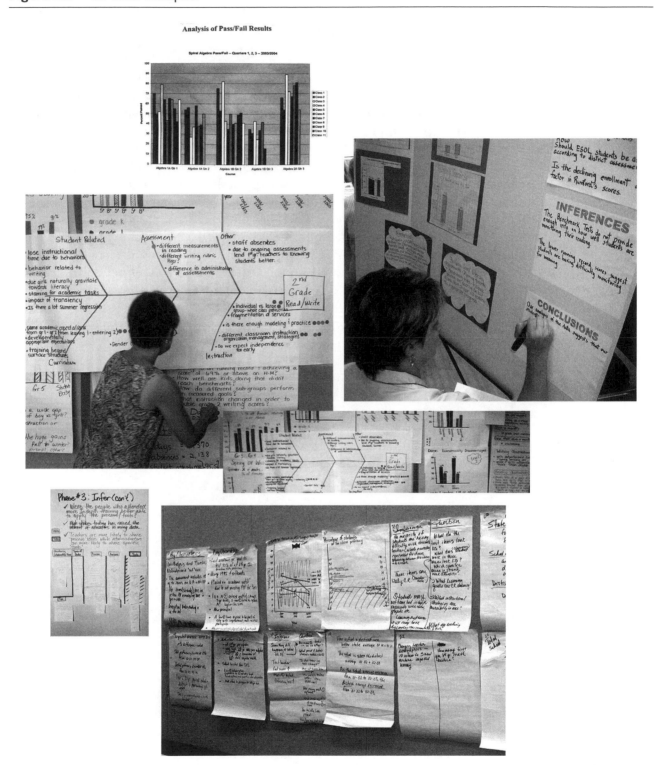

SOURCE Photographs taken by Chris Demers and Jennifer Unger. Used with permission.

Phase 3: Observe

'Tis a fatal flaw to reason whilst observing though so necessary beforehand and so useful afterwards.

—Charles Darwin

Once the data are made visual, teams are ready for the observation phase of the dialogue. This is the most difficult. It requires that the participants set aside their assumptions and focus on only what is there to be observed in the data. We have learned through experience that it is well worth taking the time to teach this phase carefully, as there is a strong tendency for participants to want to leap to explanation and interpretation before they have fully explored what can be learned from the data. The challenge in this phase is to resist that temptation and to keep the team in exploration and discovery. They will have the chance to bring their prior knowledge and experience back into the dialogue in the next phase. For now, they set those aside. The Data-Driven Dialogue description in the Toolkit provides several suggestions for helping to keep the team in the observation stage and preventing premature leaps to inference.

What makes a good observation statement? Several examples are given in Table 3.2, and below are some questions to pose to the team as they learn to refine their observations:

- Does each statement communicate a single idea about student performance?
- Are statements short and clear?
- Do the statements incorporate numbers?
- Do the statements focus on just those direct and observable facts that are contained in the data, without interpretation or inference?
- Do the statements use relevant data concepts, such as mean, median, mode, range, or distribution?

Phase 4: Infer/Question

In the last phase of the dialogue, infer/question, participants generate interpretations for the results they observed. They tap back into their prior knowledge and

Table 3.2   Rough Versus Refined Observations

Rough observation	*Refined observation*
We have lots more Latino/a students now.	Our Latino/a population increased from 10 percent in 2005 to 30 percent of the total student population in 2006.
We have a larger percentage of African American students than we do teachers.	Our student population is 85 percent African American. Our teacher population is 20 percent African American.
Our mobility rate has increased over time.	Our mobility rate has increased by 30 percent from 2002 to 2007.

assumptions to generate multiple possible explanations or implications of what they are seeing in the demographic data. Sample observations about demographic data and the kinds of questions and inferences they can generate are illustrated in Table 3.3.

Table 3.3   Observations and Inferences About Demographic Data

Observations of demographic data	Inferences/Questions
Our English Language Learner population has increased from 10 percent in 2000 to 45 percent in 2005.	Wow! We are so much more diverse than I thought. I wonder if our instructional program is geared to all of these students?
Our mobility rate increased 10 percent in the last year.	Why are so many students leaving our school? Are they choosing to go to other schools in the district?
Forty-five percent of our teachers have less than three years' experience.	What are we doing to help these new teachers? Do we have a mentoring program?
This year our free-and-reduced lunch rate went down by 10 percent.	I wonder if this is accurate. Are we getting all students who are qualified to sign up?
Our student body is 80 percent African American. Our teacher population is 5 percent African American.	What is the impact of this mismatch on our students?
Forty percent of our mathematics teachers are certified in mathematics.	Is there a relationship between teachers' certification and student performance?

The challenge in Phase 4: Infer/Question is to keep the Data Team open to multiple possible explanations and not to latch on to their first conclusion. Data-Driven Dialogue is a process of sense making and discovery, not decision making. For example, coach the team to consider all aspects of their system—curriculum, instruction, assessment, equity, teacher preparation, and so on—as possible explanations for student results. This phase is also another opportunity to stop and consider the Equity Lens we bring to the data and broaden the team's perspective by asking questions such as "How might parents and students from the diverse cultural groups in our school interpret these data? Can I stop and reframe my interpretation? What would a culturally proficient interpretation of these data be?" (See Task 3: Raise Awareness of Cultural Proficiency.)

RESOURCES

Bernhardt, V. L. (2003). *Using data to improve student learning in elementary schools.* Larchmont, NY: Eye on Education.

Bernhardt, V. L. (2003). *Using data to improve student learning in middle schools.* Larchmont, NY: Eye on Education.

Bernhardt, V. L. (2005). *Using data to improve student learning in high schools.* Larchmont, NY: Eye on Education.

Bernhardt, V. L. (2006). *Using data to improve student learning in school districts.* Larchmont, NY: Eye on Education.

Lindsey, R. B., Roberts, L. M., & CampbellJones, F. (2005). *The culturally proficient school: An implementation guide for school leaders.* Thousand Oaks, CA: Corwin Press.

Wellman, B., & Lipton, L. (2004). *Data-driven dialogue: A facilitator's guide to collaborative inquiry.* Sherman, CT: MiraVia.

MAJOR ACTIVITIES FOR TASK 2

Activity	*Time required*	*CD-ROM materials: Task 2 link*	*CD-ROM Toolkit: Relevant tools*
Activity 2.1: Create the Body of Our School	20 minutes	PowerPoint slides S2.1–S2.2	Body of Our School
Activity 2.2: Engage in Data-Driven Dialogue With Demographic Data	60 minutes	Handout H2.1: Dialogue Versus Discussion PowerPoint slides S2.3–S2.16 Data Examples and Templates	Data-Driven Dialogue Go Visual
Activity 2.3: Reflect on Program Elements Matrix of a Using Data School Culture	60 minutes	Handouts H2.2–H2.6: PEM Examples PowerPoint slides S2.17–S2.22	Program Elements Matrix (PEM) of a Using Data School Culture
Activity 2.4: Synthesize Learning	10 minutes		Body of Our School

PREPARING FOR THE TASK

Read "Background Information for Data Coaches"; see the CD-ROM: Task 2 for data examples and templates, handouts, PowerPoint slides, and sample goals and agenda; and review "Standard Procedures for Data Team Meetings" (see the introduction to Chapter 3 in this book and on CD-ROM). Although tool directions are embedded in the Data Coach Notes, you can also reference in-depth descriptions of relevant Toolkit entries on the CD-ROM.

MATERIALS PREPARATION

- Prepare to show the PowerPoint slides.

- Make one copy for each team member of Handouts H2.1–H2.6.

- Provide the team with chart paper and color markers for the Body of Our School activity.

- Make one poster-size display of each demographic data graph or table (see "Data Preparation").

DATA PREPARATION

In Activity 2.2, the team will examine demographic data about the school's and district's students, teachers, and community. The data inventory below asks you to gather five years of student demographic data. If you do not already know, find out who the best sources are for all the data you will need. Often you can find these data on your state's or district's Web sites. Or check with your district data or assessment coordinator or your school principal. If you have someone in the district helping you gather data, copy and send them the data inventory so they can begin gathering the data you will eventually need. We suggest starting this process several weeks before you start Task 2 because it may take you some time.

As you gather demographic data about students' race/ethnicity, gender, language, economic status, mobility, and educational needs, it will be important to understand what terminology is used to identify various student groups and how they are defined in your particular school and district data. There is wide variation in the terminology and definitions used.

Please note that the data the team will work with in this task is not the universe of demographic data available to schools. The purpose for looking at demographic data now is for the team to learn more about their students and teachers and the makeup of their community and to introduce the team to a unique approach for engaging with data. As the team works with later tasks, they may want to go back and collect additional demographic data that will shed light on their student-learning problem, such as dropout rates or which students are enrolled in which courses. The authors have learned from experience that Data Teams do not have all the time in the world to look at every piece of data. The checklist below is our attempt to narrow the data down to the bare essentials.

Data Inventory for Task 2

School/District Demographic Data About
Students, Teachers, and Community

- Total student enrollment in the school for five years
- Total student enrollment in the district for five years
- Student enrollment disaggregated by gender, race/ethnicity, economic status, language, educational needs, and mobility for five years for the school and the district, including both numbers and percentages
- Number of teachers in the school
- Average years of experience of teachers in the school
- Percentage of teachers who are certified in their field in the school
- Teacher population in the school disaggregated by gender and race/ethnicity (five years if possible)

- Dropout, attendance, suspension, and retention numbers and percentages (optional)
- Features of the community, for example, mean income, level of education (optional)

On the CD-ROM in the Data Examples and Data Templates links for Task 2, you will find illustrative examples of the kinds of data you will be looking for, sample data displays, and Excel templates for your own data. Prepare simple line graphs to display the student enrollment and other trend data. Don't try to put too many different groups on one graph as they may become difficult to read. For example, include race/ethnicity on one graph and gender on another. For one year of student or teacher demographic data, use a pie chart; for multiple years, use a bar or line graph. Other teacher, dropout, attendance, suspension, and retention data and features of the community may be displayed in bar graph or table form. Enlarge each of the graphs to 18″ × 24″ and provide one copy of each to the Data Team. For the prediction phase, either cover up the data on the graph with a piece of paper or create the same graphs but remove the data themselves and leave just the *x*- and *y*-axes and the titles (see example in Figure 3.3).

Figure 3.3 Demographic data graph template for prediction phase.

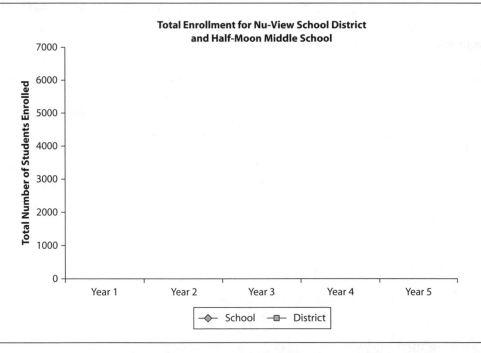

Facilitation Note: For the first data experience we suggest not introducing too many data sets at a time. With student-learning data, the team will typically be examining only one data set at a time. This is to avoid data overload—too much data to take in at once. Activity 2.2 uses several data sets because so many different student groups are included in the demographic data. Judge your team based on their level of experience with data. Be sensitive to introducing too much data at once.

DATA COACH NOTES

 ## Activity 2.1: Create the Body of Our School

1. Depending on how you decided to embed practice of your agreed-upon collaborative norms in Task 1, guide the Data Team through the process you identified.

2. Introduce the Body of Our School activity by stating that the Data Team is going to develop a poster portraying the "body" of their school that will help the team to better understand the context at their site. The poster will show what the school is like, how data are being used, what the key issues are regarding student learning, what is exciting about the school, and what are the challenges to be met.

Slide S2.2

3. Display Slide S2.2, showing the Body of Our School stick figure. Have each Data Team draw a similar stick figure on chart paper. Use the questions/prompts on the slide (or make up your own) to begin discussion/conversation within the group(s). Ask team members to write information about their school around the appropriate body part.

> **Facilitation Note**: If the Data Team is large (e.g., greater than six), have members work in groups (e.g., grade-level specific, discipline specific, grade spans). If the team is small, construct the Body of Our School together.

4. Transition to the demographic data activity by letting the team know they will now fill out more information about the Body of Our School by looking at demographic data about their students, teachers, district, and community.

Slide S2.3

Activity 2.2: Engage in Data-Driven Dialogue With Demographic Data

1. Show Slide S2.3 to introduce this activity, and let the team know the purposes for engaging with demographic data.

2. Show Slide S2.4, and explain what demographic data are and why they are important (see "Background Information for Data Coaches").

3. Explain that the team will at the same time be learning a new way of analyzing and talking about data: Data-Driven Dialogue (adapted from Wellman & Lipton, 2004; used with permission). Distribute Handout H2.1. Ask the team to read the handout, and lead a discussion of the questions provided.

Slide S2.4

Data-Driven Dialogue

Adapted from Wellman and Lipton, 2004, *Data-Driven Dialogue: A Facilitator's Guide to Collaborative Inquiry.* Sherman, CT: MiraVia LLC. Used with permission.

Using Data   Data Coach's Guide to Closing Achievement Gaps: Unleashing the Power of Collaborative Inquiry © 2007 TERC, Inc. All rights reserved.   S2.5

Slide S2.5

PHASE 1
Predict

Data-Driven Dialogue

Adapted from Wellman and Lipton, 2004, *Data-Driven Dialogue: A Facilitator's Guide to Collaborative Inquiry.* Sherman, CT: MiraVia LLC. Used with permission.

Using Data   Data Coach's Guide to Closing Achievement Gaps: Unleashing the Power of Collaborative Inquiry © 2007 TERC, Inc. All rights reserved.   S2.6

Slide S2.6

Phase 1: Predict Starters

I predict . . .
   I assume . . .
      I wonder . . .
         I'm expecting to see . . .

Using Data   Data Coach's Guide to Closing Achievement Gaps: Unleashing the Power of Collaborative Inquiry © 2007 TERC, Inc. All rights reserved.   S2.7

Slide S2.7

Phase 1: Predict

- What do you predict the patterns in total enrollment in our school will be over the last five years? In our district?
- What do you predict the patterns over the last five years will be in enrollment by race/ethnicity? Language? Economic status? Mobility? Educational status?
- How will the school's demographic patterns compare to the district's?
- What do you predict the composition of the faculty is? How will their composition compare to that of the student body?
- Document your predictions on chart paper and post.

Using Data   Data Coach's Guide to Closing Achievement Gaps: Unleashing the Power of Collaborative Inquiry © 2007 TERC, Inc. All rights reserved.   S2.8

Slide S2.8

PHASE 2
Go Visual!

PHASE 3
Observe

4. Show Slide S2.5 to provide an overview of the phases of Data-Driven Dialogue.

5. Display Slide S2.6 to illustrate the details of the four phases. Then click to animate the slide, highlighting Phase 1: Predict. Explain that the purpose of predicting is to activate prior knowledge and surface assumptions in order to maximize new learning from the data.

> **Facilitation Note**: Remember that all predictions are good whether they are ultimately proven right or wrong. Record all of the Data Team's predictions on chart paper. The team does not need to reach consensus on their predictions. Rather, elicit each individual team member's predictions.

6. Display Slide S2.7, and explain that the words on the slide are sentence starters for predictions. Tell the team that they will be making predictions about demographic data based on several graphs illustrating total student enrollment and student enrollment disaggregated by gender, race/ethnicity, economic status, language, educational needs, and mobility for five years for the school and the district.

7. Show the team the blank graph you have prepared for student enrollment trends for the school and the district with just the title and the *x*- and *y*-axes (see Figure 3.3). Give some examples of predictions (e.g., "I think that our enrollment will have decreased significantly in the last five years"; "I predict that our school has doubled the percentage of Latino/a students over the last five years.").

> **Facilitation Note**: Especially when learning the process, we recommend looking at just one data set at a time and practicing all four phases using a simple, straightforward set of data.

8. Display the questions in Slide S2.8, and give the team about five minutes to make their predictions. They can draw trend lines in on the blank graphs or generate verbal predictions.

9. Display Slide S2.9, and explain Phase 2: Go Visual, noting that in the Using Data Process the team will be using large, colorful visual displays of data to aid their collaboration and sense making. Distribute the graph comparing enrollment trends for your district and school (see example in Figure 3.4).

10. Still displaying Slide S2.9, highlight Phase 3: Observe. Explain that in this phase the team will make observations of the data.

Figure 3.4   Total student enrollment for Nu-View School District and Half-Moon Middle School, years 1–5.

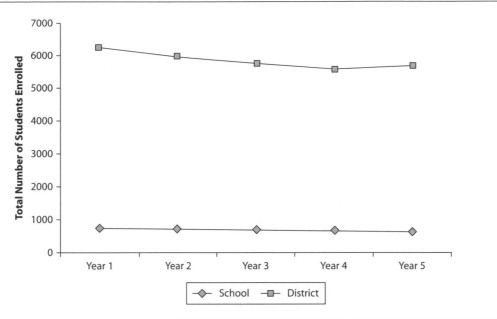

Facilitation Note: Make sure the team understands that an observation is something that can be made using the five senses and contains no explanations (inferences). For example, when reading a thermometer, "It's 52 degrees" is an observation; "52 degrees is cold" is an inference. Or "75 percent of fifth-grade students are below proficiency in geometry" is an observation; "Geometry isn't getting enough attention in our curriculum" is an inference.

Slide S2.10

Slide S2.11

Slide S2.12

11. Display Slide S2.10 to introduce the No-Because sign. Explain that this is a signal that when making observations, they do not use the word "because." "Because" signals an interpretation or explanation of the data (Phase 4), not an observation. Then display Slide S2.11, noting a few Observation reminders, and Slide S2.12 to illustrate phrases to start observations.

12. Display the questions in Slide S2.13 and have the Data Team practice making observations of the enrollment data. Record their observations on chart paper.

Slide S2.13

13. Display Slides S2.14 and S2.15 to introduce Phase 4: Infer/Question and illustrate some phrases to use to start inferences. Then show the questions in Slide S2.16, and prompt the team to make inferences and ask questions based on the data. Record these on chart paper.

PHASE 4
Infer/Question

❧

Sample Observations of Student Demographic Data

- Our Latino/a population increased by 25 percent over the last five years.
- Our district enrollment declined by 19 percent from 2000 to 2006, but our school enrollment increased by 14 percent over that same period of time.
- The percentage of students with exceptional needs decreased by 4 percent from 2004 to 2006.

❧

Sample Inferences and Questions About Student Demographic Data

- Our special education population has increased. I wonder what percentage of those students are African American boys and how that compares to the percentage of African American boys in the regular education population.
- I think students are leaving this area because the economy is so bad.
- Do we have any programs for kids who come to our school in the middle of the year to help them catch up?
- Our student population is split about 50/50 boys and girls, but we have very few male teachers. I wonder what the impact of that might be?

Slide S2.15

Slide S2.16

14. Ask the team to debrief on the process of Data-Driven Dialogue: What struck you about the process? What strategies did you use to stay open to observation and not go into inference? What are you learning about how to use data?

15. Now direct the team to repeat the process, looking at student enrollment data disaggregated by race/ethnicity, gender, language, educational status, economic status, and mobility. Figures 3.5 and 3.6 show school examples of some of these data; examples with district data are on the CD-ROM under "Data Examples."

16. Repeat Data-Driven Dialogue with data about teachers' race/ethnicity and gender as well as years of experience, percentage of teachers who are certified in their field in the school, and any other data you have prepared about teachers. See examples in Tables 3.4 and 3.5.

Figure 3.5 Student enrollment data disaggregated by race/ethnicity: Half-Moon Middle School, years 1–5.

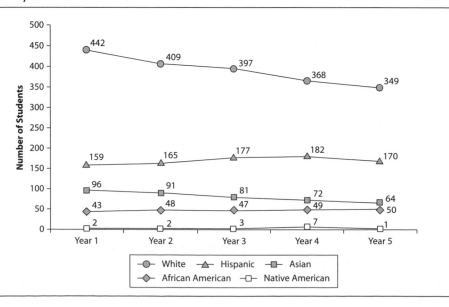

Figure 3.6   Student enrollment data disaggregated by language, educational status, economic status, and mobility: Half-Moon Middle School, years 1–5.

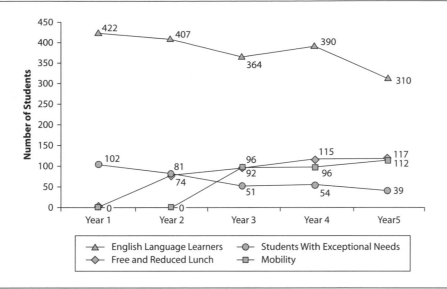

Table 3.4   Faculty Disaggregated by Race/Ethnicity and Gender: Half-Moon Middle School, Years 1–3

Year/Group	African American		Asian		Hispanic		White		Males		Females	
	#	%	#	%	#	%	#	%	#	%	#	%
3	0	0	1	2	2	5	39	93	11	27	31	73
2	0	0	0	0	1	2	47	98	12	26	36	74
1	0	0	0	0	1	2	50	98	13	26	38	74

Table 3.5   Teacher Qualifications: Half-Moon Middle School, Years 1–3

Year	Total # of teachers	Teachers licensed in teaching assignment		Total # of teachers in core academic areas	% of core academic teachers identified as highly qualified	Student-teacher ratio
		#	%			
3	42	39	92.9	39	97.4	15.2 to 1
2	48	42	87.5	41	92.6	14.2 to 1
1	51	47	91.3	47	95.7	13.9 to 1

Questions to Elicit Predictions of Teacher Demographic Data

• How experienced do you predict the faculty is?
• What percentage do you think are certified? Teaching out of field?
• How do you think our faculty's race/ethnicity and gender will compare with those of our students?

Sample Observations of Teacher Demographic Data

- Only 4 percent of our teachers are Hispanic, compared to 95 percent of our students.
- Forty percent of our mathematics teachers are teaching out of field.
- Seventy percent of our staff has 10 or more years of experience.

Sample Inferences/Questions From Teacher Demographic Data

- What are our hiring policies? How can we encourage more diversity in our staff?
- What is the impact on teaching and learning of a majority of White teachers teaching a majority of Latino/a and African American students?
- Do we have any programs in place to support our new teachers?

17. Repeat the Data-Driven Dialogue process with any additional data you have gathered on dropout rates, attendance, discipline, retention, or features of the community. See examples in Tables 3.6 and 3.7.

18. Let the team know that what they just did in this activity was use the method that they will be practicing throughout the Using Data Process. Highlight its important features: the importance of separating data from inference; going visual with data by creating large, colorful, visually vibrant displays of data; and structuring the dialogue to maximize collaboration and sense making.

Table 3.6   Half-Moon Middle School Indicators, Years 1–2

Year/Category	Dropouts		Attendance		In-school suspensions		Out-of-school suspensions		Grade retentions		Exclusions	
	#	%	Average # of absences	%	#	%	#	%	#	%	#	Rate
2	n/a	n/a	7	95.6	16	2.3	34	4.8	13	1.8	n/a	n/a
1	n/a	n/a	10	94.1	114	15.9	128	17.9	18	2.5	2	2.8

Table 3.7   Characteristics of the Community

Data descriptor	Data	
	Small urban city	State
Population	39,102	972,371
Male	18,659	499,986
Female	20,443	472,385
Unemployment	5.7%	5.3%
Median income per household	$37,004	$50,502
Population with college degrees	9.4 % (2,326)	19.5 %
Population with HS diplomas	35.2 % (8,742)	27.3 %
Average age	36.35	35.3

Activity 2.3: Reflect on Program Elements Matrix (PEM) of a Using Data School Culture

1. Introduce the Program Elements Matrix (PEM) of a Using Data School Culture (PEM template developed by K–12 Alliance/WestEd; adapted with permission). Display Slide S2.17, showing the PEM Template, and explain that the PEM is a strategic planning tool that identifies key elements of a program and enables a staff to plan for those elements over a three-year period of time. It provides a snapshot view of where your school is now and where you want it to go in the next three years.

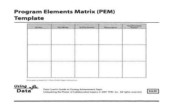

Slide S2.17

2. Explain that a goal of using data is to influence how a school operates. The PEM examples provided reflect many of the core values that the Using Data Process embraces: building collaborative communities, using data effectively, equity, quality teaching and learning, and sustainability.

> **Facilitation Note:** The example PEMs are just that—examples. Enable the Data Team to design PEMs that are meaningful and important to them. Allow them to adopt, adapt, or change the PEMs and the descriptions in each box to fit their context.

3. Distribute Handout H2.2 and display Slide S2.18, with the PEM Example for Collaborative Communities. Have groups discuss briefly and in general what a high-functioning school would look like for the three elements on the slide.

Slide S2.18

> **Facilitation Note:** The purpose of this discussion is just to "prime the pump" and get the participants engaged with the elements of this PEM.

4. Ask participants to direct their attention to the first row, the "Shared Norms and Values" element, and have them discuss the examples of a high-performing school as shown on the PEM for that element. Which do they agree with? Which would they change? What would they add?

5. Now focus participants on the "Here We Are" column, and ask them to take stock of their school/department in relation to the same element. Help them understand that the idea is to paint a picture that is true to reality, with all the blemishes and flaws included. The goal of the team/staff will be to move from where they are to where they want to be.

6. Chart ideas for the "Here We Are" column and/or chart the type of investigation/data gathering the team needs to do to brainstorm these answers.

7. Next ask the team to look at the "Just For Starters" column. Have them brainstorm possible first steps for moving toward the high-performing goal. Chart ideas and complete this column.

8. Using a similar process, ask the group to discuss what it would look like if they were making real progress toward their goals. Chart ideas and complete the "Rolling Along" column.

9. Repeat this process with each of the elements on one PEM. Have the group review the information, and make sure that everyone can "find themselves" on the chart. In other words, have them find the stage that fits where they are and how they think, and be sure they are willing to make a personal commitment to help the school move toward its goals.

10. Repeat the entire process for the rest of the PEMs with Slides S2.19 (PEM Example: Data), S2.20 (PEM Example: Teaching and Learning), S2.21 (PEM Example: Equity), and S2.22 (PEM Example: Sustainability) and with accompanying Handouts H2.3–H2.6.

> **Facilitation Note:** A PEM is a living document. Keep all of the charts the team worked on in this activity, and revisit them periodically to assess how the school/staff is moving toward its goals. In each of these reviews, the team/participants reflect on the stage they are analyzing, being critical of what they have not implemented and congratulated for what has been accomplished. The next stage is then adjusted to meet this analysis.

11. Ask the team to reflect on the work they have done in this task. How will they keep this work alive throughout the Using Data Process?

> **Facilitation Note:** For groups of 10 or more, the Consensogram (see Toolkit) is another great tool for promoting reflection on the school culture and use of data while modeling Data-Driven Dialogue and the go-visual principle. The Consensogram is not as comprehensive as the PEM, but it can provide a quick and highly engaging survey of beliefs, practices, and policies. It is also a very effective way of introducing the Using Data Process to a whole faculty and teaching basic data concepts.

 ## Activity 2.4: Synthesize Learning

1. Direct the team back to their Body of Our School chart. Ask them to summarize the key findings in each of the context boxes—students, teachers, community, and school culture—based on their analysis of demographic data and their work with the PEM.

2. Now that they have reflected on the PEM, are there additional action steps they want to add to the right foot on the Body of Our School?

3. Post the poster as the first part of the team's Data Wall (see Toolkit).

Facilitation Note: If several school teams within a district are present, have them present their stick figures to each other and identify common themes.

4. Provide time for reflection and processing of the Data Team's use of their agreed-upon collaborative norms. (See Toolkit: Seven Norms of Collaboration for suggestions on debriefing.)

Task 3: Raise Awareness of Cultural Proficiency

Task-at-a-Glance

Purpose	To raise awareness of cultural proficiency and build a common language and framework for thinking and talking about issues of race/ethnicity, class, culture, gender, and diversity throughout the Using Data Process
Data	None
Questions to ask	What do race/ethnicity, class, culture, and gender have to do with data and student learning?
	What is my own culture, and how does it shape my perceptions of myself? Of others?
	How can principles of culturally proficient leadership inform our work?
	How can we make use of the Cultural Proficiency Continuum throughout our work as a Data Team?
	How does our understanding of culture and cultural proficiency inform our understanding of achievement gaps? What is "in the achievement gap"?
Concepts	Culture
	Five principles of culturally proficient leadership
	Cultural Proficiency Continuum
Activities	Activity 3.1: Share My Culture
	Activity 3.2: Dialogue on the Principles of Culturally Proficient Leadership
	Activity 3.3: Explore the Cultural Proficiency Continuum

Vignettes: Why Raise Awareness of Cultural Proficiency as Part of a Data Process?

At a Using Data workshop, the presenters introduced a dialogue activity about race and racism. One participant asked, "What does race have to do with it?" The presenters wrote the question on chart paper and asked the group to think about that question throughout the rest of the workshop. At the end, one participant commented:

> I now see the clear connection between racism and inequities in the system and the barriers to improving learning for all children. I think that makes the Using Data [Process] almost an imperative for districts because it is the one nonpolitical and nonintrusive way of dealing with the poor learning opportunities for so many children.—Reeny Davison, Executive Director, ASSET, Pittsburgh, Pennsylvania

A Data Team was looking at disaggregated student-achievement data. One team member commented that this school was never going to be high achieving because of the number of immigrant students. "These kids just don't value education or have much interest in learning," the team member remarked. The Data Coach was shocked but not sure how to address the situation. Should he allow the conversation to continue? Stop the group? Express his anger?

When generating causes of their student-learning problem, the team kept identifying causes that blamed the students and their circumstances: "Their parents don't value education." "They get no support at home doing their homework." "These kids know they are just going to work in the mine. How are we supposed to teach them mathematics?" "They just aren't motivated. Education is not a part of their culture." There was no discussion of their teaching or curriculum. The Data Coach knew these were code words for racist beliefs about their students. She struggled with how to shift the conversation away from these disrespectful and destructive comments and toward areas where the school could take action to improve learning opportunities for all students.

WHAT IS TASK 3?

In Task 2, the Data Team examined demographic data to understand the diversity that shapes their school and district. In this task, the Data Team will gain understanding as well as tools for constructively talking about and responding to cultural differences among students. First, the team will reflect on the concept of culture by thinking about their own cultures and the dominant influence that culture has on their lives. Then they will engage in dialogue about five underlying principles of cultural proficiency, a way of being that enables individuals and organizations to respond effectively to people who differ from them (Lindsey, Nuri Robins, & Terrell, 2003). Finally, they use the Cultural Proficiency Continuum (Lindsey et al., 2003) to develop a common language for describing a range of behaviors, from culturally proficient to culturally destructive, and to reflect on their own practices.

Developing cultural proficiency happens over time and takes commitment, courage, and vigilance. Task 3 acts as a catalyst for this by establishing it as a core competency for high-functioning Data Teams. The Data Team members build the foundation for cultural proficiency early in their work so that they will continue to strengthen their will as well as their skill to close achievement gaps and raise the achievement of all students throughout the Using Data Process. They also gain experience in talking constructively and safely about the often "undiscussable" issues of race/ethnicity, class, gender, and culture. The work begun in Task 3 will continue throughout the Using Data Process.

BACKGROUND INFORMATION FOR DATA COACHES

What Is Culture?

In this book, we define culture as "everything you believe and everything you do that enables you to identify with people who are like you and that distinguishes you from people who differ from you. Culture is about 'groupness.' A culture is a group of people identified by shared history, values, and patterns of behavior"

(Lindsey et al., 2003, p. 41). Culture is broader than just race and ethnicity. It includes language, class, caste, gender, sexual orientation, geography, ancestry, physical and sensory abilities, occupation, and affiliation. It is a concept that reflects the complex realities of individuals' identities. A person may belong to several cultures.

What Is Cultural Proficiency and What Does It Have to Do With Data?

We have learned through our experience in the Using Data Project that issues of race/ethnicity, class, culture, gender, and other differences among people cannot and, more important, should not be avoided when examining data and engaging in a collaborative inquiry. Our responses and reactions to these differences deeply affect how we interpret data and have a profound impact on student learning. As discussed earlier, diversity is a reality in all schools. It can be dealt with constructively—in ways that reflect deep respect and understanding of students from diverse backgrounds and lead to closing historical achievement gaps—or destructively—reinforcing damaging racist and classist attitudes and other stereotypes and continuing a long-standing pattern of doing harm to students who do not fit the mold of the dominant culture.

The authors consider cultural proficiency to be foundational to making the changes in beliefs and practices that will close achievement gaps. Cultural proficiency is a framework for dealing with diversity in schools constructively by breaking free from damaging stereotypes and assumptions about others and by committing to life-long learning to understand and deepen respect for other cultures. Randall B. Lindsey, Laraine Roberts, and Franklin CampbellJones, in their book *The Culturally Proficient School: An Implementation Guide for School Leaders* (2005), describe cultural proficiency as "honoring the differences among cultures, seeing diversity as a benefit, and inter-acting knowledgeably and respectfully among a variety of cultural groups" (p. 54). It is also described as "a way of being that enables people to successfully engage in new environments" (p. 13). Schools have become rich in diversity of students and often poor in understanding and respect for their differences. Cultural proficiency is a concept and a framework for expanding the notion of diversity. Unlike previous trends in education, cultural proficiency is not about integration, assimilation, tolerance, or superficial multiculturalism, focused on learning about holidays or food. It is about learning to see differently through a cultural proficiency or Equity Lens—seeing culture and its influence on us all, seeing White privilege and its negative impact, and seeing students' cultures as an asset and great source of strength.

Our purpose in introducing the concept of cultural proficiency at this point is to help the Data Team develop these ways of seeing as they engage with data. Throughout the 19 tasks, the authors will remind the team to stand back and view their work through an Equity Lens, drawing on the principles of cultural proficiency and the framework of the continuum in this task.

What Are the Five Guiding Principles of Culturally Proficient Leadership?

The five principles of culturally proficient leadership, which we elaborate on in Handout H3.2 (see CD-ROM), are

1. Culture is a predominant force in people's lives.

2. The dominant culture serves people in varying degrees.

3. People have both personal identities and group identities.

4. Diversity within cultures is vast and significant.

5. Each individual and each group has unique cultural values and needs. (Lindsey et al., 2005, p. 20)

These principles reflect a transformational perspective on school change that holds that deep and lasting school improvement involves changes in relationships, interactions, and behaviors, not just in structures or practices. As the team engages in dialogue about these principles, they are preparing themselves to confront the challenges of diversity by transforming their own beliefs and relationships. These principles will also lay the groundwork for introducing the Cultural Proficiency Continuum in Activity 3.3 and for helping the Data Team to formulate and articulate their own values about student learning and equity as part of Task 4.

What Is the Cultural Proficiency Continuum?

One of the core tools of this task is the Cultural Proficiency Continuum, a framework for describing a range of responses to diversity from cultural destructiveness to cultural proficiency, derived from the work of Terry L. Cross (1989; Cross, Bazron, Dennis, & Isaacs, 1993) and adapted for educators by Randall Lindsey and colleagues (Lindsey, Nuri Robins, & Terrell, 2003; Lindsey, Roberts, & CampbellJones, 2005; see also Toolkit: Cultural Proficiency Continuum). Figure 3.7 illustrates the six dimensions of the continuum, and Table 3.8 contains more detailed examples of what educators might say or do in each stage of the continuum.

As Data Coach, you will want to become very familiar with the expressions of different stages of cultural proficiency so that you can be proactive about recognizing them, challenging assumptions, and facilitating deeper conversations about the team's responses to diversity. Using the continuum effectively is like developing new eyes and ears—to see and hear how cultural blindness and incapacity might be hampering the work of the team and to acknowledge, encourage, and celebrate growth toward cultural competence and proficiency. Eventually, the goal is for the whole team and school to see their work through the lens of cultural proficiency.

Figure 3.7   Cultural Proficiency Continuum.

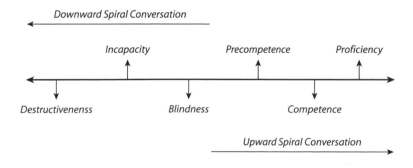

SOURCE Adapted from Lindsey, R.B., Nuri Robins, K., & Terrell, R.D. (2003), p. 85. *Cultural Proficiency: A Manual for School Leaders, 2nd Edition.* Thousand Oaks, CA: Corwin Press. Used with permission.

Table 3.8   Cultural Proficiency Continuum Descriptions

Dimension	Explanation	Examples
Cultural destructiveness	"See the difference, stomp it out": Eliminating other people's culture	• Genocide or ethnocide • Exclusion laws • Avoidance of certain curriculum topics • "Please, you cannot act Black at this school." • "If we could get rid of the special ed students, our scores would be fine."
Cultural incapacity	"See the difference, make it wrong": Believing in the superiority of one's own culture and behaving in ways that disempower another's culture	• Disproportionate allocation of resources to certain groups • Lowered expectations • My way or the highway • "I've worked at this school for 25 years and have received advanced degrees from several universities. I only work with the best and the brightest." • "It's mighty Black at the top." • "Over here are my bluebirds. They are very good students. My buzzards are not quite as talented, but they get along as best they can."
Cultural blindness	"See the difference, act like you don't": Acting as if cultural differences do not matter or not recognizing that there are differences among/between cultures	• Discomfort in noting differences • Beliefs/actions that assume the world is fair and achievement is based on merit • "I don't see color in any of my kids." • "I treat all kids the same." • "Why should we disaggregate data? Kids are kids. I don't see them as black or white or brown—I just see a classroom of kids. This exercise is just creating racial tension unnecessarily."
Cultural precompetence	"See the difference, respond inadequately": Recognizing the limitation of one's skill or an organization's practices when interacting with other cultural groups	• Delegate diversity work to others, to a committee • Quick fixes, packaged short-term programs • "Roberto, we have assigned you to work with the Latino/a parent committee" • "February is coming soon—what should we do for Black History Month?"

Dimension	Explanation	Examples
		• "I had no idea we had such a large Native American population. We really need to learn more about these students' culture. I wonder why these students are often the quietest in class?"
Cultural competence	"See the difference, understand the difference that difference makes": Interacting with other cultural groups using the five essential elements of cultural proficiency as the standard for behavior and practices	• Advocacy • Ongoing education of self and others • Support, modeling, and risk-taking behaviors • "With the addition of our new Muslim students to my classroom, the discussion among the students is so much richer." • "I see you are frustrated about teaching our kids from diverse backgrounds, but your frustration simply has not been my experience." • "There is such a difference in the make-up of our student and our teacher populations. Our staff is almost completely White. Our students are mostly Black and Hispanic. This must have a tremendous impact on our students' learning. We've got some major work to do to become more responsive to our students' cultures."
Cultural proficiency	"See the difference and respond positively and affirmingly": Esteeming culture and interacting effectively in a variety of cultural contexts	• Unabashed advocacy for culturally proficient practices in all arenas • Openness to increasing self-awareness and knowledge of others • Friendships and relationships with those of different backgrounds • Alliances with groups other than one's own • "Our Latino/a kids have to travel far out of their neighborhood to come to our school. Knowing the importance of family and community, this must have a big impact on their experience of school. Let's find ways to make them and their families feel more welcome here."

SOURCE Adapted from Lindsey, R.B., Nuri Robins, K., & Terrell, R.D. (2003), p. 85–91. *Cultural Proficiency: A Manual for School Leaders, 2nd Edition.* Thousand Oaks, CA: Corwin Press. Used with permission.

How Will I Use the Cultural Proficiency Continuum With My Data Team?

The continuum has several uses for the Data Team. In Task 3, you will ask the team to generate examples for each dimension of the continuum from their school experiences. Frequently, teams will generate many examples at the lower end of the continuum and fewer examples at the higher end. This observation makes for an interesting discussion. What often surfaces is that schools provide us with very few models of culturally proficient responses to diversity.

Introducing the continuum in Task 3 is only the beginning of its use, which is reinforced throughout the Using Data Process. For example, the team can keep the continuum posted on their Data Wall as a constant reminder that they are working toward greater cultural proficiency. The far right end of the continuum gives the team a goal to strive for. Periodically, the team can go back to the Cultural Proficiency Continuum Reflection form (see Handout H3.4) to reflect on their progress as individuals and as a team. Frequent monitoring is a powerful catalyst to change.

In addition, the continuum provides the team with a common language for reflecting on their assumptions about data and students. For example, when the team makes inferences about disaggregated data or generates possible causes for their student-learning problem, they can reflect on their assumptions using the language of the continuum. If a cause reflects cultural blindness, incapacity, or destructiveness, such as blaming the students' background for their poor performance, the team can agree to remove it from their list or revise it to be more proficient. By raising their awareness, establishing cultural proficiency goals, and developing a common language, the continuum offers Data Teams and Coaches a tool for responding more skillfully to situations where cultural blindness or precompetence arise, such as those described in the introductory vignettes.

Throughout the book, we will be pointing out ways to integrate use of the continuum with the team's work and to raise equity issues and concerns. However, the guide is not a substitute for a comprehensive diversity program. We recommend in-depth diversity or cultural proficiency training for Data Teams that are facing considerable achievement gaps and struggling with how to move away from the nonproficient end of the continuum.

How Can I Make Dialogue About Race/Ethnicity, Class, Gender, and Culture Safe, If Not Comfortable?

Most people are not comfortable talking about these issues and want to avoid them. For people of color, talk about diversity can bring up feelings of hopelessness, rage, and pain. For White people, it can trigger guilt and defensiveness. Most White people don't want to be thought of as racist and fear making racist mistakes. Facilitating what Glenn Singleton and Curtis Linton (2006) call "courageous conversations" takes courage and skill on the part of both facilitator and participants. It is important to carefully structure these dialogues and strongly enforce collaborative norms. Although the conversations will not be comfortable, they can be productive and safe for participants. Below we elaborate on some facilitation principles that guided us in constructing the activities in this task.

Start With the Personal

Experts in facilitating dialogue about race/ethnicity, class, gender, and culture such as Glenn Singleton, Curtis Linton, Brenda CampbellJones, Franklin CampbellJones, and Julian Weissglass agree that understanding these issues in our schools and our society begins with understanding ourselves, our own backgrounds, and the impact of racism and White privilege on our lives (Lindsey, Roberts, & CampbellJones, 2005; Singleton & Linton, 2006; Weissglass, 1997). Task 3 begins with Activity 3.1: Share My Culture, which invites Data Team members to think personally about their own culture. Everyone has a culture. This activity brings to life the principle that the team will be reading and talking about later: Culture is a predominant force in shaping beliefs, behaviors, values, and attitudes. It also starts the conversation on a personal level, allowing Data Team members to build trust and speak honestly about their own experiences.

Reinforce Collaborative Norms

Collaborative norms are the rules of the road that protect participants from the potential hazards of difficult conversations. In Task 1, the team committed to ways of being with each other. These agreements are going to be very important to keep in Task 3. As you introduce Task 3, we recommend that you ask the team what will make it safe for them to talk about their own culture and race/ethnicity. What collaborative norms do they especially want to attend to during the conversations? Are there other norms that they might want to agree on? This could be a time to consider whether they want to adopt the Four Agreements of Courageous Conversations recommended by Glenn Singleton and Curtis Linton (2006): Stay engaged; experience discomfort; speak your truth; and expect and accept nonclosure (p. 58; see Chapter 3: Task 1 for more information on these four agreements).

Build Foundational Knowledge

Part of the process of developing cultural proficiency is educating ourselves about students' cultures, learning about the history of racism in our society and our schools, and understanding principles that underlie cultural proficiency. In this task, the Data Team will study principles of culturally proficient leadership based on the work of Lindsey, Roberts, and CampbellJones in their book *The Culturally Proficient School* (2005). These principles provide a foundation for understanding and responding to differences that can serve as a touchstone throughout the Using Data Process.

Carefully Structure Dialogue

Dialogue is the style of conversation best suited to "courageous conversations." Through dialogue, the Data Team can explore their own assumptions and stretch themselves to understand the experiences and assumptions of others with different perspectives. We recommend carefully structuring dialogue in small groups. For example, Activity 3.2 introduces the Final Word Dialogue (see Toolkit), which provides a safe structure for dialogue by enforcing pausing and listening. Teams have a tendency to want to deviate from this structure and just talk. We suggest that you urge the team to keep to the structure, which allows all voices to be heard and minimizes reactivity. (See also Task 2, Handout H2.1: Dialogue Versus Discussion.)

What If I as the Data Coach Do Not Feel Culturally Proficient Myself?

Many of us are somewhere on the road to becoming culturally proficient, but not there yet. Be honest about where you are, and join in learning with the team. Here are some suggestions for developing your own, as well as the team's, cultural proficiency:

- Read books recommended in the Resources section of this chapter.
- Attend workshops or courses on antiracism and diversity.
- Expand your personal and/or professional relationships to include more diversity.
- Invite a diversity expert to come and work with you and the Data Team or school.
- Have a White person and a person of color co-lead activities on cultural proficiency.
- If you are White, keep a journal about your own growing awareness of White privilege. See the sample journal entry "A Day I Didn't Have to Think About Race—Which Is Just About Every Day."

A Day I Didn't Have to Think About Race—Which Is Just About Every Day

Saturday morning was errand day, then lunch with a friend. First, I walked into a bank and promptly received excellent service from the customer service representative. I put down my identification and a credit card and had no difficulty opening an account—no questions asked. I didn't have to think about whether or not I would get service because of my color.

Then I went into a local discount department store. I had to ask several times to get a case unlocked that contained expensive electric toothbrushes. Finally, someone opened the case but then quickly had to lock it again and deal with something else, leaving me stranded in front of a locked case. This happened three times with three different sales clerks. I did not have to think about my race being a factor in the poor service I received. It did not occur to me that the clerk wouldn't let me look in the case of expensive electric toothbrushes unattended because of my race. I left the store a little miffed and with no toothbrush, but my self-respect was intact.

Next I took my friend to lunch at a lovely English tearoom. There were no people of color there. I did not have to think about whether or not I belonged there. I just blended in with the tea blends, the fine china, and the White people. I didn't have to think about the legacy of tearooms as the exclusive domain of White, upper-class society—ladies of leisure sipping their tea (while their servants did the housework)—or whether I would feel comfortable there. I didn't have to be hypervigilant to stares or the quality of service I received. I just fit in. And, in the predominantly White suburbs, I did not have to think once about choosing a restaurant where I would feel comfortable as a White person. Any place would do.

While I was doing my errands, my daughter was with her father. It did not occur to me for one minute that she might have to deal with some affront to her race and her being . . . a racist insult, a snicker or snide remark, snubbing by a sales clerk or harassment by the police. Now almost middle-school age and very sensitive to acceptance by her peers, any such rejection from other children would have landed hard on her. Not an ounce of my consciousness was preoccupied with the safety and well-being of my daughter.

The fact that I get to have days like this every day is a testimony to my White privilege. I have the luxury of ignoring race unless I want to wake up to my White privilege, expand my consciousness about race, connect authentically with people of color, and take an active antiracist stance in my daily life. I choose the latter.—Nancy Love

RESOURCES

Johnson, R. S. (2002). *Using data to close the achievement gap: How to measure equity in our schools.* Thousand Oaks, CA: Corwin Press.

Lindsey, D. B., Martinez, R. S., & Lindsey, R. B. (2006). *Culturally proficient coaching: Supporting educators to create equitable schools.* Thousand Oaks, CA: Corwin Press.

Lindsey, R. B., Nuri Robins, K., & Terrell, R. D. (2003). *Cultural proficiency: A manual for school leaders* (2nd ed.). Thousand Oaks, CA: Corwin Press.

Lindsey, R. B., Nuri Robins, K., & Terrell, R. D. (2005). *Facilitator's guide: Cultural proficiency—A manual for school leaders.* Thousand Oaks, CA: Corwin Press.

Lindsey, R. B., Roberts, L. M., & CampbellJones, F. (2005). *The culturally proficient school: An implementation guide for school leaders.* Thousand Oaks, CA: Corwin Press.

McIntosh, P. (1990, Winter). White privilege: Unpacking the invisible knapsack. *Independent School Journal, 49,* 31–36.

Nuri Robins, K., Lindsey, R. B., Lindsey, D. R., & Terrell, R. D. (2005). *Culturally proficient instruction: A guide for people who teach* (2nd ed.). Thousand Oaks, CA: Corwin Press.

Nuri Robins, K., Lindsey, R. B., Lindsey, D. R., & Terrell, R. D. (2006). *Culturally proficient instruction: A multimedia kit for professional development.* Thousand Oaks, CA: Corwin Press.

Singleton, G. E., & Linton, C. (2006). *Courageous conversations about race: A field guide for achieving equity in schools.* Thousand Oaks, CA: Corwin Press.

Sparks, D. (2004). How to have conversations about race: An interview with Beverly Daniel Tatum. *Journal of Staff Development, 25*(4), 48–52.

Weissglass, J. (1997). *Ripples of hope: Building relationships for educational change.* Santa Barbara: Center for Educational Change in Mathematics and Science, University of California, Santa Barbara.

MAJOR ACTIVITIES FOR TASK 3

Activity	Time required	CD-ROM materials: Task 3 link	CD-ROM Toolkit: Relevant tools
Activity 3.1: Share My Culture	20 minutes	Handout H3.1: My Culture	My Culture
Activity 3.2: Dialogue on the Principles of Culturally Proficient Leadership	45 minutes	Handout H3.2: Five Principles of Culturally Proficient Leadership	Final Word Dialogue
Activity 3.3: Explore the Cultural Proficiency Continuum	60 minutes	Handout H3.3: Cultural Proficiency Continuum Descriptions Handout H3.4: Cultural Proficiency Continuum Reflection PowerPoint slides S3.1–S3.8	Cultural Proficiency Continuum

PREPARING FOR THE TASK

Read "Background Information for Data Coaches"; see the CD-ROM: Task 3 for handouts, PowerPoint slides, and sample goals and agenda; and review "Standard Procedures for Data Team Meetings" (see the introduction to Chapter 3 in this book and on CD-ROM). Although tool directions are embedded in the Data Coach Notes below, you can also reference in-depth descriptions of relevant Toolkit entries on the CD-ROM.

MATERIALS PREPARATION

- Make one copy for each team member of Handouts H3.1–H3.4.

- Make six charts, each labeled with one dimension of the Cultural Proficiency Continuum. Tape the charts to the wall around the room, with enough space for participants to gather around each chart.

- Prepare to show the PowerPoint slides.

- Have several Post-it pads available (one medium-size pad per table recommended).

DATA COACH NOTES

 ### Activity 3.1: Share My Culture[2]

1.   Introduce the Data Team to the overall purpose of Task 3—to raise awareness of cultural proficiency and build a common language and framework for thinking and talking about issues of race/ethnicity, class, culture, and diversity throughout the Using Data Process.

2.   Explain that the purpose of this activity is to explore their own culture and the dominant influence of culture in their lives and to begin developing an awareness that will form the foundation for the dialogue they will have throughout the task.

3.   Depending on how you decided to embed practice of your agreed-upon collaborative norms, guide the Data Team through the process you identified. Ask them if there are additional norms they want to use as they move into talking about these sensitive issues.

4.   Distribute Handout H3.1 and ask the team members to complete the chart.

---

2. SOURCE Adapted from Lindsey, R. B. and the California School Leadership Academy by Campbell Jones & Associates. Used with permission.

Handout H3.1

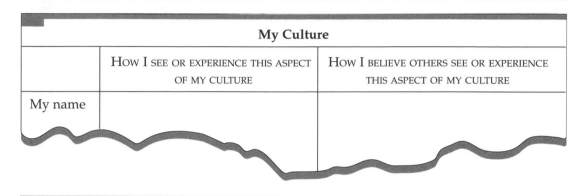

My Culture		
	HOW I SEE OR EXPERIENCE THIS ASPECT OF MY CULTURE	HOW I BELIEVE OTHERS SEE OR EXPERIENCE THIS ASPECT OF MY CULTURE
My name		

5. Have team members pair up; if possible, partners should be from different cultural backgrounds or not know each other well. Ask partners to share how they completed their charts.

6. When everyone has had a chance to share, facilitate a whole-group dialogue. Possible debriefing questions are:

- How do your own perceptions of your culture compare with your assumptions about what others perceive? With your partners' perceptions?
- What differences did you notice among us? Similarities?
- What discoveries are we making about the idea of culture? Of stereotyping?
- How might these discoveries inform our work as a Data Team?

> **Facilitation Note**: Some White participants may have difficulty with this activity because they don't identify with a particular culture; people of color often have less difficulty with the activity because they have a stronger sense of cultural identity.
>
> If the Data Team is homogeneous, consider asking others from the school with different cultures to participate in the activity so that the richness of the discussion can be enhanced with several points of view.

 ### Activity 3.2: Dialogue on the Principles of Culturally Proficient Leadership

1. Distribute Handout H3.2. Ask the Data Team to read the handout and have each person underline one statement for each principle that is particularly provocative or interesting.

2. Explain to the team that they will be reading an article or passage, using highlighters to mark important passages, and then debriefing the reading using a process called Final Word Dialogue (adapted from Wellman & Lipton, 2004; used with permission).

3. Divide the team into groups of three or four people. Distribute the reading selection and highlighters to each team member. Ask them to read and highlight two to three ideas that are particularly meaningful or provocative for them.

4. Allow appropriate time for reading.

5. Describe the round-robin structure for debriefing the reading selection:
   a. Person A begins the dialogue by reading one of his or her highlighted items to the group but making no further comment. The group listens without commenting or interrupting until Person A has finished. Then, going around the table, the other members of the group may speak in turn, commenting on what Person A read. Person A has the final word.
   b. Explain that the pattern continues until each person has had his or her final word on a dialogue he or she started.
   c. Remind the team of the power of pausing (one of the Seven Norms of Collaboration) as it gives time for everyone to think before responding, provides an opportunity for deeper thinking, and helps the group dialogue be more thoughtful.

6. Ask the groups to begin their dialogue. Allow enough time for each person to have a turn.

7. Debrief the process with the entire team by asking them to respond to questions such as, "What did it feel like to participate in the Final Word Dialogue? What impact did pausing have on each person's participation? What impact did pausing have on the group?"

8. Ask the team to reflect on what new discoveries they are making about the idea of culture. How do they want this to influence their work as a Data Team? Their core values about student learning? Equity? What light does this shed on the question, "What is in the achievement gap?"

 ### Activity 3.3: Explore the Cultural Proficiency Continuum

1. Explain the purpose of this activity (adapted from Lindsey et al., 2003; used with permission), which is to learn about a framework for thinking about a range of responses to cultural differences, from cultural destructiveness to cultural competence.

2. Display Slide S3.2, the Cultural Proficiency Continuum (see Figure 3.7). Briefly explain the continuum as a scale of behavior, language, and actions that ranges from culturally destructive to culturally proficient. Link the ends of the continuum to productive conversations. Destructive behavior contributes to a downward spiral, while proficient behavior contributes to an upward spiral.

3. Distribute Handout H3.3 (illustrated in Table 3.8) and display Slides S3.3–S3.8 to provide an overview of each dimension of the continuum.

4. Distribute Post-it pads to each table. Ask each person to think of examples for each stage of the continuum that he or she has personally experienced or observed and record these examples on Post-its, one idea per Post-it.

5. When the team has finished generating their ideas, call their attention to the charts with the different dimensions of the Cultural Proficiency Continuum that are posted around the room. Have them place their Post-its on the appropriate charts. Invite team members to walk around the room and review each chart.

6. Debrief by asking: What observations do they have about the data? Which dimension has the most examples? Which has the least? What inferences can they make about the data? Why is it lopsided? How well did the team members sort their Post-its? Are some actions more telling than others? Why?

7. Explain that a goal for the Data Team is to become more culturally proficient and for the actions of the Data Team to help change the school culture to be more culturally proficient. Select several Post-its from each chart. Read one at a time, and ask team members in partners to think about how these examples could become more proficient. For example, in cultural blindness, how would team members change the statement "I treat all of my kids the same" into a more culturally proficient statement?

8. Ask team members to share any "aha's" from this discussion.

Handout H3.4

Cultural Proficiency Continuum Reflection		
Reflect on today's meeting both as an individual and as a team At which dimension did you function for the majority of the meeting? What Is your evidence?		
Dimension	Individual	Team
Cultural Destructiveness		

9. Distribute Handout H3.4. Ask the team to reflect individually on each of the questions on the handout.

10. Ask team members to share their reflections with the whole group. On chart paper, record the team's ideas for keeping their cultural proficiency goals alive. Keep this list and post it in subsequent meetings to keep their equity work in the forefront.

Task 4: Commit to Shared Values, Standards, and Vision

Task-at-a-Glance

Purpose	To strengthen shared commitments that will guide the work of the team by agreeing to core values about student learning and equity
Data	None
Questions to ask	What are our core values related to student learning and equity? What do we want all students to know and be able to do? How will we know they have learned? What will we do if they don't learn? What kind of school do we want to be?
Concepts	Equity Vision Core values Academic content standards Benchmarks Scoring guides Rubrics
Activities	Activity 4.1: Engage With Four Variations on "All Students Can Learn" Activity 4.2: Craft Core Values About Student Learning and Equity Activity 4.3: Consider Three Key Questions About Student Learning Activity 4.4: Envision Curriculum and Instruction, Equity, and Critical Supports

WHAT IS TASK 4?

In Task 4, Data Teams strengthen their commitments to core values related to student learning and equity, a set of standards, and a shared vision. These are vital to the work of Data Teams. Without them, Data Teams can take shortcuts that benefit some students while overlooking or even harming others, meander aimlessly, or simply lose their motivation. Without clarity about desired results, it is impossible to achieve them, much less to use data to measure progress toward them.

Firmly establishing shared commitment is as difficult as it is important. It requires perseverance, time, and skilled leadership, not just of Data Coaches and Data Teams, but also of the school and district administrators. Clearly, Data Teams cannot complete this work in a few Data Team meetings. Nor can this book be a comprehensive guide to visioning; there are many good ones available; a few are suggested in the Resources section below. But Data Teams can use the activities in Task 4 to synthesize work that has already been done, take steps toward strengthening their shared commitments, and plan for how to carry forward this foundational part of the Using Data Process.

Task 4 draws on work completed in Task 2, when the Data Team used the Program Elements Matrix tool to assess what extent shared values and goals are in place in their school. In this task, they take the next step toward becoming a high-performing Using Data Culture—whether by recommitting to values and standards already in place,

Figure 3.8   Example of completed School of Our Dreams.

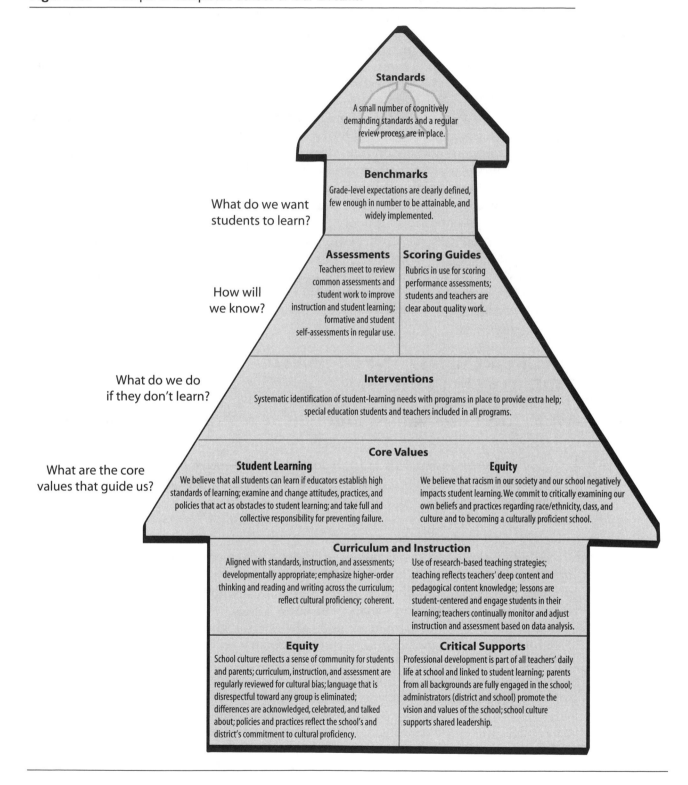

What do we want
students to learn?

How will
we know?

What do we do
if they don't learn?

What are the core
values that guide us?

Standards

A small number of cognitively
demanding standards and a regular
review process are in place.

Benchmarks

Grade-level expectations are clearly defined,
few enough in number to be attainable, and
widely implemented.

Assessments

Teachers meet to review
common assessments and
student work to improve
instruction and student learning;
formative and student
self-assessments in regular use.

Scoring Guides

Rubrics in use for scoring
performance assessments;
students and teachers are
clear about quality work.

Interventions

Systematic identification of student-learning needs with programs in place to provide extra help;
special education students and teachers included in all programs.

Core Values

Student Learning

We believe that all students can learn if educators establish high
standards of learning; examine and change attitudes, practices, and
policies that act as obstacles to student learning; and take full and
collective responsibility for preventing failure.

Equity

We believe that racism in our society and our school negatively
impacts student learning. We commit to critically examining our
own beliefs and practices regarding race/ethnicity, class, and
culture and to becoming a culturally proficient school.

Curriculum and Instruction

Aligned with standards, instruction, and assessments;
developmentally appropriate; emphasize higher-order
thinking and reading and writing across the curriculum;
reflect cultural proficiency; coherent.

Use of research-based teaching strategies;
teaching reflects teachers' deep content and
pedagogical content knowledge; lessons are
student-centered and engage students in their
learning; teachers continually monitor and adjust
instruction and assessment based on data analysis.

Equity

School culture reflects a sense of community for students
and parents; curriculum, instruction, and assessment are
regularly reviewed for cultural bias; language that is
disrespectful toward any group is eliminated;
differences are acknowledged, celebrated, and talked
about; policies and practices reflect the school's and
district's commitment to cultural proficiency.

Critical Supports

Professional development is part of all teachers' daily
life at school and linked to student learning; parents
from all backgrounds are fully engaged in the school;
administrators (district and school) promote the
vision and values of the school; school culture
supports shared leadership.

jump-starting a new visioning process, and/or mapping out how this vital work will get done. Task 4 also builds on the work the team did on cultural proficiency in Task 3. In Task 4, they apply those principles to the values that will fuel the work of the team. The final product for Task 4, a completed school vision, is illustrated in Figure 3.8. Note that the vision represented in the School of Our Dreams can be "huge and audacious," as Jim Collins (1996) says, "but ultimately achievable" (p. 19).

In Activity 4.1, the team engages with four variations on the "all students can learn" theme as a precursor to articulating their own core values. In Activity 4.2, they begin constructing the School of Our Dreams by articulating core values related to student learning and equity. In Activity 4.3, they consider the three critical questions focused on ensuring quality learning for all: (1) What do we want students to know and be able to do? (2) How will we know that students have learned? and (3) What will we do if they don't learn? (DuFour & Eaker, 1998). Finally, in Activity 4.4, the team envisions what kind of school they want to create—its curriculum and instruction, equity practices, and critical supports such as professional development—in order to achieve their vision and goals for all students. The work that the team does in Task 4 will serve as the touchstone throughout the Using Data Process for aligning their work with the principles of cultural proficiency, their shared values, their student-learning goals (standards), and a clear and compelling vision for their school.

BACKGROUND INFORMATION FOR DATA COACHES

What Are Core Values and Why Are They So Important?

A core value is a central belief deeply understood and shared by every member of an organization. Core values guide the actions of everyone in the organization; they focus its energy and are the anchor points for all its plans.

—Saphier and D'Auria, 1993, p. 3

A hallmark of successful organizations is a set of core values that the organization's members live by (Collins, 2001; Senge et al., 2000). Core values are not empty phrases that people pay lip service to or promptly forget once they are written. If a school truly embraces core values, you know it. For example, if the educators in a school commit to the core value about student learning stated in Figure 3.8, they will leap into action, designing multiple interventions to both prevent and remediate failure, motivate students to work hard, teach them about the link between effort and achievement, and offer a rigorous academic program for all students. They will not tolerate explanations for poor performance that blame students or their backgrounds.

According to Saphier and D'Auria (1993), a core value permeates the school, drives decisions, elicits strong reactions when violated, and is the very last thing you give up. In this task, we recommend that the Data Team commit to two core values—one related to student learning and one to equity. If the school has already done the work of defining their core values, then the Data Team can remind themselves of these values and think about how they will keep them alive throughout their work. If not, they will define them in this task.

What Is Equity?

Ensuring equity is at the very heart of collaborative inquiry and the Using Data Process. It is the right of every student to achieve at high levels, a right many students still do not have. The persistent achievement gaps between African American, Hispanic, and Native American students and White and Asian students and between children living in poverty and others provide overwhelming evidence that obstacles to equity—in beliefs, policies, and practices—still stand in the way of this basic right. As Love (2002) wrote,

> Education reform can proceed—states and schools can adopt standards for "all students"; schools can implement new, more challenging inquiry-based mathematics and science programs—yet little will change for . . . disenfranchised students unless we directly confront racial, class, cultural, and gender biases and the inequitable practices they spawn. Reform that does not put equity center stage has not and will not bring about high levels of mathematics and science achievement for all. (p. 253)

In Task 3, the Data Team built the foundation for understanding cultural proficiency because changes in perceptions and interactions with students' diversity are a fundamental prerequisite for achieving equity. And achieving equity is at the very heart of closing achievement gaps. Although there are many definitions of equity, we use those that define educational equity in terms of the elimination of achievement gaps. For example, Hart and Germaine-Watts define equity as "an operational principle for shaping school policies and practices which assure high expectations and appropriate resources so that all students achieve at the same rigorous standard—with minimal variance due to race, income, language, or gender" (1996, as cited in Johnson, 2002, p. 3). Similarly, Glenn Singleton and Curtis Linton (2006) define educational equity as "raising the achievement of all students while narrowing the gaps between the highest and lowest performing students; and eliminating the racial predictability and disproportionality of which student groups occupy the highest and lowest achievement categories" (p. 46).

It is useful to distinguish between equity and equality. Equity is being just, impartial, and fair. Equality is providing the same or equivalent of any resource to all people. "Equity recognizes that the playing field is unequal and attempts to address the inequality" (DeCuir & Dixson, 2004, p. 29). The remedy is not giving everybody the same thing, but giving each person what he or she needs to be successful. Think about access for people with physical disabilities. Giving everyone the same kind of access is an example of equality, but that would exclude some people. Giving people with physical disabilities access ramps and adapted facilities is equitable, but not equal. When equity is a reality in schools, all students will not just have "equal opportunities"; they will have everything they need to be successful—and that is not the same for everyone. Equity means that "students of color can rest assured that the school will meet their needs to the same degree it meets White students' needs," write Singleton and Linton (2006, p. 47). The concept of equity is introduced in this task to inform the team as they craft their own core value statement on equity.

What Are the Three Critical Questions About Student Learning?

How can you use data to drive instruction if you don't know what the instruction should be in the first place?

—Pam Bernabei-Rorrer, Mathematics and
Data Coach, Canton City, Ohio

Rick DuFour and Robert Eaker (DuFour & Eaker, 1998; Eaker, DuFour, & DuFour, 2002) argue that schools that align their practices with a commitment to all learners work together to answer three critical questions: (1) Exactly what is it we want all students to learn? (2) How do we know if they learned it? and (3) What will we do if they don't learn? Below is some background information on how to guide Data Teams in answering these questions.

Exactly What Is It We Want All Our Students to Learn?

In effective schools, every teacher is crystal clear about the learning targets they wish to reach: a set of clearly articulated learning goals for each grade and each course. At the general level, this knowledge is known as academic content standards. As defined by Douglas Reeves (1998), these are "the general expectations of what students should know and be able to do. These are typically few in number and general in scope," and they span multiple grade levels. For example,

- Students will be able to design, conduct, analyze, evaluate, and communicate about scientific investigations.
- Students will communicate clearly and effectively about science to others. (p. 16)

When the specific expectations for this knowledge and these skills are defined more specifically for grade levels, they are typically known as benchmarks. These are greater in number and more specific in scope. When students meet the benchmarks, it provides the evidence that they are meeting the standards; benchmarks are the checkpoints along the way. For example,

- By Grade 4, students will identify and describe science related problems or issues, such as acid rain and weather forecasting.
- By Grade 4, students will relate science information to local and global issues, such as world hunger and ozone depletion. (Reeves, 1998, p. 16)

Finally, there are the very specific descriptions of what student proficiency looks like on standards-based assessments, known as scoring guides or rubrics. Reeves (1998) offers the following example: "To earn a score of 'proficient,' the student will produce an informative essay with no spelling, grammar, or punctuation errors. The essay will be accompanied by at least two graphs that include data points and relationships that support the conclusions of the essay. The graphs will be mathematically correct, properly labeled, and clearly related to the essay" (p. 17). The scoring guides or rubrics enable us to know how students perform on the benchmarks.

In Activity 4.3, one of the questions the Data Team considers is "What exactly do we want students to learn?" In many schools, the background work has already been done for the Data Team to answer this question. Due mainly to increased accountability, schools have established grade-level expectations, driven by state and district standards. If this is true in your school, the Data Coach can gather relevant documents such as district curriculum guides, pacing documents, scope and sequences, and other materials that define what students should learn in the content areas and grade levels with which the team is involved. The Data Team will review these standards and benchmarks to remind themselves of why they are in business—which is to achieve these learning goals for each and every student.

If standards and benchmarks are not in place, the Data Team and Data Coach can be the catalyst for putting a process in place to establish these. In some cases the Data Team will have the authority and the responsibility for this work. For example, in Canton City, Ohio, the Mathematics and Data Coach for the four middle schools convened a Data Team comprising all the middle school mathematics teachers for a three-day retreat where they identified the critical content they expected students to master at each grade level (see Canton City example in the vignette on page 119). In other cases, the Data Team coordinates with other groups such as curriculum groups or grade-level teams to clarify these targets. In Activity 4.3 the Data Team does not complete the job of establishing standards and benchmarks if this has not yet been finished; it is too time consuming. Rather they synthesize what has already been done to date and plan for completing this major piece of work. There are many good resources to inform establishing standards and benchmarks and aligning curriculum to standards, including state and national standards documents and sources listed in the Resources section below.

Standards without standards-based assessments are merely a very expensive and time-consuming pep talk.

—Reeves, 1998, p. 35

Until we started administering our quarterly assessments, teachers were not accountable for teaching to the standards. The quarterlies got us to actually teach to the standards.

—Pam Bernabei-Rorrer, Mathematics and Data Coach, Canton City, Ohio

How Do We Know If Students Have Learned?

This is a question that good teachers are asking every day in their classrooms. Through the use of ongoing formative assessments, or assessments for learning—those that have as their purpose increasing student achievement—teachers are discovering what students learn and using what they find out to inform instruction. These assessments happen minute by minute, day to day, and include student self-assessment, descriptive feedback to students, use of rubrics, multiple methods of checking for understanding, and examination of student work as well as tests and quizzes (Stiggins, Arter, Chappuis, & Chappuis, 2004). Research provides strong evidence that these assessments contribute to significant achievement gains for students, especially those who were low performing (Black, 2003; Black & Wiliam, 1998; Bloom, 1984; Meisels et al., 2003; Rodriguez, 2004). In addition to ongoing formative assessments, common formative and benchmark assessments help teachers determine if students are learning. For more information on the use of common assessments, see Tasks 5 and 11.

What Will We Do If Students Don't Learn?

Once Data Teams establish and/or get familiar with their standards and benchmarks for student learning and assessment methods to measure learning, their ongoing work focuses on using data and answering this final question. Now, as you help the team build the foundation, is a good time to raise this question. Successful schools have a systemic response when students do not learn, including strategies to prevent failure, such as frequent monitoring of student progress, and a series of interventions to identify and support students who are not learning, such as peer tutoring systems or master schedules that allow students to receive individualized and small-group instruction. Figure 3.9 illustrates the interventions that were put in place at Adlai Stevenson High School under Rick DuFour's leadership.

Figure 3.9   Pyramid of interventions at Adlai Stevenson High School.

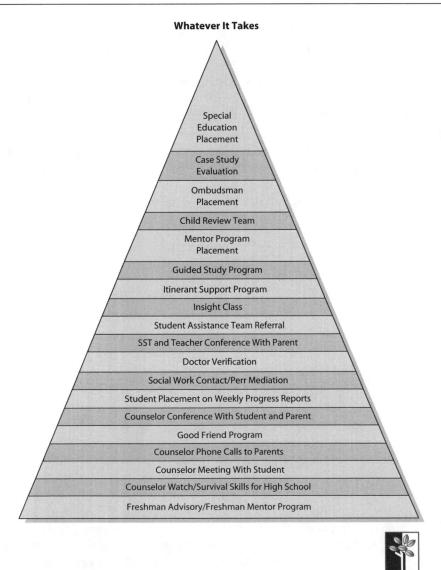

SOURCE Used with permission from *Whatever It Takes: How Professional Learning Communities Respond When Kids Don't Learn* by Richard DuFour, Rebecca DuFour, Robert Eaker, and Gayle Karhanek (p. 210). Copyright © 2004 by Solution Tree (formerly National Education Service), 304 West Kirkwood Avenue, Bloomington, Indiana 47404, 800-733-6786, www.solution-tree.com.

As discussed earlier, if your school has done none of the groundwork for answering these three questions, it is important that a process be put in place to do so. This can take several months or longer and is often beyond the scope of the Data Team. If the school does have standards, assessments, and systems to prevent failure in place, the Data Team can help to implement them properly to assure equitable learning for all. In this task, the Data Team summarizes what has been done, acts as a catalyst to further this work in the school, and recommits to achieving learning goals for all students.

Vision is simply a combination of three basic elements: (1) an organization's fundamental reason for existence . . . , (2) its timeless unchanging core values, and (3) huge and audacious—but ultimately achievable—aspirations for its own future.

—Collins, 1996, p. 19

What Is a Vision?

A vision is a compelling, desired future for your school. In the Using Data Process, Data Teams imagine the school of their dreams. The roof of the dream school is student learning, built from the core values and student-learning goals. Then they imagine what the rest of the school would look like if students—all students—were respected, encouraged, and achieving. What curriculum would they have? How would obstacles to equity be tackled? What critical supports, such as high-quality professional development and parent engagement, would be in place in this dream school?

Why take the time to dream? Because the more precise, detailed, and fully articulated our dreams are, the greater the chance of realizing them. When the team gets to the tasks of analyzing data, it is important for them to remember that collaborative inquiry is the work of dreamers; it is the relentless pursuit—one problem or goal, one "brick" or "board" at a time—of building the school of our dreams.

How Do I Keep the Work the Team Does in Task 4 Alive Throughout the Process?

Here are some ideas:

• Keep the School of Our Dreams that will be created in this task posted on the Data Wall. From time to time, refer back to it and ask the team to reflect on the extent to which their actions are aligned with their values and the principles of cultural proficiency. Encourage them to give concrete examples, which can serve as benchmarks or indicators that they are moving toward becoming the school of their dreams.

• Ask the team to remember their core values about equity and student learning each time they look at data in Tasks 6–11. Make sure that diverse students' and parents' voices and perspectives are represented in the data. As they generate inferences from their data, ask them to what extent their inferences are aligned with their values. In Tasks 13–14, ask the team to bring an Equity Lens to their exploration of causes for student learning problems.

• Use the suggested Equity Lens and School Culture Review prompts written into subsequent tasks to keep the core values and vision at the forefront of the team's work.

RESOURCES

Black, P., & Wiliam, D. (1998). Inside the black box: Raising standards through classroom assessment. *Phi Delta Kappan, 80*(2), 139–148.

DuFour, R., & Eaker, R. (1998). *Professional learning communities at work: Best practices for enhancing student achievement.* Bloomington, IN: National Educational Service.

Eaker, R., DuFour, R., & DuFour, R. (2002). *Getting started: Reculturing schools to become professional learning communities.* Bloomington, IN: National Educational Service.

Keeley, P. (2005). *Science curriculum topic study: Bridging the gap between standards and practice.* Thousand Oaks, CA: Corwin Press.

Keeley, P., & Rose, C. M. (2006). *Mathematics curriculum topic study: Bridging the gap between standards and practice.* Thousand Oaks, CA: Corwin Press.

Kendall, J., & Marzano, R. (1996a). *Content knowledge: A compendium of standards and benchmarks for K–12 education.* Alexandria, VA: Association for Supervision and Curriculum Development.

Kendall, J., & Marzano, R. (1996b). *Designing standards-based districts, schools, and classrooms.* Alexandria, VA: Association for Supervision and Curriculum Development.

Lindsey, R. B., Roberts, L. M., & CampbellJones, F. (2005). *The culturally proficient school: An implementation guide for school leaders.* Thousand Oaks, CA: Corwin Press.

Reeves, D. B. (1998). *Making standards work* (2nd ed.). Denver, CO: Center for Performance Assessment.

Saphier, J. (2005). Masters of motivation. In R. DuFour, R. Eaker, R. DuFour (Eds.), *On common ground: The power of professional learning communities* (pp. 79–84). Bloomington, IN: National Educational Service.

Singleton, G., & Linton, C. (2006). *Courageous conversations about race: A field guide for achieving equity in schools.* Thousand Oaks, CA: Corwin Press.

Stiggins, R. J., Arter, J. A., Chappuis, J., & Chappuis, S. (2004). *Classroom assessment for student learning: Doing it right—using it well.* Portland, OR: Assessment Training Institute.

See also local, state, and national standards documents, for example, National Research Council, *National Science Education Standards*; National Council of Teacher of Mathematics (NCTM), *Principles and Standards for School Mathematics*; National Council of Teachers of English, *National Standards for the English Language Arts.*

MAJOR ACTIVITIES FOR TASK 4

Activity	Time required	CD-ROM materials: Task 4 link	CD Toolkit: Relevant tools
Activity 4.1: Engage With Four Variations on "All Students Can Learn"	30 minutes	Handout H4.1: Four Variations on a Theme: All Kids Can Learn . . . Resources R4.1–R4.4: Choose Your School	Seven Norms of Collaboration

Activity 4.2: Craft Core Values About Student Learning and Equity	60 minutes	PowerPoint slides S4.1–S4.10 Resource R4.5: School of Our Dreams	Seven Norms of Collaboration
Activity 4.3: Consider Three Key Questions About Student Learning	45 minutes	Handout H4.2: Guiding Questions for the School of Our Dreams Resource R4.5: School of Our Dreams	Seven Norms of Collaboration
Activity 4.4: Envision Curriculum and Instruction, Equity, and Critical Supports	45 minutes	Handout H4.2: Guiding Questions for the School of Our Dreams Resource R4.5: School of Our Dreams	Seven Norms of Collaboration

PREPARING FOR THE TASK

Read "Background Information for Data Coaches"; see CD-ROM: Task 4 for handouts, resources, and sample goals and agenda; and review "Standard Procedures for Data Team Meetings" (see the introduction to Chapter 3 in this book and on CD-ROM). You can reference in-depth descriptions of relevant tools in the Toolkit on the CD-ROM.

MATERIALS PREPARATION

- Make one copy for each team member of Handouts H4.1 and H4.2. (Note: On Handout H4.2, replace the terms and/or definitions of standards and benchmarks with those of your school, district, and state if they are different from the definitions used on the handout.)

- Prepare four charts using Resources R4.1–R4.4 and post them on the wall, each in a different corner of the room. Cover all but the titles and descriptive paragraphs by folding and taping up the bottom of the chart. Also, prepare and post a fifth chart using Resource R4.5.

- Prepare to show the PowerPoint slides.

- Have a supply of Post-it pads available for Activities 4.2, 4.3, and 4.4.

- Gather pacing and curriculum guides, scope and sequences, and state and local standards and benchmarks in the content area(s) the team is addressing.

DATA COACH NOTES

 ### Activity 4.1: Engage With Four Variations on "All Students Can Learn"

1. Review the goals and agenda for your work with the team in Task 4. Explain that Task 4 is about creating a vision for their school.

Figure 3.10 School of Our Dreams.

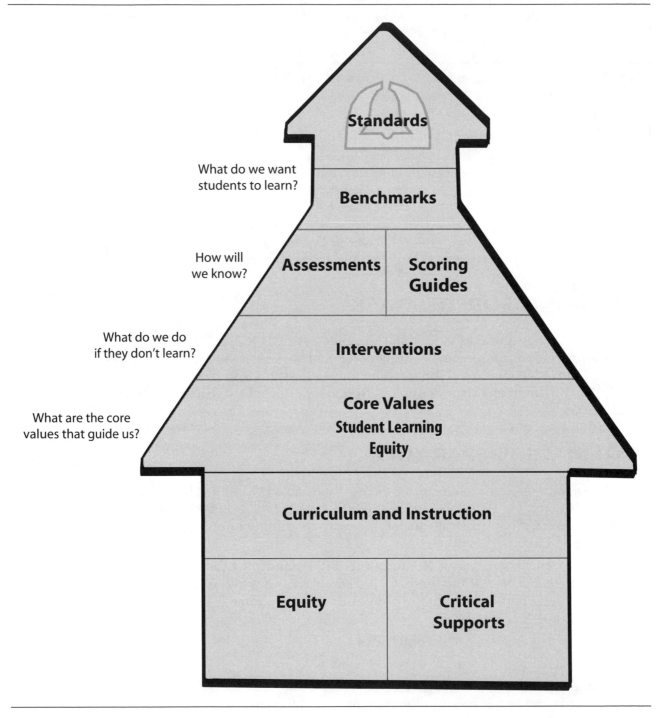

2. Refer the team to the wall chart you have created of the School of Our Dreams (see Figure 3.10). Elaborate on each of the elements of the graphic. Explain that Activity 4.1 is a precursor to formulating their core values related to student learning and equity, illustrated at the bottom of the roof in the graphic.

3. Introduce the Four Variations on "All Students Can Learn" Activity (adapted from DuFour et al., 2004; used with permission): Although educators often pay lip service to the familiar mantra that "all students can learn," what they actually mean by that can vary widely. Explain that the team will explore four different variations on beliefs about student learning and the data practices associated with each them. Note that this activity will help to prepare the team to clarify their core values about student learning and equity in Activity 4.2.

4. Distribute Handout H4.1, and ask the team to read the descriptions of the four schools, which are also depicted on the charts you have posted around the room (with the two bulleted lists from those charts covered).

5. Direct the team to choose the chart with the variation of the school that they think best represents their school and go stand by it. Ask those who gather at each chart to discuss why they chose that school, whether or not it is the school they want it to be, and why or why not. Ask for brief report-outs from each corner.

6. Ask the team to reflect on how similar or different their perceptions are of their school. Are they clustered around one description or more than one?

7. Ask the team to move now to the corner that best represents the kind of school they would want to send their own children to and discuss why they chose that school. Ask for brief report-outs from each corner.

8. Ask the team to reflect on where they went: Are they in the same corner or different ones? What does this say about their own values about student learning?

9. Untape and open up the folded charts to display the bulleted lists for what the four schools do when students do not learn and what teachers in those schools cite as the causes for students not learning. Ask the team to discuss their reactions to these lists. Does this lens on the schools alter anyone's choice of school for their own child? Why or why not? Does anyone want to change their selection? If so, have them move to another corner.

10. Ask the team members to do a written reflection on the following questions: What description did I choose for my school and why? How comfortable am I with this description? What would it take to make our school more like School D? As a Data Team member, what can I do to support that transition?

 ### Activity 4.2: Craft Core Values About Student Learning and Equity

1. Display Slide S4.2 with the definition of a core value. Explain that the purpose of this activity is for the team to formulate a set of core values related to student learning and equity. Explain that core values are the central beliefs that are understood and shared by everyone in an organization. They permeate the organization, drive decisions, elicit strong reactions when violated, and are the last thing you give up. For example, a core value might be "Effort, not ability is the prime determinant of student success. All students have sufficient intellectual capacity to do rigorous academic work at high levels" (Research for Better Teaching, 2006, p. 212).

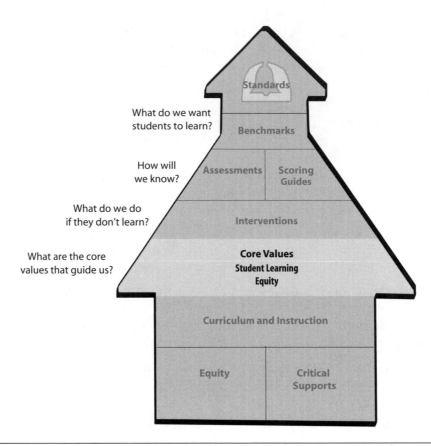

Resource R4.5a

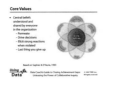

Slide S4.2

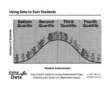

Slide S4.3

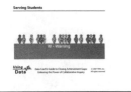

Slide S4.4

2. Display Slide S4.3, and explain that in the old model, the purpose of schooling is to sort students into different groups based on perceived ability, with each group receiving a different curriculum. Animate the slide to illustrate the four quartiles that sort students by their ability. Note that this approach contradicts the values underlying the Using Data Process of Collaborative Inquiry.

3. Show Slides S4.4–S4.9 to illustrate the approach of the Using Data Process—to serve all students and move more and more students to high levels of achievement.

4. Ask each team member to think about what they learned in Task 3 and in Activity 4.1 and to generate a definition of educational equity.

5. Display Slide S4.10 showing a definition of educational equity. Ask the team to compare their definitions with the one displayed. How do they differ?

6. Distribute Post-it pads (or portions of pads) to each Data Team member. Ask team members to individually think about their core values about student learning and equity and to write two separate statements on Post-its.

7. Then divide the Data Team into an even number of groups of two to three. Ask each small group to share their ideas and come up with two wordings that represent core values statements that they can both (or all) agree to.

8. Next, partner the partners (i.e., combine pairs or trios). Again, ask them to compare their statements and work together to come up with two statements to which everyone in the combined group can commit. For larger groups, repeat the process of combining two groups until the whole team comes to consensus about the two statements.

9. Direct the team to the Student Learning component of the School of Our Dreams wall chart. Have them post the two notes in the Core Values section at the base of the roof. Remind the team that these values will be the foundation of the rest of the work they do on the School of Our Dreams.

Slide S4.9

Slide S4.10

Activity 4.3: Consider Three Key Questions About Student Learning

1. Explain that the purpose of this activity is to acknowledge the importance of having clearly articulated student-learning goals, a plan for assessing if those goals are met, and a commitment to take essential action when students don't learn. They will also envision how to answer the questions: What do we want students to learn? How do we know if they have learned? What will we do if they don't learn?

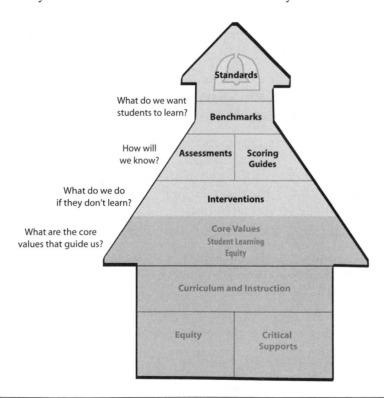

Resource R4.5b

2. Distribute Handout H4.2. Ask team members to read the definitions of standards and benchmarks and the guiding questions for student learning.

3. Ask team members to individually think about their ideal school relative to student learning. They should write specific ideas about their vision for what students should know and be able to do (based on district/school standards and benchmarks), how student learning will be assessed (assessments, rubrics, and scoring guide), and what will happen if they don't learn (interventions). Have them write one idea per Post-it and limit themselves to five Post-its for each of the five student-learning areas in the roof (standards, benchmarks, assessments, scoring goals, interventions). Encourage team members to use the questions on the handout to shape their thinking. For standards and benchmarks, rather than listing all their standards and benchmarks, they might write, "Achievement of the standards and benchmarks established by our school/district" in a particular area, such as elementary science. For curriculum they might write, "Modified standards and benchmarks for language arts that are fewer and more rigorous than what we have now." For assessment they might write, "Development of clear standards and benchmarks for all mathematics courses in our high school" (in the case where none exist).

4. Again divide the Data Team into an even number of groups of two to three. Ask partners to share their Post-its and come up with no more than five Post-its that represent their shared vision for each of the student-learning areas.

5. Next, partner the partners. Have each partner group share their Post-its and again come up with no more than five Post-its for each of the student-learning areas. For larger groups, repeat the process of combining two groups until the whole team comes to consensus.

6. Have the team post these notes in the appropriate areas in the roof of the School of Our Dreams wall chart.

 ### Activity 4.4: Envision Curriculum and Instruction, Equity, and Critical Supports

1. Now move to the Curriculum and Instruction, Equity, and Critical Supports part of the School of Our Dreams wall chart. Ask team members to think individually about their ideal school relative to these important aspects of a school and to generate Post-its with the specific ideas about their vision. Have them write one idea per Post-it and limit themselves to five Post-its for each of the three areas. Encourage the team to use the guiding questions in Handout H4.2.

2. Repeat Steps 4 and 5 from Activity 4.3 for curriculum and instruction, equity, and critical supports and then post their notes in the appropriate areas in the base of the School of Our Dreams wall chart.

3. Have the team reflect on the entire schoolhouse:
   • How does this schoolhouse compare to our current school?
   • Does it represent a vision of where we want to be? Is it feasible? What are some next steps to achieve this vision?
   • How does the schoolhouse reflect the shifts the team looked at in Task 1: Launch the Data Team and in Activity 2.3: Reflect on Program Elements Matrix (PEM) of a Using Data School Culture in Task 2?

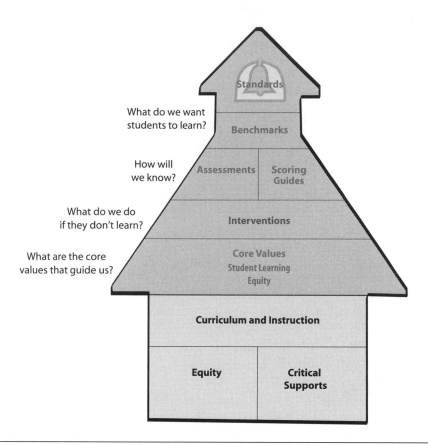

Resource R4.5c

- To what extent have we incorporated what we learned about cultural proficiency in the School of Our Dreams? Are there any changes/additions we want to make now?
- How do we want to share what we have done with other teams? With faculty?

4. Remind the team that they will use data throughout the Using Data Process to continue to inform and shape their vision. (Note: After the meeting, either tape the Post-its to the chart or write in the information for reference in future Data Team meetings.)

A Data Team in Action: Canton City Middle School Mathematics. Part I: Aligning Curriculum With Standards—Pam Bernabei-Rorrer, Mathematics and Data Coach, Canton City, Ohio

The first leg of our journey focused on designing and implementing grade-level curriculum maps based on the newly created Ohio math standards in 2002. Teachers came together in grade-level teams and dialogued about the meaning of the grade-level indicators. The result of the dialogue was a curriculum map broken into concept chunks for each of the four quarters of the school year. The mathematics curriculum in Canton City was no longer determined by the chapters in the textbook, but had a sensible flow allowing students to build upon their previous learning.

(Continued)

(Continued)

After establishing curriculum maps for each grade, representatives from each grade level met to analyze the vertical alignment of the maps. The teachers examined the vertical flow of the curriculum between the grades and evaluated the depth of each concept that extended over several grades. A logical sequence was established not only for each course, but throughout the entire mathematics program.

Since the curriculum no longer followed the outline of the textbook, the next step was to align resources to support the concept chunks in the map. Canton City's textbooks were more than 10 years old and did not include chapters on some of the Ohio standards, especially the standards involving probability and data analysis. New textbooks weren't a possibility due to budget constraints, however, so the mathematics team's solution was to collect and share their resources from various sites, including activity books from the NCTM Navigation series, Web sites, and other sources. For concept chunks that were still weak in instructional materials, new lessons were created by the mathematics team utilizing Schlechty's (2002) strategies for designing engaging student work. A notebook compiling the team's work was created and distributed to the members of the mathematics department. This became the new textbook for the district, serving to support the established curriculum maps while also establishing ownership of instruction for the teachers. (Continued in Task 11.)

Identifying a Student-Learning Problem

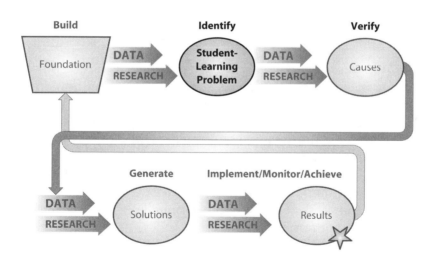

This chapter focuses on the second component of the Using Data Process, Identifying a Student-Learning Problem, and includes Tasks 5–12. The activities in these tasks lead teams through the tools and procedures associated with building data literacy and engaging in the drill-down into student-learning data. Through drilling down into the data and using multiple data sources, Data Teams pinpoint a schoolwide, grade-level, or course-specific student-learning problem and goal on which to focus their improvement efforts.

Drilling down into student-learning data is the process of analyzing a data source at several levels: aggregated, disaggregated, strand, item, and student work. It can be applied to any source of student-learning data, including state criterion-referenced tests (CRTs), district criterion-referenced tests, and benchmark common assessments. The goal is to glean as much information about student learning from the data source as you can. The tasks in this chapter guide the Data Team to drill down into multiple data sources, starting with learning how to conduct the drill-down using state criterion-referenced test data and then applying the drill-down to other data sources. Although Tasks 6–10 apply the drill-down to state criterion-referenced data, a Data Team could just as well start with Task 11 and follow the drill-down procedures with their benchmark common assessments or other local student-learning data sources. The last task in the chapter, Task 12: Identify a Student-Learning Problem and Goal, guides the Data Team to synthesize all that they have learned from the data to identify a focused student-learning problem and an accompanying student-learning goal.

During the tasks in this chapter, the Data Team continues to engage in activities that build the foundation for collaborative inquiry. They learn new tools that enhance their capacity to identify student-learning needs that will inform their implementation of improvement efforts. As a group of school leaders, they work with the Data Coach to share their learning with other faculty, build support for their schoolwide efforts through communication with key stakeholders, and develop their cultural proficiency.

The specific tasks addressed in this component of the Using Data Process and the intended outcomes of each for Data Teams are synthesized in Table 4.1.

GATHER DATA NEEDED FOR TASKS 5–12

Before starting with these tasks, you will gather the data as outlined below. The data preparation steps in each task provide further information on how to organize specific data sets to share with the Data Team; the list below is meant to provide you with some basic information about what you will want to begin gathering now. It is no small task to assemble the data you will engage with in the course of these tasks. You will use multiple measures of student-learning data (state CRT data, district CRT data, and benchmark common assessments) reported at multiple levels (aggregated, disaggregated, strand, item, and student work).

You will notice that Tasks 6–9 focus on an analysis of state criterion-referenced test (CRT) results and not norm-referenced test (NRT) results. The reason for this is that most states are using CRT rather than NRT assessments, and CRT assessments are designed to measure students' achievement of standards. However, if your state does not administer a CRT assessment and you only have access to NRT data, substitute and use the NRT student-learning results.

Below is a checklist of the different data to gather. As mentioned in Chapter 3, enlist the support of district staff who have access to these data. Meet with them, do a data inventory, and see what items in this list are available to you. Then develop a plan for how to gather additional data that are currently not available.

Table 4.1   Identifying a Student-Learning Problem: Tasks and Data Team Outcomes

Identifying a student-learning problem: Tasks	Data Team outcomes: The Data Team . . .
Task 5: Build Data Literacy	• Develops an understanding of data terminology, effective uses of data, and ways of visualizing data
Task 6: Drill Down Into State CRT Data: Aggregate-Level Analysis	• Identifies trends over time in the percentage of students meeting or exceeding the standard in the school, the district, and the state (and similar schools, if available)
Task 7: Drill Down Into State CRT Data: Disaggregate-Level Analysis	• Identifies trends in learning over time for students in specific populations achieving proficiency at a specified grade-level and within a specified content area • Identifies achievement gaps that exist between students of different racial and ethnic groups, genders, economic and educational status, and language • Uses disaggregated data as a catalyst for continuing examination of values about student learning and equity
Task 8: Drill Down Into State CRT Data: Strand-Level Analysis	• Identifies strengths and weaknesses in student learning in relation to specific content strands and learning outcomes
Task 9: Drill Down Into State CRT Data: Item-Level Analysis	• Identifies student performance on individual test items, including the percentage of items answered correctly on multiple-choice, short-answer, and extended-response items; distractor patterns; and the specific content and skills contained in frequently missed items
Task 10: Examine Student Work	• Analyzes state CRT-generated student work (if available) to further clarify and define student-learning needs within the specific content area • Gathers additional student work as a qualitative source of data to refine understanding of student-learning needs as identified through the drill-down
Task 11: Drill Down Into Common Assessments and Other Local Student-Learning Data Sources	• Conducts drill-down, from aggregate to student work levels, on one or more sources of data: common grade-level or course assessments and school or district assessments • Gathers additional student work as a source of data to refine their understanding of student-learning needs as identified through the drill-down • Uses other sources of data to confirm/refute what has been learned through the analysis of CRT data • Refines their understanding of student-learning needs within the content area
Task 12: Identify Student-Learning Problem and Goal	• Uses all data sources to articulate a clear student-learning problem and accompanying learning goal

State CRT Assessment Data (for Tasks 6–10)

You will need three, or more, sequential years of student-learning data from the state criterion-referenced or standards-based assessment in the content area under consideration for relevant grade levels, schools, and/or the district, including the following reports:

- Percentage of students at each proficiency level for the school, district, and state, and for schools similar to yours, if available
- Percentage of students at each proficiency level disaggregated by relevant populations, such as race and ethnicity, gender, economic status, language, and educational status
- Percentage correct or proficiency levels by content strands or key ideas
- Item-level data for multiple-choice, short-answer, and extended-response questions (percentage of answers correct for each item on test or percentage at or above standard for each item—however reported), including percentage of students responding to each incorrect answer and percentage receiving each of the possible scores for short-answer and extended-response items
- The actual test items or test booklets that relate to item-level data (or released sample items)
- Anchor papers and rubrics for performance tasks or short-answer and extended-response items
- Released student work generated from performance tasks or short-answer and extended-response items

Benchmark Common Assessments or Other Local Student-Learning Data (for Task 11)

You will need three, or more, sequential years of school or district criterion-referenced and performance assessments, such as common grade-level or course assessments, or end-of-unit assessments, including the following reports:

- Aggregated data on how all students in the school perform, such as percentage that meet or exceed the standard or percentage scoring at each proficiency level
- Disaggregated data by relevant student populations
- Data on how students performed on specific content within the assessment, such as science process skills or mathematical problem solving and key concepts
- Item-level data for multiple-choice, short-answer, and extended-response questions (percentage of answers correct for each item on test or percentage at or above standard for each item—however reported), including percentage of students responding to each incorrect answer and percentage receiving each of the possible scores for short-answer and extended-response items
- Test items or test booklets that relate to item-level data (or released sample items)
- Anchor papers and rubrics for performance tasks or short-answer and extended-response items
- Released student work generated from performance tasks or short-answer and extended-response items

Student Work (for Task 10)

In addition to gathering student work that has been generated through short-answer or extended-response questions on the state CRT assessment, benchmark common assessments, and other local student-learning data sources, you and the Data Team will gather additional student work during Task 10. Guidelines for gathering local student work that aligns with what has been learned from analysis of the other data sources is provided in that task.

Task 5: Build Data Literacy

Task-at-a-Glance

Purpose	Lay the foundation for data literacy through the introduction of different types and levels of data, data terminology, principles of effective data use, exploration of data misconceptions and misinterpretations, and ways of visualizing data
Data	None
Questions to ask	What are data?
	What is data literacy? What are collaborative inquiry knowledge and skills? Why are they important?
	What are the different types of data?
	What is "drilling down" into student-learning data?
	What are the different types of standardized student-learning data?
	Why does the Using Data Process emphasize CRT data?
	What are the key data terms that Data Team members should know and be able to use?
	What are high-capacity and low-capacity data use?
	What are the principles of effective data use?
	What are some data "safety regulations" to guide the use of data?
	What are some of the best practices for displaying and communicating the data and findings?
Concepts	Data
	High- and low-capacity data use
	Data literacy
	Drill-down
	Formative and summative assessments
	Norm- and criterion-referenced assessments
	Statistics concepts (see Data Glossary on the CD-ROM)
Activities	Activity 5.1: Assess Our Data Literacy
	Activity 5.2: Engage With the Data Pyramid and Drill-Down
	Activity 5.3: Compare High- and Low-Capacity Data Use
	Activity 5:4: Explore Data Principles and Safety Regulations
	Activity 5.5: Mix and Match Data Literacy Tools to Learning Goals
	Activity 5.6: Reassess Our Data Literacy

WHAT IS TASK 5?

In Task 5, the emphasis for the Data Team is on data: defining it, categorizing it, visualizing it, and exploring guidelines for using it effectively. This task also introduces the Data Team to different types of data and relevant terminology that will be used in later tasks. The Using Data Process guides the Data Team to "drill down" into multiple sources of student-learning data in order to identify the student-learning problem (Tasks 6–12). Task 5 introduces the Data Team to that process as well as to the other kinds of data they will use, such as data about people, practices, and perceptions.

Task 5 begins with a self-assessment of team members' data literacy skills. Then the Data Team explores the types of data they will use, for what purposes, and how frequently; the concept of high-capacity data use; and data principles and safety regulations. The next activity is to be customized to the Data Team's own learning goals based on their self-assessment; it is truly data-driven! As Data Coach, you will select tools from the Toolkit that align most closely with what the team (or faculty) wants to learn at this point in the Using Data Process. The data literacy tools are highly interactive, involving games, visuals, and physical-movement activities. Finally, Task 5 closes with a reassessment of the team's progress and a plan for continuing to build their data literacy. Note that the activities and tools in Task 5 can also be introduced later in the process as the need arises.

BACKGROUND INFORMATION FOR DATA COACHES

What Are Data?

One of our colleagues tells of the time he was conducting a Using Data training and, deep into the content of the second day, one of the teachers at the back of the room suddenly raised her hand. Her brow furrowed and jaw tense, she blurted out, "Okay, can someone please define the word data for me?" As the Data Coach leading the Data Team through Task 5, this is a good time not only to respond to this question, but also to go deeper.

Nancy Love, in her book *Using Data/Getting Results: A Practical Guide for School Improvement in Mathematics and Science* (2002), defines data as "the compelling evidence that grounds conclusions in actual results, not in speculation" (p. 27). Most dictionaries and statisticians agree that data (or singular, datum) can be accepted "at face value"; in other words, data are "a given," which is what the root meaning of the word "datum" means. Numbers, words, or images are used to represent data statements.

Frequently, data are confused with information. However, data in themselves have no meaning. Rather, it is engagement by Data Team members in collaborative inquiry that allows data to be "translated" into meaningful information that can then be used to make decisions and improve instruction. As Data Coach, you will want to be vigilant about the difference between data themselves and the meaning we make of them. The Data-Driven Dialogue process is designed to support this.

What Is Data Literacy? What Are Collaborative Inquiry Knowledge and Skills? Why Are They Important?

Data literacy is the ability to use multiple measures and multiple levels of data, make accurate observations, and draw sound inferences (Love, 2004, p. 22). Although data literacy does not require a degree in statistics, it does mean that the Data Team members understand and can apply basic data concepts such as those

Data Literacy Knowledge and Skills

1. Understand what kinds of data are used in collaborative inquiry, why, and how frequently and use each effectively and accurately (see Chapter 5).
2. Understand what different levels of student-learning data (aggregated, disaggregated, strand, item, and student work) are used in the drill-down, what can and cannot be learned from each, and how to use each effectively and accurately (see Chapter 4).
3. Understand the distinction between low- and high-capacity uses and responses to data (see Task 5).
4. Understand principles of effective data use and safety regulations for making data use safe for teachers (see Task 5).
5. Understand the limitations of tests and the importance of reliability, validity, fairness, and multiple measures (see Task 5).
6. Understand basic data analysis and statistics concepts and use them to accurately observe and interpret data (see Data Glossary and Task 5).
7. Make effective use of graphs and charts to display data (see Task 5).
8. Distinguish observation from inference and make sound inferences from data (see Task 2).

Collaborative Inquiry Knowledge and Skills

1. Use demographic data to accurately identify characteristics of students, teachers, and community (see Task 2).
2. Use multiple levels (aggregated, disaggregated, strand, item, and student work) and sources (e.g., CRT, common benchmark assessments, formative assessments) of student learning data to accurately identify students' learning strengths and weaknesses (see Chapter 4).
3. Use data about people, practices, and perceptions (e.g., observation, interview, survey, and enrollment data) to enhance understanding of and verify causes of student-learning problems to inform improvement planning (see Chapter 5).
4. Select and apply high-quality research to inform improvement plans (see Chapter 5).
5. Use a variety of data and planning tools (see Chapters 3–7 and Toolkit on CD-ROM).
6. Use a logic model (see Chapter 6).
7. Frequently monitor implementation and results using both student-learning data and data about perceptions and practices (see Chapters 6 and 7).
8. Use norms of collaboration (see Chapter 3).
9. Act as a champion for ensuring equity (see Chapters 1 and 3–7).
10. Engage in Data-Driven Dialogue (see Chapters 3 and 4).
11. Continually develop knowledge and skills in data literacy, collaborative inquiry, cultural proficiency, content knowledge, pedagogical content knowledge, and generic pedagogical knowledge (see Chapters 3–7).
12. Exhibit habits of mind associated with collaborative inquiry (e.g., willingness to make mistakes and share practice with colleagues, desire for knowledge, skepticism, reliance on data; see Chapter 2).

defined in the Data Glossary (CD-ROM). As Data Coach, you will be assisting them in understanding the questions that they can ask of data as well as the answers that they can and cannot draw from data. Data literacy is important because, in combination with collaborative inquiry knowledge and skills, it is a core competency for high-capacity uses of data and preventive medicine for abuses and misuses of data. Closely related, collaborative inquiry knowledge and skills are the application of data literacy to the process of using data to improve teaching and learning. (See sidebars for data literacy and collaborative inquiry knowledge and skills and Handout H5.1 for a self-assessment based on these lists.)

What Are the Different Types of Data and How Often Are They Analyzed?

The days of using data in schools once a year are over. If continuous improvement is the goal, then there is little point in examining only one source of data, state test results, which often become available only after students have moved on to the next grade and it is too late to do anything about them. Data-literate teachers use a variety of different kinds of data, some on a daily basis, some monthly or quarterly, and some annually, to continuously improve instruction and engage in collaborative inquiry. These include both formative and summative assessments. Formative assessments are assessments for learning and happen while learning is still under way and throughout teaching and learning to diagnose needs, plan next steps, and provide students with feedback. Summative assessments are assessments of learning and happen after learning is supposed to have occurred to determine if it did (Stiggins, Arter, Chappuis, & Chappuis, 2004, p. 31).

Figure 4.1 illustrates the different types of data used in the Using Data Process, including formative, summative, and other kinds of data, and gives a rough estimate of the amount of time spent with each type. (See also the table titled "Navigating Chapters 3–7" in the Introduction for an illustration of which types of data are used at which point in the Using Data Process.)

Figure 4.1   The Data Pyramid: Recommended.

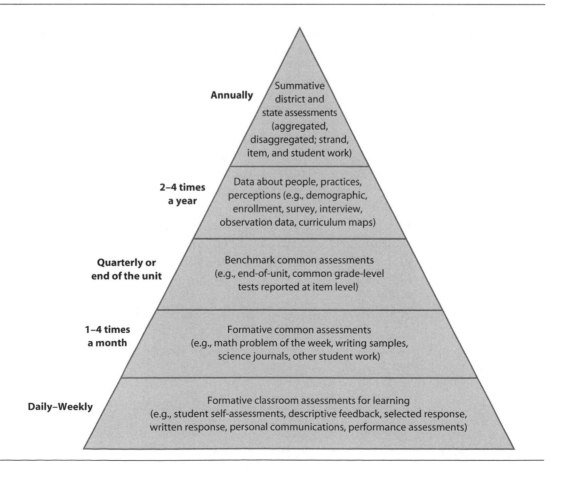

The widest part of the pyramid, at the bottom, illustrates the type of data that we suggest teachers spend the bulk of their time using—formative classroom assessments, done by teachers in their classrooms on an ongoing basis, including student self-assessments, descriptive feedback to students, use of rubrics with students, multiple methods of checking for understanding, and examination of student work as well as tests and quizzes. They inform teachers' instructional decisions—day to day, even minute by minute—and serve as the basis for feedback to students to help them improve their learning. For example, in Canton City, Ohio, the middle school Data Team members use handheld electronic devices, Texas Instruments Navigator and graphing calculators, to quickly assess student understanding of lessons while they are in progress. They then use this information to adjust their teaching, give specific feedback to students, and provide extra help for students who need it. Because of the strong research base indicating that these types of assessments improve student learning, we recommend that individual teachers spend the bulk of their data-analysis time developing, collecting, and analyzing these data (Black, 2003; Black & Wiliam, 1998; Bloom, 1984; Meisels et al., 2003; Rodriguez, 2004; Stiggins, Arter, Chappuis, & Chappuis, 2004).

The next layer of the Data Pyramid represents formative common assessments, which are frequently analyzed by the Data Team—one to four times per month. These include some of the same sources of data as the formative classroom assessments, the difference being that teams of teachers administer these assessments together and analyze them in their Data Teams. For example, the Canton City high school mathematics Data Teams administer problems of the week and meet weekly to examine student work and brainstorm ideas for improving instruction. These formative common assessments are important to the Using Data Process in identifying student-learning problems, generating short cycles of improvement, and frequently monitoring progress toward the overall student-learning goal.

The next layer of the Data Pyramid illustrates benchmark common assessments, administered at the end of a unit or quarterly to assess to what extent students have mastered the concepts and skills in the part of the curriculum recently taught. As described in Task 11, these are administered together by teachers teaching the same content, either at the same grade level or in the same subject or course. The "common" feature makes them an ideal source of data for collaborative inquiry. In fact, they are among the most important sources of student-learning data the team has because they are timely, closely aligned with local curriculum, and available to teachers at the item level (results are reported on each individual item, along with the assessment items themselves, unlike some standardized tests, where released test items are not available). Item analysis provides extremely useful information on students' misconceptions and confusions and on the specific concepts or skills that students need help with.

Benchmark common assessments can be used both formatively, to immediately improve instruction, and summatively, to inform programmatic changes in the future, such as increasing the amount of time a particular concept is taught or changing the sequence in which it is taught. In the Using Data Process, common benchmark assessments are an important part of the identification of the student-learning problem, along with the regular monitoring that is so crucial to continuous improvement. Task 11 describes how to drill down into multiple levels of common assessments, from aggregated, disaggregated, strand, and item-level to student work.

The next layer in the Data Pyramid, data about people, practices, and perceptions, is one that is often overlooked in schools, but it is extremely important. This type of data includes demographic data about student populations, teacher characteristics data, course enrollment data, and dropout rates (see CD-ROM: Data Examples for Task 2). The Data Team analyzes demographic data in Task 2 to understand who the people are who constitute the school community. This slice of data also includes survey, observation, and interview data, which provide critical information about instructional practices, policies, and perceptions of teachers, students, administrators, and parents (see CD-ROM: Data Examples for Task 14). These data become very important in exploring systemic causes of the student-learning problem identified through student-learning data and in monitoring the results of implementation of the action plan. They also help to assure that diverse voices—by role (e.g., student, teacher, parent, administrator), by race/ethnicity, and by economic, language, and educational status—are brought into the work of the Data Team. In the Using Data Process, such data are recommended for use two to four times per year.

The top of the Data Pyramid represents summative assessment data, including state assessments as well as annual district tests. These data are used to determine if student outcomes have been met and for accountability purposes. In the Using Data Process, the Data Team takes full advantage of these data, drilling down into them and analyzing them in as much detail as possible. Along with other student-learning data sources described earlier, they become the basis for identifying a student-learning problem and setting annual improvement targets. They occupy a small part of the pyramid because they are only available annually and provide limited information about what to do to improve performance (especially if item-level data are not available). In addition, these results often arrive too late for teachers who taught a group of students during the year of the test to respond to them. The inverted pyramid, Figure 4.2, illustrates the practice that we recommend schools move away from—spending most of their time and energy on state assessments.

What Is "Drilling Down" Into Student-Learning Data?

Drilling down into student-learning data is the process of looking more and more deeply at one student-learning data source to derive the greatest possible amount of information. The drill-down moves through sequential layers of analysis, from the aggregate level, to the disaggregate level, to the strand level, to the item level, and, ultimately, to analysis of student work. In the Using Data Process, the Data Team drills down into state and district summative assessment data (Tasks 6–10) as well as common benchmark assessments and other sources of student-learning data (Task 11). Figures 4.3 and 4.4 illustrate these levels of the drill-down, which can be conducted on any assessment for which they are available. Table 4.2 describes each of these five levels. For data displays of each of these levels, see the Data Examples for Tasks 6–11 on the CD-ROM. (Note that we use the term *level* to refer to the layers of the drill-down process and the term *types* to refer to the data sources, e.g., district, state, or common assessments, survey data, demographic data.)

Each level of data lends itself to answering specific questions about student learning and can contribute to your understanding of how well students are learning, which students are learning, and what content students are learning in your school. Taken as a whole process, drilling down enables you to move from answering questions about all students (e.g., "Sixth-grade students do not do well in mathematics")

Figure 4.2   The inverted Data Pyramid: Not recommended.

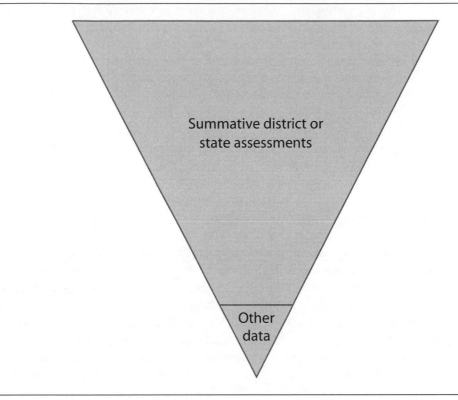

Summative district or state assessments

Other data

Figure 4.3   Drill down into state CRT data and summative district assessments.

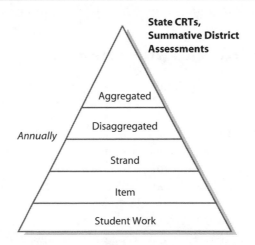

State CRTs, Summative District Assessments

Aggregated

Disaggregated

Annually

Strand

Item

Student Work

to asking questions about specific groups of students (e.g., "Why don't sixth-grade Hispanic students do as well as African American students in mathematics?") and about specific skills and knowledge (e.g., "Why don't sixth-grade students have graphing skills?"). Ideally, you can learn the most from strand, item-level, and student-work data when they are also disaggregated by race/ethnicity, language, economic level, and/or educational status. For more information on each level, see "Background Information for Data Coaches," Tasks 6–10.

Figure 4.4   Drill down into common assessment data.

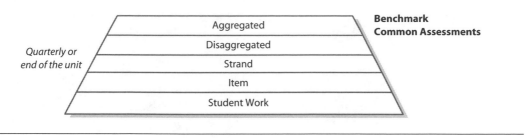

Table 4.2   Drilling Down—Five Levels of Analysis

Level	Definition	Example
Aggregated data	Student-learning data results compiled at the largest level	All sixth-grade students' performance in science
Disaggregated data	Student-learning data results separated into groups of data sets by race/ethnicity, language, economic level, and/or educational status	Sixth-grade African American, White, Latino/a, Native American, and Asian students' performance in science
Strand data	Student-learning data results separated into groups of data sets by areas within the content	All sixth-grade students' performance in physical science, life science, and the nature of science
Item-level data	Student-learning data results reported by students' performance on individual test items	All sixth-grade students' performance on all test items in each strand area in science
Student work	Artifacts that show evidence of student thinking	Written responses from sixth-grade students to a question or prompt focused on a physical science concept

What Are the Different Types of Standardized Student-Learning Data? Why Does the Using Data Process Emphasize CRT Data?

Criterion-referenced tests (CRT) and norm-referenced tests (NRT) are two types of standardized assessments. Standardized assessments are structured test materials that have formalized administration procedures and scoring methods, as well as procedures for interpreting results. This standardization makes it possible to administer, score, and interpret the tests in a controlled and consistent manner and to make comparisons between students in different contexts, such as at a school, within a district, and throughout a state. Standardized tests are used to measure progress, determine levels of performance, and compare performance and/or progress.

Figure 4.5   Criterion-referenced tests.

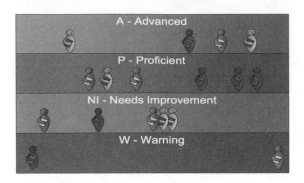

Figure 4.6   Norm-referenced tests.

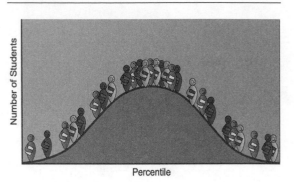

Criterion-referenced tests measure the performance of individuals relative to a set of criteria, standards, or benchmarks (see Figure 4.5). Given the purpose and design of CRTs, all students have the opportunity to succeed and master the criteria. Therefore, CRTs are primarily used to determine student mastery of the criteria. In recent years, the terminology standards-referenced tests (SRTs) has been used to further refine the definition of what type of criteria the test is based upon, in this case, content or performance standards. However, throughout the Using Data Process, the term CRT will be used to describe any test that is designed to measure students' performance relative to a set of criteria, including content and performance standards.

Norm-referenced tests measure the performance of individuals relative to the performance of a "norm" group, which is a representative sample composed of individuals for whom the test is designed, such as tenth-grade students. NRTs are designed to compare individuals to this norm, and a "normal curve," or bell-shaped curve, is used for the comparison (see Figure 4.6). The normal curve conveys data points, or test scores, distributed so that the greatest frequency of scores occur around the mean, or at the highest point of the curve, and gradually decrease in frequency to the left and right of the mean. Given the purpose and design of NRTs, some students will necessarily "fail" when compared to the normal distribution, while others will necessarily "succeed." Therefore, NRTs are primarily used to rank and sort students based on their performance in comparison to other students.

The focus of the Using Data Process is on analyzing student-learning data that is most closely associated with mastery of standards, CRT data. In addition, most schools have state CRT data available to them. However, if you have only NRT data, we recommend that you make use of it. The same drill-down process used in Tasks 6–10 for CRT data can be adapted for NRT data. (For more on CRT and NRT, see the Data Glossary and PowerPoint slides in Task 4.)

What Are the Key Data Terms That Data Team Members Should Know and Be Able to Use?

In Task 5, the Data Coach will ascertain the degree to which Data Team members are familiar with data terminology that is frequently used in the analysis of either criterion-referenced or norm-referenced assessment data. Key terms are included in the Data Glossary, found on the CD-ROM. Activity 5.5 will assist the Data Team in becoming familiar with the terminology that they will use to analyze and communicate about data. Keep in mind that these terms will be further explained and applied in Tasks 6–11.

What Are High-Capacity and Low-Capacity Data Use?

In Task 5, the Data Team will be introduced to the concepts of high-capacity and low-capacity data use. High-capacity uses are those that actually translate into improved instruction, expanded opportunities to learn for diverse learners, and improved outcomes for students. They draw on the four core competencies identified in Chapter 1: data literacy and collaborative inquiry skills; content knowledge, pedagogical content knowledge, and generic pedagogical knowledge; cultural proficiency; and leadership and facilitation skills. Low-capacity use, on the other hand, leads to inappropriate responses to data that can harm children and/or teachers. Table 4.3 contrasts high- and low-capacity use with a variety of examples. Activity 5.3 is based on these concepts, and many of the other activities in Task 5 and throughout this book are focused on assisting Data Teams and key stakeholders to move toward high-capacity data use.

What Are the Principles of Effective Data Use?

Throughout the Using Data Process, Data Teams will use the process of Data-Driven Dialogue (Wellman & Lipton, 2004) to engage teachers in making sense of data. (See Toolkit and "Background Information for Coaches" in Task 2.) This process applies several principles of data use that are fundamental to our approach to collaborative inquiry. They are

• Go visual with the data: Create large, colorful, and simple displays of data to aid understanding (see Toolkit: Go Visual).

• Use data to build understanding and ownership of problems. Engage in dialogue with data so the team owns the problem and embraces the solutions together.

• "Hang out in uncertainty": Take time to learn as much as possible from the data. The first solution might not be the best one.

• Separate observation from inference. Fully explore what is there to be learned before imposing interpretations on the data.

• Pay attention to the process: Carefully structure Data Team meetings to maximize engagement, learning, attention to equity issues, and the integrity and safety of the group.

• Assure that diverse voices are brought into the analysis. Multiple perspectives provide the richest information.

Table 4.3 Comparison of Low- and High-Capacity Data Use

Low-capacity data use	High-capacity data use
Misinterprets and misunderstands data	Accurately interprets data and discerns what they mean
Uses aggregated and disaggregated data only	Regularly uses item-level data and student work
Accepts achievement gaps as inevitable	Responds to achievement gaps with immediate concern and corrective action
Uses single measures to draw conclusions	Uses multiple sources of data before drawing conclusions
Uses only summative measures	Uses formative and summative measures
Blames students and external causes for failure	Looks for causes for failure that are within educators' control
Draws conclusions without verifying hypotheses with data	Uses student work and data about practice and research to verify hypotheses
Fails to monitor implementation and results; big surprises at the end	Regularly monitors implementation and student learning; no surprises
Responds as individual administrators and teachers	Responds in teams and as a system
Prepares for tests by drilling students on test items	Aligns curriculum with standards and assessments; implements research-based improvements in curriculum, instruction, and assessment
Tutors only those students just missing the cutoff for proficiency—"bubble kids"	Differentiates instruction; provides extra help and enrichment for all who need it
Tracks students into classes by perceived ability	Increases the rigor of the curriculum for all students; assigns the best teachers to those who need them most
Chooses strategies based on instinct or the latest educational fad	Chooses strategies that are culturally proficient and research-based and have a logical link to the intended outcome

What Are Some Data "Safety Regulations" to Guide the Use of Data?

Data are like fire. They can be very powerful and helpful, but people can get burned. The following safety regulations can prevent harmful misuses of data. Consider posting these and keeping them attached to your Data Wall.

- Don't use data to punish (administrators, teachers, students, schools).

- Don't use data to blame students or their circumstances.

- Don't jump to conclusions without ample data.

- Don't use data as an excuse for quick fixes. Focus on improving instruction!

What Are Some of the Best Practices for Displaying and Communicating the Data and Findings?

One of the important principles of the Using Data Process is going visual with the data. Data Teams are not always clear about what makes a data display or visual effective. Effective data displays are a combination of science, mathematics, and art. Table 4.4 illustrates some principles to guide you in creating effective data displays. (See also Toolkit: Best Use of Data Charts and Graphs.)

Table 4.4   Effective and Ineffective Data Displays

Effective data display	*Ineffective data display*
Communicates a clear message	Message is not clear; reader cannot determine the message
Accurately represents the data	Misleading measures or scales; inappropriate type of display; pictogram where the graphics are not proportional to the data or scale used is unclear
Can be understood quickly by intended audience	Inappropriately complex, e.g., logarithmic scale in lieu of graph, frequency tables representing complex data, and/or overwhelming numbers
Is interesting	Does not engage intended audience; does not draw their attention
Is simple and to the point	Cluttered with too much data; too many colors and/or layers
Is clearly labeled with title, legend, x- and y-axis categories, values, and measures (e.g., type of assessment)	Poorly labeled or not labeled at all; inappropriate scale; colors are difficult to differentiate; values and measures (e.g., type of assessment) are not clear

What Are the Challenges and Pitfalls Inherent in This Task?

Data Coach Lacks Confidence in His or Her Data Literacy

At this point the Data Coach may be thinking, "What have I gotten myself into?" We do not recommend that the Data Coach take time off to become a statistics teacher, but rather that you pay attention to appropriate uses and interpretations of data and are familiar with basic data concepts. (Note: None of the authors of this book consider themselves experts in statistics!)

The following are some possible ways of filling the statistical knowledge gaps:

- Identify individuals in the district and/or school with statistical and/or data analysis expertise (e.g., middle or high school mathematics teachers or district assessment specialists) and either include one on the Data Team or get a commitment from them to serve as an adviser to you and the Data Team.

- Identify and confer with a statistician outside of the school district (e.g., from a local college or business).

- Take a statistics course.

- Read books and other resources (see "Resources").

- Learn along with the Data Team!

Statistics Can Be Intimidating!

Activities for this task were designed with this challenge in mind—to reduce the threat of statistics by appealing to a variety of learning styles and including games, visuals, and physical movement. Be sure to establish a safe environment, acknowledging that members are at different levels in their understanding of data, and remind them that they do not have to be experts in statistics to use the Using Data Process.

Matching Data-Literacy Activities With Needs

The table on page 140—"Major Activities for Task 5: Data Coach's Planning Matrix"—guides you in matching data-literacy activities with the needs of the Data Team and the staff. Unlike other similar tables in this book, this one contains an extra column with the learning outcomes for each activity. In this task, the Data Team members will assess their own data literacy knowledge and skills and set learning goals. Using these data as well as the results of their PEM: Data (from Task 2), you can tailor the tools you choose to the group's learning goals. Clearly, you do not want to waste time going through material that the team already knows. Also, consider not just the Data Team but the faculty as a whole. All of the activities can be adapted for large groups, and some are exclusively for that purpose.

RESOURCES

Basic Statistics by StatSoft, Inc., available at http://www.statsoft.com/textbook/stbasic.html#Descriptive%20statisticsb

The CAESL Assessment Education Toolkit (Center for Assessment and Evaluation of Student Learning), available at http://www.caesl.org/toolkit/home/index.html

DBDM: Data-Based Decision Making—Resources for Educators by Evantia (formerly AEL) and Council of Chief State School Officers, available at http://www.ael.org/dbdm/overview.cfm

Evaluating Whole-School Reform Efforts: A Guide for District and School Staff by Kim Yap et al., available at http://www.nwrac.org/whole-school/index.html

Exciting Teachers and Improving Student Achievement With Standards-Based Assessment Data by Sandy Sanford, a Digital Workshop available at http://www.paec.org/teacher2teacher/excitingteachers.html

Introductory Statistics: Concepts, Models, and Applications by David W. Stockburger, Emeritus Professor, Missouri State University, available at http://www.psychstat.missouristate.edu/introbook/sbk00.htm

Kalie's Test: A Workshop for Parents on Standardized Testing (for teachers too!), by Michael Griffin, Stanford University, available at http://ldt.stanford.edu/~migri/kalie/report/

National Center for Education Statistics, including not only educational statistics but also Data Tools and a Kids' Site, available at http://nces.ed.gov/index.asp

Seeing Statistics by Gary McClelland, available at http://www.seeingstatistics.com/ (there is no need to register, simply click on ENTER button and click on contents icon). Also available in book form from Duxbury Press.

Statistics Primer (Revised) by Christopher L. Heffner, available at AllPsych ONLINE, http://allpsych.com/stats/index.html

SticiGui©: Statistics Tools for Internet and Classroom Instruction With a Graphical User Interface by Philip B. Start, Department of Statistics, University of California, Berkeley, available at http://www.stat.berkeley.edu/users/stark/SticiGui/index.htm

Turning Data Into Information by John Snodgrass, a Digital Workshop available at http://www.paec.org/teacher2teacher/turningdataintoinformation.html

MAJOR ACTIVITIES FOR TASK 5: DATA COACH'S PLANNING MATRIX

If the goal for the Data Team (or staff) is to . . .	Then use . . .	Time required	CD-ROM materials: Task 5 link	CD-ROM Toolkit: Relevant tools
Assess their own data literacy	Activity 5.1: Assess Our Data Literacy	30 minutes	Handout H5.1: Self-Assessment for Data Teams: Data Literacy and Collaborative Inquiry Knowledge and Skills	
Learn about the variety of types and levels of data and their uses	Activity 5.2: Engage With the Data Pyramid and Drill-Down	45 minutes	Resource R5.1: Data Pyramid Preparation Handout H5.2: Constructing a Data Pyramid Handout H5.3: The Data Pyramid Handout H5.4: What Can We Learn From the Drill-Down? Handout H5.5: Background Reading: What Can We Learn From the Drill-Down?	
Understand the difference between high- and low-capacity data use	Activity 5.3: Compare High- and Low-Capacity Data Use	30 minutes	Handout H5.6: Low-Capacity Versus High-Capacity Data Use	
Understand principles of effective data use and "safety regulations"	Activity 5.4: Explore Data Principles and Safety Regulations	30 minutes	Handout H5.7: Data Principles and Safety Regulations	
Learn one or more of the following, based on the group's learning goals:	Activity 5.5: Mix and Match Data Literacy Tools to Learning Goals			
Learn data concepts using our own version of "Pictionary"		45 minutes		Visualizing Data
Match data sets to appropriate displays		45 minutes		Best Use of Data Charts and Graphs
Learn about two data displays and data terminology through physical movement		30 minutes		Human Scatterplot, Human Bar Graph
Learn data concepts of mean, median, mode, and range by collecting, analyzing, and displaying survey data about the group itself		45 minutes		Consensogram
Reflect on progress made in developing the data literacy knowledge and set goals for the future	Activity 5.6: Reassess Our Data Literacy	20 minutes		

PREPARING FOR THE TASK

- Read "Background Information for Data Coaches"; see the CD-ROM: Task 5 for handouts, resources, and sample goals and agenda; and review "Standard Procedures for Data Team Meetings" (see the introduction to Chapter 3 in this book and on CD-ROM).

- Activities 5.1–5.4 and 5.6 are recommended for Data Teams new to the Using Data Process. Activity 5.5, however, can be customized based on the team and/or faculty learning goals. After the Data Team or other group has done its self-assessment (Activity 5.1), use the results as well as your Program Elements Matrix (PEM): Data results (Task 2) to plan Activity 5.5. As there are several data-literacy tools in the Toolkit, select those most relevant to the team and/or larger groups. (Note that Consensogram requires a minimum of 10; Human Bar Graph and Human Scatterplot, 25.) Read over the descriptions of the tools on the CD-ROM Toolkit, decide which you will use, and plan your meetings accordingly. Alternatively, develop the plan together with the Data Team. If you choose to do so, print and make copies of the descriptions of each of the relevant tools from the CD-ROM and read them together. You will need to plan at least two meetings to cover this task's activities. Note that these tools can also be used later in the Using Data Process, especially in Tasks 6–9, as the need arises.

MATERIALS PREPARATION

- Make one copy for each Data Team member of Handouts H5.1–H5.7.

- Using Resource R5.1, copy and cut out the blank pieces of the Data Pyramid, and prepare two sets of pyramid pieces for each pair on the Data Team.

- Follow the materials preparation guidelines in the Toolkit for any tools you choose for Activity 5.5.

- Bring the Program Elements Matrix (PEM): Data chart the team created in Task 2, and post it on the wall or make copies available to each team member.

DATA PREPARATION

- In Activity 5.3, the Data Team will be examining examples of aggregated, disaggregated, strand, and item-level data as well as student work, which are provided in Handout H5.4. However, if you prefer, provide the Data Team with examples from the types of data they will be examining, such as your own state, district, or common benchmark assessments. It may be better to use similar, but not the actual, data the team will be using so as not to distract them with the content of the data as they learn about the levels of data.

DATA COACH NOTES

 ## Activity 5.1: Assess Our Data Literacy

1. Let the team know that in Task 5 they will be developing their data literacy knowledge and skills. As team members will be at different levels of development, it is especially important that they create a safe environment for everyone's learning. Depending on how you decided to embed practice of your agreed-upon collaborative norms, guide the Data Team through the process you identified. Ask them if there are any in particular they want to focus on or add to assure a positive learning climate.

2. Introduce the purpose of the activity by explaining to the group that they will be exploring what they know as well as what they hope to learn about data literacy (and collaborative inquiry—optional). Let them know that this self-assessment will assist the team in formulating its plan for the activities that they will cover in Task 5 and beyond.

> **Facilitation Note**: Use either Part A or both A and B, depending on time available. Note that Task 5 focuses on data literacy. Collaborative inquiry skills are developed throughout the Using Data Process.

3. Distribute Handout H5.1. Ask each of the team members to individually review the questions and consider what they know and what they want to learn. Ask them to jot their thoughts and comments for each item in the space provided and then to set their three top data literacy and collaborative inquiry learning goals.

4. After everyone has completed the matrix, ask them to share their ratings, comments, and goals as they wish. Identify key themes and patterns.

5. Ask team members to keep their self-assessments for future use.

 ## Activity 5.2: Engage With the Data Pyramid and Drill-Down

1. Explain that the purpose of this activity is to familiarize the Data Team with the different types of data with which they will be engaging while considering when, why, and how often they will use them.

2. Ask the Data Team to divide into pairs. Distribute Handout H5.2 to each member and two sets of Data Pyramid pieces to each pair.

3. Using one set of pyramid pieces, ask each pair to construct a pyramid that represents the relative time and attention currently given to each of the five data sources (state and district annual assessment data; data about people, practices, perceptions; benchmark common assessments; formative common assessments; formative classroom assessments) by writing the name of the data in the most appropriate "layer," with the widest part of the pyramid representing where they spend the greatest amount of their time and the top of the pyramid where they spend the least

time. Then, using the second set of pieces, ask them to reconstruct the pyramid with their ideal distribution of time.

4. After the Data Team has completed their pyramids, distribute Handout H5.3. Ask them to read the handout and compare their construction of the Data Pyramid to the one in the handout. Engage them in a discussion about what their ideal Data Pyramid would look like and what steps they can take to create it.

5. Distribute Handout H5.4. Ask the team to examine examples of data at each of the levels of the drill-down and to induce what can be learned from each. Ask them to work in pairs again to fill in the table "What Can We Learn From the Drill-Down"?

6. Debrief the activity as a whole group, and clear up any confusion. Distribute Handout H5.5, additional background information provided for their reading after exploring the data examples.

 ### Activity 5.3: Compare High- and Low-Capacity Data Use

1. Introduce the purpose of the activity, which is to understand the difference between high- and low-capacity data use so that the Data Team can be more effective in their uses of data.

2. Distribute Handout H5.6, and ask participants to review the examples and talk about them with a partner.

3. Review the Program Elements Matrix (PEM): Data from Task 2. What connections do they see between the criteria in high-performing schools and high-capacity data use?

4. Note that high-capacity data is supported by shifts in professional community, equity, leadership and capacity, collaboration, data use, and instructional improvement explored in the PEM in Task 2. Use the following questions to dialogue about these ideas and how they will affect the work of the team:

- What are some of the differences between high- and low-capacity data use? What additional examples can you think of for both high- and low-capacity data use?
- Which examples on either side of the table are prevalent in our school?
- What can our school and our Data Team do to increase high-capacity data use?

 ### Activity 5.4: Explore Data Principles and Safety Regulations

1. Distribute Handout H5.7. Ask Data Team members to work in pairs. Divide the six principles in the reading evenly among the pairs, assigning each one to three principles. Ask pairs to create a visual or a slogan or jingle to teach their principle(s) to the rest of the group.

2. Facilitate a discussion about how the team will use these principles in their work.

3. Ask the Data Team to read the safety regulations and discuss the following questions:

- Which safety regulations would they like to follow as a team?
- What others can they add to assure a safe environment for Data-Driven Dialogue?
- How will the team "enforce" the safety regulations?

 ## Activity 5.5: Mix and Match Data Literacy Tools to Learning Goals

1. Based on the results of the Data Literacy Self-Assessment and their PEM on Data, select data literacy tools from the CD-ROM Toolkit that match your Data Team's learning goals (see "Major Activities for Task 5"). Alternatively, have the Data Team select tools they are most interested in by reading about the tools in the Toolkit. Work out a schedule for using these tools in the Data Team.

2. Follow directions for materials preparation and procedures in the tools you select.

3. Discuss with the Data Team which activities and tools from Task 5 to use with the entire faculty, and plan together for these sessions.

 ## Activity 5.6: Reassess Our Data Literacy

1. Tell the Data Team that having completed the activities and selected tools in Task 5, it is time to reassess what learning has occurred and what progress has been made. Refer them to Handout H5.1, and ask them to reassess their data literacy, using a different color pen or marker than they did the first time.

2. Ask team members to share their ratings and their progress. Engage them in a discussion around what growth has been made and what areas they wish to strengthen. Be sure to celebrate progress and establish team goals for continuing to develop data literacy. Note that they will continue to have opportunities throughout the remaining tasks to apply and practice the knowledge and skills that they are developing.

Thanks to Jennifer Unger, Group Works, LLC, Grafton, Massachusetts, for contributing to this task.

Task 6: Drill Down Into State CRT Data: Aggregate-Level Analysis

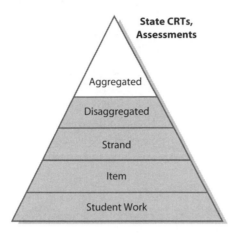

Task-at-a-Glance

Purpose	Engage in Data-Driven Dialogue to analyze state CRT data to identify trends or patterns in the percentage of students at the school, district, and state levels who are at and above proficiency over time
Data	Three or more years of aggregated state CRT data for the school, similar schools (if available), district, and state in the content area and at the grade level under consideration
Questions to ask	How do our students perform in comparison to students at similar schools and at the district and state levels?
	What trends over time in student performance do we observe?
	To what extent are we meeting our students' learning needs through our school program?
Concepts	Aggregated data
	Performance levels
	Cut points
	Test blueprints
	Trend data
	Meaningful differences
Activities	Activity 6.1: Establish Group Roles
	Activity 6.2: Facilitate Data-Driven Dialogue With Aggregated Data
	Activity 6.3: Closure and Reflection

WHAT IS TASK 6?

Drill-down refers to the process of looking deeper and deeper into data. In Task 6, the Data Team begins this process with aggregated data, student performance data reported at the largest, aggregate-group level, such as by grade level and content area for a school, district, or state. This level of analysis is important because it paints a broad-brush picture of student achievement overall and helps the Data Team understand how students in their school perform in comparison to students in similar schools (if available), in the district, and in the state. Aggregated data are the "headlines," but certainly not the "story." These data can call attention to problems in student achievement or be a cause for celebration when sustained and significant improvement is evident over time.

The team uses Data-Driven Dialogue to analyze their aggregate-data results from state criterion-referenced tests. The goal of this work is to determine whether aggregated groups of students (e.g., all fourth-grade students in the school) meet or exceed district or state performance levels and to discern patterns or trends over time in student performance. It also sets the stage for creating a historical perspective on where the school has been over time, which can easily be updated with each year's new state CRT data.

> **Facilitation Note:** While Tasks 6–10 are written for state CRT data, the Data Team can choose to start with Task 11 and do the entire drill-down first on their local assessment data.

The analysis of aggregated data guides the focus for each subsequent analysis of CRT data and serves as the first step in the drill-down process. The products for this task will be the completed Data-Driven Dialogue charts with visual representations of the aggregated data, observations, and inferences, and a synthesis statement that reflects what has been learned from this data set that is documented on the Identifying a Student Learning Problem: Data Findings chart. A sample chart, with the aggregated data findings from your first source of data filled in, is shown in Figure 4.7.

BACKGROUND INFORMATION FOR DATA COACHES

What Will I Want to Know About the State CRT Test and Results?

As a Data Coach, you will want to know as much as possible about the state CRT assessment. Below are some of the important aspects of CRT tests and the way in which the data are reported to further explore for your own state CRT test.

Performance Levels and Cut Points

Many state CRT assessments report student performance using performance levels that communicate mastery of the criteria. For example, there may be several

Figure 4.7   Identifying a student-learning problem with findings from state CRT aggregated data.

Identifying a Student-Learning Problem: Data Findings

Content Area _____ Science _____   Grade Level _____ Sixth grade _____

Levels of Data	Types of Data		
	1: ____ State CRT ____ _____ Years: 2004–2006	2: _____ _____ Years:	3: _____ _____ Years:
Aggregated results	Fifty-two percent of sixth-grade students were proficient in science, a 2 percent decrease from last year.		
Disaggregated results			
Strand results			
Item analysis			
Student work			
Student-learning problem:			

categories, such as "far below proficiency," "just below proficiency," "at proficiency," and "above proficiency" to communicate students' performance. The categories are determined by ranges on a scale in relationship to the cut point, the score at which students' performance falls above or below proficiency level. For example, a scale might span from 0 to 120, with 95 being the cut point for proficiency. Different ranges below 95 would be categorized into "just below proficiency" and "far below proficiency," while ranges above 95 would be categorized into "above proficiency" and "advanced proficiency." "At proficiency" might, in fact, be a selected range of numbers right around 95, and not only exactly at 95. The ranges are determined by the test developers and are based on educationally sound criteria. (See Table 4.5.)

Table 4.5   Cut Scores on a State Assessment Exam

Performance level	Subject area			
	Math	*ELA*	*Reading*	*Science*
Advanced	179–200	178–200	178–200	179–200
Meets standard/proficient	155–178	156–177	155–177	154–178
Needs improvement	133–154	136–155	135–154	136–153
Warning/failing	120–132	120–135	120–134	120–135

Knowing the scale, the ranges, and the cut points that are used to report student-learning data on the state CRT will help the Data Team to understand the results. If possible, knowing the number or percentage of students who score within each range and even within smaller intervals within cut-point ranges can also enhance the Data Team's understanding. Reliance on a cut point can conceal important details. The two distributions in Figures 4.8 and 4.9 have the same percentage above the cut point (represented by the vertical line), but in Distribution #1, there are more students further below the cut point, while in Distribution #2, the students are clustered more closely around the cut point.

Figure 4.8   Distribution #1 of test scores around cut point.

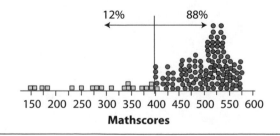

Figure 4.9   Distribution #2 of test scores around cut point.

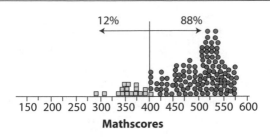

It is also very helpful to know if and how the scales, ranges, and cut points change from year to year. For example, if the cut point is lower in the current year than in the prior year and there is a higher percentage of students who are proficient in the current year, it might be due to the lowering of the cut point rather than to an actual increase in the number or percentage of students who mastered the criteria.

Test Blueprints

Information about how a test is constructed, the outcomes being measured, the number of items measuring each outcome, and additional topics is included in a document often referred to as the test blueprint. Usually, you can consult your state education Web site or contact the department of education to obtain the test blueprint for your state's CRT test. It will be important to have access to this type of information when you engage the Data Team with the student-learning results from the test. For example, all tests measure only a sample of factual or conceptual understandings within a content area, and the Data Team will need to know the specific test questions asked within the different strand areas of the discipline. "Background Information for Data Coaches" for Tasks 8 and 9 and "Data Examples" and "Data Templates" for Tasks 8 and 9 provide more detailed information on what you will want to know and understand about the test blueprints.

What Are Trend Data?

Trend data are exactly what the term implies: data that show a pattern over time. Time is the variable over which one constant is being compared. For example, open the daily newspaper and you are likely to read about crime rates over the last 10 years, unemployment rates over the last 6 years, or census statistics since 1980. Line graphs are generally preferred for displaying data over time (see example in Figure 4.11) because they clearly display how data change from year to year, although bar graphs are also used.

When looking at data to discern trends, it is important to keep in mind that the more years of data that you have, the more reliable are the trends and patterns. In Task 6, you will engage your Data Team in looking at three years of aggregated data. Statistically, three years of data just barely indicates a trend. If you have access to up to five years of state CRT data, you can have more confidence in your inferences of the observed trends.

What Can We Learn From Aggregated Data Over Time?

Aggregated data can provide the big-picture information about the school program. The key question to explore in analysis of aggregated data is "To what extent are we meeting our students' learning needs through our school program?" For example, looking at three years of aggregated data for eighth-grade mathematics can convey information about the extent to which the mathematics program is providing students with the opportunity to master content standards the test measures. Poor and stagnant performance signals that curriculum and instruction are not aligned with standards. It can also alert the team to potential equity issues and raise questions about whether all students are getting access to a rigorous curriculum aligned with standards. It also raises questions about the effectiveness of instructional strategies and materials. On the other hand, steady gains over time suggest that the program is providing students with greater opportunities to master the content the test is assessing.

What Are Some Cautions When Examining Aggregated State CRT Data?

Keep in mind that test scores can vary from year to year for reasons that have nothing to do with student learning or the quality of teaching. One study estimated that more than 70 percent of year-to-year changes in test scores were due to variations in student population and other noneducational factors rather than to changes in learning (Kane & Staiger, 2002). Below we describe some of these noneducational factors.

Sampling Error—Different Students! Different Tests!

Sampling errors relate to the "sample" of students who are tested and/or the sample of test items used to measure student achievement. State CRT tests are comparing one group of students in one year to a different group of students in another year. "The cohort of students in any one year is often very different from those in previous years, and these differences among student cohorts cause scores to fluctuate substantially from one year to the next, even if the effectiveness of the school remains unchanged" (Boudett, City, & Murnane, 2006, p. 35).

Tests change too. As noted earlier, the cut points used to report CRT assessment results can change from year to year. Simply lowering the cut point can result in a greater percentage of students scoring proficient on the test. In addition, the number of test items within content or strand areas, the difficulty of the test, and/or the emphasis of the test can change from year to year. For example, in Year 1 a sixth-grade CRT assessment might contain 15 items related to physical science and 5 items related to life science; students' responses to all 20 items determine their overall science score. In Year 2, those numbers might be reversed and include 15 life science and 5 physical science items. If the school's science program emphasizes physical science more than life science, students might do more poorly in Year 2 than Year 1. But that decrease is more likely a result of changes in the test, not changes in the school program or student learning. In another example, many states in recent years have shifted from factual-recall CRT items to higher-order thinking and problem-solving items, which often results in a drop in the percentage of students who score proficient. It is important when interpreting results to be aware of such changes.

Sample Sizes

Smaller sample sizes—whether of students or of test items—are more sensitive to variations. For example, on a test with 10 items, if a student misses 4 items, the resulting score is 60 percent correct. If another student misses just one more item, that student's score drops by 10 percentage points to 50 percent correct. On the other hand, if there are 100 items, and a student misses 4 items, the score is 96 percent correct. If another student misses one more, that student's score drops to 95 percent correct—a change of only one percentage point. A smaller number of items is much more sensitive to small changes than a larger number.

Similarly, if 10 students take the test and 8 of them score proficient or above, that means 80 percent of the students are proficient. If one more student scores proficient, that percentage jumps to 90 percent. But if 100 students take the test and the number of students scoring proficient increases from 8 to 9, the percentage proficient increases by only one percentage point. These examples point to the importance of knowing not only the percentage of students scoring proficient, but also the number of students in the sample in order to make informed interpretations of the data.

Measurement Error

Measurement error refers to inconsistencies in scores that are a result of differences in the test from year to year (as described earlier), inconsistencies in student testing performance from one day to the next, and inconsistencies in scoring accuracy. Many test developers account for measurement error associated with testing performance and scoring accuracy by reporting scores within a range, or "confidence band." For example, if an individual student scores 124, that score might more accurately be reported to fall within a range from 121 to 127.

Cultural Bias

No test is perfect—far from it. Many items on standardized achievement tests are culturally biased—more easily answered by White middle-class and affluent children. W. James Popham (2001), in his study of five national standardized achievement tests, found as many as 65 percent of language arts items and 45 percent of both science and social studies items linked to socioeconomic status.

Given all of the considerations that are related to the test, how do you know if changes in student performance scores are due to educational reasons or not? One guiding principle is that if the differences are sizeable and persistent over time, the student results are indicative of changes that have educational meaning. Another is to consider what you know about changes in tests, cut points, or student groups and factor that into your analysis of the aggregated data. Finally, you can apply the guidelines for determining "meaningful differences" that are outlined below.

What Are "Meaningful Differences"?

You should see our test scores. The increases aren't huge, but more of our fifth-grade students achieved proficiency in mathematics this year. Last year we had 65 percent of our students proficient, and this year we have 68 percent proficient—that's three percentage points higher!

The authors often hear statements such as this one, which raise the following questions: Is an increase of three percentage points meaningful? Do the data really mean that the school is improving? Could we infer that the changes in the mathematics curriculum, for example, contributed to the increased percentage of students achieving mastery? The answer to these questions relies on the concept of "meaningful differences"—how do we know if differences are meaningful? As described earlier, changes in student performance can be influenced by a variety of factors, and we need to proceed with caution before concluding that changes are due to educational factors.

John Carr has developed a guide for describing meaningful differences (see Table 4.6) that is "a mixture of statistical significance, effect size, and practical significance derived from many years of examining test results in large districts" (Carr & Artman, 2002, p. 254). Note that this table is meant to be a rough gauge rather than a precise measure of meaningful differences. In Task 6 and subsequent tasks, you will use this guide to help the Data Team interpret the significance of changes in state CRT results over time.

Table 4.6   Meaningful Differences Guide

Descriptive difference	*Total number of students being compared*			
	50	*100*	*200*	*500+*
	Percentage point difference			
None	0–12	0–8	0–5	0–3
Small	13–15	9–11	6–7	4–5
Moderate	16–19	12–14	8–10	6–8
Fairly large	20–25	15–17	11–13	9–10
Large	26–29	18–24	14–19	11–15
Very large	30+	25+	20+	16+

SOURCE Carr, J., & Artman, E. M. (2002). *The bottom-up simple approach to school accountability and improvement* (p. 254). Norwood, MA: Christopher-Gordon. Reprinted with permission.

Returning to our previous example, is an increase of three percentage points in test scores likely to be due to more than the random variation to be expected from noneducational factors? The answer is most likely no—three percentage points difference is not a meaningful difference unless the group size is well over 500. And even then, it would be important to look at multiple years to see if a trend is evident.

What More Will I Want to Think About in Terms of Using Data-Driven Dialogue With Aggregated Student-Learning Data?

In the Data Coach Notes for Task 6, we provide you with examples of aggregated data and the steps for using Data-Driven Dialogue to analyze it. We provide sample observations, inferences, and guidance to watch for inferences that blame students or use their backgrounds as an excuse or explanation for their performance. In Task 2, you and the Data Team learned to use Data-Driven Dialogue. You may want to go back and review the information provided in the "Background Information for Data Coaches" for Task 2 or on the CD-ROM (see Toolkit) to refresh your understanding of the process. It will be especially important to help the team separate observations from inferences, so provide the team with a refresher if they need it. Additionally, in this task, two new ideas about Data-Driven Dialogue are introduced: hand-drawing graphs in Phase 2: Go Visual and lining up observations and inferences in Phase 4: Infer/Question.

In Phase 2: Go Visual, we suggest that Data Teams create their own large graphs to represent the student-learning data from the state CRT assessment. (See Figure 4.10 for an example.) Graphing chart paper works especially well. This technique, although time consuming, can be especially effective in building ownership of the data and helping overcome the fear of data that some Data Team members might have. There is just something less intimidating about hand-drawn charts.

In the last phase of Data-Driven Dialogue, Phase 4: Infer/Question, the Data Team generates interpretations of the data, asking questions that the data elicit. It will be important to help the Data Team directly connect their inferences and questions to their observations. Table 4.7 illustrates three examples of inferences tied directly to observations.

The inference phase is a time for the Data Team to consider multiple and diverse perspectives, bringing a culturally proficient lens to the way in which they interpret the data. In the Data Coach Notes for Task 6, specific questions are suggested to help the Data Team do this as well as generate inferences that reflect a systemic perspective.

One of the authors first learned quite by accident about the power of having the Data Team create their own graphs. She usually brought wall-chart-size graphs of the Data Team's data, prepared in advance, usually by her artistic administrative assistant. In preparing for a workshop in St. Albans, Vermont, however, she just didn't have time to make the charts for multiple Data Teams. So she passed out the data in table form and asked the Data Team members to create their own. Soon the teams were creating bar graphs with flowers growing, representing the growth of their students. They were huddled around the charts eagerly and actively engaged with the data. The charts had become their own. From then on, having teams create their own visuals—especially early in the process—became standard procedure for the Using Data Process.

Figure 4.10   Hand-drawn data charts increase ownership and comfort with data.

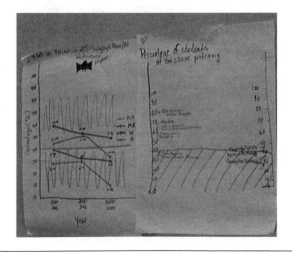

Table 4.7   Observations Linked to Inferences

Observation	Inference/Question
Our school's sixth-grade performance on the state CRT in mathematics increased from 57 percent to 63 percent from Year 1 to Year 2, and decreased to 48 percent in Year 3.	Something happened in Year 3. Maybe the state test changed in some way. Can we get copies of the released tests to understand what was different each year?
Between Years 2 and 3, students in the state, district, and school showed gradual increases (15 percent, 12 percent, and 10 percent, respectively) in mathematics proficiency scores.	Since students in all three contexts showed improvement in their performance, what contributed to this increase? Are students getting used to the test? Or can we infer that our school as well other schools in the district and state are aligning curriculum to the test and standards?
Across all three years, sixth-grade students in our school had proficiency scores in language arts that were consistently higher than all students in the district—on average, 10 percent higher.	Our school has a higher percentage of students on free and reduced lunch than most schools in the district. Yet we are performing better consistently. I think those new programs we implemented—our literacy coach, extra help for kids who needed it, and our inclusion program to meet the needs of our changing student population—are making the difference.

What Are the Challenges and Pitfalls Inherent in This Task?

Moving Too Quickly Into Generating Solutions

One possible pitfall in this task is that the Data Team will want to jump into generating solutions to solve the student-learning problem indicated in the data before first fully engaging in the inference phase or exploring additional data. Your challenge in Phase 4: Infer/Question is to keep the dialogue focused on generating multiple explanations that draw on the Data Team's knowledge of teaching and learning, cultural proficiency, and systemic thinking. It is also a time to encourage questions that will lead the team to collect additional data. For example, they may want to know how students in grade levels either above or below the one they are focused on performed in the same content area to see if there are patterns across the curriculum. These questions keep the inquiry process alive. Solutions come later, after more data analysis.

Blaming Students

Another possible challenge will be helping the Data Team stay away from placing blame on specific students and their families, or on other teachers. Your job as Data Coach is to help the team shift their conversation away from blame and toward taking collective responsibility for improving results.

If your team is stuck in blame, here are some suggestions:

• Use Phase 1: Predict, and then explore the assumptions that underlie the predictions.

• Guide team members to reframe predictions so that they do not imply that demographics alone predict performance. "We have a high percentage of free and reduced lunch students whom our school has not served well" is a way to reframe "We do poorly because of the high percentage of free and reduced lunch students in our school."

• Share research findings about schools that are high poverty, have a high percentage of students of color, and are achieving at high levels (e.g., the Education Trust's Dispelling the Myth Web site, http://www2.edtrust.org/edtrust/dtm/). Engaging in dialogue about these results can generate beneficial questions, such as How did that school achieve those results? What did they do to improve student learning so much in such a short period of time? What can we learn from what they did?

• Go back and revisit core values and commitments agreed to in Task 4.

• Establish a collaborative norm about no blame.

• Revisit the Cultural Proficiency Continuum from Task 3.

Targeting Bubble Students

As mentioned earlier, "bubble students" are those who fall just a few points short of a proficiency-level cut point. When examining aggregated data, Data Teams can get distracted by narrowly focusing on these few individual students. While extra help for these students is not bad, it is not the only implication of aggregated data. Help the team examine the larger issues of alignment of curriculum, effectiveness of instruction, and opportunities to learn for all students.

Getting Discouraged by Poor Performance

Aggregated CRT data can be discouraging. They point out the problem, but not what to do about it; and they are so often used to punish or label schools. Help the team stay focused on their role—improving student learning—and remind them that as they get into deeper analysis of the data, they will gain more useful information about who is and is not learning and what specifically they know and do not know.

Test Quality

Unfortunately, not all state assessments are of high quality. Tests can be poorly constructed, culturally biased, and lacking in rigor; items are often poorly written; content can be inaccurate. Tests originally designed as or with features of norm-referenced tests are being used as criterion-referenced tests even though they are ill-suited for that purpose. The quality of the assessment, of course, has a huge impact on the accuracy and usefulness of the data. Questions about test quality often come up in the Data Team. Until tests are consistently of high quality, this pitfall is hard to avoid. It underscores the importance of using multiple sources of student-learning data and being critical consumers of assessments. Encourage the team to learn as much as they can from the state test and to enhance that learning with analysis of the rich array of formative and summative student-learning data we recommend.

RESOURCES

Boudett, K. P., City, E. A., & Murnane, R. J. (Eds.). (2006). *Data wise: A step-by-step guide to using assessment results to improve teaching and learning.* Cambridge, MA: Harvard Education Press.

Carr, J., & Artman, E. M. (2002). *The bottom-up simple approach to school accountability and improvement.* Norwood, MA: Christopher-Gordon.

Love, N. (2002). *Using data/getting results: A practical guide for school improvement in mathematics and science.* Norwood, MA: Christopher-Gordon. (See pp. 76–82.)

See also the Education Trust, Dispelling the Myth Web site: http://www2.edtrust .org/edtrust/dtm/ and check your state department of education's Web site for relevant information on analyzing and understanding your state test results, specifically at the aggregate level.

MAJOR ACTIVITIES FOR TASK 6

Activity	Time required	CD-ROM materials: Task 6 link	CD-ROM Toolkit: Relevant tools
Activity 6.1: Establish Group Roles	15–20 minutes	Resource R6.1: Group Role Cards	Group Roles
Activity 6.2: Facilitate Data-Driven Dialogue With Aggregated Data	75–90 minutes	PowerPoint Slides S6.1–S6.5 Handout H6.1: Stoplight Highlighting: Our Criteria for Aggregated and Disaggregated Data Resource R6.2: No-Because Sign Data Examples and Data Templates	Data-Driven Dialogue, Data Wall, Stoplight Highlighting
Activity 6.3: Closure and Reflection	15–20 minutes		Group Roles

PREPARING FOR THE TASK

Read "Background Information for Data Coaches"; see the CD-ROM: Task 6 for data examples and templates, handouts, PowerPoint slides, resources, and sample goals and agenda; and review "Standard Procedures for Data Team Meetings" (see the introduction to Chapter 3 in this book and on CD-ROM). Although tool directions are embedded in the Data Coach Notes, you can also reference in-depth descriptions of relevant Toolkit entries on the CD-ROM.

MATERIALS PREPARATION

• Using Resource R6.1, print one copy of the Group Role Cards, and cut along the lines provided. Fold five 8½" × 11" sheets of heavy cardstock paper in half to create table tents (one for each role). Tape one role description to one side of each table tent and write the titles of the roles on the other side.

• Make one copy for each team member of your aggregated data reports using the data template in the Task 6 link on the CD-ROM.

• Prepare to show the PowerPoint slides or make several copies of the slides to distribute to the Data Team.

• Using Figure 4.7 or Slide S6.2 as a guide, make a poster-size chart for Identifying a Student-Learning Problem: Data Findings.

• Make one copy for the Data Team of Handout H6.1.

• Print a copy of Resource R6.2. The No-Because sign will be used throughout Tasks 6–12, so consider laminating it.

DATA PREPARATION

For Task 6, you will use three years of aggregated data from your state criterion-referenced tests (CRTs) reported at the school, district, and state levels for one grade level in one content area. If available, also obtain aggregated data for schools that are similar to yours. Based on the people who are on the Data Team, your selection of a grade level and content area to use may be readily apparent (e.g., the team is a group of eighth-grade social studies teachers, or sixth-grade teachers who want to improve science teaching and learning). But if your Data Team is composed of teachers from several content areas and/or spanning several grade levels, you may want to start this task by looking at numerous sets of aggregated date to discern the grade level and content area most in need of improvement.

To guide your preparation of the data, decide whether to provide each Data Team member with the original test reports or to condense the data into a table. There are advantages to each approach. If your purpose is to enhance team members' individual understanding of the results as reported by your state, you will want to provide the original reports. If your purpose is to expedite the drill-down process, you will want to condense the data into a format that is easy to read and use (see example in Table 4.8). In addition to providing the Data Team with information about the percentage of students who achieved or exceeded proficiency, it is important to your ability to draw useful inferences to also know the number of students.

Illustrative examples of the data for Task 6, sample data displays, and Excel templates for your own data are on the CD-ROM in the Task 6 link.

Table 4.8   Number and Percentage of Students At and Above Proficiency in Sixth-Grade Mathematics on State CRT, Years 1–3 (School, Similar School, District, State)

	Total number of students			Number of students at/above proficiency			Percentage of students at/above proficiency		
	Y1	Y2	Y3	Y1	Y2	Y3	Y1	Y2	Y3
Our school	245	240	283	108	113	94	44	47	33
Similar school	278	271	275	103	133	124	37	49	45
District	942	954	976	340	296	244	36	31	25
State	73,540	74,445	75,572	44,859	45,412	40,053	61	61	53

DATA COACH NOTES

 ### Activity 6.1: Establish Group Roles

1. Convene the Data Team and review the goals and the agenda for this meeting. Include a discussion of the drill-down process and why they will be looking at state CRT data for the next several tasks.

2. Depending on how you decided to embed practice of your agreed-upon collaborative norms, guide the Data Team through the process you identified. Let them know that another way to help them stay focused, enhance their dialogue, and increase their effectiveness as a team is to assign group roles.

3. Ask the Data Team to share experiences they have had working in groups or teams. What roles did people play on the teams?

4. Distribute one Group Role Card to each team member (adapted from Garmston & Wellman, 2002; used with permission). Ask the team to read their Role Cards and then describe the responsibilities of each role.

> **Facilitation Note:** If there are more people on the team than there are roles, consider asking several people to serve in the same group role (e.g., materials manager or recorder).

5. Answer any questions about the roles. Explain that the role of dialogue monitor includes responsibility for implementing two strategies: No-Because and Parking Lot. As they experienced in Task 2, the No-Because sign serves as a prompt to help the Data Team stay focused on Phase 3: Observe and not move into Phase 4: Infer/Question. Parking Lot is a strategy of writing comments or issues on a sheet of chart paper, "parking" them for now and leaving them to be discussed at a later time.

6. Let the Data Team know that they will use the group roles during each Data Team meeting and that they will rotate roles so that each person has an opportunity to practice different facilitation skills.

Activity 6.2: Facilitate Data-Driven Dialogue With Aggregated Data

1. Before distributing the data, review the Data-Driven Dialogue process used in Task 2 with the team members. Showing Slide S6.2 or the chart you created from it, explain that the team is beginning the process of looking at multiple data sources and levels of data to identify a student-learning problem.

2. Explain that the data set the team will be looking at is three years of student proficiency data from the state CRT assessment showing [grade-level] students' proficiency in [content area] for the school, the district, and the state. Ask the Data Team to identify their assumptions and predictions related to the data. Here are some prompts:

    *   What do you predict you will see in the data? Based on what assumptions?
    *   What do you assume about how students will perform?
    *   What trends do you expect to see over time?
    *   How will the state, district, and school compare?
    *   What are you wondering about?

3. Have the recorder document these comments on chart paper. Post the chart on the Data Wall in the section you have allocated for the student-learning data charts.

> **Facilitation Note:** Watch out for predictions that use demographics as the predictor of performance. See "Background Information for Data Coaches" for more about blaming students.

4. Ask all team members to look at the data and help the recorder create a line graph on chart paper to represent the data visually. This critical step will enable the Data Team to easily observe trends or patterns in the data. Post the graph on the Data Wall. Figure 4.11 provides one example.

5. Once the data have been visually represented, introduce Stoplight Highlighting.[1] Similar to a traffic stoplight, green will indicate proficiency data that are positive and meet your expectations, yellow will indicate proficiency data that are in the caution zone, and red will indicate proficiency data that are in the red zone and in need of urgent attention.

> **Facilitation Note:** Stoplight Highlighting works best with line graphs for aggregated data. Bar graphs can be confusing because it will appear that some of the proficient students are in the red or yellow zones.

6. Help the Data Team think about the criteria they will use to indicate each of the three different zones for the aggregate data. Two considerations are the Data

---

[1] SOURCE Adapted from *The Toolbelt: A Collection of Data-Driven Decision-Making Tools for Educators*. Copyright © 2004 Learning Point Associates. All rights reserved. Used with permission.

Figure 4.11 Percentage of students at/above proficiency in sixth-grade mathematics on state CRT, years 1–3 (school, district, state).

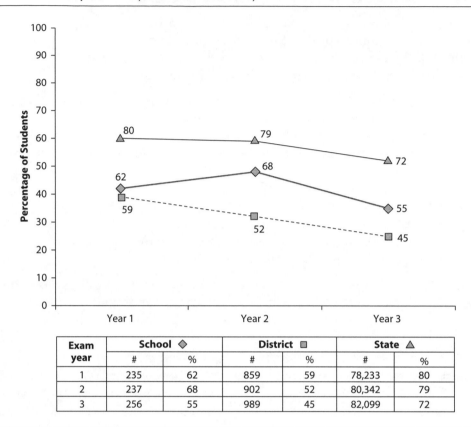

Exam year	School ◇		District ▪		State △	
	#	%	#	%	#	%
1	235	62	859	59	78,233	80
2	237	68	902	52	80,342	79
3	256	55	989	45	82,099	72

Team's vision of a great school from Task 4 and/or any national, state, or local criteria already established for expected percentage of students reaching proficiency or annual improvement. (See Table 4.9 for an example.)

7. Once the Data Team has determined the criteria, distribute one copy of Handout H6.1, and ask the recorder to write the criteria on the handout.

8. Once the criteria are determined, have the Data Team apply them to the line graph, using the colored highlighters to indicate areas in the green, yellow, and red zones. See Figure 4.12 for a black-and-white example; show Slide S6.3 as an example with color.

Table 4.9 Stoplight Highlighting: Our Criteria for Aggregated and Disaggregated Data

Highlight color	Meaning	Our cutoff: Percentage proficient or above
Green	Go! Meets expectations.	80
Yellow	Caution! Below expectations.	60–79
Red	Urgent! In immediate need of improvement.	Below 60

Figure 4.12 Stoplight Highlighting example: Percentage of students at/above proficiency in sixth-grade mathematics on state CRT, years 1–3 (school, district, state).

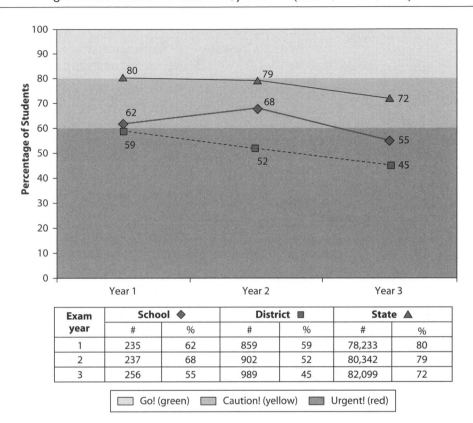

Exam year	School ◆		District ■		State ▲	
	#	%	#	%	#	%
1	235	62	859	59	78,233	80
2	237	68	902	52	80,342	79
3	256	55	989	45	82,099	72

Go! (green)   Caution! (yellow)   Urgent! (red)

9. Engage the Data Team in Phase 3: Observe. Ask the recorder to document the observations on chart paper. Remind the dialogue monitor to use the No-Because sign to help the team stay focused on observations, or to write inferences on the Parking Lot chart. Here are some sample questions to help the Data Team generate observations of the aggregated data:

- What percentage of students meet or exceed the standard?
- How does our school's performance compare to the district? The state? Similar schools?
- Looking across the data, what changes are there in the percentage of students who meet or exceed the standards?
- What are the results of the Stoplight Highlighting criteria?
- What is surprising or unexpected?

Facilitation Note: During the next phase of asking questions and generating possible explanations, be attentive to instances of blaming students, parents, or families. For instance, although an appropriate observation of the school demographic data might be "We had an increase in Hispanic students last year," this same comment is not an appropriate inference or explanation of the aggregated data: "One possible reason that our overall aggregated data decreased is because we had an increase in Hispanic students." One way to reframe that inference might be, "One possible reason that our overall aggregated data decreased is because we are not meeting the needs of our increasing Hispanic population." Throughout the next phase, help Data Team members challenge and then reframe statements that seem to blame other individuals or groups for student performance.

**Sample Observations
of Aggregated Data**

- At the state level, student performance in third-grade language arts declined in Year 3 after being stable for two years: 61 percent proficient in Year 1, 61 percent in Year 2, and 53 percent in Year 3.
- At the district level, students consistently performed below both the school and the state student performance levels in tenth-grade mathematics. For example, in Year 1, students at the district level were 8 percent below the school level and 25 percent below the state level; in Year 2, it was 16 percent and 30 percent; and in Year 3, it was 8 percent and 28 percent.
- At the district level, student performance in sixth-grade science has consistently declined over the three years: 36 percent proficient to 31 percent to 25 percent.
- At the school level, student performance in fifth-grade reading increased from Year 1 to Year 2 (44 percent proficient to 47 percent) and then declined in Year 3 (to 33 percent).

10. Using Slide S6.4, introduce the team to "meaningful differences." Ask them to review their observations using the Meaningful Differences Guide, and then to consider which differences they observe are most likely to be educationally significant and which are more likely to be attributable to noneducational factors.

11. Engage the Data Team in Phase 4: Infer/ Question. Help them connect their inferences directly to their observations. Ask the recorder to document the inferences on chart paper and post them on the Data Wall. Here are some questions to start with:

- What questions are we asking of the data?
- What inferences and explanations can we draw from the data sets?
- What additional data might we explore to verify our explanations?
- What tentative conclusions might we draw?

12. Introduce the concept of Effective Systems, using Slide S6.5 or the handouts you prepared (see also Figure 4.13). Explain that effective systems are based on alignment between the standards, the written curriculum, the curriculum as taught and implemented, and the curriculum as assessed. Ineffective systems have one or more of these components out of alignment. Encourage the Data Team to consider what, if any, of the components in their own system might be out of alignment that could provide insight into their inferences of the aggregated data. Help the Data Team explore additional inferences that may be more systemic or programmatic in nature. Here are some prompting questions:

- Did we teach the content? Did we teach it with enough depth to build conceptual and factual student understanding? Did we teach it using best practices and research-based instructional approaches?
- Does our curriculum emphasize this content? Are our instructional materials aligned with the standards and what is assessed on the state CRT? Is our curriculum focused, rigorous, and coherent, and is it designed to develop the content as students move from grade to grade or course to course?
- Are we using frequent, formative assessments to guide our instruction, provide feedback to students, and inform our teaching?
- Do all students have access to this content? Is that access equitable across classrooms or courses? Do low expectations for some students result in inequitable access? Do cultural biases in our curriculum, instruction, and/or assessment practices contribute to lack of student learning of this content for all students?
- Do we have a system in place to provide extra help for individual students who need it?
- Do we have access to high-quality professional development to help us improve our teaching?
- Are there policies in our school that have an influence on our ability to teach this content effectively?

Figure 4.13 Effective systems.

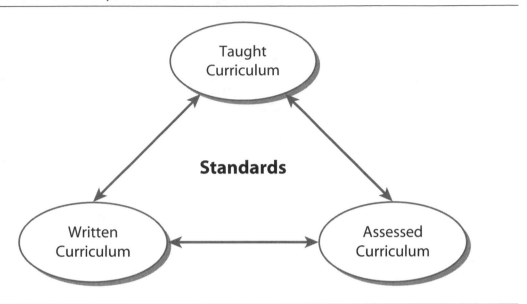

SOURCE Adapted from Fenwick W. English, *Deciding What to Teach and Test: Developing, Aligning, and Auditing the Curriculum, Millennium Edition*, 2000, p. 13. Thousand Oaks, CA: Corwin Press. Used with permission.

Sample Inferences of Aggregated Data Over Three Years

- The school and district improved in elementary mathematics because of the implementation of programs to provide extra help for students who needed it.
- The statewide scores increased because of the emphasis on increasing student achievement due to state testing and accountability in science.
- Our percentage proficient reached a plateau because of a lack of continuous funding for our language arts programs.
- District scores improved in all content areas and grade levels because some schools in the district are on a year-round schedule.
- The school mathematics results improved in tenth grade because the new mathematics program is better aligned with state standards.

13. If the Data Team has not yet surfaced important equity issues, prompt them with questions such as:
   - How might parents and students from diverse cultural groups in our school interpret these data?
   - Where would you place your response to these data on the Cultural Proficiency Continuum?
   - Does the inference blame any individual or group of individuals?
   - Does the inference imply a belief or assumption that we need to further explore or discuss?
   - Are there any inferences anyone on the Data Team cannot live with? Why? How can we reframe the statement and think through the underlying assumptions?

Activity 6.3: Closure and Reflection

Aggregated Data Cautions

- Look at trends over time.
- Consider sample size: Small numbers can lead to wide variation in results.
- Use data to improve programs for all students (not just those a point or two from the cut point).
- Remember that aggregated data are just the "headlines," not the "story."
- Keep dialogue focused on improving the system, not blaming students.
- Be aware that small fluctuations from year to year can be due to noneducational factors.

1. Engage the Data Team in a final discussion to synthesize what they have learned from the analysis of aggregated data. If they were analyzing multiple content areas and/or grade levels, guide them to identify the content area and/or grade level that is most in need of improvement. Ask the Data Team to write a summary of their learning on a sentence strip, and tape it to the appropriate section of the Identifying a Student-Learning Problem: Data Findings chart. Examples of statements that summarize what has been learned from aggregated data include

- Students in our school consistently perform below students at the district and the state levels in sixth-grade mathematics.
- Students in our school consistently perform better than similar schools in the state in eighth-grade science.
- During Year 3, fifth-grade students at the district and state levels showed a decrease in performance in language arts, while students in our school showed an increase.

2. Provide time for reflection and processing of the Data Team's use of group roles and their agreed-upon collaborative norms.

Task 7: Drill Down Into State CRT Data: Disaggregate-Level Analysis

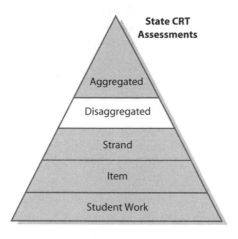

State CRT
Assessments

Aggregated

Disaggregated

Strand

Item

Student Work

Task-at-a-Glance

Purpose	Engage in Data-Driven Dialogue to analyze state CRT data to identify trends or patterns in the percentage of students within different student populations at the school who are at and above proficiency; identify any achievement gaps between students of different races/ethnicities, genders, economic and educational status, and language
Data	Three or more years of state CRT data for the school in the content area and at the grade level under consideration, disaggregated by all relevant student populations
Questions to ask of data	How do different groups of students perform? Are there achievement gaps between different groups of students? To what extent have these achievement gaps changed over time? How can we better serve all of the students in our school? To what extent do these data reflect our core values about student learning?
Concepts	Disaggregated data Achievement gaps
Activities	Activity 7.1: Facilitate Data-Driven Dialogue With Disaggregated Data Activity 7.2: Extend the Equity Conversation: Final Word Dialogue Activity 7.3: Closure and Reflection

WHAT IS TASK 7?

As a result of analyzing the aggregated data in Task 6, you and the Data Team identified a content area at a specific grade level that is most in need of improvement.

You are now ready to further drill down to answer the question, "How do different groups of students perform?"

The task is designed to drill down into the state CRT data to discover who among students in specific populations is achieving proficiency as well as to identify any achievement gaps that exist among students in different populations. This task is important because it reveals the students who may not be served well by the school and opens up dialogue about how to increase opportunities for them to learn and achieve at high levels. Disaggregated data analysis builds on dialogue the Data Team has been engaged in about their assumptions and perceptions of race/ethnicity, class, language, economic and educational status, and gender. An essential component of this task is for the Data Coach to skillfully encourage and facilitate these conversations rather than sweep them under the rug or allow them to explode into destructive conflict.

The initial process for Task 7 is similar to that used for Task 6. The difference is in the data you are using. In Task 6, the Data Team examined aggregated data; in Task 7, the Data Team examines the results by student populations relevant to the school. Although comparisons with the district and state can be useful with disaggregated data, Task 7 focuses on just the school itself and its own particular demographics. Because disaggregated data is all about equity, an added feature in this task is an opportunity for further dialogue about equity issues, values, and beliefs. The products for this task will be the completed Data-Driven Dialogue charts of your predictions, visual representations of the disaggregated data, observations, and inferences and a synthesis statement of what was learned from this data set, which is added to the Identifying a Student-Learning Problem: Data Findings chart. A sample chart, with the aggregated and disaggregated data findings from your first source of data filled in, is shown in Figure 4.14.

BACKGROUND INFORMATION FOR DATA COACHES

What Will I Want to Know About Data That Are Disaggregated?

As was true for Task 6, you will want to know and understand as much as possible about the state test and the way in which the student-learning results are reported. Most of the critical aspects identified in the "Background Information for Data Coaches" in Task 6 are also relevant here, so you may want to review that section.

Disaggregated data are simply data that have been separated into groups based on a criterion, such as student populations, grade level, or content strands. In Task 7, you will focus on state CRT data that are separated into student populations by race/ethnicity, gender, economic and educational status, language, and mobility. (See Chapter 2 for more information on these descriptors.) Because there is so much variation in how different populations are disaggregated from state to state, check your department of education's testing Web site to clarify exactly which students are placed into each group. Keep in mind that your goal during Task 7 is to answer the question "Who is and is not learning the content?" The more information you have available to you about the "who" enhances the Data Team's understanding of how the programs and policies in the schools are meeting students' learning needs.

Figure 4.14 Identifying a student-learning problem with findings from state CRT disaggregated data.

Identifying a Student-Learning Problem: Data Findings

Content Area _____ Science _____ Grade Level _____ Sixth grade _____

Levels of data	Types of data		
	1: ____ State CRT ____ _____ Years: 2004–2006	2: _____ _____ Years:	3: _____ _____ Years:
Aggregated results	Fifty-two percent of sixth-grade students were proficient in science, a 2 percent decrease from last year.		
Disaggregated results	There is a persistent achievement gap between White and Latino/a students in science; this year's gap was 38 percentage points.		
Strand results			
Item analysis			
Student work			
Student-learning problem:			

What Are Achievement Gaps?

Achievement gaps are differences in academic achievement among different groups of students. Despite decades of educational reform, achievement gaps persist: High-income, White, and Asian students continue to outperform students living in poverty and African American, Latino/a, and Native American students on standardized tests and in terms of grades, class rank, and college attendance rates (Johnson, 2002). The importance of examining achievement gaps is to call attention to the inequities of our educational system and to take action to address them.

Contrary to the view that achievement gaps are inevitable because of certain groups' inferiority or deficits, there is evidence that achievement gaps narrow and even close when the following factors are present:

- High goals, high standards, high expectations, and accountability for adults and students (Haycock, Jerald, & Huang, 2001)
- Highly qualified, culturally proficient teachers (Darling-Hammond, Berry, & Thoreson, 2001)
- Rigorous curriculum aligned to content standards (Adelman, 1999; Gamoran & Hannigan, 2000; Singham, 2003)
- Continuous inquiry and monitoring through use of data (Johnson, 1996; Sandham, 2001)

The work the Data Team does in Task 7—acknowledging achievement gaps—is the first step toward taking action to close them. This is not easy work. Some team members may hold the view that the gaps are inevitable. Others might want to avoid talking about them either because they say they view all students as the same or because of shame about a groups' performance (see "What Are the Challenges and Pitfalls Inherent in This Task"). For many Data Team members, achievement gaps have been shocking and upsetting. But the disaggregated data and the dialogue stimulated by them have transformed beliefs and practices that stand as barriers to closing achievement gaps. That is the real purpose for Task 7, and nothing the Data Team does is more important.

During Phase 4: Infer/Question in Task 7, the Data Team has an opportunity to question and explore their assumptions about achievement gaps and how those gaps are perpetuated by specific practices in the school. In Chapter 5, "Verifying Causes," the Data Team will examine research that helps them continue to think about how to close achievement gaps in ways that facilitate all students' learning.

What Are the Challenges and Pitfalls Inherent in This Task?

Blaming Students

In the authors' experience with Data Teams, this is the task most likely to result in dialogue about which students can or cannot learn. It is the time when Data Teams often point to demographic data as the explanation for student-learning problems, rather than using those data to see where changes are needed in the school's practices or policies. As the Data Coach, it is critical to facilitate dialogue, use the group's collaborative norms, and ensure a safe environment for engaging in these emotional dialogues. Keep in mind that "safe" and "comfortable" are not the same, and expect these dialogues to become uncomfortable, but do not allow them to become either emotionally unsafe or threatening.

Several strategies, including Final Word Dialogue and Why? Why? Why? (see Toolkit), are suggested to help you facilitate this task. Additionally, stay alert to those "teachable moments" (see example below).

A "Teachable Moment": How One Data Coach Confronted Negative Stereotyping

In one of the authors' experience, it was a completely unexpected topic that enabled a Data Team to confront an issue of negative stereotyping. The Data Team of 11 teachers included one African American female, one Latino, one White male, and eight White females. For several weeks, the Latino probed and challenged almost every inference of the data sets that was suggested by the mostly White team and consistently provided a different perspective about equity and diversity issues. Often, the White teachers were observed ignoring these probes and, every once in a while, engaged in behaviors that violated the group's norms, such as rolling their eyes when this person started to speak. Facilitation averted outright eruption of emotions, but the perspective of the team was far from culturally proficient.

During one meeting, the White male in the group was describing his perceptions of students in his school from single-mother homes and how those students did not have the "readiness to learn" skills. He described several factors that contributed to these students' low achievement in school: mothers working two jobs, hiring babysitters to raise their children, not overseeing the completion of homework, not reading to their children, not valuing education, and poverty. He had spoken for about two minutes when one of the White females burst into tears and yelled, "I can't believe you are saying this! I am a single parent and you are talking about every negative stereotype of single mothers. I don't do any of those things you are describing. How dare you stereotype single mothers like that!" Three of the other White women chimed in, equally as vehement, that they, too, were single parents.

The Data Coach intervened and asked everyone to pause. After about one minute, she stated, "Those of you who are single mothers just had an emotional, visceral, and very personal reaction to what was being said about single mothers. You were stereotyped in a negative way. You were lumped into a category, labeled, and had negative behaviors and attitudes attributed to you simply because you are single mothers. Now, take one silent moment to think about the comments you have heard from [the Latino] and the issues that he asks us to rethink, restate, reframe, and reconsider." After two minutes of absolute silence, one of the White women stated, simply, "Wow." The dialogue resumed at that point and there had been a distinct shift in the tone, demeanor, and overall culture of the entire Data Team, which was sustained for the rest of the school year. Look for these "teachable moments" in your own work with the Data Team.

RESOURCES

Landsman, J. (2004). Confronting the racism of low expectations. *Educational Leadership, 62*(3), 28–33.

Love, N. (2002). *Using data/getting results: A practical guide for school improvement in mathematics and science.* Norwood, MA: Christopher-Gordon. (See pp. 252–255.)

McIntosh, P. (1990, Winter). White privilege: Unpacking the invisible knapsack. *Independent School Journal, 49,* 31–36.

Singham, M. (2003). The achievement gap: Myths and realities. *Phi Delta Kappan, 84*(8), 586–591.

Sparks, D. (2004). How to have conversations about race: An interview with Beverly Daniel Tatum. *Journal of Staff Development, 25*(4), 48–52.

See also Education Trust, Dispelling the Myth Web site: http://www2.edtrust.org/edtrust/dtm/

MAJOR ACTIVITIES FOR TASK 7

Activity	Time required	CD-ROM materials: Task 7 link	CD-ROM Toolkit: Relevant tools
Activity 7.1: Facilitate Data-Driven Dialogue With Disaggregated Data	60–70 minutes	Data Examples and Data Templates	Group Roles, Seven Norms of Collaboration, Data-Driven Dialogue, Data Wall, Stoplight Highlighting, Why? Why? Why?
Activity 7.2: Extend the Equity Conversation: Final Word Dialogue	45 minutes		Final Word Dialogue
Activity 7.3: Closure and Reflection	30 minutes	Handout H7.1: Cultural Proficiency Continuum Reflection	Group Roles, Seven Norms of Collaboration, Cultural Proficiency Continuum

PREPARING FOR THE TASK

Read "Background Information for Data Coaches"; see the CD-ROM: Task 7 for data examples and templates, handout, and sample goals and agenda; and review "Standard Procedures for Data Team Meetings" (see the introduction to Chapter 3 in this book and on CD-ROM). Although tool directions are embedded in the Data Coach Notes, you can also reference in-depth descriptions of relevant Toolkit entries on the CD-ROM.

MATERIALS PREPARATION

- Make one copy for each Data Team member of the disaggregated data reports (see "Data Preparation").

- Make one copy for each team member of Handout H7.1.

- Select a short reading pertaining to equity and achievement gaps from the Resources list on page 169 or an excerpt from this book (e.g., Assumption 1 in the Introduction, or "Background Information for Data Coaches" in Task 3). Make one copy of the selection for each team member.

DATA PREPARATION

For Task 7 you will use three or more years of disaggregated data from your state criterion-referenced test (CRT) reported at the school for the grade and content area you are examining. The data will need to be disaggregated by student populations and should include both the number and the percentage of students within each population. Illustrative examples of the data for Task 7, sample data displays, and Excel templates for your own data are on the CD-ROM in the Task 7 link.

As in Task 6, decide whether to provide each Data Team member with the original data reports or to condense the data into a table. Table 4.10 provides an example of data disaggregated by race/ethnicity. For your Data Team, you will also want to create tables that disaggregate the data by gender, economic status, educational status, language, and mobility.

Table 4.10   Number and Percentage of Students At and Above Proficiency by Race/Ethnicity in Sixth-Grade Science on State CRT, Years 1–3 (School)

Student populations	Total number of students			Total number tested			Number of students at/above proficient			Percentage of students at/above proficient		
	Y1	Y2	Y3	Y1	Y2	Y3	Y1	Y2	Y3	Y1	Y2	Y3
African American	96	100	93	96	100	93	9	15	12	10	15	13
White	162	175	169	162	175	169	76	79	88	47	45	52
Latino/a	22	29	25	22	29	25	6	9	9	27	30	35
Other	3	2	0	NC	NC	NC	NC	NC	NC	NC	NC	NC

NOTE: NC = not calculated (if fewer than 10 students in the category)

DATA COACH NOTES

Activity 7.1: Facilitate Data-Driven Dialogue With Disaggregated Data

1. Convene the Data Team and ask team members to reflect on their use of the group roles during Task 6. Then rotate the roles and add any additional responsibilities for each role.

2. Depending on how you decided to embed practice of your agreed-upon collaborative norms, guide the Data Team through the process you identified.

> **Facilitation Note:** During Activity 7.3, the Data Team will engage in a process called Final Word Dialogue (see Toolkit). This tool relies on the norm of pausing and is an appropriate choice for facilitating difficult and emotional conversations. It provides time between comments for participants to reflect on their reactions, slow down the process, and stay in the spirit of dialogue.

3. Refer the team to the School of Our Dreams and the Cultural Proficiency Continuum charts on the wall. Ask members in pairs to refresh their memory about the work they did in creating their values related to equity and student learning and in generating examples for each dimension of the Cultural Proficiency Continuum. Invite the team to keep their values and awareness of cultural proficiency in the forefront as they engage in Task 7.

4. Introduce the type of data set that the Data Team will be looking at today: state CRT results in [content area] for [grade level] students disaggregated by [identify the student populations] for the school over the last three years. Ask the Data Team to engage in Phase 1: Predict and identify their expectations, assumptions, and predictions related to the disaggregated data you will examine. A suggested question to prompt predictions is "What performance gaps do we expect to see between different populations of students?" Ask the recorder to document these comments on chart paper.

> **Facilitation Note**: One idea for generating predictions is to provide time for Data Team members to pair up and document their predictions. Then ask for a report-out and record all responses on chart paper.
>
> An important point to make here is that performance gaps are not a "given"; there are many schools that are closing achievement gaps by providing opportunities for underserved students to learn a rigorous curriculum. Data Coaches can guide the team to make predictions at this point by taking into consideration what has been done to date to address achievement gaps. So, for example, if nothing has been done to address achievement gaps, a prediction could be "I predict that we will have an achievement gap between White and Hispanic students because our school has not done anything to address this problem." This is different than predicting achievement gaps solely on the basis of demographic data, which is to be avoided.

Disaggregated Data Cautions

- Don't draw conclusions from one year of data—look at multiple years and trends over time.
- Consider sample size: Small numbers within student populations can lead to wide variations in results.
- Avoid blaming students—look deeper at the systemic causes influencing achievement gaps or low proficiency.

5. Distribute the disaggregated data reports or tables and ask all Data Team members to look at the data and then make a line graph to represent the data. They may need to make several graphs to represent the data for each population of students. The line graphs will enable the Data Team to easily observe comparisons among student populations over time and note changes in any achievement gaps. Figure 4.15 provides an example based on a sample data set.

6. Using the Stoplight Highlighting criteria set for Task 6, have the Data Team apply these criteria to the disaggregated data using the three colored markers (see example in Figure 4.15).

7. Engage the Data Team in Phase 3: Observe the disaggregated data, and ask the recorder to document the observations on chart paper. Remind the dialogue monitor to use the No-Because sign to help the Data Team stay focused on observations, or to write inferences on the Parking Lot chart. Here are some guiding questions to prompt thinking and discussion during this phase:

- What changes over time are there in the percentage of students in different populations who meet or exceed proficiency?

Figure 4.15   Stoplight Highlighting example: Percentage of students at and above proficiency by race/ethnicity in tenth-grade mathematics on state CRT, years 1–3 (school).

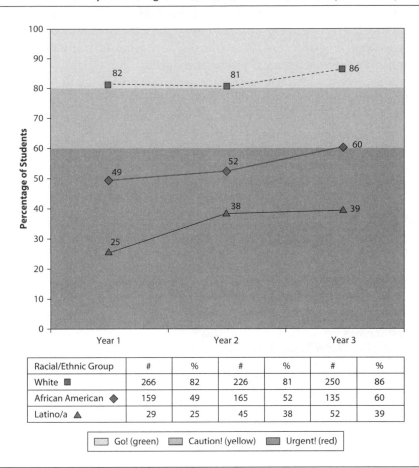

Racial/Ethnic Group	#	%	#	%	#	%
White ■	266	82	226	81	250	86
African American ◆	159	49	165	52	135	60
Latino/a ▲	29	25	45	38	52	39

☐ Go! (green)   ▨ Caution! (yellow)   ▨ Urgent! (red)

Sample Observations of CRT Disaggregated Data

- Latino/a students continue to show a downward trend in their achievement in seventh-grade mathematics; across the three years, test results showed 62 percent proficiency in Year 1, 58 percent proficiency in Year 2, and 51 percent proficiency in Year 3.
- The achievement gap in fourth-grade language arts between male and female students increases by thirteen percentage points over the three years for the school.
- In the most recent year at the school, 44 percent of sixth-grade African American students performed in the lowest performance level in science compared with 36 percent of Hispanic students and 35 percent of White students.
- In Year 1, none (0 percent) of the ninth-grade students with exceptional needs achieved proficiency in mathematics. In Year 3, 49 percent of the students with exceptional needs achieved proficiency.
- Over the three years, students who live in poverty show increased proficiency in mathematics at the third-grade level. Those increases range from 15 percent to 45 percent.

- What performance gaps exist among racial/ ethnic groups in terms of percentage proficient? Between boys and girls? Between English Proficient students and English Language Learners? Between students of different economic status? Between students who move frequently and those who do not? Between students who have been in our school for less than one year and those who have been here more than one year?
- What is the progress in reducing any achievement gaps?

8. Engage the Data Team in Phase 4: Infer/Question. Help the Data Team connect their inferences directly to their observations and to ask questions and generate possible explanations of their observations of the data. Ask the recorder to document these comments on chart paper and post them on the Data Wall. Here are some prompting questions to guide the Data Team's engagement in this phase:

- What questions are we asking of the data?
- What inferences and explanations can we draw from these data sets?
- What tentative conclusions might we draw?
- What additional data might we explore to verify our explanations, inferences, and tentative conclusions?
- Does our curriculum emphasize this content?
- Did we teach this content?
- Do all students have access to high-quality instruction of this content taught by highly qualified teachers?
- Do our beliefs, assumptions, and expectations about what students can learn limit some students from learning the content?

Sample Inferences From Disaggregated Data

- Teachers are not prepared to teach to the different needs of English Language Learners in their classrooms.
- Language on the test is not cross-cultural.
- The teen pregnancy rate in our school increased last year. Could that have an effect on girls' lower test scores last year?
- Teachers are not prepared to meet our changing population's needs.
- Our African American males are not being well served by our school.

Facilitation Note: During the fourth phase of asking questions and generating possible explanations, you need to be particularly attentive to instances of blaming students, parents, or families or attributing failure or success to a certain cultural or ethnic group of students. Listen for comments such as those below and consider the examples of how these comments can be reframed with greater cultural proficiency:

- Our Latino/a students have the lowest percentage of proficiency among all students. Most of those kids live on the east side of town and their parents don't value education. Reframe: What can we learn about our Latino/a students so that we can do a better job serving them? How can we help their parents feel more welcome in our school?
- The African American students create the biggest behavior problems in class, and we're constantly sending them to the principal's office, which means they miss a lot of math class. Reframe: What in our own biases might be influencing our discipline practices with African American boys especially? How can we more effectively engage them in the learning?
- The Asian students have the highest percentage of proficiency among all students, but we all know how hard they work at home and that their parents really push them to do well. Reframe: How can we help all of our kids connect their effort to their success? What is the diversity among our Asian students?

When you encounter comments like these, engage the Data Team in an honest and open discussion to challenge and question these statements. The strategy Why? Why? Why? (adapted from Tucker, 1996; used with permission) is helpful for delving more deeply into root causes or beliefs (see Toolkit and Data Coach Notes, Task 9).

9. Ask Data Team members to identify one inference that appears to blame students or families. Help the Data Team explore their beliefs or assumptions about student learning that underlie this inference. Have them respond to the prompt, "Why?" and have the recorder document their responses on chart paper. Then ask "Why?" again about the preceding response, and record their responses on the chart. Repeat the "Why?" question at least three times, or until the Data Team believe they have surfaced the "root" or underlying belief about the inference. Table 4.11 offers two examples.

CULTURE REVIEW
√ Equity
√ Teaching and Learning
√ Data
√ Collaboration
√ Leadership and Capacity

Table 4.11   Examples of Why? Why? Why?

Inference: Our students do not know how to graph data.

Why? Students have limited opportunities to learn how to graph.

Why? The instructional materials do not include graphing.

Why? The instructional materials are outdated and do not align with the standards.

Inference: Our English Language Learners have the lowest proficiency scores in science because they don't know basic science concepts and processes.

Why? They have a language problem.

Why? They get pulled out of science class for language tutoring.

Why? We hold the assumption that all English Language Learners need remediation and are not ready to learn science.

10. After engaging the Data Team members in this strategy to explore some of their inferences, invite them to rephrase, delete, or amend any that do not reflect their intent.

11. Ask the Data Team to revisit the final list of inferences and to consider them one more time in light of the following questions:

- How might parents and students from diverse cultural populations in our school interpret these data?
- Where on the cultural proficiency continuum is my response to these data?
- Do any inferences continue to blame individuals or groups of individuals?
- Are there any inferences we cannot live with? Why? How can we reframe the statements so that they are more culturally proficient?

Activity 7.2: Extend the Equity Conversation: Final Word Dialogue

1. Explain to the Data Team that they will read an excerpt from this book or an article you have selected and engage in Final Word Dialogue (see Toolkit or Task 3) to surface their beliefs and values about achievement gaps.

2. Distribute a highlighter and a copy of the reading selection to each team member. Ask them to read the article and highlight two or three ideas that are particularly meaningful or provocative for them.

3. Have the team engage in a round-robin dialogue about the reading selection, giving each person a chance to have the first and last word about items he or she highlighted.

4. Once the round-robin dialogue is complete, invite the team to respond to these questions: "What did it feel like to participate in this process? What impact did pausing have on each person's participation? What impact did pausing have on the group?"

⇒ Activity 7.3: Closure and Reflection

1. Engage the Data Team in a final discussion to synthesize what they have learned from the analysis of disaggregated data. Ask them to write a summary of their learning on a sentence strip and tape it to the appropriate section of the Identifying a Student-Learning Problem: Data Findings chart. Examples of statements that summarize what has been learned from the disaggregated data include
  - In our school, we have a consistently increasing achievement gap between sixth-grade students of color and White students in language arts proficiency.
  - The mathematics test scores for 10th-grade Asian students increase each year.
  - The achievement gap between White students and African American students narrows each year for our third-grade students' science proficiency scores, but there is a widening gap between White and Latino/a students.

2. Invite the Data Team to reflect on what they learned in this task and how their observations and inferences relate to the vision and goals they identified earlier.

3. Distribute Handout H7.1. Ask each member to reflect on his or her own and the team's cultural proficiency at the meeting today. Facilitate a dialogue about the commitments they wrote on the handout.

4. Provide time for reflection and processing of the Data Team's use of group roles and their agreed-upon collaborative norms.

Task 8: Drill Down Into State CRT Data: Strand-Level Analysis

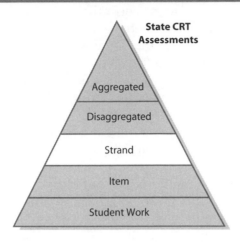

Task-at-a-Glance

Purpose	Engage in Data-Driven Dialogue to analyze state CRT data to identify trends or patterns in the percentage of students in the school who are at and above proficiency (or percentage correct) in each content strand area over a three-year period; determine the relative strengths and weaknesses in student performance in relation to the content standards or learning outcomes
Data	Three or more years of strand data for the school in the content area and at the grade level under consideration, accompanying standards or learning outcomes, and state test information on strands
Questions to ask	What content strands is the test measuring? What standards or learning outcomes are being tested within the content strands? Over time, what are areas of relative strength and weakness in our students' performance on content strands?
Concepts	Strand-level data Vertical plot graph
Activities	Activity 8.1: Facilitate Data-Driven Dialogue With Strand Data Activity 8.2: Closure and Reflection

WHAT IS TASK 8?

As a result of engaging with aggregated and disaggregated data in prior tasks, the Data Team has identified trends in the percentage of students proficient and above in the state CRT and uncovered content areas and grade levels in need of improvement. The Data Team also knows if there are differences in the extent to which different populations of students are achieving proficiency on the state CRT in the content area and grade levels being examined. In Task 8, the Data Team drills down into the third level of analysis: strand-level data. Looking at these data enables the

Data Team to further refine their answers to the question, "What specific content are students learning and not learning well?"

Task 8 involves examining student performance on content strands within a discipline or subject area to determine relative strengths and weaknesses in relation to the standards, or learning outcomes, that are measured by the state CRT assessment. Strand-level data (sometimes referred to as clusters, content or process skills, standards, domains, key ideas, subscales, or learning objectives) are student performance results that have been separated into groups of concepts or skills that fall into a common domain. For example, in mathematics, common strands include algebra; geometry; number sense; patterns, relations, and functions; and data analysis. Many state CRT assessments measure not only student mastery of knowledge and skills within strand areas, but also "cross-cutting" understandings, such as application and problem solving in mathematics or scientific processes and inquiry in science. Knowing which strands are difficult for students enables the Data Team to focus on what students do and do not understand within specific areas within the content.

The products for this task will be the completed Data-Driven Dialogue charts that capture predictions, visual representations of the strand data, observations, and inferences, and a synthesis statement that reflects what has been learned from this data set that is added to the Identifying a Student-Learning Problem: Data Findings chart. A sample chart, with the aggregated, disaggregated, and strand data findings from your first source of data filled in, is shown in Figure 4.16.

BACKGROUND INFORMATION FOR DATA COACHES

What Will I Want to Know and Understand About Strand Data?

The first thing to clarify is how your state's CRT assessment refers to strand-level data. Tests use varying terms—such as strand, cluster, content or process skills, standard, domain, key idea, subscale, or learning objectives—to refer to the specific subcontent areas within a discipline. Throughout this book we consistently use the term *strand*, but you should use the appropriate term from your state's test with your Data Team.

Next, find out what strands are assessed within the discipline and at the grade level that you are investigating. For example, strand areas within science can include life, physical, and Earth science; literacy/language arts can include writing application, language conventions, and vocabulary. In addition to these content-specific strand areas, your state test may also assess cross-cutting themes, processes, or abilities. For example, one state test that the authors are familiar with includes three levels of understanding in K–8 mathematics that cut across all of the other strands: conceptual understanding, knowledge and skills, and application and problem solving. Find out both the cross-cutting themes and content strands for the discipline and grade level that you and your Data Team are focusing on.

Once you have identified the strand areas, obtain the learning outcomes or standards that are included within each strand area. This information can be found in state standards documents and on your state testing Web site. These documents will most likely contain definitions of each standard and/or include

Figure 4.16 Identifying a student-learning problem with findings from strand data.

Identifying a Student-Learning Problem: Data Findings

Content Area _____ Science _____ Grade Level _____ Sixth grade _____

Levels of data	Types of data		
	1:_____State CRT_____ _____ Years: 2004–2006	2:_____ _____ Years:	3:_____ _____ Years:
Aggregated results	Fifty-two percent of sixth-grade students were proficient in science, a 2 percent decrease from last year.		
Disaggregated results	There is a persistent achievement gap between White and Latino/a students in science; this year's gap was 38 percentage points.		
Strand results	For two years, the lowest percentage of students were proficient in the physical science strand; 31 percent last year, 28 percent this year.		
Item analysis			
Student work			
Student-learning problem:			

specific skills, knowledge, and abilities that align with each standard or learning outcome. For example, in sixth-grade mathematics, the strand called "patterns, relations, and functions" might include two learning outcomes: "1). apply the relation between doubling the side of a regular figure and the corresponding increase in area, and 2). determine the rule, identify missing numbers, and/or find the nth term in a sequence of numbers or a table of numbers involving one operation or power" (Ohio Department of Education, 2003). Often these outcomes are assigned a number. This level of accompanying information provides you and your Data Team with a deeper understanding of what the test is assessing within each strand area.

Next, find out how many items appear on the test within each strand and, if possible, what kinds of items are included in each strand, including multiple-choice, short-answer, and extended-response items. Background documentation for the state CRT, sometimes referred to as the "test blueprint," usually contains this type of information. See an example in Table 4.12.

Finally, find out how the strand data are reported. Typically, strand data are reported either by the percentage correct of possible points within each strand or by the percentage of students at each proficiency level.

Once you have compiled all of the test blueprint information, you will want to know how the strand data are scored or calculated. This is a challenging question and one that is often not easily answered. Many test developers score the individual items based on difficulty or complexity, and individual test items can assess more than one standard or learning outcome. For example, the discussion about

Table 4.12 Sixth-Grade Mathematics Strands, Learning Outcomes, and Number of Items on the CRT

Strand	Learning outcome number	Items on test per strand (total items on test = 46)
Patterns, relations, and functions	1, 2	4
Problem-solving strategies	3, 4, 5	5
Numbers and number relations	6, 7, 8, 9, 10	9
Geometry	11, 12	4
Algebra	13, 14, 15	6
Measurement	16, 17, 18	5
Estimation and mental computation	19, 20	4
Data analysis and probability	21, 22, 23, 24	9
Conceptual understanding	Cross-cutting	Approximately 40% of items
Knowledge and skills	Cross-cutting	Approximately 20% of items
Application and problem solving	Cross-cutting	Approximately 40% of items

SOURCE From the Ohio Department of Education. *Guide to Test Interpretation for Ohio Sixth-Grade Proficiency Tests, 2003.* Reprinted with permission of the Ohio Department of Education.

cross-cutting themes or concepts within strand areas (e.g., conceptual understanding or application and problem solving in mathematics) illustrates that any one test item may assess, for example, both algebra and conceptual understanding. In the authors' experience, most test developers are hesitant to release detailed information about the ways in which their test items are weighted, scored, and compiled to obtain overall scores. It is less important for you and your Data Team to know the detailed scoring information than it is for you to understand that items are weighted and scored in various ways.

Some strand data may not make sense at first glance. Here's a concrete example: If 33 percent of students are above proficiency in science, how can 65 percent of the students be above proficiency in life science? Knowing that individual test items are not scored equally (e.g., each test item is not worth 1 point) and that items may assess more than one strand area helps make this seeming discrepancy more understandable. Perhaps the best way to approach strand data is from a "whole-to-parts" perspective: Aggregated and disaggregated data help you understand how students achieve in the overall content area, and strand data help you understand which specific areas within the content are weaker or stronger than others.

Why Do We Continue to Look at Multiple Years of Strand Data and Disaggregate by Student Populations If Possible?

Looking at the strand data over multiple years enables the Data Team to continue to observe patterns and trends and make inferences about the content area program over time and is preferable to one year of data. Also, because tests vary from year to year, you can have greater confidence in your conclusions from multiple years of data. For example, on some state tests, items of the greatest difficulty are placed in a different strand each year. As a result, students may perform poorly in the strand that happens to have the most difficult items in that particular year. When the more difficult items are moved to another strand the next year, that strand shows up as the weakest area. Similarly, if a state test includes more multiple-choice items in one strand and more short-answer or extended-response items in another strand, students' performance may reflect those differences. Although multiple years of strand data can help teams draw sounder conclusions, be careful that state standards have not changed significantly, making year-to-year comparisons impossible. If student populations are large enough, further disaggregating strand data by student populations is very useful for identifying achievement gaps in specific content strands.

What Kinds of Graphs Are Used to Display Strand Data?

In Task 8, as in previous tasks, the Data Team will create graphic representations of students' proficiency in each strand area. For multiple years of strand data, use either bar graphs or vertical plots—a display that illustrates comparisons among strands by placing them in sequential order. (See examples in Figure 4.17 and Table 4.13.)

Figure 4.17 Percentage proficient and above on tenth-grade science strands on state CRT, years 1–3.

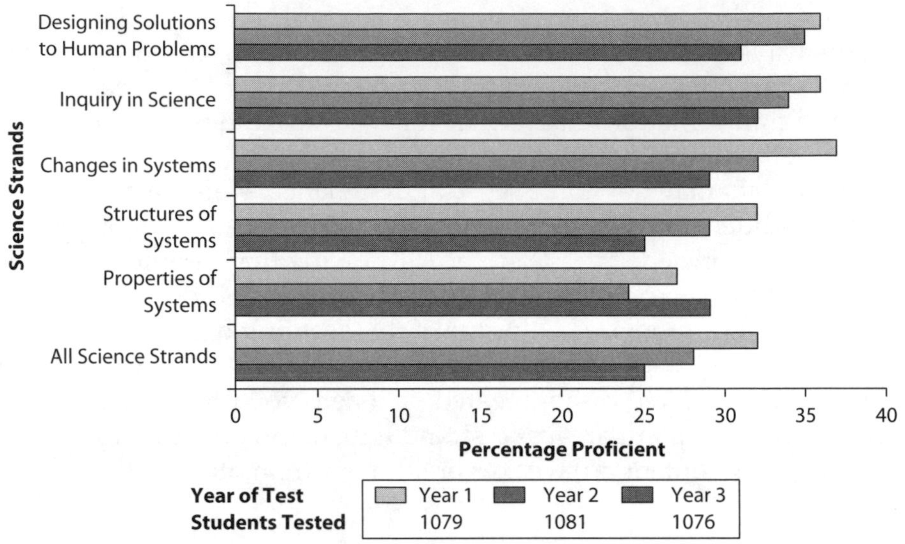

% Proficient			
Designing solutions to human problems	31	35	36
Inquiry in science	32	34	36
Changes in systems	29	32	37
Structures of systems	25	29	32
Properties of systems	29	24	27
All science strands	25	28	32

What Are the Challenges and Pitfalls Inherent in This Task?

Drawing Conclusions

The same factors that point to the importance of using multiple years of strand data make drawing sound conclusions from just one year of strand data challenging. In addition, a small number of items can skew results (see "Background Information for Data Coaches" in Task 6). Strand data are most useful when combined with item and student work analysis and other data sources (Tasks 9, 10, and 11).

Blaming Students and/or Teachers

Similar to Tasks 6 and 7, there is the challenge of helping the Data Team move away from inferences that blame students. For example, if students are placed in science classes based on their ability—they are tracked—one inference drawn from higher student proficiency in life science than in general science might be: "The lower-achieving students are in the general science courses and, therefore,

Table 4.13 Percentage Proficient and Above on Eighth-Grade Mathematics Strands on State CRT, Years 1–3

Percentage	Mathematics strands and levels of understanding		
	Year 1 (n=201)	Year 2 (n=230)	Year 3 (n=191)
100			
95			
90			
85			
80			Geometry 78%
75			
70			
65		Data analysis/probability 66%	
60	Number sense 62%		Data analysis/probability 61%
55	Data analysis/probability 60% Algebra 59%	Number sense 59% Geometry 59% Algebra 58%	Measurement 58% Number sense 54%
50	Geometry 53% Measurement 50%	Measurement 51% Computation 50%	
45	Computation 45%		
40			Algebra 40%
35			Computation 38% Knowledge and skills 35%
30		Knowledge and skills 31%	Conceptual understanding 30%
25	Knowledge and skills 26%	Conceptual understanding 27%	Application/problem solving 27%
20		Application/problem solving 18%	
15	Conceptual understanding 17% Application/problem solving 16%		
10			
5			
0			

obviously have lower test scores." You can help the Data Team reframe such an inference by starting a dialogue that focuses on how well the science program is structured to meet all students' learning needs. You might ask them to reflect on questions such as: "What criteria do we use to place students in each course? Do we place more students of color in the lower-track courses than the higher-track ones? Are our most highly qualified teachers only teaching the higher-track courses? To what extent do all students have equal access to excellent instructional materials?" These, and other, questions keep the focus on the program and not on individual students.

In addition, this task often lends itself to inferences related to individual teachers within the school. For example, if students' performance in algebra is lower than their performance in geometry over three years, there can be a tendency to blame the algebra teachers. As Data Coach, you can help Data Teams reframe their inferences so that the focus stays on what they can do to enhance the program (e.g., the curriculum, the instructional materials, or the overall program's emphasis on one strand or another) and improve their own teaching.

MAJOR ACTIVITIES FOR TASK 8

Activity	Time required	CD-ROM materials: Task 8 link	CD-ROM Toolkit: Relevant tools
Activity 8.1: Facilitate Data-Driven Dialogue With Strand Data	60–70 minutes	Data Examples and Data Templates Handout H8.1: Stoplight Highlighting: Our Criteria for Strand Data	Data-Driven Dialogue, Data Wall, Group Roles, Seven Norms of Collaboration, Stoplight Highlighting, Why? Why? Why?
Activity 8.2: Closure and Reflection	15–20 minutes		Group Roles, Seven Norms of Collaboration

PREPARING FOR THE TASK

Read "Background Information for Data Coaches"; see the CD-ROM: Task 8 for data examples and templates, handout, and sample goals and agenda; and review "Standard Procedures for Data Team Meetings" (see the introduction to Chapter 3 in this book and on CD-ROM). Although tool directions are embedded in the Data Coach Notes, you can also reference in-depth descriptions of relevant Toolkit entries on the CD-ROM.

MATERIALS PREPARATION

• Make one copy for each team member of the strand data reports (see "Data Preparation").

• Make one copy for the Data Team of Handout H8.1.

• Make sure the chart for Tasks 6 and 7, Identifying a Student-Learning Problem: Data Findings, is posted on the wall.

DATA PREPARATION

For this task, gather the reports and test information from the state CRT assessment for the strand areas in the content area and grade level under consideration. Guidelines for gathering each are listed here, and examples of the data for Task 8, sample data displays, and Excel templates for your own data are on the CD-ROM in the Task 8 link.

Learning Objectives

Gather the learning objectives or standards for the content area and grade level under consideration, including definitions of specific skills, abilities, and knowledge for each objective or standard and any cross-cutting themes or concepts. Examples of learning outcomes and cross-cutting themes are provided on the CD-ROM in the Task 8 link.

Strand Areas, Outcomes, and Number of Test Items

Using the template provided on the CD-ROM, compile a table that synthesizes each strand area aligned with the learning objectives or standards and with the number of items on the test for each strand area (see Table 4.12 for an example).

Strand-Level Student-Proficiency or Percentage-Correct Data

Using the templates provided on the CD-ROM, organize the student-proficiency results for the strand-level data for the grade level and content area under consideration for three years, including the percentage of students proficient in each strand area (see Table 4.14) or the percentage correct (see Table 4.15), depending upon how your data are reported. Also gather strand data disaggregated by student populations if it is available (see Table 4.16).

Table 4.14   Percentage At and Above Proficient 10th-Grade Mathematics Strands on State CRT, Years 1–3

Year of test	Year 1	Year 2	Year 3
Number of students tested	521	539	534
Mathematics strand	*% proficient*	*% proficient*	*% proficient*
Number sense	24	41	59
Patterns, relations, functions	37	34	38
Measurement	28	49	59
Geometry	28	63	47
Data Analysis	34	76	90
Algebra	44	89	69
Knowledge/skills	18	53	55
Conceptual understanding	50	56	63
Application/problem solving	8	43	49

Table 4.15   Percentage Correct on Fourth-Grade Language Arts Strands, Years 1–3

Year of test	Year 1	Year 2	Year 3
Number of students tested	87	101	98
Language arts strand	% correct	% correct	% correct
Language	55	58	62
Reading/literature	53	53	60
Topic development	43	46	46
Conventions	68	67	70
Writing	50	55	53

Table 4.16   Percentage At and Above Proficient on Sixth-Grade Writing Application (Open-Ended) Strand, by Race/Ethnicity, Years 1–3

Student population	Number of valid tests			Number of students at/above proficient			Percentage of students at/above proficient		
	Y1	Y2	Y3	Y1	Y2	Y3	Y1	Y2	Y3
African American	121	124	93	69	57	61	57	46	66
Latino/a	18	32	31	9	17	20	50	53	65
Multiracial	16	15	16	10	9	10	56	67	56
White	198	184	177	153	138	142	77	75	80

DATA COACH NOTES

 ### Activity 8.1: Facilitate Data-Driven Dialogue With Strand Data

1. Convene the Data Team and ask team members to reflect on their use of the group roles during Task 7. Then rotate the roles, and add any additional responsibilities for each role.

2. Depending on how you decided to embed practice of your agreed-upon collaborative norms, guide the Data Team through the process you identified.

3. Distribute the strand-level test information (but not the student-proficiency data) to the Data Team: learning outcomes or standards, definitions of strand areas and any cross-cutting themes or levels of understanding, and strand areas aligned with each learning outcome or standard and the number of test items for each. Help the Data Team to look at each set of information in order to understand what strand-level data assesses. Prompt them to investigate these documents using the following questions:

- What are the major content strands? Cross-cutting themes or levels of understanding?
- What are the specific concepts and skills within those strands?
- How many items are in each content strand? Cross-cutting strand?

4. Based on their understanding of what the CRT is assessing within the strand areas, engage the Data Team in Phase 1: Predict. Ask them to identify their expectations, assumptions, and predictions related to the student-proficiency data they will examine. Ask the recorder to document these comments on a sheet of chart paper. Here are some suggested questions to prompt the teams' predictions:

- In which strand areas do you expect to have the lowest percentage of proficient students (or percentage correct)? The highest?
- In which levels of understanding or cross-cutting themes do you expect to have the lowest percentage of proficient students (or percentage correct)? The highest?
- What predictions do you have for how these results may have changed, or not, over the three years?

Sample Predictions of Strand Data

- Teachers have been attending workshops focused on higher-level thinking, which should result in higher scores on the literacy strand of fact/opinion and purpose.
- More students will master the strand of language-in-use writing because the school implemented the criterion-based writing program last year.
- The teachers identified that we need to strengthen teaching strategies for helping students with language conventions, so I predict that students do not do well in that strand.
- The new scope-and-sequence we implemented last year should show us improved scores in all strand areas.

5. Distribute the student-proficiency data and ask the Data Team to make a bar graph (see Figure 4.17) or vertical plot (see Table 4.13) to represent the data.

6. Distribute Handout H8.1. Ask the Data Team to consider their criteria for Stoplight Highlighting, since they may be different for strand data than for aggregated or disaggregated data. For instance, if the strand data are reported based on the percentage of correct items, the Data Team will set different criteria than those for aggregated and disaggregated data. Or the state or district may have their own criteria (e.g., 80 percent correct or more is considered mastery) that the team may choose to use as their guidelines. Once the criteria are established, write them on the handout. See Table 4.17 for an example of criteria filled in.

7. Using their criteria, have the Data Team Stoplight-Highlight their strand data on either a bar graph (see Figure 4.18) or a vertical plot (see Table 4.18).

Table 4.17 Stoplight Highlighting Example for Strand Data

Highlight color	Meaning	Our cutoff: Percentage proficient or above
Green	Go! Meets expectations.	75
Yellow	Caution! Below expectations.	60–74
Red	Urgent! In immediate need of improvement.	Below 60

Figure 4.18   Stoplight Highlighting bar graph example: Percentage proficient and above on eighth-grade mathematics strands on state CRT, year 3.

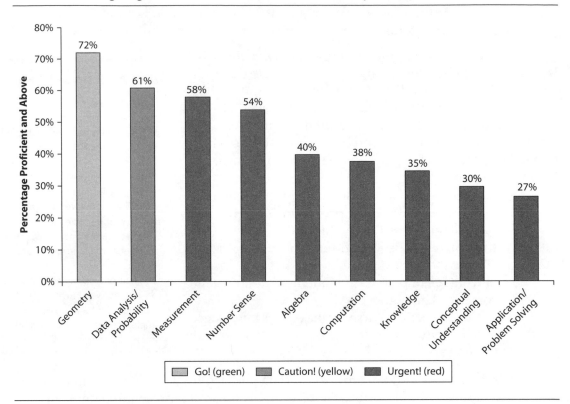

Sample Observations of Strand Data

- From Year 1 to Year 3, student performance in life science increased each year (62 percent to 70 percent to 74 percent), while performance in physical science remained stable (63 percent, 64 percent, and 64 percent).
- Student performance in all levels of understanding in mathematics was lower than any of the content strand areas in each of the three years.
- Our strand in most urgent need is comprehension of informational text.

8. Engage the Data Team in Phase 3: Observe of the strand data, and ask the recorder to document the observations on chart paper. Remind the dialogue monitor to use the No-Because sign to help the Data Team stay focused on observations, or to write inferences on the Parking Lot chart. A suggested prompt for engaging in this phase is: What are the areas of relative strength and weakness in our student performance on content strands? How does this change over the three years?

9. Engage the Data Team in Phase 4: Infer/Question. Help the Data Team ask questions and generate possible explanations of the strand data. Ask the recorder to document these comments on chart paper and post them on the Data Wall. Here are some prompting questions to guide the Data Team's engagement in this phase:

- What do students understand in this content area? What do students not understand?
- What about our curriculum, instructional materials, or teaching strategies might contribute to student understanding or lack of understanding in this content area?
- What policies, such as ability grouping or tracking, could be contributing to students' poor performance?

Table 4.18   Stoplight Highlighting Vertical Plot Example: Percentage Proficient on Eighth-Grade Mathematics Strands on State CRT, Year 3

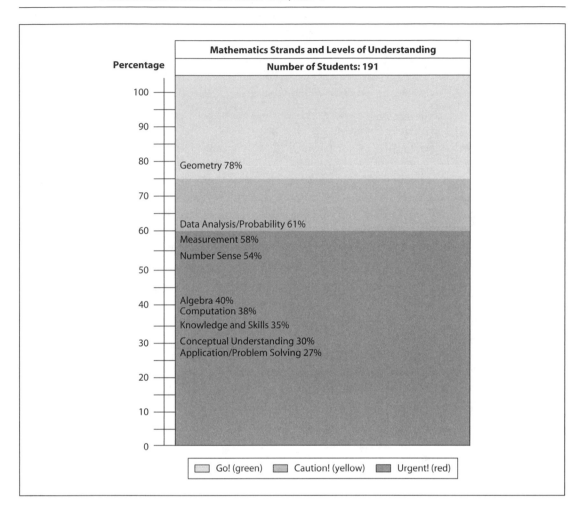

Mathematics Strands and Levels of Understanding

Number of Students: 191

Percentage

- Geometry 78%
- Data Analysis/Probability 61%
- Measurement 58%
- Number Sense 54%
- Algebra 40%
- Computation 38%
- Knowledge and Skills 35%
- Conceptual Understanding 30%
- Application/Problem Solving 27%

Go! (green)   Caution! (yellow)   Urgent! (red)

- What might we infer about the test itself given the number of items in each strand area?
- What questions about student learning has strand-level analysis prompted us to wonder about? What additional data or information do we need to answer those questions?

10. Help the Data Team explore the beliefs or assumptions about student learning that underlie their inferences. Facilitate a discussion of the following questions:

- Do all students have access to high-quality content and instructional materials? Effective instructional and assessment strategies? Teachers who are certified?
- Do our beliefs and assumptions about student learning result in instructional, program, or policy decisions that prohibit some students from learning?

Sample Inferences of Strand Data

- Our science curriculum emphasizes life science more than physical science.
- Our mathematics teaching is more procedural than conceptual. That's why we have such low student performance on the levels of understanding.
- Three years ago, we implemented a reading comprehension program, and we're seeing results in the reading comprehension strand—student scores in this area have gradually increased each year.
- Student performance in algebra and geometry reversed the trend of improvement in Year 3. We wonder if that is an indication of something specific to the test rather than to our students' learning.

- How might parents and students from diverse cultural populations in our school interpret these data?
- Where on the cultural proficiency continuum is my response to these data?
- Are there any inferences we cannot live with? Why? How can we reframe the statements and rephrase them so that they are more culturally proficient?

> **Facilitation Note:** As noted earlier, during the inference phase be attentive to comments that suggest an assumption that the student performance is based solely on students' background and/or perceived ability, or that blame others (e.g., parents). When you encounter inferences that blame or reflect low expectations of some students, prompt the Data Team to consider issues related to curriculum, instructional materials, assessment, schoolwide policies or practices in placing students, and instructional practices. This is another appropriate place to engage your Data Team in the Why? Why? Why? strategy (see Toolkit) to explore the beliefs and values underlying some of their comments.

Strand Data Cautions

 Activity 8.2: Closure and Reflection

- Look at trends over time.
- Remember that a small number of items within a strand can skew results. Small numbers are sensitive to greater variation.
- Combine strand analysis with item and student-work analysis to gain greatest insights.
- Know what outcomes are included within a particular strand on the particular test you are using, as strand definitions vary from test to test.
- Keep inferences focused on curriculum and instruction and away from blaming students and teachers.

1. Engage the Data Team in a final discussion to synthesize what they have learned from the analysis of strand data. Ask them to write a summary statement of their learning on a sentence strip and tape it to the appropriate section of the Identifying a Student Learning Problem: Data Findings chart. Examples of statements that summarize what has been learned from the strand data include:

- Number sense and problem-solving strategies are two areas within sixth-grade mathematics in our school that are most in need of improvement.
- Ninth-grade students consistently perform poorly in all levels of understanding in science.
- Twelfth-grade students show improvement each year in comprehension in language arts.

2. Provide time for reflection and processing of the Data Team's use of group roles and their agreed-upon collaborative norms.

Task 9: Drill Down Into State CRT Data: Item-Level Analysis

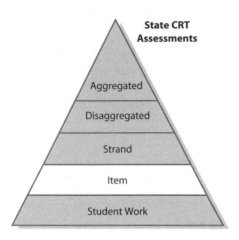

State CRT Assessments

- Aggregated
- Disaggregated
- Strand
- Item
- Student Work

Task-at-a-Glance

Purpose	Engage in Data-Driven Dialogue to analyze state CRT data to identify student performance on individual test items, including the percentage of items answered correctly, distractor patterns, rubric scores on open-response items, and the specific content and skills contained in frequently missed items
Data	Most recent year of item-level data for the content area and grade level under consideration; released test items; learning outcomes or standards; and state test information on items, including rubrics and scoring guides
Questions to ask	What kinds of items are on the test? In what content strands? At what level of difficulty?
	What knowledge, skills, and concepts are required for students to be successful with a particular item?
	What specific skills and understandings are our students' strengths? Which pose difficulties for them?
	For which items are students frequently giving the same incorrect answer?
	On what types of questions, such as short answer, extended response, or multiple choice, do our students perform well? Which pose difficulty?
	Why are our students doing well or missing points on their open-response questions?

(Continued)

Task-at-a-Glance (Continued)

Concepts	Item-level analysis—four approaches: • Multiple choice: Percentage correct • Multiple choice: Distractor patterns • Open response: Percentage at each possible score • Task deconstruction
Activities	Activity 9.1: Facilitate Data-Driven Dialogue With Multiple-Choice Item Data: Percentage Correct and Distractor Patterns Activity 9.2: Facilitate Data-Driven Dialogue With Open-Response Item Data Activity 9.3: Engage in Task Deconstruction Activity 9.4: Closure and Reflection

WHAT IS TASK 9?

Through engagement with Tasks 6–8, the Data Team has answered "Who is and is not learning at high levels?" and continued to learn more about "What are students learning and not learning?" Task 9 helps the Data Team continue the drill-down to examine student performance on individual test items, adding further information to their understanding of what students are and are not learning.

In this task, the Data Team investigates item-level data through four approaches:

1. Looking at the percentage of items answered correctly for multiple-choice items

2. Analyzing multiple-choice items to identify distractor patterns—patterns in students' choice of incorrect responses

3. Analyzing open-response items to determine the percentage scoring at each possible rubric score

4. Investigating individual test items to discern the knowledge, skills, and concepts that are being assessed through the process of task deconstruction

Most Data Teams find that item-level data is one of the most valuable data sets for understanding student-learning needs. The process enables the Data Team to further drill down into the state CRT to identify students' specific strengths and weaknesses within content areas and strands, especially since they narrow their focus and only look at item-level data from the most recent year of the state CRT assessment. The products for this task will be the completed Data-Driven Dialogue charts of predictions and visual representations of the data, observations, and inferences, as well as a synthesis statement that reflects what has been learned from this data set that is added to the Identifying a Student-Learning Problem: Data Findings chart. A sample chart, with the aggregated, disaggregated, strand, and item-level data findings from your first source of data filled in, is shown in Figure 4.19.

Figure 4.19 Identifying a student-learning problem with findings from item-level data.

Identifying a Student-Learning Problem: Data Findings

Content Area _____ Science _____   Grade Level _____ Sixth grade _____

	Types of data		
	1: ___ State CRT ___ _____ Years: 2004–2006	2: _____ _____ Years:	3: _____ _____ Years:
Levels of data			
Aggregated results	Fifty-two percent of sixth-grade students were proficient in science, a 2 percent decrease from last year.		
Disaggregated results	There is a persistent achievement gap between White and Latino/a students in science; this year's gap was 38 percentage points.		
Strand results	For two years, the lowest percentage of students were proficient in the physical science strand; 31 percent last year, 28 percent this year.		
Item analysis	Of the eight physical science multiple-choice items, students performed worst on the three items pertaining to floating and sinking, with 23–30 percent proficient.		
Student work			
Student-learning problem:			

BACKGROUND INFORMATION FOR DATA COACHES

What Will I Want to Know and Understand About Item-Level Data?

After engaging in Task 8, you and the Data Team already have much of the information that you need to analyze item-level data. For example, you have investigated the learning objectives or standards being assessed in the content area, the definitions of the strands and cross-cutting themes, and how many items on the test are designed to assess each strand and cross-cutting theme. You will revisit those documents during this task.

In addition to the information you have, you will gather and compile student performance data on each test item for the most recent year of the state CRT assessment results. Table 4.19 provides an example of what these data look like.

What information is included in this table? First, the column labeled "Test part" indicates the content area; in this case, "M" indicates that the data are from the mathematics portion of the test. "NU" in the "Strand" column indicates that all of the items in the table are ones that align with the content strand "Numbers and Number Relations." In the "Outcome #" column, each number aligns with one of the learning objectives in mathematics. Looking at the outcome numbers, you can see that two test items are designed to assess understanding of outcome number 10: items number 1 and number 7, both of which appear in the "Item #" column. The next

Table 4.19   Item Analysis

Test part	Strand	Outcome #	Item #	Correct answer	A — 0	B — 1	C — 2	D — 3	4	Blank	Bldg %	Dist %	State %	N = Bldg
M	NU	10	1	C	15	23	49	12	0	0	49	48	62	282
M	NU	10	7	S	47	32	12	0	0	10	12	9	20	282
M	NU	06	16	D	4	7	4	85	0	0	85	81	87	282
M	NU	07	19	S	47	15	28	0	0	9	28	23	45	282
M	NU	08	20	D	6	27	11	56	0	0	56	59	73	282
M	NU	06	22	B	16	38	26	20	0	1	38	37	53	282
M	NU	09	35	D	50	0	33	17	0	0	17	25	40	282
M	NU	08	41	D	9	12	39	37	0	3	37	27	44	282
M	NU	06	45	B	33	50	8	4	0	6	50	48	58	282
M	NU	09	39	E	6	60	20	3	3	9	6	7	17	282

NOTE: S = short answer (2 possible points), proficient = 2; E = extended response (4 possible points), proficient = 3 or 4.

SOURCE Adapted from the Ohio Department of Education, data reporting table for student item-level test data, 2003. Used with permission of the Ohio Department of Education.

column, "Correct answer," indicates the correct answer for multiple-choice, short-answer, and extended-response items. Those items designated "A," "B," "C," or "D" indicate multiple-choice items; those with an "S" refer to short-answer items, which are scored using a two-point rubric; those designated "E" refer to extended-response items, which are scored using a four-point rubric.

Short-answer items: Test questions that require students to either complete a statement (fill in the blank) or answer a direct question using a single word or brief phrase.

Extended-response items: Open-ended questions that require students to provide written answers varying in length from a short paragraph to a detailed multipage composition.

The next five columns provide information on the percentage of students responding to each answer option on a multiple-choice item (A, B, C, or D) or receiving each possible rubric score on short-answer items (0, 1, or 2) or receiving each possible rubric score on extended-responses items (0, 1, 2, 3, or 4). Look at item number 20: What is the correct answer? What percentage of students responded correctly to that item? What percentage of students responded to the answer option A? What percentage of students left that item blank? The answer to that last question is in the column labeled "Blank."

The next three columns indicate the percentage of students in the school, at the district level, and in the state who answered each multiple-choice test item correctly or the percentage of students who received a rubric score of 2 on the short-answer items or a 3 or 4 on the extended-response items, which are considered proficient on this particular test. The final column in the table, "N = Bldg," provides information on the number of students who were tested in the school. Look at item number 20 again: How does student performance at the school compare to performance at the district level? At the state level? How many students in the school were tested?

By examining the data, you can learn how students performed on each test item, how they responded to each answer option for each test item, how they performed on open-response items, and how students' performance at the school compares to students at the district and state level.

The data as organized in Table 4.19 may not look identical to the data from your own state CRT, but these are the sets of information you will want to compile in order to engage the Data Team in item-level analysis. You will want to learn how the item-level data are reported for multiple-choice, short-answer, and extended-response items. Test items that ask students to provide a written response are often referred to as short-answer, extended-response, open-response, or applied writing items or tasks. Find out and use the terms that are used in your state test to refer to these items. In addition, you will need to gather the scoring rubric for short-answer and extended-response items as well as any anchor papers (student work samples used as benchmarks for criteria from the rubric and representing a range of possible points). If your state releases any of the test items, gather those to help the Data Team engage in the task deconstruction portion of this task. You may only have access to released short-answer or extended-response items and not multiple-choice items; either type of test item will be useful for analysis.

What Are the Four Approaches the Data Team Will Use to Analyze Item-Level Data?

As you and your Data Team engage in item-level analysis, you will use four distinct approaches to looking at the student-learning data, each providing valuable insight into student understanding of the content.

1. Percentage Correct: Looking at Item Data for the Percentage of Students Who Responded Correctly

In this approach, the Data Team looks at how students performed on all test items within strand areas to identify students' strengths and weaknesses. For example, Data Teams look at a table similar to Table 4.20, which shows only the correct answer for each multiple-choice item and the percentage of students at the school, district, and state level who responded correctly. Note that the short-answer and extended-response items have been removed, as they will be analyzed in a later activity.

2. Distractor Patterns: Looking at Multiple-Choice Items to Determine Which Incorrect Answers a High Percentage of Students Are Choosing

The term distractor refers to any multiple-choice answer option that is not the correct answer. For example, look at item number 35 in Table 4.21. The correct answer is D, which means that answer options A, B, and C are all distractors. Patterns emerge when students consistently provide the same incorrect answer. For example, the correct answer to item 35 is D, but, as shown in the same table, 50 percent of the students selected answer option A. That test item reflects a pattern among student answers: Half of the students provided the same wrong answer. An inference of the data is that there is some content or concept within the test item and/or the answer options that consistently "distracts" students and leads them to provide the incorrect answer. The Data Team will analyze those test items (if available) to further understand students' misconceptions of the content.

Table 4.20   Item Analysis: Multiple Choice Percentage Correct

Test part	Strand	Outcome #	Item #	Correct answer	Bldg %	Dist %	State %	N = Bldg
M	NU	10	1	C	49	48	62	282
M	NU	6	16	D	85	81	87	282
M	NU	8	20	D	56	59	73	282
M	NU	6	22	B	38	37	53	282
M	NU	9	35	D	17	25	40	282
M	NU	8	41	D	37	27	44	282
M	NU	6	45	B	50	48	58	282

SOURCE Adapted from the Ohio Department of Education, data reporting table for student item-level test data, 2003. Used with permission of the Ohio Department of Education.

Table 4.21 Item Analysis: Multiple Choice Percentage Correct and Percentage Choosing Each Distractor

Test part	Strand	Outcome #	Item #	Correct answer	A	B	C	D	Blank	Bldg %	Dist %	State %	N = Bldg
M	NU	10	1	C	15	23	49	12	0	49	48	62	282
M	NU	06	16	D	4	7	4	85	0	85	81	87	282
M	NU	08	20	D	6	27	11	56	0	56	59	73	282
M	NU	06	22	B	16	38	26	20	1	38	37	53	282
M	NU	09	35	D	50	0	33	17	0	17	25	40	282
M	NU	08	41	D	9	12	39	37	3	37	27	44	282
M	NU	06	45	B	33	50	8	4	6	50	48	58	282

SOURCE Adapted from the Ohio Department of Education, data reporting table for student item-level test data, 2003. Used with permission of the Ohio Department of Education.

3. Open-Response Items Analysis: Analyzing Percentage Proficient or Passing for Short-Answer and Extended-Response Items

This analysis examines the results for short-answer and extended-response items on the test. Table 4.22 illustrates the percentage of students receiving each of the possible points on the rubric for both short-answer and extended-response items. It also compares the percentage of students receiving a passing or proficient score at their school to the district and the state.

4. Task Deconstruction: Looking at Multiple-Choice, Short-Answer, and Extended-Response Test Items to Identify the Knowledge, Skills, and Concepts That Students Should Know and Understand in Order to Respond Correctly to a Test Item

By "deconstructing" a test item into the knowledge, skills, and big ideas or concepts that students need to know in order to correctly answer it, the Data Team is

Table 4.22 Item Analysis: Percentage Scoring Each of the Possible Points on Open-Response Items

Test part	Strand	Outcome #	Item #	S or E	0	1	2	3	4	Blank	Bldg %	Dist %	State %	N = Bldg
M	NU	10	7	S	18	12	70	–	–	10	70	68	75	282
M	NU	6	19	S	26	22	52	–	–	9	52	55	60	282
M	NU	7	20	E	6	60	20	3	3	6	6	7	17	282

NOTE: S = short answer (2 possible points), proficient = 2; E = extended response (4 possible points), proficient = 3 or 4.

SOURCE Adapted from the Ohio Department of Education, data reporting table for student item-level test data, 2003. Used with permission of the Ohio Department of Education.

able to make better informed inferences about what specific content students do not know or understand. Figure 4.20, which includes the accompanying Task Deconstruction Table, shows an example of task deconstruction.

Figure 4.20   Task deconstruction example.

Test item #5 asks:

Which number does the point on the number line represent?

A. 5/2
B. .25
C. 1.75
D. 12/16 [correct answer]

Task Deconstruction Table

Item #	Knowledge	Skills	Big ideas/concepts
5	Fraction and decimal representations of a number	Converting between fractions and decimals	There is a relationship between decimals and fractions
	Relative distance between numbers on a number line	Comparing and ordering decimals	A number line shows relationships between numbers
	Equivalent fractions	Reducing fractions to the lowest terms	

Since task deconstruction is an in-depth process, the Data Team will focus their efforts on analyzing either frequently missed items within one strand, items for which many students chose the same incorrect answer, or short-answer and/or extended-response items for which a high percentage of students did not receive a passing or proficient rubric rating. The Data Team can use the Stoplight Highlighting criteria they determine in the Go Visual phase of their Data-Driven Dialogue to narrow down which items to deconstruct.

What Are the Challenges and Pitfalls Inherent in This Task?

No Access to Item-Level Data or Released Test Items

Some state CRT assessments do not provide item-level data, nor do they release test items. In this case, it is very important that your Data Team obtain item-level data from another source, such as common benchmark assessments and district tests. If you analyze item-level data from a second data source, read ahead to Task 11, where you will find information concerning consulting a second source of data.

Another possibility is that your state may provide item-level data but only release sample test items, not the actual test items. In this case, you may not be able to look at every individual test item that you would like to. There is still much to be learned by looking at only a sample of released items, particularly if the released items align with the strand area you and the Data Team are investigating.

Test-Item Quality

The quality of test items frequently comes up during item analysis. Unfortunately, there is wide variability in the quality of state tests. Typically, Data Teams find some items poorly worded, confusing, incorrect, and/or ineffective at assessing the intended learning outcome. Until test quality is consistently high, this is an unavoidable pitfall. The advantage of item analysis, however, is that it gets the team to closely examine the quality of items and factor that into their analysis. It also reinforces the importance of using multiple measures and of well-written, reliable, valid, and bias-free test items.

Data Team Members' Own Content Knowledge

Especially during the task deconstruction approach, it may become apparent that Data Team members do not have adequate content knowledge to deconstruct tasks thoroughly or to diagnose students' misconceptions. If so, you may want to schedule an extra meeting. You can use this opportunity to enhance their understanding by examining state or national standards, engaging them in a process called Curriculum Topic Study (Keeley, 2005; Keeley & Rose, 2006—see Resources), studying cognitive research about student misconceptions or alternative conceptions related to the content strand or outcomes of concern, or providing other content-based professional learning opportunities.

Keeping the Task Manageable

Item-level data provides a wealth of information and could occupy the Data Team for weeks. For example, the Data Team could explore all of the strand areas, identifying all of the strengths and all of the weaknesses in student understanding. They could engage in task deconstruction for numerous test items. However, this may not be practical for your team. You will want to prioritize your efforts and stay focused on the overall purpose: What are the specific skills, knowledge, and concepts within the content and strand area that are most in need of improvement? Generally, Data Teams zoom in on items related to the content strands on which their students performed the most poorly and deconstruct only those items that are highlighted red or urgent in their Stoplight Highlighting. Other suggestions for keeping each approach in this task focused on that purpose are provided throughout the procedures for this task.

RESOURCES

Keeley, P. (2005). *Science curriculum topic study: Bridging the gap between standards and practice.* Thousand Oaks, CA: Corwin Press.

Keeley, P., & Rose, C. M. (2006). *Mathematics curriculum topic study: Bridging the gap between standards and practice.* Thousand Oaks, CA: Corwin Press.

WestEd, & WGBH Educational Foundation. (2003). *Teachers as learners: A multimedia kit for professional development in science and mathematics.* Thousand Oaks,

CA: Corwin Press. (For an image of a group of high school mathematics teachers engaging in dialogue about a test item and what students need to know in order to solve the problem on the test, see the *Teachers as Learners* videotape entitled *Examining Content and Student Thinking*.)

Local, state, and national standard documents, for example, National Research Council, *National Science Education Standards*; National Council of Teacher of Mathematics, *Principles and Standards for School Mathematics*; National Council of Teachers of English, *National Standards for the English Language Arts*.

Your own test documentation and blueprint.

MAJOR ACTIVITIES FOR TASK 9

Activity	Time required	CD-ROM materials: Task 9 link	CD-ROM Toolkit: Relevant tools
Activity 9.1: Facilitate Data-Driven Dialogue With Multiple-Choice Item Data: Percentage Correct and Distractor Patterns	60 minutes	Handout H9.1: Stoplight Highlighting: Our Criteria for Percentage Correct on Multiple-Choice Items Handout H9.2: Stoplight Highlighting: Our Criterion for Distractor Patterns Data Examples and Data Templates	Data-Driven Dialogue, Data Wall, Group Roles, Seven Norms of Collaboration, Stoplight Highlighting, Why? Why? Why?
Activity 9.2: Facilitate Data-Driven Dialogue With Open-Response Item Data	30 minutes	Handout H9.3: Stoplight Highlighting: Our Criteria for Percentage Passing or Proficient on Open-Response Items Data Examples and Data Templates	Data-Driven Dialogue, Data Wall, Group Roles, Seven Norms of Collaboration, Stoplight Highlighting, Why? Why? Why?
Activity 9.3: Engage in Task Deconstruction	20 minutes per task	Handout H9.4: Task Deconstruction Example Handout H9.5: Task Deconstruction Table	Data-Driven Dialogue, Data Wall, Group Roles, Seven Norms of Collaboration, Stoplight Highlighting, Why? Why? Why?
Activity 9.4: Closure and Reflection	10 minutes		Group Roles, Seven Norms of Collaboration

A Data Team in Action: Item-Level Analysis—Kristy Welsh, Mathematics and Data Coach, Canton City, Ohio

All of the mathematics Data Teams at our district's high schools look forward to getting data from our common assessments as well as from the Ohio Graduation Test since the tests look not only at the big picture but at each item. Getting down to the nitty-gritty results in making changes to instruction and reteaching concepts that have not been learned has benefited our students.

Below is an example of an item that our students had great difficulty with last year. The percentage of students who picked each choice is listed next to the choice. The analysis that follows this item illustrates the kind of discussion that takes place as we go through each common assessment.

The test item reads:
What is the solution to this system of equations?

$7x + 3y = -8$

$-4x - y = 6$

A. $(-2, -2)$	15%
B. $(-2, 2)$ [correct answer]	48%
C. $(2, -2)$	24%
D. $(2, 2)$	7%
Left blank or multiple answers	6%

When the Data Team first looked back at this question, they predicted that at least 60 percent of the students would get it correct. They reasoned that at the very least students could plug all four choices in to find the correct answer. When we looked at the breakdown of how the students answered, however, there was shock and frustration. Then we began to talk about what had happened and how could this be retaught. Some of the comments centered around the idea that the students apparently didn't know how to plug the solution choices in to check their answers. The idea that came from this was that in the future and when reteaching, the teachers would begin by offering students two choices as solutions to a system of equations and the students would choose the correct choice by plugging the answers in. They hope that this will help the students understand what a solution is and how to check their own answers better when solving equations. All of the teachers admitted that previously they had rushed through checking solutions and at times skipped the step altogether. Another thought that emerged was that the question only asked for a solution and didn't tell the students what method to use. Some teachers guessed that students became confused because they had to choose a method. The strategy that the teachers decided to use during reteaching was more practice with each method without telling the students which method to use. As for when the material would be retaught, there were two ideas: The first was to use similar problems as warm-up problems during regular class time; the second was to address it in the "homework club" (an opportunity to get after-school tutoring with regular classroom teachers three days a week).

PREPARING FOR THE TASK

Read "Background Information for Data Coaches"; see the CD-ROM: Task 9 for data examples and templates, handouts, and sample goals and agendas; and review "Standard Procedures for Data Team Meetings" (see the introduction to Chapter 3 in this book and on CD-ROM). Although tool directions are embedded in the Data Coach Notes, you can also reference in-depth descriptions of relevant Toolkit entries on the CD-ROM.

You may want to conduct two Data Team meetings in order to complete the activities in this task. Meeting lengths will vary depending on the number of strands and items being analyzed. You may also want to hold a third meeting to study content related to deconstructed tasks.

MATERIALS PREPARATION

- Make one copy for each Data Team member of the item-level student performance data (see "Data Preparation").
- Make one copy for the Data Team of Handouts H9.1–H9.3.
- Make one copy for each Data Team member of Handout H9.4.
- Make one copy for each pair of Data Team members of Handout H9.5.
- Make sure the chart from Tasks 6, 7, and 8, Identifying a Student-Learning Problem: Data Findings, is posted on the wall.

DATA PREPARATION

- Make sure that you have the following documents from Task 8: learning objectives for the content and grade level that you have identified as most in need of improvement; definitions of cross-cutting content or process themes and the percentage of items on the test for each theme; the table synthesizing the strand areas, outcome numbers, and items on the test aligned with each strand area; and any other test documentation that you may have collected that will give you and the Data Team an understanding of item-level data on the test.

- Before compiling the item-level data, decide whether the team is going to examine item-level data for all strands or only for those strands identified in Task 8 as most in need of improvement. You may want to provide data that focuses on both the content strand areas and the cross-cutting concepts, especially if the cross-cutting concept areas were in need of improvement. Once you have made your decision, gather released test items or released sample items from the most recent state CRT assessment that align with the strand area or areas that you are investigating. Then make one copy for each Data Team member of all of these test items or released test items.

- Provide copies of the scoring guide for short-answer and extended-response items, including rubrics and anchor papers.

- Create three poster-size charts (18" × 24" is recommended) with your item-level data using the data templates on the CD-ROM.

DATA COACH NOTES

Activity 9.1: Facilitate Data-Driven Dialogue With Multiple-Choice Item Data: Percentage Correct and Distractor Patterns

1. Convene the Data Team, and ask team members to process their use of the group roles during Task 8. Then rotate the roles, and add any additional responsibilities for each role.

2. Depending on how you decided to embed practice of your agreed-upon collaborative norms, guide the Data Team through the process you identified.

3. Distribute the test information used in Task 8 (described in "Data Preparation") and ask the team to review it.

4. Let the team know they will now engage in Data-Driven Dialogue and Stoplight Highlighting with multiple-choice items. Distribute the released multiple-choice test items that align with the strand area you are investigating. Ask the Data Team to review the items and have them engage in Phase 1: Predict about how students might perform on each of these items. Ask the recorder to document these predictions on chart paper. Here are some suggested questions to prompt the team's predictions:

- What specific skills and understandings are our students' strengths?
- What specific skills and understandings pose difficulties for our students?
- What might we expect on those test items that also assess cross-cutting concepts?
- Which particular items do you think students will do well on? Have the most difficulty with? Why?

Sample Predictions of Item-Level Data: Percentage Correct

- Students struggle with the concept of buoyancy. I think they will do poorly on question 23.
- The content of this nonfiction text is unfamiliar to our students. I think they will perform poorly on question 12.
- Graphing is always easy for our students, so we should see higher scores on all questions that involve graphing skills.
- Our students seem to constantly confuse converting decimals to fractions and converting fractions to decimals. We expect to see low performance on questions 8, 15, and 38.

5. Beginning Phase 2: Go Visual, direct the Data Team's attention to the chart you have prepared with the percentage correct information for multiple-choice test items (see example in Table 4.20). Talk through the table and ensure that all Data Team members understand the way in which the data are reported.

6. Give the copy of Handout H9.1 to the Data Team, and guide them to establish criteria for Stoplight Highlighting based on the percentage correct. For example, 80–100 percent correct might be "green," 60–79 percent correct "yellow," and 59 percent and below "red." Or you may decide to set criteria based on the percentage above or below the student performance at the district or state levels. Ask the recorder to document the Data Team's criteria on the handout. (See example in Table 4.23.)

7. Once you have established the criteria, ask the Data Team to Stoplight-Highlight rows on the percentage correct table that meet each of the three criteria. (See example in Table 4.24 and in color in the Task 9 Data Examples link on the CD-ROM.) Post the highlighted table on the Data Wall.

Table 4.23   Stoplight Highlighting: Our Criteria for Percentage Correct on Multiple-Choice Items

Highlight color	Meaning	Our cutoff levels (percentage correct)
Green	Go! Meets expectations.	70
Yellow	Caution! Below expectations.	50–60
Red	Urgent! In immediate need of improvement.	Below 50

Table 4.24   Item Analysis: Multiple Choice Percentage Correct, With Stoplight Highlighting

Test part	Strand	Outcome #	Item #	Correct answer	Bldg %	Dist %	State %	N = Bldg
M	NU	10	1	C	49	48	62	282
M	NU	6	16	D	85	81	87	282
M	NU	8	20	D	56	59	73	282
M	NU	6	22	B	38	37	53	282
M	NU	9	35	D	17	25	40	282
M	NU	8	41	D	37	27	44	282
M	NU	6	45	B	50	48	58	282

	Go! (green)
	Caution! (yellow)
	Urgent! (red)

SOURCE Adapted from the Ohio Department of Education, data reporting table for student item-level test data, 2003. Used with permission of the Ohio Department of Education.

8.   Continue with Phase 2: Go Visual, and direct the Data Team's attention to the chart you have prepared with the percentage of students answering each option for the multiple-choice items on the test (see example in Table 4.21). If you have prepared more than one chart, you may want to ask Data Team members to investigate the charts in pairs. Talk through the table and ensure that all Data Team members understand the way in which the data are reported.

9.   Introduce the concept of distractor patterns. Make sure that they know that their purpose is to call attention to the high-frequency incorrect answers that reflect a pattern of student misunderstanding.

10. Give the copy of Handout H9.2 to the Data Team, and ask them to establish their criterion for highlighting frequently chosen distractors with the red highlighter; for example, highlight instances where more than 20 percent of the students chose the same wrong answer (see Table 4.25).

Table 4.25 Stoplight Highlighting: Our Criterion for Distractor Patterns

Highlight color	Meaning	Percentage choosing the distractor
Red	Urgent! In immediate need of improvement.	20 percent or more

11. Once you have established the criterion, ask the Data Team to Stoplight-Highlight the distractors on the Multiple-Choice Distractor Pattern Table. (See example in Table 4.26 and in color in the Task 9 Data Examples link on the CD-ROM.) Post the highlighted table on the Data Wall.

Table 4.26 Item Analysis: Multiple Choice Percentage Correct and Percentage Choosing Each Distractor, With Stoplight Highlighting

Test part	Strand	Outcome #	Item #	Correct answer	A	B	C	D	Blank	Bldg %	Dist %	State %	N = Bldg
M	NU	10	1	C	15	23	49	12	0	49	48	62	282
M	NU	06	16	D	4	7	4	85	0	85	81	87	282
M	NU	08	20	D	6	27	11	56	0	56	59	73	282
M	NU	06	22	B	16	38	26	20	1	38	37	53	282
M	NU	09	35	D	50	0	33	17	0	17	25	40	282
M	NU	08	41	D	9	12	39	37	3	37	27	44	282
M	NU	06	45	B	33	50	8	4	6	50	48	58	282

	Go! (green)
	Caution! (yellow)
	Urgent! (red)

SOURCE Adapted from the Ohio Department of Education, data reporting table for student item-level test data, 2003. Used with permission of the Ohio Department of Education.

**Sample Observations of Multiple-Choice Item-Level Data:
Percentage Correct and Distractor Patterns**

- For the three items designed to assess learning outcome number 4, students did not perform better than 34 percent correct.
- For item number 8, which is assessing learning outcome number 11, students in our school performed worse than did students at the district or state levels: 17 percent correct compared to 25 percent and 40 percent, respectively.
- Five out of seven items are in the red, or urgent, zone.
- On test item number 12, assessing students' understanding of the needs of living organisms, 32 percent of the students responded to the incorrect answer option of B.
- All test items that assess students' understanding of algebraic equations are highlighted in red.
- Test item numbers 7, 12, and 35 are designed to assess students' understanding of learning objective 6. All of those items contain high-frequency incorrect responses.
- For test item number 15, 22 percent of the students responded to A, 20 percent responded to B, and 18 percent responded to D. C was the correct answer, and 40 percent of the students answered correctly. The pattern for incorrect answers is spread across the three incorrect answer options.

12. Engage the Data Team in Phase 3: Observe about both the percentage correct and the distractor patterns. Ask the recorder to document these comments on chart paper and post them on the Data Wall. Remind the dialogue monitor to use the No-Because sign to help the Data Team stay focused on observations, or have the recorder write inferences on the Parking Lot chart. Suggested prompts for engaging in this phase include

- Which learning objectives pose the greatest difficulty for our students?
- How does student performance at the school level compare with the district level? The state level?
- Looking at all of the items with distractor patterns, which learning objectives do they align with?
- Which test items have incorrect answers spread across three answer options? Which ones have incorrect answers focused mostly on one answer option?
- How do the distractor pattern items line up with the percentage correct items? Are any of the distractor pattern items in the "yellow" zone, or are all of them in the "red" zone?

> **Facilitation Note**: Discourage the team from going back and examining the items while in Phase 3: Observe. It is hard to stay in observation while looking at the test items.

13. Direct the Data Team to the released items that have either percentage correct or distractors highlighted as urgent. As they examine these items, engage the Data Team in Phase 4: Infer/Question, generating possible explanations for why students may have missed that item or chosen a particular distractor. Ask the recorder to document the comments on chart paper and post them on the Data Wall. Prompt them to consider the following questions:

- Which learning objectives are associated with the lowest percentage correct and greatest number of distractor patterns? What do we think contributes to students' misunderstandings of those learning objectives?

- Are there patterns across items that are emerging? For example, are there related weak or strong concepts and skills across items?
- What specifically might students have been confused by in a particular item? What misconceptions might they have?
- What questions do we have about the test items themselves?
- What about our curriculum or instructional materials might contribute to this result? Do all students have access to this content?
- What about our teaching practices might contribute to students' strengths? Their relatively poor performance?

Sample Inferences From Multiple-Choice Item-Level Data:
Percentage Correct and Distractor Patterns

- Students seemed confused about the motion of objects. In this case, 28 percent of the students chose answer B, which suggests they were thinking that a moving object stops when its force is "used up," a commonly held idea.
- It seems like students who chose answer D did not find a common denominator, but simply added the two different denominators. They seem confused about how to add fractions.
- We only have access to sample test items, and we wonder what the actual test items are assessing. Specifically, we want to better understand what students do and do not know about discerning fact from fiction, and we won't know that without more information; we just know that test items aligned with that objective were frequently missed and that 20 percent or more of students chose the same distractors.
- There were no commas in the numbers. I think that confused the students.
- Our language arts curriculum does not include a balanced approach to teaching students decoding skills and reading comprehension skills.
- I think we need more strategies for teaching students to draw inferences.
- Our science program does not provide students with experience in understanding the nature of science.

 ## Activity 9.2: Facilitate Data-Driven Dialogue With Open-Response Item Data

1. Let the team know they will now engage in Data-Driven Dialogue and Stoplight Highlighting with just the open-response items.

2. Distribute the open-response items and scoring guide, and ask the team to familiarize themselves with these.

3. Ask the team to engage in Phase 1: Predict about how they think students will perform on these items. Ask the recorder to document these predictions on chart paper. Here are some suggested questions to prompt the team's predictions:

- How do you think students will perform on these items overall? How will this compare to their performance on multiple-choice items?
- How will performance on short-answer items compare with extended-response items?
- Which particular items will students perform well on? Have the most difficulty with? Why?

Sample Predictions on
Open-Response Items

- We've done so much work on nonroutine mathematics problem solving. I think our students are going to perform really well on extended-response questions.
- Students will do better overall on short-answer than extended-response items.
- There are so many steps in this item. I think the students are going to get confused.
- Our emphasis on writing this year is going to pay off in improved performance on the five-paragraph essay. Our students were doing really well with these on our common assessments.

4. Beginning Phase 2: Go Visual, direct the team to the chart you have prepared of the open-response results (see example in Table 4.22). Talk through the table and ensure that all Data Team members understand the way in which the data are reported.

5. Give the copy of Handout H9.3 to the Data Team, and guide them to establish criteria for Stoplight Highlighting based on either percentage passing or percentage proficient on open-response items. They might set different criteria for two-point and four-point questions, as illustrated in Table 4.27. Ask the recorder to document the criteria on the handout.

Table 4.27 Stoplight Highlighting: Our Criteria for Percentage Passing or Proficient on Open-Response Items

Highlight color	Meaning	Our cutoffs: 2-point questions	Our cutoffs: 4-point questions
Green	Go! Meets expectations.	80–100	70–100
Yellow	Caution! Below expectations.	60–79	50–69
Red	Urgent! In immediate need of improvement.	Below 60	Below 50

6. Once you have established the criteria, ask the Data Team to Stoplight-Highlight rows on the table with the open-response item data that meet each of the three criteria. (See example in Table 4.28 and in color in the Task 9 Data Examples link on the CD-ROM.) Post the highlighted table on the Data Wall.

Table 4.28 Item Analysis: Percentage Scoring Each of the Possible Points on Open-Response Items, With Stoplight Highlighting

Test part	Strand	Outcome #	Item #	S or E	0	1	2	3	4	Blank	Bldg %	Dist %	State %	N = Bldg
M	NU	10	7	S	18	12	70	–	–	10	70	68	75	282
M	NU	6	19	S	26	22	52	–	–	9	52	55	60	282
M	NU	7	20	E	6	60	20	3	3	6	6	7	17	282

	Go! (green)
	Caution! (yellow)
	Urgent! (red)

NOTE: S = short answer (2 possible points), proficient = 2; E = extended response (4 possible points), proficient = 3 or 4.

SOURCE Adapted from the Ohio Department of Education, data reporting table for student item-level test data, 2003. Used with permission of the Ohio Department of Education.

7. Engage the Data Team in Phase 3: Observe about the open-response item data. Ask the recorder to document these comments on chart paper and post them on the Data Wall. Suggested prompting questions to guide the Data Team include

- Which items met our criteria for success?
- How did their performance on short-answer items compare with performance on extended-response items?
- On which outcomes did students perform well? On which did they struggle?
- How does their performance on these outcomes compare with performance on the same outcomes on multiple-choice items?
- What surprises or intrigues us about these results?

8. Engage the Data Team in Phase 4: Infer/Question about these data. Facilitate a discussion to help the Data Team ask questions and generate possible explanations of the data. Ask the recorder to document the comments on chart paper and post them on the Data Wall. Prompt them to consider the following questions:

- What can we infer about which kinds of items are most difficult for our students?
- What can we infer about the particular outcomes that students do well with? Have difficulty with?
- To what extent does our curriculum prepare students to be successful on open-response items? Our instruction and assessment practices?
- What are we doing well that we can do more of?
- Why didn't our students get full credit for their responses?
- What particular parts of the items were challenging for students?

Sample Observations of Open-Response Items

- Sixty-two percent of our students were proficient or above on the extended-response item in physical science.
- Ten percent of our students left question 3 blank.
- Thirty percent of our students received one point on the two-point question about three-dimensional shapes, while 75 percent of students got the multiple-choice question right on the same outcome.
- Fifty-six percent of our students scored a three or four on their writing sample.

Sample Inferences From Open-Response Items

- Mathematical reasoning and communication are not emphasized enough in our curriculum.
- Our students are not used to explaining their work. They didn't explain the rule.
- Our students are having difficulty with multistep problems because they are making simple computation errors.
- They haven't had enough practice applying the scientific method.
- Our extra practice with writing prompts and rubrics paid off!

Item-Level Data Cautions

When looking at test items, make sure that the following questions are asked:
- Is the test item valid for its purpose—does it measure what it is supposed to measure?
- Is the test item accurate in its content? Is the correct answer accurate in its content?
- Do the items elicit varying levels of student understanding, from factual recall to conceptual understanding?
- Is the test itself fair and unbiased in its cultural references, language use, and reading levels?

When drawing conclusions and inferences:
- Don't assume that items within a strand are classified in the way that you might classify them or that aligns with your curriculum or instructional materials.
- Remember that conclusions are best drawn from patterns of items rather than from individual items.
- Resist the tendency to disregard a test item that you may consider to be invalid—it may need further investigation.
- Keep your focus on content understanding as well as on achievement gaps.

CAUTION

Activity 9.3: Engage in Task Deconstruction

1. Introduce the idea that task deconstruction provides an opportunity to further explore the test items to identify the specific knowledge and skills that the items are assessing, explore whether answer options for test items include common misconceptions in addition to the correct answer, and determine the quality of the assessment and scoring criteria (i.e., is the test language fair and unbiased, valid, reliable, and accurate?). Task deconstruction can lead the team to deepen their inferences from the item analysis while deepening their understanding of the content that is being taught and assessed.

2. Make sure the Data Team has copies of relevant standard and local curriculum documents. Distribute Handout H9.4 (see Figure 4.20) to each Data Team member. Using that example, help the Data Team distinguish between the terms knowledge, skills, and big ideas/concepts:
   - *Knowledge*: The discrete facts that are known within the content area.
   - *Skills*: The procedures and processes that are needed within the content area.
   - *Big ideas/concepts*: The larger learning objectives within the content area.

3. Ask Data Team members to pair up with a partner. Have each pair select one red-highlighted test item that they feel confident in analyzing based on their own content knowledge and their comfort with teaching it. If possible, make sure that the Data Team selects a combination of multiple-choice items and short-answer and extended-response items. Distribute to each pair the released test item and a copy of Handout H9.5.

Handout H9.5

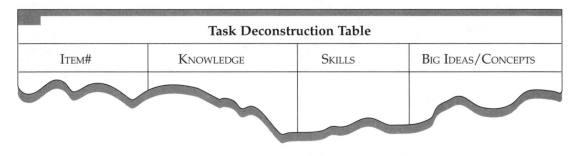

	Task Deconstruction Table		
ITEM#	KNOWLEDGE	SKILLS	BIG IDEAS/CONCEPTS

Facilitation Note: Task deconstruction requires a firm knowledge of standards and the structure of the discipline under consideration. It is often helpful to have an instructional specialist at the meeting. Task deconstruction can also lead to deeper inquiry into what standards mean, what student work looks like when students meet standards, and how concepts and skills are developed through the curriculum. Your Data Team may want to delve more deeply into topics, concepts, or skills in their curriculum using a study process such as Keeley's curriculum topic studies for mathematics and science (see Resources above).

4. Ask each pair to use the task deconstruction table to "deconstruct" their test item by identifying the knowledge, skills, and ideas/concepts that students would need to know and understand in order to complete the task successfully or answer the question correctly.

5. Invite the pair to share their analyses of the items selected and post their tables on the Data Wall. Ask the entire Data Team to discuss their observations of the items that have been deconstructed, and have the recorder document these comments on chart paper.

Sample Task Deconstruction Observations

- Three of the five test items contain more skills than they do concepts.
- The knowledge that is assessed by items 4, 15, and 23 is aligned with learning objectives that we don't teach at this grade level.
- All of the skills students need to correctly answer test item number 42 are similar to those needed to answer test item number 3.

6. Ask the team to revisit and deepen the inferences generated in Activities 9.1 and 9.2. Ask the recorder to document the comments on chart paper and post them on the Data Wall. Some prompting questions to guide the Data Team's engagement in this phase include

- Do student response patterns indicate the specific knowledge, skills, and concepts that they do or do not know, understand, or have mastery of?
- What are the specific knowledge, skills, or concepts that students know, and what are some reasons for their mastery and understanding? What specific knowledge, skills, or concepts do they not know, and what are some possible reasons for their lack of mastery or understanding?
- What about our curriculum or instruction might contribute to the student-learning strengths? Weaknesses?
- Are there issues of equity that are contributing factors?
- Did language used in the test items contribute to the responses?
- Are the items valid for their purposes? Fair and unbiased?
- Do any inferences blame individual students or students of different populations? If so, how can we reframe those inferences?

Sample Inferences After Task Deconstruction

- Some of the test items were culturally biased, and we don't feel confident in those items' ability to assess student understanding.
- Most of our task deconstruction tables indicate more concepts than skills that students would need to understand in order to correctly answer the test item. Thinking about what we teach, we don't think we emphasize the concepts enough.
- The physical science test items contained wording that could have contributed to the distractor patterns. But if students truly understood the concepts, the wording probably would not have resulted in so many incorrect answers. They had the most difficulty with the force and motion questions.
- It seems clear that in mathematics/number sense, students have the greatest difficulty understanding how to convert decimals into fractions.
- We identified numerous skills that students would need to know in order to correctly answer the geometry questions, but only a few concepts.
- We weren't sure what the overarching life science concepts would be for many of the test items. We wonder whether our own understanding of the content is lacking.

Activity 9.4: Closure and Reflection

1. Facilitate a discussion to help the Data Team synthesize what they learned from the item-level analysis. Ask them to document their learning on sentence strips and post them on the Identifying a Student-Learning Problem: Data Findings chart. Examples of statements that summarize what has been learned from the item-level data analysis include

- Within the strand area of data analysis and probability, students have the most difficulty with interpreting data that are graphically displayed and with explaining the data. Student performance on both multiple-choice items and short-answer items contributed to this finding.
- In physical science, students had the greatest difficulty with predicting the influences of motion of some objects on other objects.
- In language arts, students had the greatest difficulty in reading with word recognition and fluency.

2. Ask the Data Team to generate a list of questions that they still have about student learning in the content strand. Prompt them to consider whether they have a robust picture of student thinking, understanding, and misconceptions of the content within the strand area. What would they need in order to better understand student thinking? Document the questions on chart paper.

3. Build on the questions raised to help the Data Team focus on the questions they will investigate in the next task. Ask them to consider the following questions:

- What questions were asked today that can be answered by looking at student work?
- For which short-answer and extended-response test items will it be important to see the students' actual written responses?

4. Provide time for reflection and processing of the Data Team's use of group roles and their agreed-upon collaborative norms.

Task 10: Examine Student Work

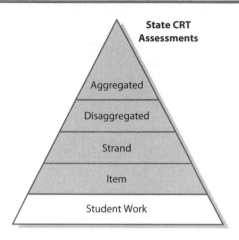

State CRT Assessments

Aggregated

Disaggregated

Strand

Item

Student Work

Task-at-a-Glance

Purpose	Engage in Data-Driven Dialogue to further clarify and define student-learning needs within the specified content area and grade level, using state CRT-generated student work and/or additional sources of student work
Data	Released student responses to short-answer and extended-response items on the state CRT (if available) and/or samples of student work aligned with the student-learning problem collected in the school
Questions to ask	What questions about student thinking and understanding will we further explore through analyzing student work?
	What skills, knowledge, and concepts do students have mastery or understanding of as evidenced by the student work? In which have they not gained mastery or understanding?
	Are the observations and inferences that surfaced in our analysis of CRT data validated by what we see in samples of student work? If not, how do we explain the data findings?
	What additional insights are we gaining about student thinking?
Concepts	Student work as evidence of understanding
Activities	Activity 10.1: Facilitate Data-Driven Dialogue With Student Work
	Activity 10.2: Closure and Reflection

WHAT IS TASK 10?

By now the Data Team has accomplished a great deal. They have examined results from the state CRT assessment and identified the content strands that students have difficulty with as identified by the CRT data. They have analyzed individual items on the CRT assessment to identify the knowledge, skills, and concepts students do and do not understand. As a result of their data analyses in each task, they have generated tentative conclusions, inferences, and questions about student understanding within the content area. Each subsequent task has helped the Data Team drill down into more detailed understanding of students' learning needs.

At the end of Task 9, the Data Team identified additional questions about student-learning needs that could not be answered through analysis of the item-level data. Investigating student work and student thinking can now address many of those questions. In Task 10, the Data Team looks at student work to further clarify the student-learning needs. Two sources of student work can be used in this task: either released short-answer or extended-response answers from the state assessment or student work gathered from students in the school.

If the Data Team examines student work that has been generated from the state CRT, they are continuing the drill-down at the fifth level (see Task 10 Data Pyramid at the beginning of this chapter). If student work is gathered from classrooms, the Data Team is moving into examination of a second source of student-learning data. In either case, the purpose is to learn more about student misconceptions and misunderstandings. The products for this task will be the completed Data-Driven Dialogue charts of inferences, as well as synthesis statements that reflect what has been learned from the state CRT-generated student work and/or classroom student work. These are added to the Identifying a Student-Learning Problem: Data Findings chart. A sample chart, which now includes the findings from a second source, a classroom performance task on floating and sinking, is shown in Figure 4.21. In this example, the state provided no student work samples, so the team collected their own data to further investigate students' understanding of sinking and floating. The second column of the chart illustrates the team's findings from examining student work, especially their insights into student thinking. In addition, since the work came from a performance task with a rubric, aggregated, disaggregated, and item analysis results are also included.

BACKGROUND INFORMATION FOR DATA COACHES

Why Is Student Work So Valuable as a Source of Data?

Examining student work has become an increasingly widespread practice among teachers, and for very good reasons. Through analysis of student-generated artifacts (journals, projects, reports, drawings, performance tasks, or writings), teachers gain insight into students' thinking and the extent of their understanding of the concepts, skills, and knowledge within content areas. Knowing not only what students know or do not know but also how they think about and process their knowledge provides teachers with valuable information to guide instruction and

Figure 4.21 Identifying a student-learning problem with findings from student work.

Identifying a Student-Learning Problem: Data Findings

Content Area _____ Science _____   Grade Level _____ Sixth grade _____

Levels of data	Types of data		
	1: ___ State CRT ___ _____ Years: 2004–2006	2: Classroom performance task on floating and sinking (4–0 point scoring rubric) Years: 2005–2006	3: _____ _____ Years:
Aggregated results	Fifty-two percent of sixth-grade students were proficient in science, a 2 percent decrease from last year.	Sixty-five percent of all sixth-grade students scored a rubric rating of 2 or below.	
Disaggregated results	There is a persistent achievement gap between White and Latino/a students in science; this year's gap was 38 percentage points.	Of the students who scored a rubric rating of 2 or below, 70 percent were Latino/a and 52 percent were White.	
Strand results	For two years, the lowest percentage of students were proficient in the physical science strand; 31 percent last year, 28 percent this year.	N/A (the assessment focused on one strand area)	
Item analysis	Of the eight physical science multiple-choice items, students performed worst on the three items pertaining to floating and sinking, with 23–30 percent proficient.	Students performed poorly on the part of the task that required them to explain why objects floated or sank.	
Student work	N/A (no state data provided)	Showed evidence of student misconceptions of the relationship between an object's composition and its buoyancy; students consistently relied on the object's size to determine its buoyancy.	
Student-learning problem:			

improve teaching and learning. For an example of student work, see vignette on page 218. Additional examples can be found on the CD-ROM, Task 10 (Data Examples).

Although there are numerous purposes for examining student work—assessing the quality of the assignment, providing an opportunity for teacher learning and professional development, looking for evidence of specific learning, determining whether all students have equal opportunities for challenging learning, or determining whether students' learning is aligned with standards—the focus in the Using Data Process is on gaining a better understanding of the student-learning problem the Data Team is uncovering. Scores on a rubric or percentage correct on multiple-choice items provide little insight into student thinking. Through examining student work, however, the team gathers additional evidence about what students understand, what they are confused about, and what might be causing that confusion. They also learn which skills students have mastered and which need improvement.

Based on what was learned from strand and item-level data analysis, the team will gather student work that provides evidence of student thinking related to the specific skills and knowledge identified as most in need of improvement. For example, a Data Team finds that students are having difficulty with fractions, decimals, and percentages, but they are not yet certain what students are confused about and what they currently think about these ideas. In this task, the team will gather student work using assessment prompts that elicit student thinking. Then the Data Team will analyze the work to uncover student-learning needs and confirm or refute earlier inferences drawn from item-level data. Examining the students' written responses can provide deeper insights into the patterns observed in the item-level data—for example, why students chose a particular distractor, what misconception or confusion they generally hold, or whether their poor scores in reading informational text resulted from a particularly difficult reading passage or from an actual skill deficit.

What Are the Challenges and Pitfalls Inherent in This Task?

No Access to State CRT-Generated Student Work

Some, but not all, states make the actual student work for short-answer and extended-response questions available to teachers. If you do not have access to released student written work from the state CRT assessment, not to worry! You can gather your own student work from students in your school.

Staying Objective

It is easy, when examining student work, to get distracted by messiness, amount written, or other factors that do not reflect the criteria for success. It will be important to guide the Data Team to examine the work only in relation to the criteria and, to the extent possible, put their biases aside. It is also suggested that teachers examine the work of other teachers' students, not their own students. And, of course, in the observation phase of the Data-Driven Dialogue, it is particularly important that Data Team members stick to "just the facts."

Sharing Student Work Publicly

Putting student work on the table for examination by colleagues can be threatening, especially if this is not the norm in your school. Often, teachers are most comfortable sharing only their "best" students' work. You will want to assure the Data Team that the student work will not be used to assess either the teacher or the student, but to inform the team's understanding of all students' knowledge and skills. In this task, teachers will be examining random samples of student work, not identified by teacher or by student. It will still be important, however, to create a safe environment for examining the work by reinforcing your group norms and making sure that blame and judgment are not a part of the conversation.

Teacher Content Knowledge

Sometimes teachers share some of the same misconceptions or confusion about a concept that the students have. If this is the case, introduce some research about student misconceptions or alternative conceptions and some material that will help teachers strengthen their own content knowledge, such as national standards documents and other resources cited below.

RESOURCES

Keeley, P. (2005). *Science curriculum topic study: Bridging the gap between standards and practice.* Thousand Oaks, CA: Corwin Press.

Keeley, P., Eberle, F., & Farrin, L. (2005). *Uncovering student ideas in science: 25 formative assessment probes* (Vol. 1). Arlington, VA: National Science Teachers Association Press.

Keeley, P., & Rose, C. M. (2006). *Mathematics curriculum topic study: Bridging the gap between standards and practice.* Thousand Oaks, CA: Corwin Press.

WestEd & WGBH Educational Foundation. (2003). *Teachers as learners: A multimedia kit for professional development in science and mathematics.* Thousand Oaks, CA: Corwin Press. (See Videotape 3, Program 3, Assessing student work, Arizona State University East, Mesa, Arizona, and Videotape 4, Program 5, Examining content and student thinking, Urban Calculus Initiative, TERC, Cambridge, Massachusetts.)

Student work Web sites:

Harvard Graduate School of Education's Project Zero: http://www.pz.harvard.edu/

Looking at Student Work: http://www.lasw.org

Education Trust's Standards in Practice (SIP): http://www2.edtrust.org/EdTrust/SIP+Professional+Development/

WestEd's Center for Science Education and Professional Development: http://www.wested.org/cs/we/view/pj/214/

MAJOR ACTIVITIES FOR TASK 10

Activity	Time required	CD-ROM materials: Task 10 link	CD-ROM Toolkit: Relevant tools
Activity 10.1: Facilitate Data-Driven Dialogue With Student Work	Variable for gathering student work from classrooms but plan on one to two weeks; 90–120 minutes for analyzing the work	Handout H10.1: Ground Rules for Looking at Student Work Handout H10.2: Student Work Protocol Data Examples	Data-Driven Dialogue, Data Wall, Group Roles, Seven Norms of Collaboration
Activity 10.2: Closure and Reflection	30 minutes		Group Roles, Seven Norms of Collaboration

Vignette: Examining Student Work

The analysis of the eighth-grade CRT science strand data for "investigation and experimentation" indicated that 42 percent of the students scored at the proficient level. Item-level data revealed that three questions about plotting and interpreting graphs had the lowest percentage of correct answers. Even with this drill-down, the Data Team was left with lingering questions about why students were not able to answer these questions.

It was evident to the team that only analyzing multiple-choice questions would not help them understand students' naive or alternative conceptions about graphing. The teachers knew that in order to enhance their instruction, they needed to know exactly the concepts or content students were struggling to master.

The Data Coach brought the national and state science standards to the table for discussion. Using the documents helped the team to clarify their own content knowledge and build a common understanding of what eighth-grade students should know about charting, graphing, and summary statements. The list of concepts included appropriate graphic representation (e.g., bar, line, pie), orientation of x- and y-axes, parallel and perpendicular lines, labeling of manipulated (independent) variables and responding (dependent) variables, and analysis of the relationship of manipulated and responding variables.

The team also discussed their experiences with teaching graphing and where students seem to "always struggle." Reviewing research on student learning helped the team confirm that two of the most common misconceptions involved use of appropriate graphs to display the data and understanding the relationship between the variables.

Their interest was further piqued. What could they do to gather student work on this subject? The team decided to create an open-ended assessment prompt that asked students to graph data from a table that clearly labeled the variables and to make a summary statement from the graphic representation. They asked all eighth-grade science teachers to randomly select 10 students in their classes to take the open-ended assessment. This resulted in 50 pieces of student work (see example in Figure 4.22).

Figure 4.22 Student work example.

Open-Ended Prompt

Please write (or draw) your answer directly on the lines or in the space provided

- You are the owner of a company that supplies local florists with tulips. Last year the tulips you produced tended to be smaller than usual and you wonder if it had something to do with the soil temperature in the winter.
- You recorded the ground temperature where the tulip bulbs were dormant and the average height of the plants when they sprouted. Your data chart look like this:

HEIGHT OF TULIP PLANTS
ONE WEEK AFTER BREAKING THROUGH SOIL

	AREA A	AREA B	AREA C
Ground Temperature in Winter	7 C	2 C	0 C
Average Height of Plants	4 cm	8 cm	14 cm

1. Graph the data on the grid below. Remember to label the graph.

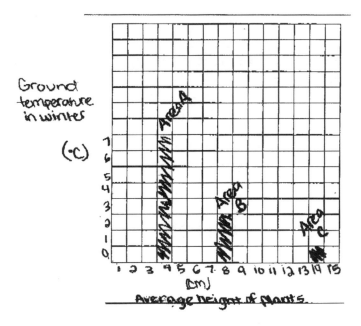

2. Based on the data from the graph, describe the relationship between ground temperature in winter and the height of tulip plants after a week of visible growth.

    The relationship is the more the temperature goes down the height gets taller.

SOURCE Adapted from the Fall 2004 Partnership for Student Success in Science student assessment. Used with permission. Designed by Dr. Shavelson of Stanford University.

(Continued)

(Continued)

To interpret the student work, the Data Team invited all teachers who gave the assessment to join in the analysis. First the teachers reviewed the scoring criteria (rubric) for expected student answers. Then they sorted the work into high-, medium-, and low-quality piles based on the scoring criteria and discussed the characteristics of each group. How was student understanding represented in the high-quality pile? What was lacking in a student's knowledge that indicated an intermediate level of understanding? What types of instructional interventions would be necessary to move a student from the low-quality to the medium-quality pile?

These rich discussions resulted in the team documenting the following inference about student understanding: Students have difficulty understanding the difference between when to use a bar graph (discontinuous data) and a line graph (continuous data). They are also not using data as evidence when writing a summary statement of the data.

Of course, this led to a discussion of how graphing was taught, and it was apparent that math and science teachers don't articulate their content or their strategies. It was also apparent that there were no common criteria for a quality graph or summary statements for Grades 6–8. The team wrote up their observations for use in the "verify causes" phase and starred their inferences for possible intervention strategies in "generating solutions."

PREPARING FOR THE TASK

Read "Background Information for Data Coaches"; see the CD-ROM: Task 10 for data examples, handouts, and sample goals and agenda; and review "Standard Procedures for Data Team Meetings" (see the introduction to Chapter 3 in this book and on CD-ROM). Although tool directions are embedded in the Data Coach Notes, you can also reference in-depth descriptions of relevant Toolkit entries on the CD-ROM.

MATERIALS PREPARATION

• Make one copy for each Data Team member of either released state CRT student responses or student work collected from classrooms in the school, along with relevant scoring guides and anchor papers (see "Data Preparation" below).

• Make one copy for each Data Team member of Handouts H10.1 and H10.2.

• Post the item-level data charts from Task 9 on the wall.

• Make sure that the chart from Tasks 6–9, Identifying a Student-Learning Problem: Data Findings, is posted on the wall.

DATA PREPARATION

Based on the availability of state CRT-generated student work, decide what source of student work the Data Team will examine in this task. If you have released student work from the state test that aligns with items, concepts, and skills that you want to investigate further, we recommend you start with those. Once you have examined those samples, however, you may still want to gather student work from classrooms to expand the Data Team's understanding of student thinking. The guidelines here provide information on gathering student work from both sources; if you are examining student work from only one source, disregard the other set of guidelines.

State CRT-Generated Student Work

If available, gather student written responses for the released short-answer and extended-response items that the Data Team has identified are most in need of improvement or about which they have further questions. For example, they may have generated questions about student understanding based on a high percentage of students receiving a rubric score of "0" or "1" for a specific extended-response item and therefore want to examine the student responses to better understand student thinking and misconceptions. Make sure you have enough student work samples for each pair of Data Team members to have at least four or five different samples. Here are some guidelines for selecting the samples:

- Two to four samples that show that the student understands the knowledge, skills, or concepts;
- Two to four samples that show that the student does not understand the knowledge, skills, or concepts;
- Two to four samples that are confusing to you as the teacher; or
- Two to four interesting or unusual samples.

Classroom Student Work

If you do not have access to state CRT-generated student work, identify appropriate assessment prompts to elicit student thinking about the content you are focused on. Using the item-level data charts from Task 9, focus on weak items and strands as the criteria for identifying appropriate student work to gather. Consider asking students to provide more in-depth written responses to any of the multiple-choice or short-answer items on which they seemed confused or performed poorly. If you have already examined state-CRT generated student work, use your unanswered questions to guide development of appropriate assessment prompts. For example, if you are still not sure what is confusing to students about the idea of sound, use a prompt such as the one illustrated in Figure 4.23. The student explanations generated from the Making Sound prompt would provide insight into their thinking about vibrations and the production of sound. Through examining those explanations, a Data Team would have greater understanding of students' current conceptions of sound.

Once you and the Data Team have selected the assessment prompts for generating the student work, ask team members and, if possible, other teachers at the same grade level and same content area to give the assessment in their classrooms. One option is to gather student work on the same task from as many students as possible. However, this may produce more student work samples than the team can analyze. Another option is to gather samples of student work from a selection of

Figure 4.23   Making sound.

Physical Science Assessment **Probes**

Making Sound

All of the objects listed below make sounds. Put an X next to the objects you think involve vibrations in producing sound.

_____ guitar strings

_____ drum

_____ dripping faucet

_____ barking dog

_____ piano

_____ screeching brakes

_____ radio speaker

_____ crumpled paper   _____ wind   _____ hammer

_____ car engine   _____ Wood saw   _____ flute

_____ chirping cricket   _____ clapped hands   _____ thunderstorm

_____ singer   _____ bubbling water _____ two stones rubbled together

_____ popped ballooon   _____ rustling leaves _____ snapped fingers

Explain your thinking. What "rule" or reasoning did you use to decide which objects involve vibrations in producing sound?

_____

_____

_____

_____

_____

_____

SOURCE Keeley, Eberle, & Farrin. _Uncovering Student Ideas in Science: 25 Formative Assessment Probes, Volume 1_, p. 43. 2005. Arlington, VA: National Science Teachers Association Press. Reprinted with permission.

students. Remember that the purpose is to examine patterns of thinking to see if the same problems that surfaced in item-level analysis are also evident in classroom-generated student work; at this time, you will not analyze student work to individualize instruction (although you will use student work for this purpose later as you implement and monitor your action plans).

However, do make sure that you have a diverse range of student work samples that represent the racial/ethnic, gender, language, educational status, and economic diversity of the students. Also, follow the guidelines given above for state CRT-generated student work. Once the student work samples have been collected, organize them so that pairs of Data Team members will have at least four or five different samples. Additionally, remove any student identification information so that the work remains anonymous.

DATA COACH NOTES

 ### Activity 10.1: Facilitate Data-Driven Dialogue With Student Work

1. Convene the Data Team, and ask the team members to process their use of the group roles during Task 9. Then rotate the roles, and add any additional responsibilities for each role.

2. Depending on how you decided to embed practice of your agreed-upon collaborative norms, guide the Data Team through the process you identified.

> **Facilitation Note:** Probing for specificity is a norm that is especially helpful during the engagement with student work. If it is not one of your selected norms, you may wish to add it at this point. The norm involves the use of gentle open-ended probes or inquiries to increase the clarity and precision of the Data Team's thinking. Practicing this norm during the dialogue about student work and students' thinking can enhance the Data Team's learning from student artifacts.

3. Distribute Handout H10.1. Engage the Data Team in a discussion about the ground rules, and invite them to add guidelines that they have used in the past that will contribute to the dialogue of the student work.

Ground Rules for Looking at Student Work

- Engage in dialogue during which team members seek to understand each other and probe for understanding.
- Focus on the evidence, not on what you think or infer that the student meant.
- Be aware of personal biases (such as disliking "messy" work) and ask others to help you avoid them in your analysis.
- Follow a protocol to guide dialogue and analysis of the student work.

4. Distribute Handout H10.2, and review the protocol steps with the Data Team.

5. Share the test item or prompt that is the source of the student work. Ask the Data Team to work in pairs to complete the same task for which you have gathered student work. If there is a rubric for the task, ask the partners to review the rubric and discuss how it matches with their expected student responses.

6. Facilitate a dialogue during which various solutions or responses can be shared. Encourage Data Team

Student Work Protocol

- Complete the task with a partner.
- Discuss solutions or responses with the Data Team.
- Clarify the knowledge, skills, and concepts that are needed to successfully complete the task.
- Predict what student work will show.
- Observe what is evident in the student work.
- Infer what you now think about student understanding and misunderstandings of the content or mastery of skills.
- Generate additional questions and possible causes.

Sample Predictions About Student Work (based on open-ended prompt in Figure 4.22)

- I think that the students won't do very well because they are not very experienced at generating a graph from observational or experimental data.
- Students don't often have to explain a figure; therefore, they might not understand how to interpret the graph.
- Students will make a bar graph because that is the only type of graph they have been taught in elementary school.
- Students will label the *x*- and *y*-axes but won't know which one is the manipulated (independent) variable and which is the responding (dependent) variable.
- Students will plot points correctly.
- Students will use data to make their summary statement.

pairs to share their solutions or responses visually. Make sure each member understands what the prompt is asking and what would make a high-quality student response. Ask the team to clarify the knowledge, skills, and concepts needed to successfully complete the task as they did in Task 9, Task Deconstruction.

7. Before looking at the student work, ask the pairs to engage in Phase 1: Predict about what students' responses will show. Remind the Data Team to consult the Data Wall and their sentence strips for the item-level analysis findings to inform their predictions. Prompt the Data Team to consider the following questions:

- How do you think the students will perform on the task?
- What do you think the students will demonstrate an understanding of?
- What do you think the students will have difficulty with?

8. Distribute the samples of student work (Phase 2: Go Visual), and ask pairs to engage in Phase 3: Observe. Document their observations on chart paper. Prompt pairs to think about the following questions:

- What is the evidence that students do or do not have understanding and/or mastery of the knowledge, skills, and concepts in the task?
- What are the differences between student work samples that are of high, medium, and low quality?
- Based on the questions and inferences generated from item-level analysis, what do we now know about student learning?

9. Engage the Data Team in sharing what they observed with each other. Document the key points on chart paper.

Sample Observations of Student Work (based on student work examples on CD-ROM)

- Paper A uses a bar graph rather than a line graph.
- Papers A, B, and D have no title.
- Papers A and B have mixed up the variables, plotting the manipulated variable (ground temperature) on the *y*-axis instead of the *x*-axis.
- Most data points are plotted correctly.
- Papers A, B, and C don't use data from the graph to explain the changes, although they do state the change (colder temperature, taller plants).
- Paper D has a wrong relationship (warmer ground, taller plants).
- Paper E is the only one to use actual data numbers.

10. Ask the Data Team to engage in Phase 4: Infer/Question, considering these questions:

- What new insights do you have about the student-learning problem?
- What causes do you think are contributing to the lack of student understanding?
- Does your examination of student work confirm or refute the tentative conclusions from the item analysis?
- What additional questions are raised by the student work? What additional data could help answer these questions?

Sample Inferences From Student Work (based on student work examples on CD-ROM)

- For the most part, students have the skill of coordinate plotting on the graph, and most understand the x- and y-axis orientations. For those students misusing the axis orientation, we need to know if it was a skill-based mistake or a misconception about what the data chart indicates.
- In our sample, only one student used a bar graph. We are curious if this is an accurate representation of students who have this misconception. We want to look at other student work to see how often students use bar graphs when a line graph is the appropriate type of graph.
- It is obvious from this sample of student work that students don't understand how to write a summary statement that uses data from the graph. Their statements are general (it went up or went down) without numerically describing the change, or the rate of change.
- Students don't understand that this is continuous data and should be represented on a line graph.
- The science department does not coordinate with the mathematics department about how graphing is taught.
- Some students don't know how to label the title and the x- and y-axes.
- Some students don't understand that the title is a relationship of the variables.
- Do we have criteria for making graphs and summary statements that all teachers use?
- How do our texts from Grades 6–8 teach graphing?
- What supplemental graphing activities do we use at our grade level?
- How much modeling of graphing and forming summary statements do we do in our teaching? Do teachers use similar approaches?

Analysis of Student Work Cautions

Before confirming conclusions about student understanding, make sure that the following questions have been asked:

- Was the task valid for its purpose, i.e., did it measure what it was supposed to measure?
- Did the task elicit student understanding or factual recall?
- Was the task fair and unbiased in its cultural references, language use, and reading levels?
- Did we let our personal biases interfere with our observations of the student work? For example, did we allow messy papers or misspelled words to interfere with our interpretation of student understanding?
- Did we allow inferences to slip into our observations?

11. Facilitate a dialogue with the Data Team to help them synthesize everything they learned from examining student work. Ask them to document their learning on sentence strips and tape them to the Identifying a Student-Learning Problem: Data Findings chart. Also, if the work is based on a performance task with rubric scores, add findings in the aggregated, disaggregated, and item-level rows as applicable.

12. Engage the Data Team in a dialogue about what they have learned and where they currently are in their understanding of the student-learning problem. Ask them to consider the question, "Now that we have analyzed student work, what questions do we still have?" Document their questions on chart paper.

13. If the Data Team still has unanswered questions about student understanding, let them know that they can gather additional student work from their, and other teachers', classrooms or consult relevant cognitive research about student thinking about the particular concept or skill.

Activity 10.2: Closure and Reflection

1. Ask the Data Team to return to the list of questions generated in Activity 10.1, Step 12, and ask them to discuss the following questions:

- Did the student work help us answer the questions we highlighted?
- What other questions on the list can we answer through analysis of common classroom-based assessments? Highlight those questions with a marker for further exploration in Task 11.

2. Provide time for reflection and processing of the Data Team's use of group roles and their agreed-upon collaborative norms.

Task 11: Drill Down Into Common Assessments and Other Local Student-Learning Data Sources

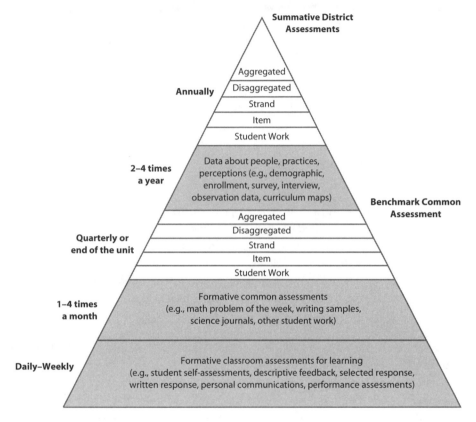

Task-at-a-Glance

Purpose	Consult local student-learning data sources to further verify and deepen the current understanding of student-learning needs as identified from the state CRT assessment and classroom student work
Data	Common classroom-based assessments, such as end-of-unit assessments or performance-based tasks, districtwide benchmark and/or annual assessments
Questions to ask	What questions about student thinking and understanding will we address by examining our own common assessments and our district assessments?
	What skills, knowledge, and concepts do students have mastery of as evidenced by these additional assessments? Which have they not mastered?
	Are the observations and inferences that surfaced in our analysis of state CRT assessments and examination of student work validated by what we see in these additional assessments? If not, how do we explain the contradictory evidence?
	What additional insights can we gain about student thinking and understanding?
	Have we verified a student-learning problem?
Concepts	Common classroom-based assessments
	Drill-down into common assessments
Activities	Activity 11.1: Facilitate Data-Driven Dialogue and Conduct Drill-Down Into Common Assessments and Other Local Student-Learning Data Sources

---

Vignettes: The Importance of Multiple Measures

When we looked at our state CRT data, life science was our weakest strand in sixth grade. We couldn't believe that. We thought we had a pretty strong life science program. It wasn't until we looked at our own local assessments and saw the same weakness that we became convinced we had to take a look at our life science curriculum.

On our state test, our students performed poorly in nonfiction reading comprehension. We looked at the passage and thought that they did poorly because there were many vocabulary words that were unfamiliar to our students. Then we looked at our district test. The passage seemed easier, but students still did poorly. Now we can say with more certainty that our students need help with this particular skill.

Our students did much better in mathematics problem solving on our state test than on our common assessments. This confused us at first. But when we looked more closely, we discovered that mathematics problem solving on the state test did not include any nonroutine mathematics problems. They were simple word problems. Our common assessments gave us a much fuller picture of students' problem solving. They need help breaking down the problems and using problem-solving strategies. We could never have figured that out from just our state test.

The Data Team learned from their drill-down into the state CRT strand, item-level, and released extended-response writings that their sixth-grade students are weak in physical science, specifically in understanding series and parallel circuits. To consult a second source of data, the Data Team gathered student work that asked students to describe their understanding of series and parallel circuits. The Data Team is now ready to drill down into the district's end-of-unit assessments that are administered to all sixth-grade students at the completion of the electric circuits unit.

WHAT IS TASK 11?

Tasks 6–10 focused on drilling down into state CRT data. The Data Coach used this data source to teach the entire drill-down process to the Data Team. However, there are limitations to any one data source in telling the whole story about student learning. For example, the state assessment may contain only four items in a particular content strand, not enough to draw solid conclusions; or item-level data and released items may not be available; or the state test may not be closely aligned with certain aspects of the local curriculum. In addition, any test is subject to measurement and sampling errors. Other sources of student-learning data, including district benchmark and/or annual assessments and common grade-level and course assessments, can be equally or even more valuable for identifying student-learning needs, particularly when these sources are closely aligned with local standards and curriculum, contain robust performance tasks, and are reported at the item level with released items.

In this task, the Data Team takes advantage of the local student-learning assessments they have available to them. They will again engage in Data-Driven Dialogue and use the same drill-down process as in Tasks 6–10, but now with district assessments and/or common classroom-based assessments—assessments that all students in the content area, course, and/or grade level under consideration have completed.

The team may do an entire drill-down on a new source of data or a partial one. For example, they might examine the aggregated district data for their school and then zero in on areas of interest such as the item-level data. More guidance on when to use which level is given in "Background Information for Data Coaches" below.

Overall, the goal of Task 11 is to enrich the data analysis and confirm or refute the findings from state CRT analysis and examination of student work. The Data Team examines common classroom-based assessments and/or district benchmark and summative assessments as additional sources of data to see whether the same findings or patterns continue to appear across the data sets. If they see discrepant data across the sources, they can consider if there are some situations for which the findings vary and ask why this might be so. If they see supporting data, they are in a better position to pinpoint what students are having difficulty with and choose areas for interventions. (Note: In Task 18, the Data Team will come back to common assessments to monitor student progress and implement short cycles of improvement.)

> **Facilitation Note:** While Tasks 6–10 are written for state CRT data, the Data Team can choose to start with Task 11 and do the entire drill-down first on their local assessment data.

The products of this task will be completed Data-Driven Dialogue charts for each of the four phases and each of the levels of drill-down being conducted. The Data Team will document their findings on the Identifying a Student-Learning Problem: Data Findings chart. An example of a completed chart, which now includes the data findings from the district common benchmark assessment as the third data source, is shown in Figure 4.24. In this example, the analysis of state CRT data (source 1) and classroom performance assessment data (source 2) led the team to analyze their district common benchmark assessment in physical science. The third column of the chart shows the results of undertaking the activities in Task 11: the team's findings from the aggregated and disaggregated data, item analysis, and examination of student work samples from that assessment.

BACKGROUND INFORMATION FOR DATA COACHES

What Are Common Assessments and Why Are They So Important?

We talked about standards. But it wasn't until we implemented common assessments that our teachers starting teaching to the standards.

> —Pam Bernabei-Rorrer, Mathematics and
> Data Coach, Canton City, Ohio

In Task 4 your team addressed the questions "How do we know if students have learned? What will we do if students don't learn?" Schools that are organized to know if students learn, and that intervene when they don't, make use of common assessments administered at the school or district level to students in a common grade level or content area. If all teachers at a specific grade level or within a content area administer the same assessments, they are considered "common" assessments.

In the Using Data Project, the sites that had benchmark common assessments in place along with quick access to item-level data and student work from those

Figure 4.24 Identifying a student-learning problem with findings from common assessments and other local sources.

Identifying a Student-Learning Problem: Data Findings

Content Area _____ Science _____   Grade Level _____ Sixth grade _____

Levels of data	Types of Data		
	1: _____ State CRT _____	2: Classroom performance task on floating and sinking (4–0 point scoring rubric)	3: District common benchmark assessment in physical science (multiple choice and open response)
	Years: 2004–2006	Years: 2005–2006	Years: 2005–2006
Aggregated results	Fifty-two percent of sixth-grade students were proficient in science, a 2 percent decrease from last year.	Sixty-five percent of all sixth-grade students scored a rubric rating of 2 or below.	Sixty percent of all sixth-grade students passed the physical science assessment.
Disaggregated results	There is a persistent achievement gap between White and Latino/a students in science; this year's gap was 38 percentage points.	Of the students who scored a rubric rating of 2 or below, 70 percent were Latino/a and 52 percent were White.	There was an achievement gap of 28 percentage points between White and Latino/a students.
Strand results	For two years, the lowest percentage of students were proficient in the physical science strand: 31 percent last year, 28 percent this year.	N/A (the assessment focused on one strand area)	N/A (the assessment focused on one strand area)
Item analysis	Of the eight physical science multiple-choice items, students performed worst on the three items pertaining to floating and sinking, with 23–30 percent proficient.	Students performed poorly on the part of the task that required them to explain why objects floated or sank.	Students performed most poorly on the 10 items assessing buoyancy, with an average of 22 percent proficient; six of these items asked students to predict which objects would either float or sink.
Student work	N/A (no state data provided)	Showed evidence of student misconceptions of the relationship between an object's composition and its buoyancy; students consistently relied on the object's size to determine its buoyancy	Showed evidence of misconceptions with the concept of buoyancy and of how the composition of an object relates to its buoyancy
Student-learning problem:			

assessments were those that made the greatest progress in closing achievement gaps and improving student learning (Zuman, 2006). A big advantage of the common assessments is that teachers can readily access the actual test items and item-level data, which are among the most valuable levels of analysis for instructional improvement and are not always available from state CRTs. And the data are available in a timely fashion, not at the end of the year, after the students have moved on. In addition, because they are "common" among teachers teaching the same content, they provide an ideal data set for collaborative inquiry. For all these reasons, common assessments become the engine for continuous improvement.

Common assessments are most typically used to monitor student progress on a regular basis—weekly, monthly, and/or quarterly. They are reviewed by teams of teachers, who make immediate adjustments in instruction to meet the needs of more students. In Task 11, however, the Data Team will use common assessments for a different purpose: to deepen their understanding of a student-learning problem on which to focus their improvement plan. They will design multiple strategies to address the student-learning problem later in the Using Data Process. In Task 18, the team will use common assessments for their more "common" purpose of frequently monitoring student learning.

Often teachers themselves create common assessments. In Canton City, Ohio, the Data Coaches created these assessments with input from the Data Team. In other cases, the school or district purchases commercially available benchmark assessments or makes use of assessments that are embedded in their curriculum materials.

A Data Team in Action: Canton City Middle School Mathematics. Part II: Developing Common Assessments—Pam Bernabei-Rorrer, Mathematics and Data Coach, Canton City, Ohio (continued from Task 4)

The mathematics Data Team now had their curriculum maps and the resources to teach their curriculum, but the driving force of their instruction was still missing. The crucial missing component was the collection of data that would enable the teachers to know how the students were performing so that adjustments could be made early in order to avoid the downward spiral of remediation. As Mathematics Coach, I developed common short-cycle assessments for each grade level in order to assess the students' understanding of the curriculum chunks. Not only did the assessments provide valuable data for the team, but the questions themselves assisted the teachers in understanding the meaning behind some of the vague state standards. These assessments were given at the end of each quarter, with the data analyzed quickly so that the grade-level teams could make effective instructional decisions based on the learning needs of their students. The common assessments were designed using the state achievement tests as a guideline, with 15 multiple-choice questions, two two-point short-answer questions, and one four-point extended-response question.

Rubrics were developed for the free-response questions to provide an outline of what was expected for the maximum points. The free-response questions were scored during departmental meetings at each of the schools. Not only did this assist me with the scoring, but it also gave teachers greater insight into student understanding. (Continued at the end of this task.)

What Kinds of Common Assessments Are There?

Common assessments can be either formative or summative. Summative common assessments are designed to measure students' learning and understanding at the conclusion of the teaching of the content, such as at the end of a unit or a quarter. We refer to these common assessments as benchmark common assessments.

Formative common assessments are designed to gauge student learning and understanding prior to and during the teaching of the content and to inform instructional decisions. This type of common assessment includes mathematics problems of the week, writing samples, science journals, and other student work that are administered by all teachers teaching the same grade level, content, or course. They are used regularly in the classroom and reviewed by the Data Team weekly or monthly. Summative assessments are often referred to as "assessments *of* learning," while formative assessments are "assessments *for* learning." In Task 11, the Data Team will be looking primarily at their common benchmark assessments, although they might select a particular formative assessment most relevant to the student-learning problem they are investigating.

Common assessments vary in format, from paper and pencil tests to performance-based tasks. The most robust of these common assessments, whether formative or summative, include both selected-response (multiple-choice) and performance assessments, which require students to generate rather than choose a response to accomplish complex tasks or solve realistic and authentic problems. Performance assessments are important to answering the question about whether students have learned for several reasons. Douglas Reeves (1998) argues that they are fairer than traditional pencil and paper tests because all students know the rules of the game—the specific expectations around what they know and what constitutes quality work. The specifics of what they measure are another advantage: Performance tasks are useful because they not only can assess procedural knowledge, but they can also provide a lens into application and thinking, for example, the extent to which students use mathematical reasoning, represent their work effectively, demonstrate understanding of specific concepts, or communicate about their thinking in writing or oral presentations.

Performance-based common assessments also encourage students to self-assess, revise, and continuously improve their product; both the process and the product are important. As Black and Wiliam (1998) note, "Self-assessment by pupils, far from being a luxury, is in fact an essential component of formative assessment" (p. 143). Love (2002) adds that performance assessments are learning experiences in themselves for students and help teachers gain rich insights into student thinking. Finally, they facilitate the very specific feedback—what students can do to close the gap between the learning goal and their current performance—associated with achievement gains (Black & Wiliam, 1998). Putting such assessments in place, if they are not already in use, will be an important part of the Data Team's work.

Making use of performance assessments (whether the team decides to create or adopt them) requires the team to clarify the criteria—the scoring guides or rubrics—by which they will judge the work and then learn to apply those criteria consistently. Using these guides helps teachers recognize quality while helping students know what they are aiming for and how to assess and improve their own work. Even in the many schools where standards and benchmarks are in place, it is not a given that teachers have studied what they mean or have developed the scoring guides or rubrics and common agreements about how student work should be assessed and what quality work actually looks like when these benchmarks are achieved. This will be important work for the Data Team and/or other relevant teams in the school to accomplish.

What Does It Mean to Engage in the Drill-Down Into Common or Other District Assessments?

In this task, the Data Team drills down into benchmark common assessment data using the same drill-down process they learned in Tasks 6–10. (See Task 5 for a refresher of the five levels of analysis in drill-down.) Ideally, the Data Team will apply the complete drill-down process they learned with CRTs to their own local data. But a full drill-down is not always necessary. If the student group sizes are small (roughly fewer than 15), disaggregated data will not be useful, and that level of analysis can be skipped. If the team's questions are very specific at this point, related to specific outcomes within a strand, they might skip directly to item analysis. Or they can focus on only the common assessments that tested the same skills and knowledge identified as problematic on the state CRT. Time is always a factor. They might take a quick look at aggregated and strand data, and then concentrate their energies on item analysis and student work.

What Are the Challenges and Pitfalls Inherent in This Task?

Desire to Move Ahead Faster

You and the Data Team have been working together for several months to learn as much as possible about student-learning needs from the state CRT and classroom student work. At this point in the process, the Data Team may ask, "Why do we have to look at yet another set of data?" It will be important for you to help them recognize the value of using an additional data source to validate and confirm the student-learning problem. In the authors' experience, too many school improvement teams start down the path of implementing "quick fixes" to problems that are not their real problems, leading to frustration and dead ends. Although the Data Team may think they are ready to move into resolving the student-learning problem after looking at CRT data, you will probably note a major shift in their perceptions once they begin the drill down into their common assessments. These are the data sets that are often most relevant to school-based educators: They are generated from their current students, using assessments that align with what is being taught and learned in the classroom, and provide data on what the current students know and do not know about the content. As a result, teachers often value them a great deal more than state-generated tests.

Access to Common Assessments

Ideally, your school or district already has a common assessment data collection system in place. More and more schools do. If this is the case for you and your Data Team, you will probably be able to obtain the data at aggregate, disaggregate, strand, item, and student work levels. However, if you do not have such a system in place, you and the Data Team can take on the responsibility of working with the principal or curriculum leaders in the school or district to develop, implement, and gather data from common assessments.

In some cases, the Data Team can get this process started themselves. If the team constitutes all of the fifth-grade mathematics teachers in the school, they might start with a common assessment given to all of their fifth-grade students. If the team is a cross-grade Data Team, the members might work with the teachers in their grade level to gain agreement to collect common assessment data. Once Data Teams see the value of common assessments, they are eager to get an organized data collection system in place. In one of the Using Data Project sites, the Data Team led the effort to obtain the software and hardware that made it possible to quickly scan and score classroom assessments; from that point on, gathering common assessments that could be disaggregated to the item level became common practice. The Resources section below provides suggestions for initiating schoolwide or districtwide common assessment systems.

Comparing Apples With Oranges

As the Data Team begins to look across multiple sources of student-learning data, it is important to know what can and cannot be compared. Different tests frequently define content strands and outcomes differently. For example, "mathematics in context" on one test may refer to simple word problems where students choose the operation and calculate. Another test may not have such a category, or may give it a different name, or may have a category of the same name but mean something very different. Use the test blueprints that delineate the specific outcomes and skills within strands and examine individual test items to determine these distinctions so you will know whether you are comparing "apples with apples" or "apples with oranges."

RESOURCES

Assessment: General

Atkin, J. M., Coffey, J. E., Moorthy, S., Sato, M., & Thibeault, M. (2005). *Designing everyday assessment in the science classroom.* New York: Teachers College Press.

Black, P., Harrison, C., Lee, C., Marshall, B., & Wiliam, D. (2003). *Assessment for learning: Putting it into practice.* Maidenhead, Berkshire, England: Open University Press.

Black, P., & Wiliam, D. (1998). Inside the black box: Raising standards through classroom assessment. *Phi Delta Kappan, 80*(2), 139–148.

Brown, J. H., & Shavelson, R. J. (2001). *Assessing hands-on science: A teacher's guide to performance assessment.* Thousand Oaks, CA: Corwin Press.

DiRanna, K., Osmundson, E., Topps, J., Barakos, L., Gearhart, M., Cerwin, K., et al. (2008). *Assessment-centered teaching: A reflective practice.* Thousand Oaks, CA: Corwin Press.

DuFour, R., Eaker, R., & DuFour, R. (Eds.). (2005). *On common ground: The power of professional learning communities.* Bloomington, IN: National Educational Service.

Hein, G. E., & Price, S. (1994). *Active assessment for active science: A guide for elementary teachers.* Portsmouth, NH: Heinemann.

Herman, J. L., Aschbacher, P. R., & Winters, L. (1992). *A practical guide to alternative assessment.* Alexandria, VA: Association for Supervision and Curriculum Development. (Out of print but available at http://www.cse.ucla.edu/CRESST/pages/products.htm/)

McTighe, J., & Ferrara, S. (1998). *Assessing learning in the classroom: Student assessment series.* Annapolis Junction, MD: National Education Association.

National Research Council. (2001). *Classroom assessment and the national science education standards.* Washington, DC: National Academy Press.

Pelligrino, J., Chudowsky, N., & Glaser, R. (Eds.). (2001). *Knowing what students know: The science and design of educational assessment.* Washington, DC: National Academy Press.

Popham, W. J. (2005). *Classroom assessment: What teachers need to know* (4th ed.). Boston: Allyn & Bacon.

Stiggins, R, J. (2006). *Student-involved classroom assessment* (4th ed.). Upper Saddle River, NJ: Prentice Hall.

Assessment: Common Assessments

Ainsworth, L. B., & Viegut, D. J. (2006). *Common formative assessments: How to connect standards-based instruction and assessment.* Thousand Oaks, CA: Corwin Press.

DuFour, R. (2004). What is a "professional learning community"? *Educational Leadership, 61*(8), 6–11.

Martin, R. A. (2006). Wake-up call brings a jolt of alignment to the curriculum: Teacher leaders hear the warning and develop common assessments to improve student achievement. *Journal of Staff Development, 27*(1), 53–55.

Stiggins, R., & Chappuis, J. (2006). What a difference a word makes: Assessment FOR learning rather than assessment OF learning helps students succeed. *Journal of Staff Development, 27*(1), 10–14.

Wiggins, G. (1998). *Educative assessment: Designing assessments to inform and improve student performance.* San Francisco: Jossey-Bass.

Assessment: Rubrics

Ainsworth, L., & Christinson, J. (1997). *Student-generated rubrics: An assessment model to help all students succeed.* Lebanon, IN: Dale Seymour.

Arter, J., & Chappuis, J. (2006). *Creating and recognizing quality rubrics.* Princeton, NJ: Educational Testing Service.

Arter, J., & McTighe, J. (2001). *Scoring rubrics in the classroom: Using performance criteria for assessing and improving student performance.* Thousand Oaks, CA: Corwin Press.

MAJOR ACTIVITIES FOR TASK 11

Activity	Time required	CD-ROM materials: Tasks 6–10 links	CD-ROM Toolkit: Relevant tools
Activity 11.1: Facilitate Data-Driven Dialogue and Conduct Drill-Down Into Common Assessments and Other Local Student-Learning Data Sources	Up to five Data Team meetings of variable length, depending on the levels of drill-down to be done	All handouts and resources from Tasks 6–10	All tools from Tasks 6–10

PREPARING FOR THE TASK

Follow the guidelines in Tasks 6–10 to prepare materials for each drill-down engagement.

MATERIALS PREPARATION

Follow the guidelines in Tasks 6–10 to prepare materials for each drill-down engagement.

DATA PREPARATION

Prior to gathering the common assessment and other district student-learning data, you will want to convene the Data Team to identify what data you will use as the basis for analysis in Task 11. Building on what you learned in Tasks 6–10 from the state CRT data and student work, you and your Data Team will want to identify local assessment data that help you better understand the student-learning problem or answer outstanding questions. For example, you may want to look at each of the quarterly benchmark assessments or just at one that assesses the same strand that was lowest in the state CRT. Or, if you have a lingering question about students' confusion about fractions, decimals, and percentages, you may want to use samples of the common problem-of-the-month that include this content.

Once you have settled on what data to collect, follow the guidelines for data preparation in Tasks 6–10, as the data at each level of the drill-down will be quite similar for your local and common assessments. Use or modify the data templates for Tasks 6–10 as needed to match how your local and common assessment data are reported. Often Data Teams work with common assessment data summarized for their grade level or common course, while individual teachers receive their own classroom data. It may be important for the safety of the group to keep individual classroom results anonymous.

> **Facilitation Note:** Several inexpensive software and scanning programs are available to provide quick turn-around on common assessments at the item level. Use of such programs is strongly recommended and has resulted in breakthroughs in the use of common assessments in many schools implementing the Using Data Process.

Additional Data Preparation Guidelines

Aggregated Data

Common assessments can be aggregated so that the Data Team is looking at student data from all classrooms in the school, in the district, and/or in schools similar to their own. Based on the way in which the data are reported, you may have the percentage of students "passing" or "failing" the assessment or the percentage of students meeting criteria for proficiency. If available, examining these data over three or more years is recommended. (See Data Examples and Data Templates, Task 6, on the CD-ROM.)

Disaggregated Data

Common assessments can be disaggregated by race/ethnicity, gender, economic status, educational status, language, and/or mobility if the numbers of these student populations are large enough. If available, examining these data over three or more years is recommended. (See Data Examples and Data Templates, Task 7, on the CD-ROM.) Common grade-level or course assessments are often also disaggregated by individual classrooms.

Strand Data

Depending on the common assessment, the entire assessment may focus on only a single strand area. For example, an end-of-unit assessment might focus on students' understanding of statistics and probability. In other cases, you might be able to cluster items on the assessment in ways that allow the Data Team to focus on very specific concepts within the strand area, such as series and parallel circuits within physical science. If available, examining these data disaggregated by relevant student populations is recommended (See Data Examples and Data Templates, Task 8, on the CD-ROM.)

Item-Level Data

If you have access to a data system that compiles student responses on the assessments, you will more than likely be able to engage in all four approaches to item-level data analysis, as described in Task 9. Each different type of software generates its own reports, which typically include the percentage responding to each possible multiple-choice answer in a way that is similar to the tables illustrated in Task 9 (see Data Examples and Data Templates, Task 9, on the CD-ROM).

Table 4.29 illustrates a computer-generated report from a local common assessment. The first column represents the test questions. The columns labeled 0–4 represent the multiple-choice options. The rows include the percentage of students responding to each option for questions 1–20. The underlined percentages are the correct responses.

Student Work

Student work can be collected from common assessments that contain short-answer or extended-response items. If your common assessments do not contain these items, you can use the guidelines provided in Task 10 to direct your collection of appropriate student work from classrooms.

DATA COACH NOTES

Activity 11.1: Facilitate Data-Driven Dialogue and Conduct Drill-Down Into Common Assessments and Other Local Student-Learning Data Sources

Follow the Data Coach Notes specific to Tasks 6–10 as you engage the Data Team in the drill-down into the common assessments. Provided here are some overarching guidelines to inform the Data Team's work:

- Identify the question(s) you want to answer through further data analysis.
- Identify existing sources of common assessments and district benchmark or annual assessments.
- Gather those data most relevant to your student-learning problem and outstanding questions.
- Organize and display the data for each level of the drill-down.
- Engage in Data-Driven Dialogue, recording predictions, observations, and inferences/questions on the Data Wall.
- Facilitate a discussion to help the Data Team synthesize what they learned from analyzing the common assessments. Ask them to document their learning on sentence strips and tape them to the Identifying a Student-Learning Problem: Data Findings chart.
- Reflect on new insights gained from examining multiple data sources.

Table 4.29 Sample Item-Level Report From Local Common Assessment, 10th-Grade Geometry, First Quarter

Res =	0	1	2	3	4
1		8%	2%	87%	4%
2	2%	6%	87%	2%	4%
3		2%		98%	
4		4%	8%	6%	83%
5				98%	2%
6		2%	4%		94%
7	2%	4%	71%	17%	6%
8		60%	4%	12%	25%
9		10%	12%	63%	15%
10			12%	4%	85%
11		2%		85%	13%
12		13%	6%	77%	4%
13	2%	8%	10%	2%	79%
14		69%	27%	4%	
15	2%		8%	4%	87%
16		98%		2%	
17		2%	27%	69%	2%
18	2%	12%	54%	23%	10%
19	6%	15%	46%	13%	19%
20			98%	2%	

Common Assessment Cautions

- Ensure that common assessments are not used to compare or evaluate teachers' effectiveness at a supervisory level. Do encourage teachers to share and learn from each other concerning effective teaching practices they are implementing in their classrooms.
- Use common assessments to celebrate and spread successes, not just to highlight weaknesses.
- Ensure that the assessments used are in fact "common," that is, that they align with the instructional materials and what is being taught in all classrooms.
- Consider validity and reliability as you create, adapt, or adopt common assessments. It is important that items measure what is intended and would produce a similar result if administered again.
- Carefully review assessments for cultural biases.
- If developing your own assessments, make sure that teachers have had adequate training in writing valid, reliable, and bias-free items.
- Use scanning devices and software to reduce time and effort compiling and reporting common assessment data.

A Data Team in Action: Canton City Middle School Mathematics. Part III: Using Common Benchmark Assessments—Pam Bernabei-Rorrer, Mathematics and Data Coach, Canton City, Ohio (continued from earlier in Task 11)

The next step along the pathway to increasing student achievement was to hold quarterly grade-level meetings to analyze the results of our common assessments. During these collaborative meetings, the team shared in Data-Driven Dialogue where they explored the data by creating visual representations of their own data, analyzed the data for root causes, and generated an action plan to improve student learning.

The quarterly assessments provided the mathematics Data Team with a picture of the students' thinking. By reviewing the item analysis from these assessments, we have been able to pinpoint exactly what the students' misconceptions are so that we can correct them in our instruction. For example, one question assessed student understanding that the slope of perpendicular lines are negative reciprocals of each other.

The question is as follows:

The equation of a line a is $y = 2x + 6$. Which equation represents a line that is perpendicular to a?

A. $y = -\frac{1}{2}x - 9$
B. $y = 2x - 6$
C. $y = \frac{1}{2}x + 6$
D. $y = 2x + 9$

When reviewing the item analysis, 42 percent of the students chose the equation with the negative y-intercept (B) rather than the negative slope (A). This showed that not only did the students not understand the idea of a negative reciprocal, but they were also confused as to what the numbers represent in the slope-intercept form of an equation. Rather than continue on with their teaching, the teachers chose to stop and implement more

(Continued)

(Continued)

activities that allowed the students to explore the difference between slope and y-intercept. For example, the Texas Instruments graphing calculators were very effective tools in cementing the students' understanding of these vital concepts of algebra. The Navigator system also allowed the teachers to do a quick assessment at the end of the instruction on slope and y-intercept to determine if the activities that they used in class were effective at increasing their students' understanding. The results showed that the students were able to address their own misunderstandings and had a more secure understanding of the algebra concepts. (Continued in Task 18.)

Task 12: Identify a Student-Learning Problem and Goal

Task-at-a-Glance

Purpose	Synthesize findings from data sources to articulate a clear student-learning problem and accompanying learning goal
Data	Student-learning data from Tasks 6–11
Questions to ask of data	Looking across all of the data, what are our student-learning problems?
	What evidence do we have that confirms these problems?
	If we have multiple student-learning problems, how do we prioritize them?
	What is our student-learning problem?
	What is our student-learning goal?
Concepts	SMART Goal
Activities	Activity 12.1: Walk Across the Data
	Activity 12.2: Identify and Prioritize Student-Learning Problems
	Activity 12.3: Articulate a Draft Student-Learning Goal Statement
	Activity 12.4: Plan to Engage Stakeholders and Review School Culture

WHAT IS TASK 12?

In Task 12, the Data Team synthesizes their findings from the drill-down into student-learning data to clearly define student-learning problems indicated in the data sources, prioritize problems based on those most in need of immediate attention, and articulate a draft student-learning goal. In the first three activities of this task, the Data Team members make sure that they are focusing on the "right" problem to solve, choosing areas that are most likely to have a positive impact on student learning and that address achievement gaps. They then begin to craft an effective, or "SMART," goal statement: one that is specific, measurable, attainable, relevant, and time bound.

The last activity in the task engages the Data Team in planning to engage other stakeholders and reflecting on their progress in "building the foundation" by revisiting the Program Elements Matrix (PEM) of a Using Data Culture from Task 4. The products for this task will be the final student-learning problem statement and the accompanying draft student-learning goal statement. (See examples in Tables 4.30 and 4.31, which are the problem and goal statements based on the student-learning data findings example at the beginning of Task 11.)

Table 4.30   Student-Learning Problem Statement: Example

Sixth-grade students at Lincoln Elementary School are below proficiency in science. A weak strand is physical science, particularly in buoyancy, as evidenced by these data:

- Fifty-two percent of students were proficient on last year's state science CRT; 28 percent were proficient in the physical science strand.
- Sixty-five percent of students scored a rubric rating of 2 or below on this year's school-administered performance task on floating and sinking.
- Sixty percent of students passed the most recent district common benchmark assessment in physical science.
- Twenty-three to thirty percent of students were proficient on test items relating to buoyancy on last year's state CRT; students also performed poorly on items relating to buoyancy on the other two data sources.

Within this subject area, a performance gap was noted between White and Latino/a students as evidenced by

- An achievement gap of 38 percentage points on last year's state CRT.
- Fifty-two percent of White students scored a rubric rating of 2 or below on this year's school-administered floating and sinking performance task, compared to 70 percent of Latino/a students.
- An achievement gap of 28 percentage points on the most recent district common benchmark assessment in physical science.

Table 4.31   Draft Student-Learning Goal Statement: Example

By next year we will improve sixth-grade students' learning in physical science and narrow achievement gaps between White and Latino/a students.

BACKGROUND INFORMATION FOR DATA COACHES

How Do We Identify the Student-Learning Problem to Address?

In Task 12, the Data Team will synthesize all that they have learned about student-learning problems. The first activity in this task engages them in a "walk-through" of their findings and suggests tools to help them prioritize when they have identified two or more student-learning problems. In the authors' experience, clarity about the problem to be solved is one of the most critical points in the process in terms of improving teaching and learning. You and the Data Team are well versed in the specific learning needs of the students at the grade level and in the content area that you have been investigating. This activity simply guides the Data Team to craft a data-based student-learning problem statement.

What Is a Good Goal Statement?

Effective goal statements are achievable and include enough information so that you will know when you have achieved them. Data Teams set SMART goals (Doran, 1981), which are

Specific: The goal identifies what will happen and with whom.

Measurable: The goal includes clear indicators of success.

Attainable: The goal can be accomplished with the strengths, abilities, and resources available.

Relevant: There is a documented need for the goal, and it is something you want to do.

Time Bound: The goal includes the time frame for when it will be met.

In Task 12, the Data Team will craft a preliminary goal statement based on their student-learning problem; the goal is the problem solved. The reason we call it preliminary is that the goal will not yet be completely "SMART." At this point in the process, the Data Team will write the goal statement so that it is specific, attainable, relevant, and time bound, but it will not yet include all of the measurable indicators of success. The Data Team will revisit the preliminary goal statement later when they add their solutions and clarify specific measures and indicators they will use to monitor the goal. Table 4.32 provides several examples of goals that are in this draft form and reflect the type of goal statement that the Data Team will write in this task.

What Are the Challenges and Pitfalls Inherent in This Task?

Scope of the Goal Statement

Depending on the scope of the Data Team's work and roles, the team will craft a preliminary goal statement that may be "large" or "small." For example, if the Data Team is a grade-level or content-area team, their goal will focus on improving student learning at the specific grade level or within the specific content area.

Table 4.32   Student-Learning Goals of Differing Scope

Grade-level- or content-area-specific goals	Schoolwide goals
By June, we will improve eighth-grade students' performance in our algebra strand and narrow achievement gaps between White students and Latino/a students.	By June, we will improve first-grade through fifth-grade students' performance in mathematical problem solving and narrow achievement gaps between African American and Latino/a students.
By February of next year, we will improve fourth-grade students' performance in scientific reasoning in life science and narrow achievement gaps between males and females.	By February of next year, we will improve seventh-grade through ninth-grade students' performance in scientific reasoning in all science strand areas and narrow achievement gaps between students on free and reduced lunch and those who are not.
Within one year, we will improve 10th-grade students' performance in language fluency and narrow achievement gaps between English Language Learners and students for whom English is a first language.	Within one year, we will improve all high school students' performance in reading comprehension and narrow achievement gaps between English Language Learners and students for whom English is a first language.

However, if the Data Team includes school staff from multiple grade levels or content areas, the goal will be broad enough so that students in all grades and each content area will be reached. What is important in this task is that the preliminary goal statement aligns with what has been learned through the drill-down into student-learning data. Table 4.32 provides examples of these two "sizes" of goals.

RESOURCES

Cozemius, A., & O'Neill, J. (1999). *The handbook for SMART school teams.* Bloomington, IN: National Education Service.

Cozemius, A., & O'Neill, J. (2006). *The power of SMART goals: Using goals to improve student learning.* Bloomington, IN: Solution Tree.

Love, N. (2002). *Using data/getting results: A practical guide for school improvement in mathematics and science.* Norwood, MA: Christopher-Gordon. (See pp. 106–109.)

MAJOR ACTIVITIES FOR TASK 12

Activity	Time required	CD-ROM materials: Task 12 link	CD-ROM Toolkit: Relevant tools
Activity 12.1: Walk Across the Data	60 minutes		Data Wall, Group Roles, Seven Norms of Collaboration
Activity 12.2: Identify and Prioritize Student-Learning Problems	60 minutes	Handout H12.1: Student-Learning Problem Statement: Example	Group Roles, Seven Norms of Collaboration, Spend-a-Buck, Student-Learning Problem Statement Template
Activity 12.3: Articulate a Draft Student-Learning Goal Statement	30 minutes	Resource R12.1: Student-Learning Problem Statement Template Resource R12.2: Draft Student-Learning Goal Statement Template Handout H12.2: Draft Student-Learning Goal Statement: Example	Group Roles, Seven Norms of Collaboration
Activity 12.4: Plan to Engage Stakeholders and Review School Culture	45 minutes		Group Roles, Seven Norms of Collaboration

PREPARING FOR THE TASK

- Read "Background Information for Data Coaches"; see the CD-ROM: Task 12 for handouts, resources, and sample goals and agenda; and review "Standard Procedures for Data Team Meetings" (see the introduction to Chapter 3 in this book and on CD-ROM). Although tool directions are embedded in the Data Coach Notes below, you can also reference in-depth descriptions of relevant Toolkit entries on the CD-ROM.

- Reorganize the Data Wall by grouping all of your graph charts together in a row. To the right of or below this grouping, create two rows of charts from Tasks 6–11. Row 1 will include all of the Observations charts; Row 2 will include all of the Inferences/Questions charts. Figure 4.25 illustrates this new arrangement. On the far right of all charts, post the Identifying a Student-Learning Problem: Data Findings chart with all of the sentence strips synthesizing learning from each analysis of data.

MATERIALS PREPARATION

- Make sure the charts from the Program Elements Matrix (PEM) of a Using Data School Culture (see Task 2) are posted on the wall.

- Make one copy for each Data Team member of Handouts H12.1 and H12.2.

- Add to the Toolbox four round color-coding labels for each Data Team member.

- Using Resources R12.1 and R12.2 as guides (see Figures 4.26 and 4.27), make large poster-size charts.

DATA PREPARATION

You will not need to do any data preparation prior to this task.

DATA COACH NOTES

 ### Activity 12.1: Walk Across the Data

1. Convene the Data Team, and ask team members to reflect on their use of the group roles during Task 11. Then rotate the roles, and add any additional responsibilities for each role.

2. Depending on how you decided to embed practice of your agreed-upon collaborative norms, guide the Data Team through the process you identified.

Figure 4.25 A reorganized data wall.

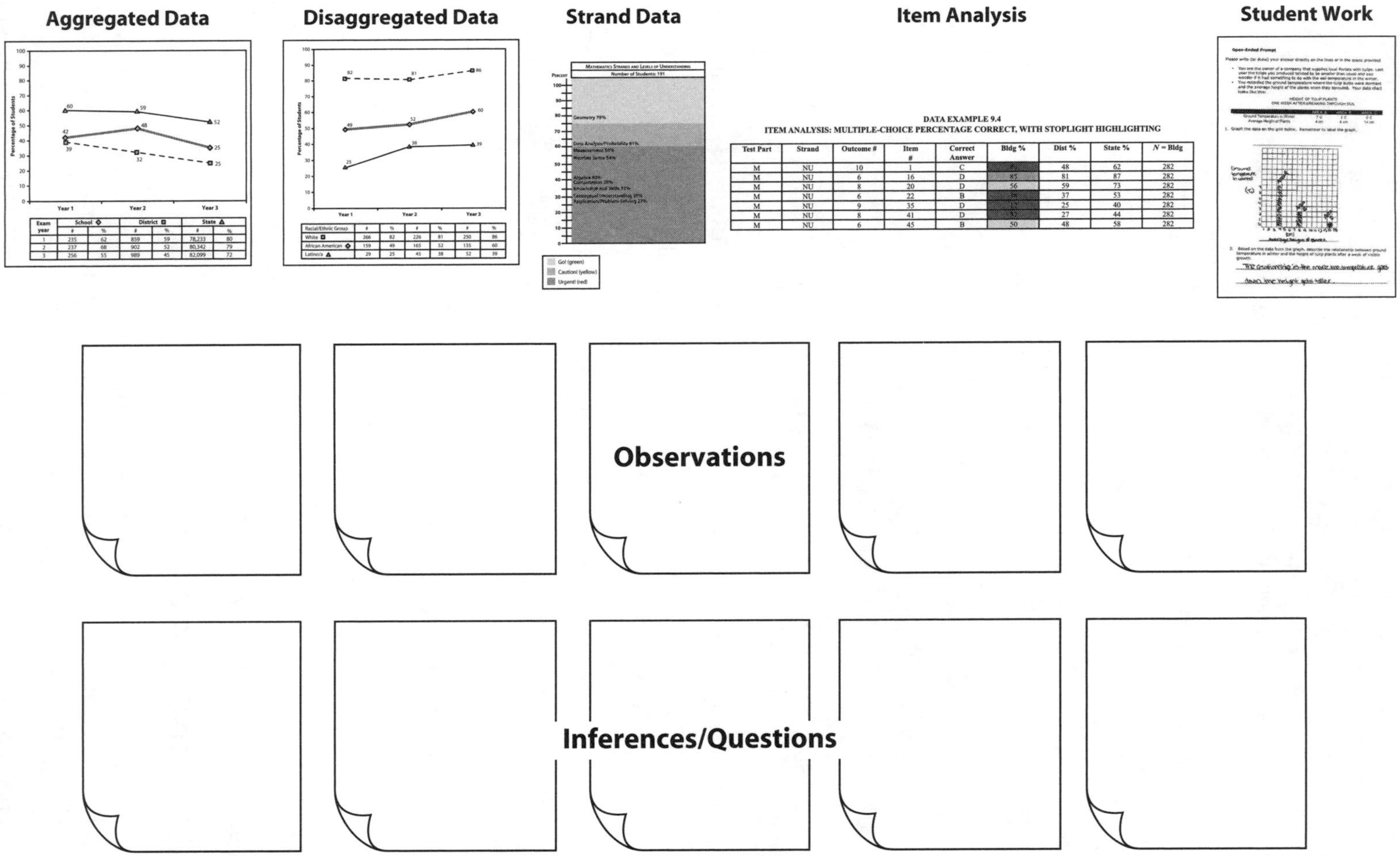

Aggregated Data

Disaggregated Data

Strand Data

Item Analysis

Student Work

Observations

Inferences/Questions

Figure 4.26 Student-learning problem statement template.

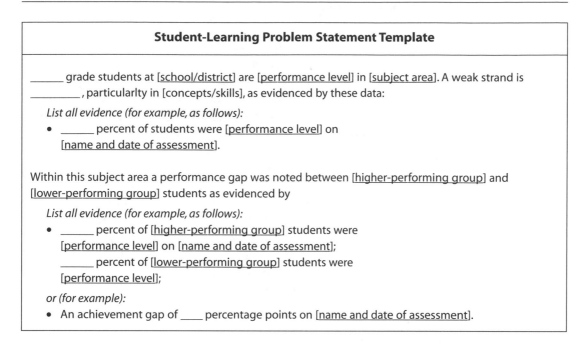

Student-Learning Problem Statement Template

_____ grade students at [school/district] are [performance level] in [subject area]. A weak strand is
_____ , particularlty in [concepts/skills], as evidenced by these data:

> List all evidence (for example, as follows):
> - _____ percent of students were [performance level] on
>   [name and date of assessment].

Within this subject area a performance gap was noted between [higher-performing group] and
[lower-performing group] students as evidenced by

> List all evidence (for example, as follows):
> - _____ percent of [higher-performing group] students were
>   [performance level] on [name and date of assessment];
>   _____ percent of [lower-performing group] students were
>   [performance level];
>
> or (for example):
> - An achievement gap of ____ percentage points on [name and date of assessment].

Figure 4.27 Draft student-learning goal statement template.

Draft Student-Learning Goal Statement Template

By [date], we will improve [grade or course] students' learning in [content strand] and narrow
achievement gaps between [higher-performing group] and [lower-performing group] students.

---

3. Direct the Data Team's attention to the reorganized Data Wall and the completed Identifying a Student-Learning Problem: Data Findings chart.

4. Facilitate a dialogue about what the Data Team has learned about the student-learning problem from their drill-down into each data source. Prompt them to consider the following questions:
- What connections do we see across the data findings?
- What data seem to support each other?
- What data are confounding? How do we explain these differences?
- Do we have a verified student-learning problem?

Sample Observations From a Walk Across the Data

- Mathematics problem solving shows up consistently as a weak area in our state and local assessments.
- Across the board, our students perform more poorly in reading comprehension with nonfiction than fiction.
- There is a pattern across all the data in statistics and probability. It is the lowest strand on our state and common assessments.
- Achievement gaps between our White and African American students are evident in our state as well as our district assessments.

Activity 12.2: Identify and Prioritize Student-Learning Problems

1. Familiarize the Data Team with the key aspects of the criteria for formulating an actionable student-learning problem statement. These are

Caution: When comparing different assessments, be careful that you are comparing apples with apples. Different tests define content strands and outcomes differently. (See challenges and pitfalls in "Background Information for Data Coaches" in Task 11.)

- Who? Clearly state the students impacted by the learning problem, including grade level and the race/ethnicity, gender, economic status, language, and/or educational needs of the students among whom achievement gaps have been identified.
- What? Clearly state the performance level (e.g., percentage below proficiency) as well as information about the content area and the knowledge, skills, and concepts that are in need of improvement.
- Based on what evidence? State the percentage of students scoring at what performance level and include the types of assessments, the component or skill area in need of improvement, and the dates of the source of the data set.

2. Distribute Handout H12.1. Then direct the Data Team's attention to the chart you prepared, Student-Learning Problem Statement Template (see Figure 4.26), and point out that the template incorporates all of the criteria. Engage the team in a discussion of how to translate the criteria into an actionable problem statement.

> **Facilitation Note:** It is important to distinguish a "student-learning problem" from a problem with the students themselves. The student-learning problem defines the specific content areas and achievement gaps on which the Data Team will focus their improvement efforts. By identifying the learning problem, the team is demonstrating its commitment to every student's learning, not blaming the students for the problem. Some Data Teams may want this point clarified.

3. Engage the Data Team in writing student-learning problem statements on chart paper, following the criteria and student-learning problem statement guidelines. Encourage them to focus on the findings that reflect "critical weaknesses" for students' learning. Post all student-learning problem statements on the Data Wall.

> **Facilitation Note:** Defining the student-learning problem can be very straightforward or very messy! For example, one Data Team discovered that all their greatest needs fell into just two concept areas in mathematics and showed up at only two grade levels. They were able to clearly articulate their data sources, which populations were affected, and the specific content that was weak. However, this situation is rare. More often, Data Teams find that there are multiple learning problems across multiple grade levels in multiple concept areas.
>
> Even though you will choose one priority goal to focus on, at this point the Data Team should write a student-learning problem statement for each critical weakness area they identified through the drill-down.

4. The Data Team will now prioritize the student-learning problem statements and decide which one needs to be immediately addressed and improved. Let the team know that they will be using a strategy called Spend-a-Buck (adapted from Kagan, 1997; used with permission).

5. Ask the Data Team to identify criteria they will use to choose priorities from among the student-learning problem statements. Post the criteria on chart paper.

Prioritizing Student-Learning Problem Statements

For every Data Team, one criterion will be that the student-learning problem reflects a critical weakness in student performance that needs to be addressed. In addition, schools operate in different contexts and within diverse settings, which will influence the priority placed on some of the other student-learning problems that have been identified. With your Data Team, consider what is important in your own context. Some other possible criteria to consider are the extent to which the problem

- Is systemic (e.g., a failure to develop understanding of pre-algebra concepts in sixth and seventh grade that results in "math phobia" and prevents students from performing well in high school mathematics and physics);
- Addresses critical inequities in your school (e.g., lack of access to higher-level mathematics or science courses);
- Is one of "high stakes" for meeting school, district, or state testing accountability and/or a graduation requirement; or
- Aligns with other school or district priorities (e.g., focusing on scientific language and communication because this aligns with a district focus on enhancing literacy).

6. Distribute four round color-coding labels to each person. Using the agreed-upon criteria to guide decisions, ask each person to "spend" the labels on the various student-learning problem statements by placing them next to the statements he or she thinks best meet the criteria, with a maximum of three spent on any one statement.

7. After each person has "spent" their round labels, rearrange the order of the student-learning problem statement sheets from those with the most votes to those with the least votes. Let the Data Team know that they will use the student-learning problem statement with the most votes to guide their next steps and improvement efforts. Assure them that they will revisit this prioritized list and continue to address each student-learning problem over time.

> **Facilitation Note**: If you are working with a Data Team that spans multiple grade levels and/or content areas, you may decide to have a smaller grade-level or content-area team address one or two of the student-learning problems, enabling you to address all of the problems that have been identified at one time.

 ### Activity 12.3: Articulate a Draft Student-Learning Goal Statement

1. Let the Data Team know that it is time to turn the student-learning problem into a goal that they will focus on for the rest of this round of the Using Data Process. This draft goal statement is simply a statement of the problem solved, and it will be refined and clarified in later tasks. Distribute Handout H12.2. Then direct the Data Team's attention to the chart you prepared, Draft Student-Learning Goal Statement Template (see Figure 4.27), and guide the Data Team to write a goal statement for the student-learning problem.

Think-Pair-Share Strategy

1. Each person thinks quietly about the statement.
2. Each person turns to one other person and shares his or her thoughts and ideas.
3. The team engages in a large-group sharing of the ideas.

2. Post the draft goal statement on the Data Wall.

3. Ask each person to engage in a "think-pair-share" dialogue (see sidebar). Use one or more of the prompts below for this activity:

- One concern I have about achieving the student-learning goal is. . . .
- One thing that excites me about achieving the student-learning goal is. . . .
- I know that achieving the student-learning goal will benefit students in my class by. . . .

 ## Activity 12.4: Plan to Engage Stakeholders and Review School Culture

1. Facilitate a discussion by asking Data Team members to focus on these questions:
   - What have been our most important learnings in Tasks 5–12?
   - What do we want to share with others?
   - How will we share what we learned with others?

2. Develop a short plan for how and with whom each person, as well as the entire team, will communicate the progress of the Data Team.

Involving Key Stakeholders

As the Data Coach, you may want to make plans for ensuring that the findings to date are shared and that there is support for the next steps in the process. Talk with other staff who have been involved with you in this process and share the student-learning problem and goal that you and the Data Team have identified. This is a good point in the process to schedule a meeting with staff, administrators, parents, community representatives, and/or the school board to report on the process and identify the areas on which you and the Data Team are focused as a result of analyzing the data. Such meetings may help foster "buy-in" for the action plans that the team will develop in later tasks.

Depending on the venue for presenting and sharing your lessons learned and findings, you can take sections of your Data Wall with you to show how the team has progressed and to illustrate the process they engaged in to reach their conclusions about the student-learning problems. Alternatively, you may find it easier to use electronic forms and charts that include photographs or graphics of your Data Wall. Whether communicating through short reports in faculty meetings, one-on-one conversations, or formal presentations, encourage everyone to highlight the following ideas:

- Purpose: Enhanced student learning
- Process: Thorough, collaborative, and research-based inquiry into student-learning data
- Findings: Confirmed student-learning problem through analysis of student data and verified causes based on research and local data
- Next steps: Make a compelling argument for support to take the necessary actions to engage in research and collect local data to verify the causes of the student-learning problems

CULTURE REVIEW
✓ Equity
✓ Teaching and Learning
✓ Data
✓ Collaboration
✓ Leadership and Capacity

3. Engage the Data Team in assessing where they are in building their foundation. Refer them back to the Program Elements Matrix of a Using Data School Culture they filled out in Task 2. What progress have they made so far on building collaborative communities? Using data? Equity? Celebrate progress and recommit to goals for improvement.

4. Provide time for reflection and processing of the Data Team's use of group roles and their agreed-upon collaborative norms.

5

Verifying Causes

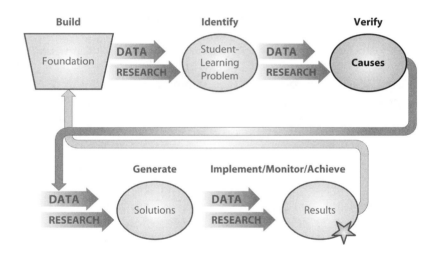

This chapter focuses on the third component of the Using Data Process, Verifying Causes, and includes Tasks 13 and 14. The activities in these two tasks enable you and your Data Team to identify and then verify the causes of your selected student-learning problem. You will use several tools to generate, organize, and prioritize the factors in your school contributing to the student-learning problem. The overall goal of this component is to verify the causes with data and research and select those causes that, when addressed, will most likely solve the problem. This is a critical juncture in the process. Too often, educators respond to student-learning problems prematurely, before they explore fully what practices in their system may be contributing to the problem and what research has to say about that problem. The Verifying Causes tasks keep educators from wasting time by pursuing unproductive solutions.

The specific tasks addressed in this component of the Using Data Process and the intended outcomes of each for Data Teams are synthesized in Table 5.1.

Table 5.1 Verifying Causes Tasks and Data Team Outcomes

Verifying causes: Tasks	*Data Team outcomes: The Data Team. . . .*
Task 13: Conduct Cause-and-Effect Analysis	• Identifies and prioritizes the possible causes contributing to the student-learning problem • Generates research questions for further investigation
Task 14: Verify Causes Through Research and Local Data	• Verifies the contributing causes by consulting relevant research and gathering and analyzing local data

GATHER DATA NEEDED FOR TASK 14

Prior to starting Task 6, you assembled a great deal of student-learning data using the data inventory list. You will now gather additional data to support the Data Team's work during Task 14 (none is required in Task 13), in this case data about school practices in the areas of curriculum, instruction, assessment, equity, and critical supports. Although you and the Data Team will determine the exact local data questions and sources during Task 14, anticipate that you will be gathering data related to the identified student-learning problem. If you have access to any data that have been collected at a prior time that directly relate to the teaching and learning of the content at the grade level for which you and the Data Team have identified the student-learning problem, you can expedite Task 14 by compiling the data in advance. Collaborate with your district administrative office, assessment department, and/or external project evaluators to obtain as much of the previously collected data as possible.

A suggested inventory list for Task 14 data is included below. For examples of some of these data, see CD-ROM: Task 14, Data Examples.

Possible sources of data about curriculum, instruction, and assessment practices in the content area and grade level of focus for the Data Team and about equity and critical supports include

- Teacher surveys
- Student surveys
- Parent surveys
- Administrator surveys
- Textbook or programs adopted
- Courses taught
- Curriculum documents
- Assessments being used
- Records of kit use in science
- Student interviews
- Teacher interviews
- Parent interviews
- Classroom observations
- Teacher qualifications
- Teacher certification
- Enrollment data, disaggregated by student populations
- Enrollment data, cross-tabulated by students scoring proficient and above
- Professional development offered
- Teacher participation in professional development
- Culture surveys
- Leadership surveys
- Professional development surveys
- Classroom and school walk-throughs

Task 13: Conduct Cause-and-Effect Analysis

Task-at-a-Glance

Purpose	Identify and prioritize the causes that contribute to the student-learning problem and engage in dialogue about assumptions and beliefs
Data	Student-Learning Problem Statement from Task 12; Phase 4: Infer/Question charts from Tasks 6–11
Questions to ask	What do we believe are the causes that contribute to the student-learning problem?
	What causes lie within the areas of curriculum? Instruction? Assessment practices? Equity issues? Critical supports? Teacher preparation?
	How do we keep the causes focused on classroom and schoolwide practices and not blame students or their backgrounds?
	Which causes are most closely linked to student learning?
	How do we prioritize our list of causes?
	Which causes warrant further investigation through research?
	What guidelines should we use to inform the research we gather?
Concepts	Cause-and-effect analysis
	Primary versus secondary sources
Activities	Activity 13.1: Generate Possible Causes
	Activity 13.2: Dialogue About Causes and Their Underlying Assumptions
	Activity 13.3: Identify Causes for Further Verification
	Activity 13.4: Frame Research Questions Based on Causes

A Data Team in Action: Fishbone Cause-and-Effect Analysis

After drilling down into student-learning data, the sixth-grade science teachers from different elementary and middle schools in one school district began the process of generating their ideas for the possible causes to the student-learning problem by using a Fishbone graphic organizer. The Data Coach provided a context for true brainstorming to occur, and the team generated the causes illustrated in Figure 5.1.

The Data Coach then asked, "Which of these causes do we have control over? Which ones can we address in our schools?" The Data Team began generating ideas for addressing some of the causes. For example, they suggested providing supplemental activity-based ideas for parents to engage with at home to address the cause "lack of exposure to scientific concepts at home." From this emerged the idea of tracking students into remedial courses to help students "get up to speed."

One of the teachers stated, "No, we can't do that. We tried tracking at our school two years ago and it was a disaster. The students who normally did well started to do poorly in all subject areas. The students who were already struggling did even worse. We eliminated the tracking process within three months of starting it. Our school assessments, student work, and grades showed almost

(Continued)

(Continued)

Figure 5.1   First-draft Fishbone.

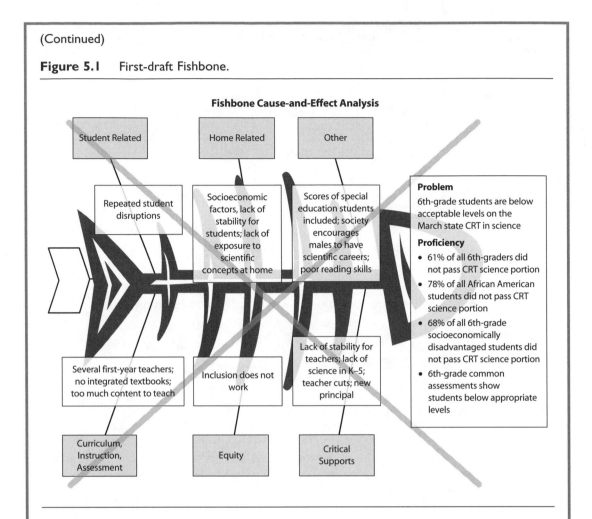

immediate evidence that the idea was ineffective for all students. But what did work, especially for our highly disruptive students, was to do some hands-on science stations in class."

A second teacher added, "Yeah, last month we did the same thing in my class. It has been impossible to manage the disruptive students, and I have a class that is 55 percent students with exceptional needs. Another teacher helped me and we set up these hands-on stations that the kids rotated to. It was amazing! All of the students were engaged for over an hour and there were no behavior problems!"

This prompted another teacher to ask, "Well, this makes me think that a lot of our possible causes don't have anything to do with how to really solve our student-learning problem. Maybe it's what we are, or aren't, doing in our classrooms. The only thing we do have control over and can really change is how we deliver content and how we teach. What if we all tried to do more with these hands-on stations?"

The Data Coach suggested that, instead of moving too quickly to determine strategies to solve the problems, they revisit the Fishbone and think through the causes. The team eagerly agreed and decided to start a new Fishbone graphic. One of the teachers started a Parking Lot sheet and noted "hands-on learning," "need to assess learning," and "need new instructional materials" to make sure that when they were ready for generating solutions they remembered this conversation.

In later Data Team meetings, they verified and confirmed the cause, "Our instructional practices do not help students learn science," and their first strategy was, "Sixth-grade teachers meet during the summer to develop hands-on and inquiry-based lessons and activities that lead to a common science curriculum."

WHAT IS TASK 13?

The purpose of Task 13 is to identify the possible causes to the student-learning problem. This is another critical juncture in the Using Data Process. Often, Data Teams are anxious at this point to move away from data collection and start taking action. It is important to help the Data Team understand that their success requires tackling the most important causes of the student-learning problem as well as those that are within their control and are verified through research and local data. When schools move too quickly to resolve a cause before verifying that it is in fact the cause, they can end up on the wrong road.

For example, Victoria Bernhardt, noted for her work in using data analysis with schools, tells the story of one California school that received data showing that 90 percent of their high school graduates were dropping out of college in the first year. Initially assuming that the cause was lack of social skills, they were about to spend time and money to solve that problem, but fortunately they decided to slow down and collect data from the students. What they discovered was that the problem did not result from poor social skills, but from poor writing skills (V. Bernhardt, personal communication, 2001). (See the Clark County, Nevada, case study in Chapter 8 for an additional example of the value of verifying causes before taking action.) In other cases, the team might choose a cause that is inconsistent with research. For example, they might decide to institute tracking of students by ability, as was suggested and ultimately rejected in the Data Team in Action scenario.

In Task 13, the Data Team takes the first step toward solving the right problem. They conduct a cause-and-effect analysis, prioritize the causes, and identify causes to further verify and research before and during Task 14. The team engages in facilitated dialogue about the causes of the student-learning problem and probe the underlying assumptions and beliefs of those causes. Throughout Task 13, the Data Coach plays a critical role in helping the Data Team assess whether the causes they are generating reflect diverse perspectives, focus on systemic causes, and do not blame students, families, or the community. The Data Coach also guides the team to reflect on their own instructional practices, as the need to reteach, teach in a different way, teach in more depth, or teach at a different point in the curriculum frequently underlie problems related to student understanding.

The products for this task will be a list of prioritized possible causes of the student-learning problem (see Verify Causes Tree example in Figure 5.2) and a set of questions to guide the collection and analysis of the research to further investigate these (see examples in Table 5.2). Between Tasks 13 and 14, the Data Team will gather research that they will study and act on in Task 14. In Task 14, they complete the Verify Causes Tree.

BACKGROUND INFORMATION FOR DATA COACHES

What Is Cause-and-Effect Analysis?

"We cannot fix anything until we know what is wrong. By focusing on dissolving the most fundamental causes for problems, we then select strategies that are properly targeted on the cause rather than on the symptoms," explains Paul Preuss (2003, p. 2). This is the purpose of cause-and-effect analysis—to identify causes that,

Figure 5.2 Verify Causes Tree example for the end of Task 13.

Student-Learning Problem	Sixth-grade students at Nevazoh Middle School are performing below proficiency in mathematics. A weak strand is mathematics problem solving. There is an achievement gap of 37 percent between White and African American students.				
	Curriculum	**Instruction**	**Assessment**	**Equity**	**Critical Supports**
Possible Causes	Does not emphasize mathematics problem solving	Classes are too heterogeneous	Not using performance assessment tasks with rubrics	Tracking: lower-track students get more drill and practice	Teachers do not feel prepared to teach nonroutine problem solving
Research Findings					
Local Data Findings					
Verified Causes					

Adapted from Preuss (2003) used with permission.

if acted on, will have a positive effect on solving the student-learning problem. There are several tools (see Toolkit) that can be used for cause-and-effect analysis, including the following:

- Cause Cards, a tool with multiple possible causes listed on cards for the team's consideration
- Fishbone Cause and Effect, a graphic organizer to help the Data Team identify and visually depict systemic causes to the student-learning problems
- Impact/Effort Matrix, for prioritizing causes
- Verify Causes Tree, which incorporates the use of research and local data before verifying a possible cause
- Why? Why? Why? for probing more and more deeply into why the student-learning problem exists

This task is written based on the Verify Causes Tree. However, you can substitute one of the others or use them in combination, as discussed in the Toolkit for each and in the Data Coach Notes below.

What Will I Want to Consider and Be Prepared to Do to Facilitate Effective and Respectful Dialogue During This Task?

Facilitating dialogue about possible causes can be challenging. Although your Data Team has been discussing inferences about the data throughout the Using Data Process, Task 13 moves them into new territory and is when the "blame game" can surface or resurface. For example, you may hear Data Team members suggesting causes such as "Students just don't have the motivation," "Parents aren't interested in education," or "Students with exceptional needs are unable to learn the content." This task opens up the opportunity for deep reflection about Data Team members' beliefs and assumptions and about how their own practices may be contributing to the student-learning problem. Such discussions require a culture that supports safe and honest self-reflection.

Throughout the Using Data Process you and the Data Team have consistently relied on your collaborative norms to promote constructive dialogue and enhance your team's effectiveness, and during Task 13 the norms continue to play a critical role. One norm in particular, paraphrasing, can be especially helpful. It is a norm that Garmston and Wellman (1999) see as essential for group understanding and is very important in teamwork for the following reasons:

- It allows a speaker to know that he or she has been heard and understood.
- It honors the worth of group members by recognizing their contributions.
- It moves the process forward by synthesizing or summarizing what has been said.
- It allows for any vagueness, lack of clarity, or imprecision to be corrected.
- It opens the way for probing for details and elaboration.

If you have not been using this norm, you may suggest that the group add it to your collaborative norms during this task.

What Guidelines Should We Use to Inform the Research We Gather?

Between Tasks 13 and 14, the Data Team will work in small groups to gather the research needed to address each of the areas identified in this task as a possible cause. Here is a set of questions to guide your selection of quality resources:

- Is the author an authority on the subject? Has he or she contributed empirical work on the subject? Have others based their work on this author's work?
- When was the material written? (More recent materials reflect the most up-to-date information.)
- What was written about or tested? Does the material contain research that supports your needs?
- Does the source provide a well-designed study? A thoughtful analysis? An original way of viewing the topic?

In addition to these questions, you and the Data Team can set other criteria for selecting articles, books, or studies. For example, U.S. Department of Education guidelines urge educators to use research studies that are scientifically based. Scientifically based studies use rigorous data analysis; provide reliable and valid data; use experimental or quasi-experimental designs that assign subjects to different conditions with appropriate controls, with a preference for random-assignment experiments; and have been accepted by a peer-reviewed journal or approved by a panel of independent experts through a comparably rigorous, objective, and scientific review. In recent years, several studies following these guidelines have been published and are readily available.

If possible, make sure that you and the Data Team gather research from multiple sources, both primary and secondary. Primary sources are reports of research written by the researchers themselves. These sources are often found in peer-reviewed journals, books, dissertations, summaries of research, conference proceedings, and evaluation reports. Secondary sources are reports or discussions of someone else's work or research. These sources are often found in books, articles in periodicals, point-of-view or opinion pieces, and how-to manuals.

A list of print and Web-based research sources and organizations is on the CD-ROM in Handout H13.2.

What Are the Challenges and Pitfalls Inherent in This Task?

As noted previously, one of the greatest challenges in this task is shifting the Data Teams' conversation from blame to collective responsibility. Part of building the foundational culture of the Data Team and the entire school is to ensure that all teachers and school personnel are committed to their role and responsibility to improve teaching and learning and close achievement gaps (see Task 4). In Task 13, it is especially important that the team act consistently with that commitment.

During this task, you will facilitate dialogue about assumptions and beliefs. What do you do when things go "wrong"? Listed here are some strategies to help you promote deep and respectful dialogue and reflection. (Special thanks to Franklin CampbellJones, Brenda CampbellJones, and Kimberly Kinsler for many of these suggestions.)

Dialogue Suggestions

Discuss undiscussables. On an index card each team member writes a topic that is "undiscussable" but does not sign the card. The cards are placed in the center of the table and team members select a card, one at a time, and engage in facilitated dialogue of the topic.

Final Word Dialogue (see Toolkit). This process can be particularly effective for facilitating dialogue since it gives time for each person to think and reflect before responding. You can choose for dialogue an article that illustrates how schools are closing achievment gaps and improving student learning (see the "Dialogue About Research" suggestion and the Resources section below).

Facilitation Suggestions

Scaffold the cause-and-effect analysis by providing the categories. Rather than have the Data Team generate its own categories for causes either on the Fishbone or on the Verify Causes Tree, supply the categories to guide their brainstorming. For example, label the Possible Causes boxes on the Verify Causes Tree or the spines of the Fishbone with "Curriculum," "Instruction," "Assessment," "Equity," and "Critical Supports" (e.g., professional development, leadership, and school culture), as illustrated in Figure 5.2. As the team gains more experience, they can generate their own categories.

Fishbone redo. If you select the Fishbone cause-and-effect tool and find that the Data Team generates causes that blame others, you might consider this strategy: Tear up the first Fishbone graphic, as was done in the vignette on page 253, and start again. While this might seem drastic, some teams have so many insights after dialoguing about their assumptions and reading about equity issues that they want to consider the first Fishbone as a warm-up and start fresh with a new one that is guided by their new ideas.

Use white-out tape. Once the Verify Causes or Fishbone graphic organizer has been developed, ask the Data Team if there is anything on the graphic that anyone in the group cannot live with. If so, cover these comments up with white-out tape and facilitate a dialogue about why the cause was unacceptable. Then help the Data Team reframe the causal statement. For example, one Data Team reframed a cause that blamed students' cultural backgrounds to "Our curriculum does not reflect the diversity of our students."

The Cultural Proficiency Continuum (see Toolkit). Revisit the Cultural Proficiency Continuum introduced in Task 3. Ask the Data Team to consider where on the continuum their causes might fall, and help them reframe causes so that they are closer to the culturally proficient end of the continuum.

Use of Research or External Resources

Dialogue about research. Introduce the Data Team to real-world examples of schools that have improved in ways that meet all students' learning needs and are making progress in narrowing or closing achievement gaps. For example, research conducted in the Pittsburgh public schools demonstrated that when African American students had access to a rigorous mathematics curriculum, the achievement gap between African American and White students closed (Briars & Resnick, 2002). Engaging the team in dialogue about research findings such as these can be eye-opening and build new understanding of what is possible.

Provide examples from reflective practitioners. Reflective practitioners such as Vivian Gussin Paley, author of *White Teacher* (2000), provide models of educators who are confronting their own racism and transforming their teaching and relationships with children. Reading *White Teacher*, for example, can be inspirational and seed rich dialogue.

Invite a skilled facilitator. An outside expert can be very helpful in leading challenging and important dialogues. Consider inviting such a person to help your Data Team.

RESOURCES

Resources for cause-and-effect analysis and dialogue

Briars, D., & Resnick, L. B. (2002). *Standards, assessments—and what else? The essential elements of standards-based school improvement* (CSE Technical Report 528). Los Angeles: National Center for Research on Evaluation, Standards, and Student Testing.

Haycock, K., Jerald, C., & Huang, S. (2001). Closing the achievement gap: Done in a decade. *Thinking K–16, 5*(2), 3–22.

Love, N. (2002). *Using data/getting results: A practical guide for school improvement in mathematics and science.* Norwood, MA: Christopher-Gordon. (See pp. 102–106.)

Paley, V. G. (2000). *White teacher.* Cambridge, MA: Harvard University Press.

Preuss, P. G. (2003). *Root cause analysis: School leader's guide to using data to dissolve problems.* Larchmont, NY: Eye on Education.

For selected print sources of primary and secondary research and Web-based research sources, see CD-ROM: Handout H13.2.

MAJOR ACTIVITIES FOR TASK 13

Activity	Time required	CD-ROM materials: Task 13 link	CD-ROM Toolkit: Relevant tools
Activity 13.1: Generate Possible Causes	15 minutes	PowerPoint Slides S13.1–S13.2	Cause Cards, Fishbone Cause-and-Effect Analysis, Verify Causes Tree, Why? Why? Why?
Activity 13.2: Dialogue About Causes and Their Underlying Assumptions	30–45 minutes		Group Roles, Seven Norms of Collaboration
Activity 13.3: Identify Causes for Further Verification	15 minutes		Spend-a-Buck or Impact/Effort Matrix, Verify Causes Tree
Activity 13.4: Frame Research Questions Based on Causes	20 minutes	Handout H13.1: Verify Causes Table: Research Handout H13.2: Selected Research Sources	Group Roles, Seven Norms of Collaboration

PREPARING FOR THE TASK

Read "Background Information for Data Coaches"; see the CD-ROM: Task 13 for handouts, PowerPoint slides, and sample goals and agenda; and review "Standard Procedures for Data Team Meetings" (see the introduction to Chapter 3 in this book and on CD-ROM). Although directions for the Verify Causes Tree tool are embedded in the Data Coach Notes below, you can also reference in-depth descriptions of other relevant tools on the CD-ROM. Read through those and select which additional ones, if any, you will use with your Data Team.

MATERIALS PREPARATION

- Make one copy for each Data Team member of Handouts H13.1 and H13.2.
- Post the Student-Learning Problem Statement, Draft Student-Learning Goal Statement, and all Phase 4: Infer/Question charts from Tasks 6–11 on the wall.
- On chart paper, create two tables using the examples of Slide S13.2 (Verify Causes Tree) and Handout H13.1 (Verify Causes Table: Research).
- Prepare to show PowerPoint slides.

DATA COACH NOTES

 ### Activity 13.1: Generate Possible Causes

1. Guide the Data Team through the process you have identified for engaging with your agreed-upon collaborative norms and group roles.

2. Review the purpose of Task 13 with the Data Team. Ask them to focus on the Phase 4: Infer/Question charts from Tasks 6–11 to initiate their thinking about the possible causes of the student-learning problem.

Slide S13.2

3. Display Slide S13.2 (Verify Causes Tree), and explain that the team will have an opportunity to use this graphic to help determine possible causes for the identified student-learning problem.

> **Facilitation Note:** If you are using another tool (e.g., Fishbone, Cause Cards, or Why? Why? Why?) to generate possible causes, simply substitute their Toolkit directions for the steps in this activity. Then resume following these Data Coach Notes again with Activity 13.2.

4. Explain that the Verify Causes Tree tool (adapted from Preuss, 2003; used with permission) is predicated on the belief that problems are best solved by addressing root causes, rather than by merely addressing the immediately obvious symptoms.

5. Use the graphic to describe the iterative nature of the process. The student-learning problem is placed in the box provided. The team will then organize their inferences generated to date and synthesize them into possible causes. They will determine if there are additional possible causes they have not yet considered. Through a winnowing process, such as Spend-a-Buck (see Toolkit) or the Impact/Effort Matrix (see Toolkit), the team will limit the number of possible causes to those that they think can be addressed effectively. The possible causes should be under the team's and/or school's control and "do no harm" to any group of students. Additionally, these causes should be of sufficient significance to create change to improve student learning. Finally, in Task 14, the team will verify causes through research and examination of local practice. Those possible causes that are confirmed by both investigations will be considered verified causes and will form the basis for generating solutions.

6. Post the Verify Causes Tree chart on the wall. Encourage the team to use the same categories from the School of Our Dreams (see Task 4) as organizers for their inferences—curriculum, instruction, assessment, equity, and critical supports (e.g., policies, technology, professional development, school culture)—but they may also choose to create categories of their own. Have the team review their inferences from Tasks 6–11 and, using those and others that now occur to them, create lists of possible causes for each of the categories.

Activity 13.2: Dialogue About Causes and Their Underlying Assumptions

1. The Data Team will now take a reflective look at the causes they have identified. This dialogue is the first step in helping the team identify possible causes that they can verify and confirm through research and local data. Use the following questions to facilitate the Data Team's dialogue:

- Is the way in which the cause is stated harmful to any person or group of persons?
- Is the stated cause based on assumptions that blame any person or group of persons?
- Does the cause imply a belief or assumption that we need to further explore or discuss before allowing it to remain on the graphic organizer?
- Have we included causes that diverse populations might consider important?
- Have we fully considered the ways in which classroom practices contribute to the student-learning problem?
- Have we considered systemic causes?
- Which of these causes are within our control to act upon?
- Which ones are closer to the "proficiency" end of the Cultural Proficiency Continuum?
- Which can have the greatest impact on solving the student-learning problem?
- Which can be verified with additional data and research?
- Which can be addressed given our resources and time constraints?
- Which do we want to investigate further?

> **Facilitation Note:** As you facilitate this dialogue, pay attention to these critical aspects of the dialogue and your role as the facilitator:
>
> - Are we using our norms of collaboration to enhance our dialogue?
> - Are we practicing paraphrasing to clarify assumptions?
> - Are we referencing data that provides the evidence for our assumptions?
> - Are we challenging causes that blame any population? Are we surfacing the assumptions that underlie those causes?

 ## Activity 13.3: Identify Causes for Further Verification

1. Use a winnowing process, such as Spend-a-Buck, the Impact/Effort Matrix (see Toolkit), or the Symbol Winnowing Process (see box), to narrow down possible causes in each category. Transfer the "winners" to large Post-its, and place them in the Possible Causes row on the Verify Causes Tree, one Post-it per box.

Symbol Winnowing Process

Another winnowing process involves asking the team to identify the criteria they will use to prioritize the causes, assigning a symbol or code for each criterion, and then marking the symbol next to the causes that meet their criteria. Four criteria are suggested below. Expand on or modify this list as appropriate:

- Place a ▲ next to the causes you think you have control to change.
- Place a ☺ next to the causes that can have the greatest impact on student learning.
- Place a ★ next to the causes that you are most eager to investigate further through research and local data.
- Place a $ next to the causes that you believe you have the time and resources to address.

Ask the team to identify up to four causes that have the most symbols next to them (i.e., meet the most criteria). These will be the possible causes they will investigate further.

---

2. Make sure that the team agrees that the topics in each Possible Cause box is under their control, will do no harm to any group of students, and has the possibility of being solved through a rigorous action plan.

 ## Activity 13.4: Frame Research Questions Based on Causes

1. Explain that in this step the team will determine if the possible causes are supported by research. If so, they will verify the extent to which this cause is occurring

Handout 13.1

Verify Causes Table: Local Data		
Research Question	Research Source	Research Findings

Table 5.2 Two Types of Research Questions

Questions to determine whether research validates this as a possible cause	Questions to elicit what we can learn from research about this cause
Does tracking contribute to achievement gaps between White and African American students? To poor mathematics achievement overall?	What kinds of grouping practices help students succeed? What are the short- and long-term effects of tracking?
Does inclusion have a positive effect on students with exceptional needs? On general education students?	What are the features of a successful inclusion program?
Is class size a factor in student achievement?	What class size is optimal for students?
Does the use of manipulatives help students with proportional reasoning?	What are best practices for helping students master proportional reasoning?

in their school in Task 14. If not supported by research, the cause is deleted and another one can be put in its place to be verified.

2. Distribute Handout H13.1, and display the chart of the Verify Causes Table: Research. Assist the team to develop research questions to ask about their possible causes by introducing two types of questions: (1) questions to determine whether research validates this as a possible cause and (2) questions to elicit what we can learn from research about this cause (see examples of each in Table 5.2). The answers to both kinds of questions will help them as they verify causes and develop action plans. Ask the team to generate both kinds of questions and add them to their handout. Record their questions on the Verify Causes Table: Research chart.

3. Distribute Handout H13.2, and discuss resources the team can use to verify their cause through research. Add these to the chart, and ask members to add them to their handouts.

4. Assign research questions to pairs of team members, and provide ample time for them to gather, read, and analyze the research between meetings. Ask them to record their findings on Handout H13.1 and bring them to the next meeting. Offer your assistance in gathering relevant research as needed. (Alternatively, bring relevant research to the next meeting for team study; see Task 14.)

5. Ask each Data Team member to write a brief statement summarizing what he or she has learned today, and then facilitate sharing. Provide time for reflection and processing of the Data Team's use of group roles and their agreed-upon collaborative norms.

> **Facilitation Note:** Some Data Teams have found they wanted more time to examine the assumptions and beliefs that surfaced when they identified causes of the student-learning problem. If needed, schedule a separate meeting (prior to the next scheduled one, where you will investigate the research) to continue your dialogue and delve further into the assumptions and beliefs that may be getting in the way of providing rich educational opportunity for all students. This may be especially appropriate if you decide to bring in an external facilitator to help the team dig more deeply into these issues to strengthen their foundation and/or want to read and discuss research or examples of reflective practitioners, but did not have time available during this Data Team meeting.

Task 14: Verify Causes Through Research and Local Data

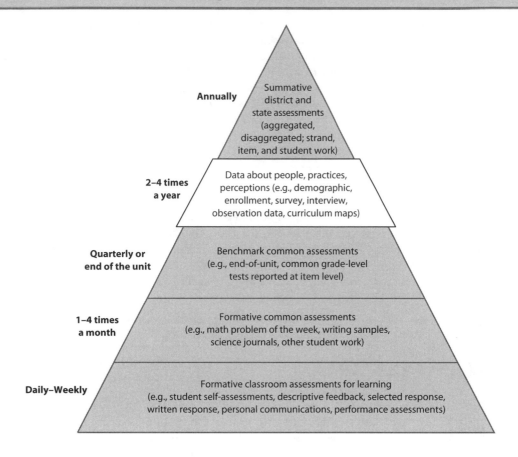

Annually — Summative district and state assessments (aggregated, disaggregated; strand, item, and student work)

2–4 times a year — Data about people, practices, perceptions (e.g., demographic, enrollment, survey, interview, observation data, curriculum maps)

Quarterly or end of the unit — Benchmark common assessments (e.g., end-of-unit, common grade-level tests reported at item level)

1–4 times a month — Formative common assessments (e.g., math problem of the week, writing samples, science journals, other student work)

Daily–Weekly — Formative classroom assessments for learning (e.g., student self-assessments, descriptive feedback, selected response, written response, personal communications, performance assessments)

Task-at-a-Glance

Purpose	Study the research and gather and analyze local data to verify causes that contribute to the student-learning problem
Data	Research and local data related to the identified causes (e.g., enrollment, survey, interview, and observation data)
Questions to ask	Which causes are validated through the research? What can we learn from research about the causes? To what extent does a research-validated cause exist within our context? Is there a relationship between two or more factors in our school (e.g., course enrollment and achievement) that point to a particular cause?
Concepts	High-quality research Data about people, practices, and perceptions
Activities	Activity 14.1: Study the Research Activity 14.2: Frame Questions for Local Data Collection Activity 14.3: Develop the Local Data Collection Plan Activity 14.4: Analyze Local Data and Verify Causes Activity 14.5: Plan for Engaging Stakeholders and Review School Culture

---

A Data Team in Action: Verify Causes, Part I

The Data Team at Nevazoh Middle School chose the following as one possible cause for poor performance in mathematics and achievement gaps between African American and White students: Our sixth-grade general mathematics classes are too heterogenous. Students would do better if we added a third level of mathematics, in addition to our advanced and regular mathematics courses, for our students who are doing the most poorly. This possible cause generated the following research questions: Does heterogeneous grouping contribute to achievement gaps between White and African American students? To poor mathematics achievement overall? What kinds of grouping practices help students succeed? What are the short- and long-term effects of tracking? With the help of the Data Coach, the team collected and studied a combination of secondary and primary sources about grouping practices and documented their findings. From their research they learned that, contrary to their expectations, heterogeneous groupings benefit most learners. Differentiating instruction within the classroom, creating flexible groups, providing extra help for students who need it, and using a variety of research-based instructional strategies were recommended in the research. The team realized they had been barking up the wrong tree. Tracking, not heterogeneous groupings, was a more likely cause of their student-learning problem. They went back to their Verify Causes Tree (see Figure 5.3) and revised their possible causes accordingly. Now the team wanted to learn more about their own grouping practices and their impact on students. (Continued at the end of this chapter.)

WHAT IS TASK 14?

In this task, the Data Team completes the process of verifying causes begun in Task 13. They begin the task by collecting and analyzing the research to answer their questions: Is our cause verified by research? What else can we learn about this and other causes and best practices related to our student-learning problem? After discarding unproductive causes, the team decides which causes warrant further investigation in their school.

Then the Data Team generates questions about their own local practice and collects and analyzes local data, such as survey, interview, enrollment, or classroom observation data. Local data provide evidence of what is happening in the school in relationship to each cause, so that the Data Team verifies that the cause is not only supported by research, but is also of concern in their own school. For example, they may have a hunch that teachers are not fully implementing their mathematics curriculum but need more data to determine to what extent the curriculum is being implemented as intended. The local data collected in Task 14 also provide baseline data about curriculum, instruction, assessment, grouping, or other practices. Later, in Task 19, the team can compare how this baseline changes as they implement solutions.

The products for this task are a summary of findings from research and local data and a few verified causes of the student-learning problem. In Task 13, the team completed the Possible Causes row of the Verify Causes Tree. In this task, they complete the remainder of the Tree, recording their findings from research and local data analysis and discarding or revising possible causes based on what is learned, as illustrated in Figure 5.3. (See Clark County, Nevada, case study in Chapter 8 for an extended example of verifying causes).

Figure 5.3 Verify Causes Tree example at the end of Task 14.

Possible Causes[a]	Curriculum	Instruction	Assessment	Equity	Critical Supports
Possible Causes[a]	Does not emphasize mathematics problem solving enough	~~Classes are too heterogeneous~~ Not using best practices consistently		Tracking	Teachers do not feel prepared to teach nonroutine problem solving
Research Findings	Rigorous curriculum benefits students and narrows achievement gaps (NRC, 2005; Singham, 2003)	Heterogeneous groupings with differentiated instruction, flexible groupings, extra help for students, and varied instructional approaches that build on students' understandings are recommended (NCTM, 2000; NRC, 2005; Oakes, 1993)		Tracking has a negative impact on students in low tracks, who receive less rigorous curriculum and less effective instruction; African American students are disproportionately represented in low tracks (Oakes, 1993; Singham, 2003)	Teacher preparation is an important factor in student achievement (Ma, 1999; NCTM, 2000; NRC, 2005; Singham, 2003)
Local Data Findings	Problem solving emphasized more in advanced mathematics classes, less in regular mathematics classes (observation and student interview data)	Best practices more in evidence in advanced mathematics classes (observation and student interview data)		11 percent of African Americans are enrolled in advanced math versus 44 percent of Whites; 75 percent of students in advanced mathematics classes scored proficient in mathematics compared with 10 percent of students in regular mathematics; 82 percent of African Americans in advanced mathematics scored proficient (enrollment and most recent state CRT data)	Most teachers report feeling "somewhat" or "inadequately" prepared to teach mathematics on most dimensions of preparation surveyed (teacher survey)
Verified Causes	Lack of emphasis on problem solving, especially in regular mathematics classes	Not using best teaching practices consistently, especially in regular mathematics classes		Tracking	Teachers do not feel prepared to teach nonroutine problem solving

Adapted from Preuss (2003). Used with permission.

a. Possible causes that are shaded indicate that they were maintained or added after studying research; cause that is crossed out was determined not to be confirmed by research.

BACKGROUND INFORMATION FOR DATA COACHES

What Kinds of Questions Can We Ask to Guide Local Data Collection?

Once the Data Team has verified through research a few causes to investigate with local data, they focus on generating two types of questions to guide their collection of data: "to what extent" questions and "correlational" questions. "To what extent" questions focus on gathering local data that provide evidence that a condition either does or does not exist within the school, and, if it does, to what extent. The first sidebar provides several examples of this type of question. The data that are collected in response to questions of this type simply provide information on whether or not the practice is occurring in the school. For example, in the Clark County, Nevada, case study in Chapter 8, the Data Team wanted to know to what extent teachers were implementing the reform mathematics curriculum the school had adopted.

"Correlational" questions focus on gathering data that provide evidence of whether there is a relationship between two factors. For example, a question of this type might be, "In classrooms where teachers implement inquiry-based teaching strategies, is there evidence that students have higher achievement scores?" The question focuses on comparing two factors: inquiry-based teaching practices and student learning. However, the purpose of these questions is simply to determine if there is a relationship between the factors, not to determine cause-and-effect. Cause-and-effect data require conducting rigorous research and controlled studies in order to confirm a causal relationship. The second sidebar provides several examples of correlational questions. These questions will lead the Data Team to cross-tabulate data, another way to slice and dice data by showing the relationship between two or more factors. For example, the first correlational question example cross-tabulates course enrollment with proficiency on the state assessment.

"To What Extent" Local Data Questions

- To what extent is our mathematics curriculum being implemented?
- To what extent are we using higher-order questioning in our classrooms?
- To what extent do teachers feel prepared to teach the module on floating and sinking?
- To what extent do students have opportunities to engage in increasing their reading fluency?

"Correlational" Local Data Questions

- Who is enrolled in our high-track and low-track mathematics courses? How are students in different tracks performing on our state assessments? (correlation between tracking and achievement)
- Do students in low-track classes receive a different type of instruction than do students in high-track classes? (correlation between tracking and instruction)
- How much time do teachers spend teaching science? Are students in classrooms where more time is spent achieving better? (correlation between time spent on teaching and achievement)

What Are the Challenges and Pitfalls Inherent in This Task?

Gathering Local Data

There are numerous sources of local data that can help the Data Team answer their questions and confirm or refute the existence of specific practices in the school and the relationship between those practices and student learning. These are the types of data illustrated in the Data Pyramid at the beginning of this task as data about people, practices, and perceptions, and they include sources such as enrollment, survey, observation, and interview data. See Table 5.3 in Activity 14.3 for more specific examples of local sources of data you might use to investigate a variety of questions.

Gathering data of this type is different from gathering student-learning data. We routinely assess, measure, and evaluate the extent to which students are learning. We rarely gather information about instructional practices such as materials used, time spent, rigor, use of questions, or nature of learning activities. As a result, these data are not readily available. While the Data Team will take advantage of survey, observation, or interview data already collected in the school, teams often have to invest time and effort to collect these data themselves.

This leads to a second challenge. It will be important to have the school building administrator's and the faculty's cooperation and support for your local data collection efforts. Make sure to share information and plans, ask for feedback, and address concerns, since the process of gathering the local data can sometimes feel threatening. Assure the staff that the data being collected will not be used in an evaluative way. Rather, the intent is to learn about what is happening in all relevant classrooms to improve all students' learning of the content.

RESOURCES

Guskey, T. R. (2000). *Evaluating professional development.* Thousand Oaks, CA: Corwin Press.
Love, N. (2002). *Using data/getting results: A practical guide for school improvement in mathematics and science.* Norwood, MA: Christopher-Gordon. (See pp. 35, 125, 219–224, 301–308, and 361–546.)
Nunnaley, D. (2004). Test scores: What can they tell us? *Hands On!, 27*(1), 4–7.

Council of Chief State School Officers' *Surveys of the Enacted Curriculum* (http://www.ccsso.org/projects/Surveys_of_Enacted_Curriculum/) has surveys for mathematics, science, and language arts.

Horizon Research, Inc. (http://www.horizon-research.com/instruments/) has observation protocols and survey instruments.

MAJOR ACTIVITIES FOR TASK 14

Activity	Time required	CD-ROM materials: Task 14 link	CD-ROM Toolkit: Relevant tools
Activity 14.1: Study the Research	60–120 minutes	Handout H13.1: Verify Causes Table: Research	Final Word Dialogue, Key Concepts/ Key Words, Verify Causes Tree
Activity 14.2: Frame Questions for Local Data Collection	60 minutes	Handout H14.1: Verify Causes Table: Local Data	Verify Causes Tree

(Continued)

Major Activities for Task 14 (Continued)

Activity	Time required	CD-ROM materials: Task 14 link	CD-ROM Toolkit: Relevant tools
Activity 14.3: Develop the Local Data Collection Plan	30 minutes	Handout H14.1: Verify Causes Table: Local Data Handout H14.2: Local Data Sources	Interview Design and Dialogue, Levels of Use, Stages of Concern, Verify Causes Tree
Activity 14.4: Analyze Local Data and Verify Causes	60–120 minutes	Handout H14.1: Verify Causes Table: Local Data	Data-Driven Dialogue, Group Roles, Seven Norms of Collaboration
Activity 14.5: Plan for Engaging Stakeholders and Review School Culture	30 minutes		

PREPARING FOR THE TASK

• Read the "Background Information for Data Coaches"; see the CD-ROM: Task 14 for data examples, handouts, and sample goals and agenda; and review "Standard Procedures for Data Team Meetings" (see the introduction to Chapter 3 in this book and on CD-ROM). Although tool directions are embedded in the Data Coach Notes, you can also reference in-depth descriptions of relevant and optional Toolkit entries on the CD-ROM.

• Task 14 will span more than one Data Team meeting. Prior to convening the Data Team for the first meeting, work with the smaller groups formed at the end of Task 13 to gather the research they will need for this task. Decide whether Data Team members will read the research prior to or during the first Data Team meeting for Task 14. In either case, ask them to bring Handout H13.1 (Verify Causes Table: Research) to the meeting. The first meeting will focus on discussing the research, framing local data questions, and developing a local data collection plan. The Data Team will then gather the local data, and reconvene for the second meeting to analyze the local data.

MATERIALS PREPARATION

• Make one copy per team member of Handouts H14.1 and H14.2.

• Make copies of the research that will be reviewed by Data Team members (see "Data and Research Preparation").

• Using Handout H14.1, create a chart of the Verify Causes Table: Local Data and post it on the wall.

• Post the Verify Causes Tree and Verify Causes Table: Research charts used in Task 13.

DATA AND RESEARCH PREPARATION

Between Tasks 13 and 14, help the team gather research related to their questions and sources they generated in Task 13 (see Task 13, "Background Information for Data Coaches," and Handout H13.2). Then prepare for engaging the Data Team with the research that has been gathered. Decide whether to have the Data Team members read the research prior to convening for Task 14 (this is ideal since it will save time) or during the Data Team meeting, and whether to have each person read every source of research or to divide the resources among individuals based on the research questions. If reading at the meeting, consider whether to use Key Concepts/Key Words (see Toolkit) or the Jigsaw Strategy (described below in the Data Coach Notes).

Later, you will be helping the team to collect local data. Consult the data inventory in the introduction to this chapter, and identify what data are already available to guide the team's planning. Once you determine what data sources will be used, help the team organize and display the data for their analysis. These data will be both qualitative and quantitative. For the qualitative data, help the team organize the data for ease of analysis. For example, see the student interview data in the Data Examples on the CD-ROM, which is separated into comments from students in regular mathematics and advanced mathematics classes. Quantitative survey data can be displayed with results for each question inserted into the survey itself, with bar graphs or in table form, showing the results for each question. Graphs of surveys can even be Stoplight-Highlighted using criteria such as "a rating of 3 or above on a scale of 1–5 is green; 2 is yellow; below 2 is red." See the CD-ROM: Data Examples for sample interview, classroom observation, survey, and enrollment data.

DATA COACH NOTES

 Activity 14.1: Study the Research

Handout H13.1

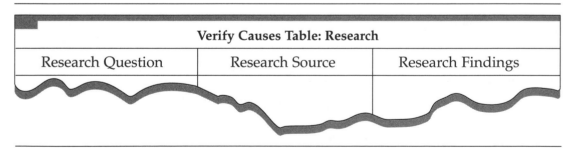

Verify Causes Table: Research		
Research Question	Research Source	Research Findings

1. Ask Data Team members to report their findings from their research, which they have recorded on their copy (Handout H13.1) of the Verify Causes Table: Research. Record their findings on the Verify Causes Tree chart in the appropriate row.

> **Facilitation Note:** If the research was not read prior to the meeting, allow time to read using Key Concepts/Key Words or the Jigsaw Strategy (see sidebar). Ask team members to record their findings on the Verify Causes Table: Research chart.

---- ✄ ----

Jigsaw Strategy

Jigsaw is a good strategy for quickly assimilating a lot of material and can be used effectively for studying research:

- Divide the Data Team into smaller groups of three to four.
- Divide the reading material into the same number of sections as there are members in the small group.
- Make as many copies of each section as there are groups.
- Have each person in the smaller group read a different section, so that as a whole, the small group reads the full selection of reading material. (For example, for two groups of three members each, you would need two copies of the full reading selection, which is divided into three sections.)
- If time permits, direct those who read the same material to meet in "expert groups" to synthesize the key points and prepare to teach their material to the rest of their small group (optional).
- Have each person teach the material he or she studied to the rest of the small group, noting key ideas that relate to the causes you are investigating.

2. Engage the Data Team in an analysis of their findings using these questions as prompts:

- Which causes are validated from the key findings in the research?
- For those causes that are not validated, did we learn anything from the research to help us refine or adapt our causes? Or, based on the research, should the cause be eliminated?
- If none of the causes is validated, what are alternative causes that we did not consider before? What did we learn in the research that informs our list of causes?
- What are the most important findings that we want to remember to consider when generating solutions to the student-learning problem?

3. If the cause is verified through research, continue with the next step. If not, remove this cause from the Verify Causes Tree, and discuss a possible replacement. If another cause is added, it must also undergo the research process for verification.

 ## Activity 14.2: Frame Questions for Local Data Collection

Handout H14.1

Verify Causes Table: Local Data		
Question for Local Data Collection	Local Data Sources/Tools	Findings

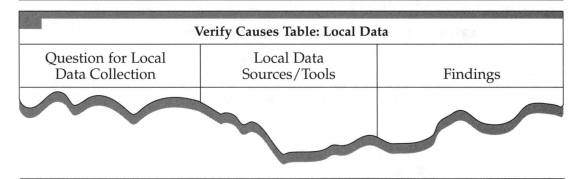

1.   Post the Verify Causes Table: Local Data chart, and distribute Handout H14.1. Assist the team to develop questions concerning their school practice that will yield data about the identified possible causes. Two types of questions, "to what extent" and "correlational," can be useful at this point (see "Background Information for Data Coaches"). Give the team time to practice generating both types of questions. Then add their questions for local data collection to the chart and have team members add them to their handouts.

> **Facilitation Note:** Here are two important ways to streamline this activity: (1) If the team already has enough information about a practice to confirm that it is a problem in their school (e.g., "our curriculum is not aligned with standards"), there is no need to frame questions for local data collection for that possible cause. Investigate only those causes for which evidence is needed. (2) Every cause does not need to be explored with "to what extent" and "correlational" questions. Data Teams can use one, the other, or both as relevant.

2. Facilitate a large-group sharing to finalize the questions for local data collection. This is a good time to prompt the team to consider equity issues such as opportunities for all students to learn (e.g., are some racial or gender groups underrepresented in advanced courses or high-ability tracks or overrepresented in special education programs?) and to ask questions that probe practices that might be contributing to achievement gaps.

 ### Activity 14.3: Develop the Local Data Collection Plan

1. Engage the Data Team in a discussion to help them identify the kind of data that are needed to answer each question. You will want to keep the data collection plan as simple as possible by only collecting data related to the questions identified.

Table 5.3 Local Data Sources

Local data questions	Data sources
What are the course patterns in grades 5–12? How many courses are offered at different levels? Who teaches which types of classes?	• Course offerings from school's master schedule • District archival data on enrollment and teacher assignments
Who is enrolled in which classes?	• Enrollment data disaggregated by race/ethnicity, gender, language, economic, and educational status • Student and/or parent focus groups
To what extent are best-practice instructional strategies implemented in classes?	• Classroom observation protocols or checklists • Student and/or teacher interviews or surveys • Teacher self-assessments or rubric ratings • Toolkits: Interview Design and Dialogue, Levels of Use, Stages of Concern • Classroom walk-throughs (to gather observational data)
To what extent are teachers implementing the instructional materials?	• Classroom observation protocols or checklists • Student and/or teacher interviews • Student, teacher, and/or parent focus groups • Teacher self-assessments or rubric ratings • Toolkits: Interview Design and Dialogue, Levels of Use, Stages of Concern • Student notebooks and/or portfolios representative of work from each lesson
Is there a relationship between how students achieve on the state test and course enrollment?	• State test results for school disaggregated by course enrollment
To what extent do teachers feel prepared to teach new content?	• Teacher surveys or interviews • Focus groups • Toolkit: Interview Design and Dialogue
Is there a relationship between teacher preparation and student learning?	• Teacher certification levels • Documentation of teachers' years of experience • Teacher surveys or checklists • State test results disaggregated by classroom

For example, limit data collection to a few survey questions or a few interviews. If you plan to observe classrooms, keep the focus on one or two aspects of instruction or learning. Consider data that you may already have access to, such as those gathered by a study group or action research project in the school or by a funded project's evaluator. Also consider using or adapting protocols, surveys, or other data collection processes that have been used effectively in the past, rather than creating new tools or instruments. Distribute Handout H14.2 (illustrated in Table 5.3), and use those ideas to help the Data Team identify appropriate, and easily collected, data.

2. Engage the Data Team in a review of the data sources before finalizing the plan, asking them to consider these questions: Will the data gathered from the sources we have identified answer the local data questions? Have we included diverse voices in the data collection (teachers, students, parents, administrators, community members, and other stakeholders)? Have we included data sources that reflect the diverse populations in our school? Is our plan doable and realistic?

3. Finalize the data collection plan by identifying who will take responsibility for obtaining or creating data collection tools or instruments, who will gather the data, and by when the team will reconvene with all of the data collected. Provide ample time for team members to conduct their investigation and prepare their data for the Data Team.

Activity 14.4: Analyze Local Data and Verify Causes

1. Once the local data have been collected, reconvene the Data Team for a second meeting. Use Data-Driven Dialogue to review and analyze the data. Document findings on the Verify Causes Tree chart.

> **Facilitation Note**: If time is short, ask the Data Team members who collected the data to conduct the analysis and share their findings rather than having the team analyze all the local data. Ask them to come to the meeting with the Verify Causes Table: Local Data filled out with their findings.

2. Use the findings to determine whether or not the cause is verified by local data. If a possible cause is confirmed in research and in practice, the Post-it can now be moved to the Verified Cause box. If a possible cause is not confirmed in both research and practice, do not move it to the Verified Cause box.

Activity 14.5: Plan for Engaging Stakeholders and Review School Culture

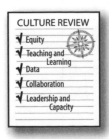

1. Conduct a think-pair-share activity, and ask Data Team members to focus on these questions: What have been our most important lessons learned in Tasks 13 and 14? What do we want to share with others? How will we share what we learned with others?

2. Develop a plan for how the team will communicate their progress, including what each team member will do. See the Involving Key Stakeholders box at the end of Task 12 for some suggestions.

3. Engage the Data Team in reflecting on and assessing where they are in relation to the School of Our Dreams (Task 4), particularly the core values they identified. To what extent are these values reflected in the work the Data Team has done so far? What will they commit to do to keep those values alive as they move to the next part of the Using Data Process?

A Data Team in Action: Verify Causes, Part II (continued from beginning of Task 14)

The Nevazoh Middle School Data Team framed their questions for investigating their own tracking practices and determined the data they would use to answer their questions. They examined their enrollment data disaggregated by race/ethnicity and student performance on the state assessment disaggregated by both race/ethnicity and level of mathematics in which the student was enrolled. They also collected student interview and observation data in each of the levels of mathematics (see CD-ROM: Task 14, Data Examples). They analyzed these data using Data-Driven Dialogue and recorded their findings on their Verify Causes Table: Local Data chart. They were stunned to learn that African American students were so disproportionately represented in the low-level course and so underrepresented in the advanced course. At the same time, African American students enrolled in the advanced course performed very well. The team then revisited their Verify Causes Tree and came up with their final verified causes, which included their tracking practices.

6

Generating Solutions

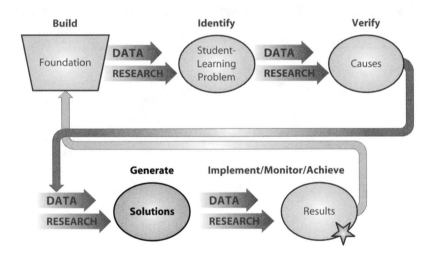

Build		Identify		Verify
Foundation	DATA / RESEARCH	Student-Learning Problem	DATA / RESEARCH	Causes

		Generate	Implement/Monitor/Achieve
	DATA / RESEARCH	Solutions	DATA / RESEARCH → Results

This chapter focuses on the fourth component of the Using Data Process, Generating Solutions. The Data Team builds on their work in Task 14 where they learned from research and verified through local data the specific causes that are contributing to the student-learning problem. The activities in Tasks 15, 16, and 17 help you lead the Data Team to refine their preliminary student-learning goal, clarify the outcomes and results that they want to achieve, determine strategies that will help them achieve their outcomes and goal, and identify data collection tools that will provide evidence that they are achieving the outcomes and goal. The Data Team's focus during the three tasks in this component of the Using Data Process is on three questions: (1) What do we want to achieve? (2) How will we achieve it? and (3) How will we know if we have achieved it?

In the three tasks in this chapter, the Data Team engages in an iterative process using a Logic Model of their thinking about how to move from the student-learning problem to the results. A Logic Model is simply a graphic representation of the logical and sequential thinking that moves from the problem to the results. In other words, it graphically models the answer to the question: "If we want to achieve specific outcomes and goals, what strategies do we implement and how will we know if we have met our outcomes and goals?"

The specific tasks addressed in this component of the Using Data Process and the intended outcomes of each for Data Teams are synthesized in Table 6.1.

Table 6.1   Generating Solutions Tasks and Data Team Outcomes

Generating solutions: Tasks	*Data Team outcomes:The Data Team . . .*
Task 15: Build Your Logic Model	• Refines the Draft Student-Learning Goal Statement to make it SMART • Identifies the strategies, intended outcomes, and data for monitoring outcomes that will address the verified cause and result in achieving the student-learning goal
Task 16: Refine Outcomes and Strategies	• Revisits the Logic Model and refines the sequence and combination of strategies and outcomes • Ensures that the Logic Model plan includes strategies to address all aspects of the student-learning problem
Task 17: Develop a Monitoring Plan	• Revisits the Logic Model and refines the monitoring tools • Develops a realistic and manageable plan for gathering data to monitor implementation of the strategies and progress toward achievement of the outcomes and the student-learning goal

GATHER DATA NEEDED FOR TASKS 15–17

There are no specific data sets that you will gather prior to these three tasks. However, in these tasks, you and the Data Team will build on the analysis of student-learning data, local data, and the research from previous tasks, and it will be important to have that information available.

Task 15: Build Your Logic Model

Task-at-a-Glance

Purpose	Identify the strategies, intended outcomes, and data for monitoring outcomes that will address the verified cause and achieve the student-learning goal
Data	None
Questions to ask	How do we refine the student-learning goal to include the "measurable" aspect of SMART goals?
	What are the specific outcomes we expect to achieve in our program and policies? In teacher knowledge, skills, beliefs, and/or practices? In student learning? What did we learn in Task 14 from the local data that informs these changes?
	What strategies do we believe will solve the verified causes of the student-learning problem and achieve these outcomes?
	What do research and best practice say about effective strategies?
	If we implement those strategies, will they help us achieve all of our outcomes and the student-learning goal?
	How will we know?
Concepts	Logic Model
	Verified cause
	Strategies
	Outcomes
	Monitoring tools
Activities	Activity 15.1: Refine the Student-Learning Goal
	Activity 15.2: Build Your Logic Model

WHAT IS TASK 15?

At this point in the Using Data Process, the Data Team is ready to consolidate all of their learning about student-learning needs and verified causes into a plan to achieve the student-learning goal and improve teaching and learning in the school. In Task 15, the Data Team first refines the draft student-learning goal statement they completed in Task 12. Now they add the evidence that will let them know to what extent they have achieved the goal, the "measurable" part of their SMART (Specific, Measurable, Attainable, Relevant, and Time-Bound) goal (Doran, 1981) that was missing in their draft goal statement.

Next, through an iterative process, the Data Team builds a Logic Model—a graphic representation of the logical and sequential steps involved in achieving their goal (see Figure 6.2). They have already verified their causes in Task 14. Now they generate strategies that will address these causes, represented by the triangles in the graphic. They also think through the intended outcomes for each of their strategies, represented by the boxes under the strategies (labeled Program or Policy Outcomes, Teacher-Learning Outcomes, Teacher-Practice Outcomes, and Student-Learning

Figure 6.1 First-draft Logic Model.

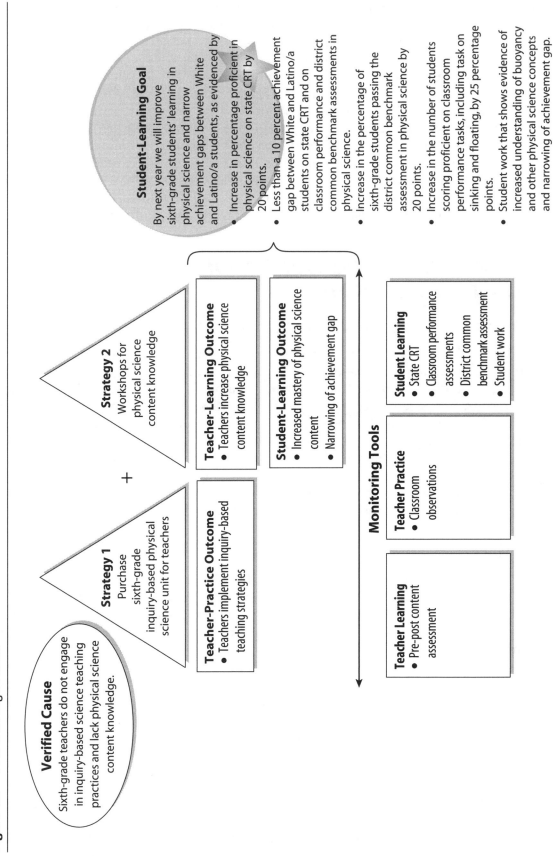

Verified Cause

Sixth-grade teachers do not engage in inquiry-based science teaching practices and lack physical science content knowledge.

Strategy 1

Purchase sixth-grade inquiry-based physical science unit for teachers

+

Strategy 2

Workshops for physical science content knowledge

Teacher-Practice Outcome
• Teachers implement inquiry-based teaching strategies

Teacher-Learning Outcome
• Teachers increase physical science content knowledge

Student-Learning Outcome
• Increased mastery of physical science content
• Narrowing of achievement gap

Student-Learning Goal

By next year we will improve sixth-grade students' learning in physical science and narrow achievement gaps between White and Latino/a students, as evidenced by

• Increase in percentage proficient in physical science on state CRT by 20 points.
• Less than a 10 percent achievement gap between White and Latino/a students on state CRT and on classroom performance and district common benchmark assessments in physical science.
• Increase in the percentage of sixth-grade students passing the district common benchmark assessment in physical science by 20 points.
• Increase in the number of students scoring proficient on classroom performance tasks, including task on sinking and floating, by 25 percentage points.
• Student work that shows evidence of increased understanding of buoyancy and other physical science concepts and narrowing of achievement gap.

Monitoring Tools

Teacher Learning
• Pre-post content assessment

Teacher Practice
• Classroom observations

Student Learning
• State CRT
• Classroom performance assessments
• District common benchmark assessment
• Student work

Outcomes). Finally, they begin to consider what tools they will use to monitor these outcomes as they implement their plan. They can start building their Logic Model with strategies and then go to outcomes or reverse the order. It doesn't matter as long as they answer the following questions: (1) What strategies will we implement to address the verified cause and achieve the student-learning goal? (2) What outcomes do we expect to achieve along the way? and (3) How will we know if we have met our outcomes and achieved the student-learning goal?

The product for this task will be their initial Logic Model graphic, illustrated in the example in Figure 6.1, which includes a SMART student-learning goal, strategies, intended outcomes, and monitoring tools that will serve as evidence that outcomes and the goal have been achieved. In Tasks 16 and 17, the Data Team will further refine their strategies, outcomes, and monitoring tools. The example in Figure 6.1 is not a completed Logic Model, just a first draft. See Task 17 for a fully developed example.

BACKGROUND INFORMATION FOR DATA COACHES

What Is the "Logic Model" Approach?

Logic Models come in many shapes and forms, and you and the Data Team may already be familiar with one or more such model. For example, some Logic Model graphics are used by project designers, evaluators, or funding agencies to identify the resources needed to conduct specific activities that will result in specific outcomes. No matter what the Logic Model looks like, however, they all serve the same purpose: to engage people in thinking through the logical and sequential steps that will move them from the particular problem to the desired results and outcomes.

Figure 6.2 depicts the specific Logic Model graphic that you and the Data Team will use in this task and shows the various components: the verified cause, the strategies, the outcomes, the monitoring tools, and the student-learning goal.

Verified Cause

At the end of Tasks 13 and 14, the Data Team verified through research and local data one or more causes that contribute to the student-learning problem. For each verified cause, the Data Team will now create a Logic Model that represents the steps they will take to address the cause. They will also think through whether the causes can be combined and whether individual causes may in fact be attributed to one overarching causal area. For example, one cause might be "lack of instructional time spent on non-routine problems." A second might be "lack of instructional materials for mathematics problem solving," and a third might be "teachers are not comfortable teaching non-routine problem solving." These three verified causes could be combined into "curriculum, instruction, and teacher preparation for mathematics problem solving."

Strategies

Strategies are the specific activities the Data Team will implement to respond to the verified cause and that lead to the achievement of the student-learning goal. The Data Team returns to what was learned from the research and local data to guide these decisions. For example, strategies might include working with the

Figure 6.2   Using Data Process Logic Model.

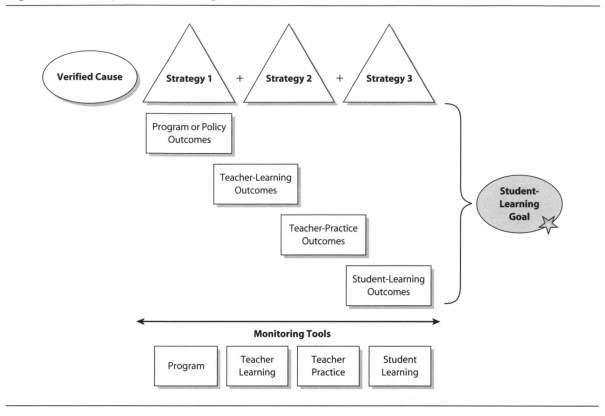

building administrator to eliminate tracking, adopting new instructional materials, conducting study groups or workshops to deepen teachers' content knowledge, implementing use of formative assessments, identifying and systematically offering extra help to students who need it, or providing coaching opportunities to help teachers practice specific skills. A critical concept that emerges during the identification of strategies is that it is the combination of strategies together, rather than any one strategy, that will help you meet your student-learning goal. Figure 6.2 has three triangles to represent strategies, but you and your Data Team may have more or fewer strategies.

Features of Strategies

- Have a clear purpose
- Combine with other strategies
- Make a positive difference
- Can be monitored
- Logically linked to the outcomes
- Supported by research and best practice

Outcomes

This component of the Logic Model asks the Data Team to identify what they expect to have happen as a result of the implementation of their strategies. They will focus on four potential outcome areas: (1) What do we expect to see as a result of changes in our content-area program, teaching, or educational policies? (2) What do we expect teachers to know, understand, be able to do, and/or believe? (3) What do we expect to see happening in classrooms in terms of teacher practice? and (4) What do we expect students to know, understand, be able to do, and/or believe? The intent of clarifying what they expect to "see," versus what they expect to "do," is to help the

Data Team zero in on the results of their actions. For example, a strategy to "conduct study groups focused on inquiry-based teaching and learning" might have an expected teacher-learning outcome that "teachers deepen their knowledge of inquiry-based approaches to teaching and learning" and a teacher-practice outcome that "teachers implement inquiry-based teaching strategies in their classrooms." Figure 6.2 shows boxes that indicate the four outcome areas your team will be considering.

Monitoring Tools

Monitoring tools are the sources of data that the Data Team will collect before, during, and/or after the implementation of the strategies to provide evidence of the extent to which each of the outcomes is being met. The team will revisit the local data collection tools they used in Task 14 and learn about additional tools and processes that will help them gather evidence to continuously adjust their plan to ensure that they meet the outcomes and the student-learning goal. The monitoring tools are indicated by the squares at the bottom of Figure 6.2. Once the Logic Model is completed in Task 17, there will be monitoring tools to align with each outcome.

Monitoring Slogans

- Measure what you treasure.
- Do less, monitor more.
- Don't bite off more than you can monitor.
- Quantify your outcomes: How much? How often?

Student-Learning Goal

This is the draft student-learning goal statement from Task 12 to which the Data Team will now add SMART evidence—what are the expected goals stated in measurable terms? In Activity 15.1, the team identifies this evidence. They may add further sources of evidence in the student-learning goal later during the "outcomes" discussion in Activity 15.2.

Engaging with the Logic Model is iterative, and the Data Team will find that focusing on one component leads into a focus on another. As the Data Coach, having an understanding of the intent of the Logic Model process and the type of information that will be documented in each component will enable you to guide the Data Team through a productive discussion. It will be extremely helpful for you to look ahead to Tasks 16 and 17 to see one example of a Logic Model as it evolves in this component of the process.

In this task, Activity 15.2 provides a structure for leading the iterative process that allows for maximum flexibility to "meander" through the Logic Model and still end up with a cohesive and logical plan for achieving outcomes and goals. The scenario below provides one example of this productive meandering. Note that this is a different example than the one depicted in Figure 6.1.

Scenario: Productive "Meandering" Through the Logic Model

Here's our verified cause: Eighth-grade algebra teachers don't have access to instructional materials that emphasize algebraic thinking, and they don't feel confident in their own understanding of algebraic thinking.

Here's our preliminary student-learning goal: By February of next year, we will improve eighth-grade students' performance in mathematics and understanding of algebra and narrow achievement gaps between White and African American students.

If we achieve that goal, what evidence will we have that will let us know that we have met the goal?

1. A 20 percent increase in the percentage of all eighth-grade students who achieve mathematics proficiency on the state CRT

2. A decreased percentage gap in mathematics proficiency scores between White and African American students on the state CRT

3. A higher percentage of eighth-grade students who achieve proficiency in the algebra strand on the state CRT

4. Enhanced algebraic thinking as evidenced by increases on monthly common assessments and periodic analysis of student work

Now that we have identified the sources of evidence that will let us know if we have achieved the student-learning goal, we can add that information to the goal statement on the Logic Model so that it is SMART. We've also started our list of what we'll do to monitor our progress along the way before we get the state test information back: monthly assessments and examining student work.

If that's what we expect, what do teachers need to know and do differently in their classrooms?

- Local data in Task 14 showed that mathematics teachers do not feel confident in their ability to teach algebraic thinking, so we need to help them deepen their own content knowledge, and one teacher-learning outcome is: Teachers better understand algebraic thinking.

- Teachers don't have instructional materials that help them emphasize algebraic thinking, so one mathematics program outcome is: Teachers have access to better instructional materials.

- Teachers will need to learn how to use those new materials, so a teacher-practice outcome is: Teachers will use the new materials in their classrooms.

If those are our outcomes, we can now identify several strategies to help us achieve those outcomes:

- To find new mathematics instructional materials and provide them to the teachers, we will convene a group of teachers to research instructional materials and find supplementary units that we can add to our existing materials since we can't adopt a whole new program right now.

- To help teachers learn how to use those materials, we will conduct a workshop.

- To help teachers deepen their content knowledge, we will conduct a study group led by the mathematics department chair.

What if we combined learning the content and learning how to use the materials? We could do a workshop to provide an overview of the new materials and then hold weekly study groups to walk through every lesson in the materials with a focus on understanding the content in each lesson and how to teach each lesson.

If we implement these strategies, we'll have helped teachers develop the knowledge and skills to use the new materials, but we still need to give teachers a way to practice with these new materials. If we don't, we'll most likely not have student-learning outcomes. So, after a few months

(Continued)

(Continued)

of the study group, we can have teachers start trying them in their classrooms, and we'll work with the principal to get release time so that we can observe each other. Our study group could then be about helping each other problem-solve while we teach. It could also be a way for teachers to bring student work to the table to check whether students' understanding is improving.

So, what do we have now?

Program outcome: New instructional materials available to teachers.

Teacher-learning outcome: Deeper understanding of algebraic thinking.

Teacher-practice outcome: Implementation of new instructional materials.

Student-learning outcome: Improved ability to engage in algebraic thinking.

Strategy 1: Obtain new instructional materials.

Strategy 2: Conduct a workshop overview.

Strategy 3: Start the study groups and later add in the peer observations and examination of student work.

Monitoring 1: Did we get the materials? Are they really better than what we already had?

Monitoring 2: Did the workshop help teachers get an overview of the new materials? We could do a survey.

Monitoring 3: Are the study group and peer observation working? We could do interviews and get surveys from teachers to see if they are learning the new content, take notes during the conference after peer observations to see what teachers are talking about and focusing on, conduct informal classroom walk-throughs to see what's happening in classes, and ask teachers to complete a pre–post short-answer item to see if their content knowledge is increasing.

Monitoring 4: Are students learning? We'll look for evidence in the student work and the monthly assessments. We'll need to develop a rubric or criteria to determine what we mean by "evidence" of increased learning.

Have we completely addressed all aspects of the verified cause and the student-learning goal? Do we believe that these strategies and outcomes will contribute to closing the achievement gap between White and African American students, or do we need additional strategies that focus on that specific student-learning problem? We need to go back into our Logic Model and rethink the relationship between the outcomes and the strategies to make sure.

In this scenario, the Data Team starts with refining the student-learning goal so that it is SMART, which is where you and the Data Team will start in Task 15. However, your own meandering may look very different from the scenario. For example, once the evidence of success is identified for the student-learning goal, your Data Team may move directly into identifying strategies, rather than outcomes. Or they may generate ideas for other sources of evidence they might want to gather that would lead them into monitoring tools. Activity 15.2 provides a structure and process that enables you to document the Data Team's thinking no matter which path they take through the Logic Model. What is important is that the Data Team end up with a logical representation of what they think needs to happen, with what results, and how they will know if they are successful in achieving the outcomes and the student-learning goal.

What Are the Challenges and Pitfalls Inherent in This Task?

The tasks and activities in this component of the Using Data Process help Data Teams move away from educational "quick fixes" toward sustained and ongoing cycles of continuous improvement. As you start the processes in the Generating Solutions tasks, one challenge for the Data Team may be impatience. You may hear them ask, "Why can't we just decide what we are going to do and start doing it?" If this sentiment is raised, engage the Data Team in a dialogue to explore what has been done in the school in the past to address student-learning problems. Encourage them to think about some of the following questions: "How often do we do what we have always done, with the same results? How many of the solutions have in fact resulted in improved student learning? How do we know? How many of the solutions are still sustained and in use?" Let them know that "slowing down in order to go fast" at this point will enable them to develop logical and research-based approaches to solving the student-learning problem and to sustain their collaborative inquiry into improving teaching and learning. (See also the Human Chain activity in the Data Coach Notes in this task for a motivating and fun way to provide the rationale for the Logic Model for a group of 10 or more.)

RESOURCES

Books on logic models, strategies, and monitoring

Guskey, T. R. (2000). *Evaluating professional development*. Thousand Oaks, CA: Corwin Press.

Keeley, P. (2005). *Science curriculum topic study: Bridging the gap between standards and practice*. Thousand Oaks, CA: Corwin Press.

Keeley, P., & Rose, C. M. (2006). *Mathematics curriculum topic study: Bridging the gap between standards and practice*. Thousand Oaks, CA: Corwin Press.

Killion, J. (2002). *Assessing impact: Evaluating staff development*. Oxford, OH: National Staff Development Council.

Loucks-Horsley, S., Love, N., Stiles, K. E., Mundry, S., & Hewson, P. W. (2003). *Designing professional development for teachers of science and mathematics* (2nd ed.). Thousand Oaks, CA: Corwin Press.

Love, N. (2002). *Using data/getting results: A practical guide for school improvement in mathematics and science*. Norwood, MA: Christopher-Gordon. (See pp. 109–115.)

W. K. Kellogg Foundation. (2001). *Logic model development guide: Using logic models to bring together planning, evaluation, and action*. Battle Creek, MI: Author.

Web links to centers and organizations that synthesize research on best practice and effective strategies

American Association of School Administrators (AASA): http://www.aasa.org/

American Educational Research Association (AERA): http://www.aera.net/

Annenberg Institute for School Reform: http://www.annenberginstitute.org/

Association for Supervision and Curriculum Development (ASCD): http://www.ascd.org/

Bill and Melinda Gates Foundation: http://www.gatesfoundation.org/

Center for Comprehensive School Reform and Improvement: http://www.centerforcsri.org/

Center on Reinventing Public Education: http://www.crpe.org/

Consortium for Policy Research in Education: http://cpre.org/

National Center for Research on Evaluation, Standards, and Student Testing (CRESST): http://www.cresst.org/

Education Development Center (EDC): http://main.edc.org/

Education Trust: http://www2.edtrust.org/edtrust/

Education Week: http://www.edweek.org/

ERICDigests.org: http://www.ericdigests.org/

goENC.org: http://www.goenc.org/

Institute for Learning Technologies: http://www.ilt.columbia.edu/

The Knowledge Loom: http://knowledgeloom.org/

Learning Point Associates: http://www.learningpt.org/

Learning Research and Development Center: http://www.lrdc.pitt.edu/

Mid-continent Research for Education and Learning (McREL): http://www.mcrel.org/

Minority Student Achievement Network: http://www.msanetwork.org/

National Academies Press: http://www.nap.edu/

National Comprehensive Center for Teacher Quality: http://www.ncctq.org/

National Staff Development Council (NSDC): http://www.nsdc.org/

Professional Development for Mathematics and Science Teachers: http://www.pdmathsci.net/

Schools Moving Up: http://www.schoolsmovingup.net/cs/wested/print/htdocs/home.htm/

Southwest Educational Development Laboratory: http://www.sedl.org/

TERC: http://www.terc.edu/

WestEd: http://wested.org/

MAJOR ACTIVITIES FOR TASK 15

Activity	Time required	CD-ROM materials: Task 15 link	CD-ROM Toolkit: Relevant tools
Activity 15.1: Refine the Student-Learning Goal	30 minutes		
Activity 15.2: Build Your Logic Model	60–120 minutes	Handout H15.1: The Using Data Process Logic Model PowerPoint Slides S13.1–S13.2	Group Roles, Introducing the Logic Model, Seven Norms of Collaboration

PREPARING FOR THE TASK

Read "Background Information for Data Coaches"; see the CD-ROM: Task 15 for PowerPoint slides and sample goals and agenda; and review "Standard Procedures for Data Team Meetings" (see the introduction to Chapter 3 in this book and on CD-ROM). Although tool directions are embedded in the Data Coach Notes below, you can also reference in-depth descriptions of relevant Toolkit entries on the CD-ROM.

MATERIALS PREPARATION

- Identify an area of the wall that can be used to build the Logic Model.

- On two sheets of 8½" × 11" paper, prepare one sign with an identified student-learning problem and a second sign that says "Student Achievement Improves."

- Cut out shapes for the Logic Model components: one white oval for each verified cause, one green triangle for each strategy, one blue sheet of 8½" × 11" paper (i.e., rectangle) for each outcome, one yellow square for each monitoring tool, and a white circle for the student-learning goal. Make each shape as large as the 8½" × 11" sheet will accommodate.

- On 8½" × 11" sheets, write the names of each component—Verified Cause, Strategies, Outcomes, Monitoring Tools, Student-Learning Goal—and put them aside for now (to be posted in Activity 15.2).

- Make one copy for each Data Team member of Handout H15.1.

- Prepare to show PowerPoint slides.

- Post the Verify Causes Tree from Task 14.

- Post the student-learning problem statement and the draft student-learning goal statement on the wall.

DATA PREPARATION

You will not need to do any data preparation prior to this task.

DATA COACH NOTES

 ### Activity 15.1: Refine the Student-Learning Goal

1. Convene the Data Team, and ask team members to reflect on their use of the group roles during Task 14. Then rotate the roles, and add any additional responsibilities for each role.

2. Depending on how you decided to embed practice of your agreed-upon collaborative norms, guide the Data Team through the process you identified.

3. Review the purpose of Task 15, and engage the Data Team in a brief discussion to emphasize the importance of this task to improving teaching and learning.

4. Let the Data Team know that they will begin the process of generating solutions by reviewing their verified causes. Direct their attention to the charts from Task 14 on which they documented their verified causes. Facilitate a discussion to see if they think they can condense or group any of the causes into one larger and overarching causal area, such as "implementation of instructional materials that promote scientific inquiry." Let the Data Team know that they will develop an implementation plan for each cause and that by condensing causal statements they will be better prepared to address them. Document each cause statement on an oval cut-out (to be posted later on the Logic Model they will build).

5. Direct their attention to the draft student-learning goal statement. Ask them, "If we achieve our student-learning goal, what evidence will we have that will let us know that we have met the goal? How can we make it SMART by adding the evidence that we will use to measure whether the goal has been met?" Document their list of evidence statements on a sheet of chart paper. Once they have generated the list, clarify which ones they want to include on their student-learning goal statement and add these to the goal. Post the final student-learning goal statement on the Logic Model wall. Encourage the team to include multiple measures of student learning, not just the state CRT. Evidence statements might include

- There is a 20 percent increase in the percentage of all eighth-grade students who achieve mathematics proficiency on the state CRT.
- The gap in mathematics proficiency scores between White and African American students on the state CRT narrows by 10 percentage points.
- Twenty percent more eighth-grade students achieve proficiency in the algebra strand on the state CRT.
- Seventy-five percent or more of students achieve a score of three or above on the monthly common performance assessment.
- Students' work shows evidence of algebraic thinking.

⇒ Activity 15.2: Build Your Logic Model

1. Introduce the concept of a Logic Model by engaging the Data Team in the Human Chain activity (adapted from Killion, 2003, pp. 32–34, with permission of the National Staff Development Council; see Toolkit: Introducing to the Logic Model).

2. Hand the student-learning problem sign to one team member, and ask him or her to stand against one wall and hold the sign so that it is visible. Hand the student achievement sign to another team member, and ask him or her to stand next to the first person. Then ask the team to discuss what is wrong with this picture. What interventions/strategies might be necessary to make this "line-up" result in increased student achievement?

a. Have the person who suggests the first intervention or strategy write it on a piece of paper and stand between the person representing the goal and the person representing the problem. As each additional suggestion is made and written down, ask that person to determine where he or she might logically stand in the growing sequence of interventions and strategies between the problem and the goal.

b. Ask the team members to look at their strategies and organize them into those that could be combined. Ask what is missing. Record the responses.

c. Then ask team members to consider what might happen as a result of each strategy: What will the outcome be? Who will learn or do something differently as a result of this strategy? As team members suggest outcomes and results, ask each person to write the outcome on a piece of paper and stand in front of the strategy resulting in the outcome he or she noted. (If the group is too small, record the outcomes on separate pieces of paper and give them to the person representing the strategy related to that outcome.)

d. Review the Human Chain by following the logic of moving from the student-learning problem to the increase in student achievement. Point out that the Logic Model helps avoid what too often occurs in education: jumping too quickly from problem to solution. These chains represent the complexity of thought that describes a Logic Model, an articulated plan that addresses an identified problem and verified causes through a series of strategies; these strategies in turn achieve outcomes, which lead toward the accomplishment of the student-learning goal.

3. Display PowerPoint Slide 15.2, and distribute Handout 15.1 (both illustrated in Figure 6.2). Post the sheets of paper with the five components of the Logic Model on the wall so that they approximately match the configuration on the model: one verified cause on the left; the related strategies, outcomes, and monitoring tools in a tier beside that; and the goal on the right.

4. In pairs, have team members discuss the visual and how it relates to the activity they just did. Have partners share their comments with the whole group. Make the following points in the discussion:

- Outcomes and strategies are aligned.
- Outcomes can be teacher-, student-, or policy- or practice-based.
- Outcomes need to be monitored.
- Changes in strategies are based on a monitoring plan.

5. Show the Data Team the shapes that you have cut out to represent the different components of the Logic Model. Let them know that the following questions will guide their building of the Logic Model: "In order to achieve the student-learning goal by addressing this verified cause, what will we do? If we want students to develop certain knowledge, skills, abilities, and/or beliefs, what do teachers need to know and be able to do in their classrooms? What instructional materials will they need? What outcomes do we expect to see based on what we do? How will we know whether we have met each outcome? What tools will we use to gather evidence?"

6. Post one of the verified causes (on oval cut-outs) that the team generated earlier. Using the following sets of questions, guide the Data Team to write their ideas for each additional component on the corresponding cut-out shapes and post them on the Logic Model wall. Anticipate that the Data Team may not focus on only one component at a time. For example, discussion during the generating of outcomes may produce ideas for strategies. Whenever ideas are suggested for any component, make sure they are documented on the appropriate shape and posted on the Logic Model wall. Let the Data Team know that they will have time to revisit these ideas and ensure that there is a logical and sequential relationship among all components; their purpose now is to brainstorm what they will do, what they expect to have happen, and how they will know that what they have done is effective.

> **Facilitation Note:** At this point in the process, the Data Team may feel more confident moving into one component of the Logic Model than others. Using the information provided in "Background Information for Data Coaches", facilitate the development of each component of the Logic Model in the order that the Data Team feels comfortable with.

Expected Outcomes

Note: Depending on the verified cause, you may not have outcomes in each of the following areas. Engage the Data Team only in exploring outcomes that relate to the verified cause.

- What do we expect to see as a result of changes in the content area program or educational policies?
- What do we expect teachers to know, understand, be able to do, and/or believe? What are the knowledge, skills, abilities, and understandings that we expect them to have?
- What do we expect teachers to do? What will we see happening in classrooms as a result of the knowledge, skills, or beliefs that teachers develop?
- Based on our student-learning problem, what do we expect students to know, understand, and/or believe? What are the specific skills, knowledge, and concepts that we expect them to have mastery of?
- What do we expect students to do? What will we see happening in classrooms as a result of the knowledge, skills, or beliefs that students develop?

Strategies to Address the Verified Cause and Achieve the Student-Learning Goal and Intended Outcomes

- Based on all of our intended outcomes, what strategies do we want to implement that will enable teachers and students to achieve the outcomes?
- What did we learn from the research in Task 14 that informs our selection of strategies that emphasize best practices? Is there additional research we will want to consult to be sure our strategies are based on research and best practices?
- What did we learn from the local data in Task 14 that helps us better understand what the current practices are in our school and what needs to change?
- To what extent will any one strategy "reach" all the way to student outcomes? If it doesn't, what accompanying strategies might we implement?
- What strategies will enable us to meet all aspects of the verified cause?
- What strategies will enable us to meet all aspects of the student-learning goal? For example, have we included strategies that we believe will increase student learning and close the achievement gap?

Monitoring Tools

- How will we know if the outcomes are met?
- What tools will we use to gather evidence?
- How will we know if the strategies are effective?

- How can we use the same data collection tools from Task 14 to gather similar data?
- What evidence of our student-learning goal is also a source of data to monitor student learning "along the way" as we implement strategies?
- Are some of the student-learning goal indicators or evidence also "benchmarks" for achieving the larger goal? Do we have other benchmarks that would indicate evidence of learning?

7. Once the Data Team has generated ideas for each component, let them know that they will revisit the overall relationships among the components in the next two tasks in order to refine the Logic Model and create a realistic and doable plan. At this point, their Logic Model will resemble the degree of completion illustrated in Figure 6.1.

8. Provide time for reflection and processing of the Data Team's use of group roles and their agreed-upon collaborative norms.

9. Make sure that the Logic Model wall stays intact and, if possible, remains on the wall until the next Data Team meeting. However, if necessary, ask the materials manager to help you remove the components and carefully organize them so that it can be reassembled prior to the next meeting.

Task 16: Refine Outcomes and Strategies

Task-at-a-Glance

Purpose	Refine the sequential ordering of strategies and outcomes on the Task 15 Logic Model
Data	None
Questions to ask	Do the strategies address every aspect of the student-learning problem?
	Are all the strategies of the same scale and complexity? Are some larger in scale (e.g., conduct study groups with teachers) while others are smaller (e.g., teachers read articles)? Could we combine some of the smaller ones into the larger ones?
	Do we have the resources needed to implement these strategies? Are there some we want to eliminate?
	In what order could we implement the strategies? Are there some that necessarily need to come before others?
	Are we missing any steps in the sequence of helping teachers develop new knowledge and then translate that knowledge into practice?
	Do the strategies address the needs of student populations most in need of our attention? Are they likely to result in closing achievement gaps?
	Do these strategies reflect a knowledge of and respect for students from different racial/ethnic, cultural, and economic backgrounds? Would students and their parents agree?
Concepts	Change as a process
Activities	Activity 16.1: Refine the Logic Model: Outcomes and Strategies

WHAT IS TASK 16?

Task 16 provides an opportunity for the Data Team to refine their Logic Model strategies and outcomes to develop an action plan to achieve results. Specifically, they will determine the order in which they will implement the strategies, identify when they might expect to see evidence of specific outcomes, and clarify when they will gather monitoring data. Working through the process of moving from problems to solutions may be a new experience for the Data Team, but it is an important one for sustaining continuous improvement. The product for this task will be a revised Logic Model graphic, illustrated in the example in Figure 6.3, which now includes the final plan for the implementation of the strategies and the expected outcomes.

Figure 6.3   Refined Logic Model strategies and outcomes.

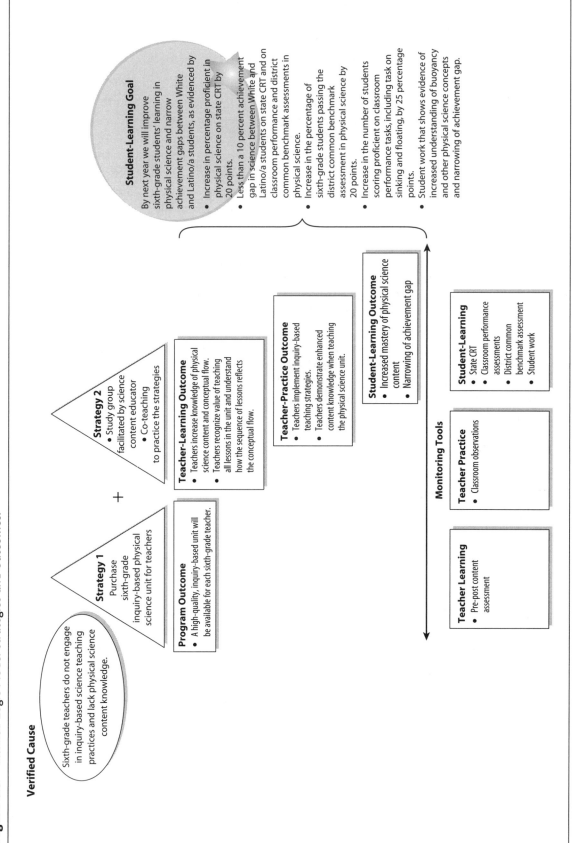

Verified Cause

Sixth-grade teachers do not engage in inquiry-based science teaching practices and lack physical science content knowledge.

Strategy 1

Purchase sixth-grade inquiry-based physical science unit for teachers

Program Outcome

- A high-quality, inquiry-based unit will be available for each sixth-grade teacher.

+

Strategy 2

- Study group facilitated by science content educator
- Co-teaching to practice the strategies

Teacher-Learning Outcome

- Teachers increase knowledge of physical science content and conceptual flow.
- Teachers recognize value of teaching all lessons in the unit and understand how the sequence of lessons reflects the conceptual flow.

Teacher-Practice Outcome

- Teachers implement inquiry-based teaching strategies.
- Teachers demonstrate enhanced content knowledge when teaching the physical science unit.

Student-Learning Outcome

- Increased mastery of physical science content
- Narrowing of achievement gap

Student-Learning Goal

By next year we will improve sixth-grade students' learning in physical science and narrow achievement gaps between White and Latino/a students, as evidenced by

- Increase in percentage proficient in physical science on state CRT by 20 points.
- Less than a 10 percent achievement gap in science between White and Latino/a students on state CRT and on classroom performance and district common benchmark assessments in physical science.
- Increase in the percentage of sixth-grade students passing the district common benchmark assessment in physical science by 20 points.
- Increase in the number of students scoring proficient on classroom performance tasks, including task on sinking and floating, by 25 percentage points.
- Student work that shows evidence of increased understanding of buoyancy and other physical science concepts and narrowing of achievement gap.

Monitoring Tools

Teacher Learning

- Pre-post content assessment

Teacher Practice

- Classroom observations

Student-Learning

- State CRT
- Classroom performance assessments
- District common benchmark assessment
- Student work

BACKGROUND INFORMATION FOR DATA COACHES

What Do We Need to Know About Change as a Process?

One of the key concepts that will help the Data Team refine their Logic Model is that change is a process—it doesn't happen overnight, and it is not an "event" that is over and done with. Rather, change takes time and involves moving through various stages at various times in the process of making the change. The Logic Model plan that the Data Team will implement requires change on someone's part, for example, teachers using new instructional materials, students engaging in a new approach to learning, or new policies that guide how courses are offered. Each strategy is intended to achieve certain outcomes, and the Data Team will think through the order of implementing strategies and how this influences which outcomes they might expect to see evidence of and when. Figure 6.3 illustrates the development of the Logic Model example shown in Task 15 (see Figure 6.1), with the strategies and outcomes further refined.

Notice in Figure 6.3 that student-learning outcomes are not expected until after there is evidence of changes in teachers' practice. Additionally, the sequence of strategies provides opportunities for teachers to learn new content, understand the skills inherent in using that new content, and then practice the new knowledge and skills in their classrooms, with opportunities for reflection and continuous improvement.

During this task, it will be important to help the Data Team think through the realistic expectations for implementing strategies, achieving the desired outcomes, and gathering monitoring data. You may want to read Stages of Concern and Levels of Use (see Toolkit), as well as "Background Information for Data Coaches" in Task 18 to further your own understanding of the concepts associated with the change process.

What Are the Challenges and Pitfalls Inherent in This Task?

Perhaps the greatest challenge will be to help the Data Team create a realistic and manageable Logic Model plan. If they generate too many strategies, they may be overwhelmed with what is required to implement them. If they identify too many outcomes, they will constantly be gathering data to determine whether the outcomes have been met. If they generate too many or complex monitoring tools and processes, they will be overwhelmed with data. The questions that are provided in this task can help you guide the Data Team to develop a manageable and yet comprehensive Logic Model plan that they can use to guide their improvement efforts.

RESOURCES

Guskey, T. R. (2000). *Evaluating professional development*. Thousand Oaks, CA: Corwin Press.

Killion, J. (2002). *Assessing impact: Evaluating staff development*. Oxford, OH: National Staff Development Council.

Loucks-Horsley, S., Love, N., Stiles, K. E., Mundry, S., & Hewson, P. W. (2003). *Designing professional development for teachers of science and mathematics* (2nd ed.). Thousand Oaks, CA: Corwin Press.

Love, N. (2002). *Using data/getting results: A practical guide for school improvement in mathematics and science.* Norwood, MA: Christopher-Gordon. (See pp. 109–115, 125, 219–224, 301–308, and 361–546.)

W. K. Kellogg Foundation. (2001). *Logic model development guide: Using logic models to bring together planning, evaluation, and action.* Battle Creek, MI: Author.

MAJOR ACTIVITIES FOR TASK 16

Activity	Time required	CD-ROM materials: Task 16 link	CD-ROM Toolkit: Relevant tools
Activity 16.1: Refine the Logic Model: Outcomes and Strategies	60 minutes		Group Roles, Introducing the Logic Model, Levels of Use, Seven Norms of Collaboration, Stages of Concern

PREPARING FOR THE TASK

Read "Background Information for Data Coaches"; see the CD-ROM: Task 16 for sample goals and agenda; and review "Standard Procedures for Data Team Meetings" (see the introduction to Chapter 3 in this book and on CD-ROM). Although tool directions are embedded in the Data Coach Notes below, you can also reference in-depth descriptions of relevant Toolkit entries on the CD-ROM.

MATERIALS PREPARATION

- Reassemble the Logic Model from Task 15 if necessary.
- Using the guidelines in Task 15, Materials Preparation, prepare additional cut-out shapes for components of the Logic Model, as needed.

DATA PREPARATION

You will not need to do any data preparation prior to this task.

DATA COACH NOTES

 ### Activity 16.1: Refine the Logic Model: Outcomes and Strategies

1. Convene the Data Team, and ask the team members to process their use of the group roles during Task 15. Then rotate the roles, and add any additional responsibilities for each role.

2. Depending on how you decided to embed practice of your agreed-upon collaborative norms, guide the Data Team through the process you identified.

3. Review the purpose of Task 16, and provide time for the Data Team to orient themselves to the Logic Model as they developed it in Task 15.

4. Using the following questions, guide the Data Team to decide on the sequence in which they will implement their strategies and when they might expect to see evidence of the identified outcomes. As they engage in this dialogue, move the cut-out shapes within the Logic Model to reflect their decisions. If the Data Team generates new ideas, have them write the ideas on the appropriate cut-out shapes and add them to the Logic Model.

Refining the Strategies

• Are the strategies all of the same scale and complexity? Are some larger in scale (e.g., conduct study groups with teachers) and others smaller (e.g., teachers read articles)? Could we combine some of the smaller ones into the larger ones?

• Do we have the resources needed to implement these strategies? Are there some we want to eliminate?

• In what order could we implement the strategies? When we think about how teachers learn and implement new practices in their classrooms, what are the sequences of steps that enable them to do so? How does that idea inform the sequence of our strategies? Are there some that necessarily need to come before others? Some that might be implemented simultaneously?

• Can some of the strategies be combined or grouped in ways that make this design more manageable?

Refining the Outcomes

• Do two or more strategies result in the same outcomes? If so, how might we combine them?

• Have we thought through the sequence in which we might expect to see each outcome? Are there some outcomes that are dependent on achieving others before they might be realized, for exmple, change in teacher practice precedes change in student learning?

• Are we missing any steps in the sequence of helping teachers develop new knowledge and then translating that knowledge into practice?

Reviewing the Overall Logic Model

• Do the strategies address every aspect of the student-learning problem? If not, what have we missed?

EQUITY

• Do the strategies address the needs of student populations most in need of our attention?

- Are they likely to result in closing achievement gaps?

- Do these strategies reflect a knowledge of and respect for students from different racial/ethnic, cultural, and economic backgrounds? Would our students and their parents agree?

- Do any of the strategies harm or neglect any group of students or teachers?

5. If there are other verified causes that the Data Team wrote on ovals in Task 15, repeat the Logic Model building process for those causes. Once completed, engage the Data Team in looking across all Logic Model plans to avoid redundancy and duplication. Use the questions suggested in Step 4 to refine all Logic Model plans.

6. Engage the Data Team in thinking about how they might share their progress with the larger school faculty and/or key stakeholders. See Toolkit: Introdution to the Logic Model.

7. Provide time for reflection and processing of the Data Team's use of group roles and their agreed-upon collaborative norms.

8. Make sure that the Logic Model wall stays intact and, if possible, remains on the wall until the next Data Team meeting. However, if necessary, ask the materials manager to help you remove the components in exactly the order in which they are currently organized so that the model can be reassembled prior to the next meeting.

Reflection on Strategies and Outcomes

- Strategies work in combination with each other to ensure reaching student-knowledge outcomes.
- All strategies in combination move you toward achieving the student-learning goal; in most cases, no one strategy will accomplish the goal.
- In order to achieve all identified outcomes, strategies will need to be implemented in a logical sequence.
- Reviewing the outcomes can help you refine the implementation sequence of the strategies.
- The end product should logically lead to the achievement of the student-learning goal and result in changing the verified cause.

Task 17: Develop a Monitoring Plan

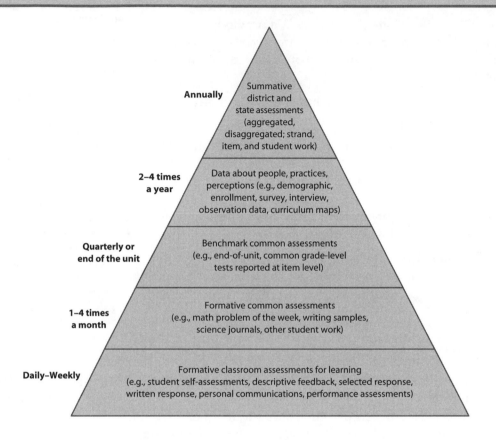

Annually — Summative district and state assessments (aggregated, disaggregated; strand, item, and student work)

2–4 times a year — Data about people, practices, perceptions (e.g., demographic, enrollment, survey, interview, observation data, curriculum maps)

Quarterly or end of the unit — Benchmark common assessments (e.g., end-of-unit, common grade-level tests reported at item level)

1–4 times a month — Formative common assessments (e.g., math problem of the week, writing samples, science journals, other student work)

Daily–Weekly — Formative classroom assessments for learning (e.g., student self-assessments, descriptive feedback, selected response, written response, personal communications, performance assessments)

Task-at-a-Glance

Purpose	Learn about tools that can be used to gather data to monitor achievement of the outcomes and the student-learning goal; refine the Logic Model Monitoring Plan
Data	None
Questions to ask	What specific monitoring tools will we use?
	What data do different kinds of tools result in?
	Are there several outcomes that might be monitored using only one tool or process?
	When should we gather this evidence? What outcomes might we expect to see before or after other outcomes?
	Do we have the resources available to implement the Monitoring Plan?
Concepts	The importance of monitoring
	Monitoring versus evaluation
Activities	Activity 17.1: Expand Our Repertoire of Monitoring Tools
	Activity 17.2: Refine the Monitoring Plan
	Activity 17.3: School Culture Review

WHAT IS TASK 17?

In Task 17, the Data Team revisits their original ideas for gathering monitoring data, learns about additional tools, and fleshes out their Monitoring Plan. As noted in Task 15, monitoring is the process of conducting structured data collection to gather evidence on how well the strategies for improvement are being implemented and whether they are having the intended outcomes. These data also provide information to help the team decide how to refine and/or improve the implementation of their strategies. The product of this task, illustrated in the example in Figure 6.4, will be the final Logic Model plan listing the specific tools that will be used to monitor the implementation of the strategies and the achievement of the outcomes and student-learning goal.

BACKGROUND INFORMATION FOR DATA COACHES

A true learning community identifies, honors, and provides opportunities for any and every successful team or teacher to share his or her methods and successes with colleagues.

—Schmoker, 2004a, p. 88

Monitoring Tools: Developing a Shared Vision and Gathering Data

In two of the Using Data Project sites, project leaders facilitated the use of an existing evaluation instrument developed by Horizon Research, Inc.—a classroom observation protocol for use in evaluating science and mathematics teaching and learning in elementary and middle schools. In Arizona and Ohio, project leaders adapted the observation instrument and created a short synopsis of the observable student and teacher behaviors that are aligned with best practices in science and mathematics. During teacher institutes and other professional development opportunities, the synopses were shared with the teachers and served as a catalyst for discussions about improving teaching. These synopses were then used to gather monitoring data during the implementation of the strategies. Using the protocol that teachers were familiar with and were using themselves to guide improvements in their teaching contributed to a confidence and comfort level for having observers in classrooms.

Why Is Monitoring So Important?

For more than 30 years, educators have introduced innovations aimed at improving student outcomes. Yet time after time, professional development, curriculum adoptions, policy changes, and other interventions fail to be fully implemented because they lack follow-up and monitoring to assess whether the change has been made, and whether it has had the desired effect on student learning. We cannot expect to see improvements in learning unless we know there have been changes in practice. The Using Data Process stresses the need for Data Teams to continue to gather and analyze data as their schools take action to learn what is being implemented and what is and is not working. Schools that were most successful in improving student achievement through the Using Data Project were those that regularly monitored student progress as strategies were being implemented. We are more likely to change what we monitor!

That is why in this component of the Using Data Process, the Data Team develops a data collection plan to monitor results as the entire school (or a specific department or group in the school) takes action to address the identified student-learning problem. While the focus in the earlier tasks has been on gathering and analyzing data to pinpoint student-learning problems and choosing the right solutions, the Data Coach and Data Team are now responsible for ensuring that a set of coordinated actions designed to reach the intended outcome are launched and carefully monitored.

Figure 6.4 Logic Model with refined monitoring tools.

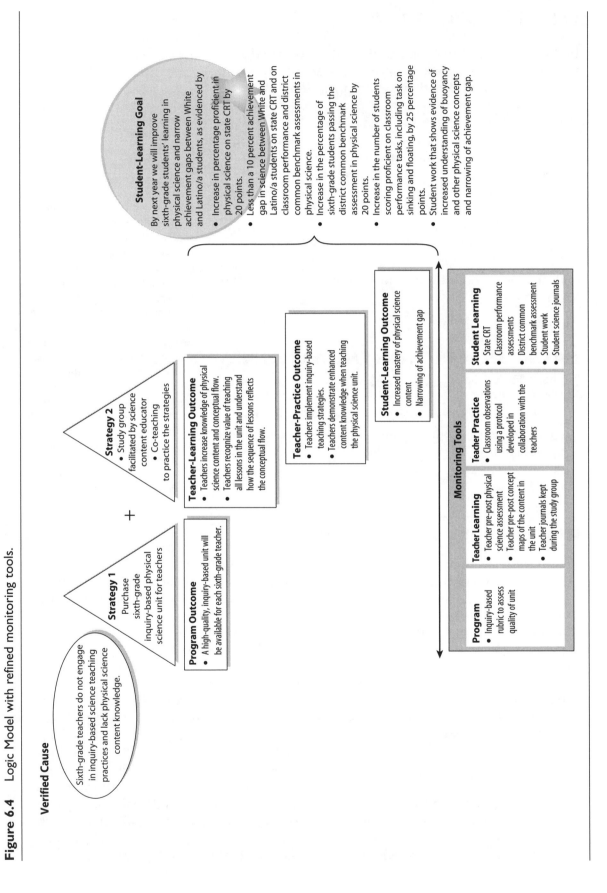

How Do I Help the Data Team Understand Their Role and See the Difference Between Program Monitoring, on the One Hand, and Program Evaluation and Rigorous Research on the Other?

In evaluation and research efforts, researchers are often trying to draw conclusions about the direct cause-and-effect relationships between the implemented strategies and the intended outcomes. In monitoring, the purpose is to gather data about effectiveness, rather than causality, that will be used to make adjustments, improvements, and adaptations during the implementation. The process is similar to conducting formative and summative assessment of student learning—using formative data to know what is being learned along the way and to adjust instruction (or, in the case of the action plan, the strategies) to improve learning, and using summative data to know if the goal and outcomes have been met. In addition, teachers are monitoring their own teaching for the purposes of improving their practice, not for evaluation purposes.

For example, if a Data Team learns that student understanding of the content is not improving based on the data they gather through monthly common assessments, they have an opportunity to improve one, or more, of the strategies they are implementing. Perhaps the study group is not providing teachers with the content knowledge needed to teach the lessons. Or teachers may not be implementing that new learning in their classrooms. The monitoring data provide feedback on how the implementation strategies are working and give the Data Team an opportunity to adjust and refine their overall plan.

In Task 15, We Identified Several Tools for Monitoring—What More Will We Want to Think About to Finalize Our Plan?

Preimplementation and Postimplementation Data

The Data Team already has experience gathering data to inform their understanding of current practices and conditions within the school. In Task 14, the local data that they gathered provided information about what is happening in classrooms and whether there was a relationship between different factors such as course enrollment and student learning. Those data now serve as a baseline of where they currently are; data gathered through the same tools and processes can inform them of changes along the way.

Using the tools from Task 14 can be one way that the Data Team gathers data both before and after implementation. One such tool is a walk-through, a systematic and purposeful means of collecting interview and observation data by walking around the school and/or through classrooms with a specific question or questions as a focus. For example, if the Data Team conducted classroom walk-throughs to gather data on the extent to which teachers were implementing inquiry-based teaching strategies, those data serve as preimplementation data. Once the Data Team implements the strategies designed to enhance teachers' learning and practice, they can conduct walk-throughs again and gather postimplementation data. The two sets of data allow the Data Team to compare teacher learning and practice before and after the implementation of the strategies. In addition, student-learning data that are gathered before and after the implementation can inform the Data Team of the extent to which changes in teacher practice contributed to student learning.

Quantitative and Qualitative Data

This task helps the Data Team learn more about monitoring tools that are designed to gather specific types of data, such as qualitative data—which provide robust descriptive information—and quantitative data—which provide specific frequency or percentage information. Both are recommended to provide the fullest picture of changes.

Objective and Subjective Data

The Data Team will also explore the idea of balancing objective data and subjective data. Objective data are facts and precise measurements that involve minimal judgment, such as how much time is spent teaching science in elementary classrooms. Subjective data result from personal opinion or judgment, such as self-report data on a survey. Both are important—you want to know what teachers or students believe and think but also to have more objective data.

Diverse Voices

It will probably be evident to the Data Team that they will want to gather data from both students and teachers as they monitor their results. However, it is also important to consider gathering data from other people in the community, including parents, administrators, and others who play a role in the school. For example, sending home a parent questionnaire can be a way to learn whether students' perceptions or attitudes are changing.

Monitoring Tools

Table 6.2 provides a list of the Logic Model outcome areas, examples of questions to guide data collection, and suggested data tools that could be used to monitor whether the outcomes are met. During Activity 17.1, you and the Data Team will use the information in this table to guide your final selection of monitoring tools. In addition, if the Data Team wants to learn more about designing their own instruments and/or using existing instruments for gathering monitoring data, the Resources below as well as "Background Information for Data Coaches" in Task 18 list several excellent sources that provide more in-depth guidance.

What Are the Challenges and Pitfalls Inherent in This Task?

A Manageable Monitoring Plan

The greatest challenge the Data Team will face is keeping the Monitoring Plan manageable. Guide the team to strike a balance in the amount of data they gather, aiming for enough to inform progress but not so much that they don't have the time to process it all. The questions and guidelines in Activity 17.2 can help move the Data Team toward a realistic plan.

Table 6.2   Tools for Monitoring Implementation of Strategies and Outcomes

Logic Model outcomes	*Questions to guide monitoring data collection*	*Suggested monitoring tools*
Program or policy outcomes	• Were the program or policy changes implemented? • Was the quality of the implementation as we expected? • Were resources allocated to support the changes?	• Course offerings • Course enrollment data • Program placement data • Graduation rates • Retention rates • Discipline or suspension data • Absenteeism rates • Questionnaires • Surveys • Interviews • School walk-throughs
Teacher-learning outcomes (knowledge, skills, and/or attitudes)	• What are teachers learning? • Are teachers learning new knowledge or acquiring new skills as intended? • What changes in attitudes or beliefs are being made?	• Teacher questionnaires • Teacher surveys • Teacher interviews • Teacher focus groups • Teacher logs/journals • Teacher self-reflections or self-assessments • Classroom observations with protocols • Observations of professional development sessions • Concept maps • Content assessments • Teacher portfolios
Teacher-practice outcomes	• Are teachers implementing their new learning in their classrooms? • To what extent are teachers implementing new strategies as intended?	• Teacher/student questionnaires • Teacher/student surveys • Teacher/student interviews • Teacher/student focus groups • Teacher self-reflections or self-assessments • Classroom observations with protocols or checklists • Demonstration lessons • Classroom walk-throughs
Student-learning outcomes (knowledge, skills, and/or attitudes)	• What are students learning? • Are students learning new knowledge or acquiring new skills as intended?	• Classroom and common content assessments • Student portfolios • Student work • Student questionnaires • Student surveys • Student interviews • Student focus groups • Student logs/journals • Student self-reflections or self-assessments • Classroom observations with protocols • Classroom walk-throughs

RESOURCES

Barnes, F. V., & Miller, M. (2001, April). Data analysis by walking around. *The School Administrator*, 20–25.

Bernhardt, V. L. (1998). *Data analysis for comprehensive school improvement*. Larchmont, NY: Eye on Education. (See pp. 233–264.)

Guskey, T. R. (2000). *Evaluating professional development*. Thousand Oaks, CA: Corwin Press.

Guskey, T. R. (2003). How classroom assessments improve learning. *Educational Leadership, 60*(5), 6–11.

Kaufman, R., Guerra, I., & Platt, W. A. (2006). *Practical evaluation for educators: Finding what works and what doesn't*. Thousand Oaks, CA: Corwin Press.

Killion, J. (2002). *Assessing impact: Evaluating staff development*. Oxford, OH: National Staff Development Council.

Love, N. (2002). *Using data/getting results: A practical guide for school improvement in mathematics and science*. Norwood, MA: Christopher Gordon. (See pp. 35, 83–89, 94–99, 421, 429, 440, 455–462, 464, 465–468, 489–490, 531.)

Sanders, J. R., & Sullins, C. D. (2006). *Evaluating school programs: An educator's guide* (3rd ed.). Thousand Oaks, CA: Corwin Press.

Shaha, S. H., Lewis, V. K., O'Donnell, T. J., & Brown, D. H. (2004). *Evaluating professional development: An approach to verifying program impact on teachers and students*. Oxford, OH: National Staff Development Council.

Council of Chief State School Officers' *Surveys of the Enacted Curriculum* has surveys for mathematics, science, and language arts: http://www.ccsso.org/projects/Surveys_of_Enacted_Curriculum/

Horizon Research, Inc., has observation protocols and survey instruments: http://www.horizon-research.com/instruments/

MAJOR ACTIVITIES FOR TASK 17

Task-at-a-Glance

Activity	Time required	CD-ROM materials: Task 17 link	CD-ROM Toolkit: Relevant tools
Activity 17.1: Expand Our Repertoire of Monitoring Tools	30–60 minutes	Handout H17.1: Tools for Monitoring Implementation of Strategies and Outcomes	Group Roles, Introdution to the Logic Model, Seven Norms of Collaboration
Activity 17.2: Refine the Monitoring Plan	20–40 minutes		
Activity 17.3: School Culture Review	10–20 minutes		

PREPARING FOR THE TASK

Read "Background Information for Data Coaches"; see the CD-ROM: Task 17 for handout and sample goals and agenda; and review "Standard Procedures for Data Team Meetings" (see the introduction to Chapter 3 in this book and on CD-ROM). You can reference in-depth descriptions of relevant Toolkit entries on the CD-ROM.

DATA PREPARATION

You will not need to do any data preparation prior to this task.

MATERIALS PREPARATION

- Make sure that the Logic Model components from Task 16 are posted and accessible.

- Make one copy for each Data Team member of Handout H17.1.

- Post the chart from Task 14, Verifying Causes: Local Data, to use to guide ongoing data collection that was already started in that task.

- If needed, make additional yellow squares for finalizing the monitoring tools.

DATA COACH NOTES

 ### Activity 17.1: Expand Our Repertoire of Monitoring Tools

1. Convene the Data Team, and ask members to process their use of the group roles during Task 16. Then rotate the roles, and add any additional responsibilities for each role.

2. Depending on how you decided to embed the practice of your agreed-upon collaborative norms, guide the Data Team through the process you identified.

3. Distribute Handout H17.1. Using the "Background Information for Data Coaches" and the content on the handout, facilitate a discussion that helps the Data Team explore some of the options for tools. Introduce them to the idea that they will want to gather pre- and postimplementation data, objective and subjective data, and quantitative and qualitative data.

4. Direct the Data Team's attention to the Logic Model plan posted on the wall, focusing specifically on the outcomes that they have indicated. Ask the team what additional tools they might want to add to their Monitoring Plan based on the new information they have gained. For each outcome, engage the Data Team in a discussion using the questions below:
   - Given this outcome, what do we really want to know? Do we want to know if it happened and/or how well it happened?
   - Do we want to know what teachers and students think about their own learning, beliefs, skills, or attitudes? And/or do we want to know what others think about teachers' and students' learning?

Monitoring Tips

- Quantify your outcomes: How much have we improved? How often are we gathering data to assess our improvement?
- Multiple outcomes can be assessed using one monitoring tool or process—go for multiple mileage!
- To document changes, gather pre- and postimplementation data.
- When gathering data through interviews, surveys, or focus groups, ensure that diverse voices are included.
- Be specific about what you want to learn (i.e., what evidence you want) before deciding on a monitoring tool.
- Measure what you treasure—make sure you are gathering data on outcomes that really matter.
- Be realistic and make sure that the plan is manageable and doable as well as comprehensive.

Examples of Monitoring Tools for Multiple Outcomes

- Classroom observations can be a source of data for teacher practices in the classroom and evidence of student engagement and/or learning.
- Student work or journals provide evidence of student thinking and teachers' sequencing of conceptual flow or lessons.
- Student interviews provide insight into what students are learning and their perceptions of changes in the classroom.

- What tools did we use in Task 14 that provided preimplementation data? Can we use those same tools to provide data during the implementation of the strategies and postimplementation?
- Do we have tools that provide both qualitative and quantitative data?
- If we gather these data, will we have evidence that the outcome has been achieved? Will we have evidence that the student-learning goal has been achieved?
- Do we have any outcomes for which we do not have a monitoring tool?

5. During the discussion, as new tools are identified, write them on yellow squares and add them to the Logic Model.

 ## Activity 17.2: Refine the Monitoring Plan

1. Guide the Data Team to refine their Monitoring Plan. Use the following questions to guide this discussion:

- Do we have too many tools? Is the Monitoring Plan manageable?
- Are the tools in the "right" sequence? Are we gathering monitoring data on an outcome before we really think that outcome might be in evidence? Do we need to rethink the sequence of the outcomes as well as when we might gather monitoring data?
- Does any one tool gather data to assess the effectiveness of more than one outcome? If so, what implications does that have for how often we will administer that tool? For example, if a classroom observation can help us gather data about teachers' practices and student learning, do we want to conduct these observations before we implement a strategy, during the implementation of a strategy, and/or after it is implemented?
- Do we have monitoring tools that enable us to gather evidence on how students are learning and on whether we are helping them move toward achievement of the student-learning goal?
- Have we included data gathered from diverse audiences?
- Will it be manageable for us to gather all of these sets of data? Do we have the resources? Do we have access to specific monitoring tools? If not, how do we find them?

2. Finalize the list of monitoring tools and their alignment with outcomes. If the Data Team wants to explore specific tools and/or learn more about designing their own, either provide time now or schedule a time prior to the next Data Team meeting for them to investigate existing tools, such as those suggested in the "Background Information for Data Coaches." Before Task 18, the Data Team will want to identify the specific instruments, protocols, or processes for each monitoring tool they have identified.

3. Provide time for reflection and processing of the Data Team's use of group roles and their agreed-upon collaborative norms.

4. Conduct a think-pair-share activity, and ask Data Team members to focus on these questions: What have been our most important learnings in Tasks 15–17? What do we want to share with others? How do we want to share what we have learned with others? Develop a plan for how and with whom each person, as well as the entire team, will communicate the progress of the Data Team. Encourage them to consider how they will share the Logic Model plan with others so that teachers and other key personnel are aware of the strategies and the monitoring plans. (See Toolkit: Introducing the Logic Model.)

 ## Activity 17.3: School Culture Review

1. Engage the Data Team in reflecting on and assessing where they are in building the school culture. Refer the Data Team to the School of Our Dreams vision they created in Task 4. What progress have they already made toward that vision? How will the solutions generated in these last tasks bring them closer to their vision?

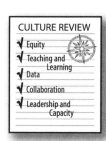

2. Ask the materials manager to help you organize the Logic Model sheets in exactly the order in which they appear on the wall. The Data Team will transfer the Logic Model and its components to a detailed action plan in Task 18.

7

Implementing, Monitoring, and Achieving Results

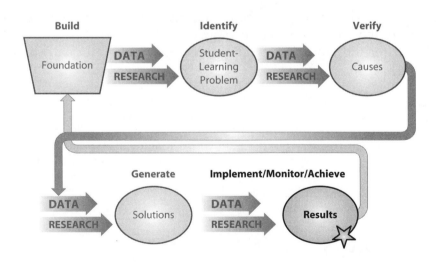

This chapter focuses on the fifth component of the Using Data Process—Implementing, Monitoring, and Achieving Results. It includes Task 18: Take Action and Monitor Results and Task 19: Celebrate Success and

Renew Collaborative Inquiry. The activities in these tasks lead the Data Team to develop and then implement Action Plans and carefully gather and monitor data on implementation and results. They also document and celebrate achievement of the student-learning goal. In this component, the Data Team addresses various questions, including: To what extent are the strategies being implemented? What barriers to implementation are we facing, and how will we address them? Are the necessary skill, will, and resources in place to enable action? To what degree are we making progress toward our stated outcomes and student-learning goal? What should we do next? (e.g., What do we do if we don't achieve our results? If we are making progress, what additional intervention is needed? If we attain our outcomes, what can we do to sustain what's working? What new areas of improvement will we address next?) How will we report and share our results and with whom? What will we celebrate? What and who will be rewarded and recognized? How will we celebrate? How will we sustain and renew our practice of using collaborative inquiry to ensure student learning? How will we amplify our successes and engage others in the Using Data Process?

The specific tasks addressed in this component of the Using Data Process and the intended outcomes of each for Data Teams are synthesized in Table 7.1.

GATHER DATA NEEDED FOR TASKS 18–19

In Tasks 15–17, the Data Team developed their Logic Model of improvement efforts, including identifying the strategies to implement and the monitoring tools to use to gather data. In this task, the Data Team creates a detailed Action Plan and initiates

Table 7.1 Implementing, Monitoring, and Achieving Results Tasks and Data Team Outcomes

Implementing, monitoring, and achieving results tasks	Data Team outcomes: The Data Team. . . .
Task 18: Take Action and Monitor Results	• Finalizes a detailed Action Plan • Implements chosen strategies and/or enables other staff to implement the strategies • Monitors the implementation of the plan and collects monitoring data • Makes suggestions about how to adjust implementation, as needed, based on monitoring data
Task 19: Celebrate Success and Renew Collaborative Inquiry	• Plans and carries out celebrations to acknowledge achievement of benchmarks • Identifies next steps for collaborative inquiry • Assesses the school culture and continues to strengthen

the implementation of the strategies and gathering of monitoring data. Unlike earlier tasks, you won't have all the data when you begin. Part of the Data Team's and Data Coach's work in Task 18 is to identify who will gather monitoring data and when it will be ready for the team to analyze.

Task 18: Take Action and Monitor Results

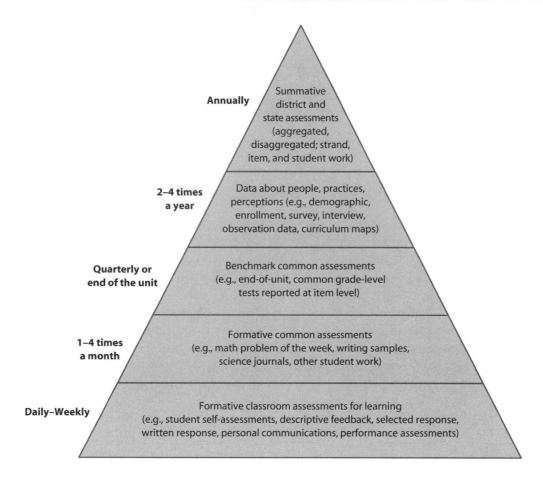

Task-at-a-Glance

Purpose	Develop and carry out the Action Plan to solve the identified student-learning problem and achieve the student-learning goal; work closely with decision makers and other stakeholders to encourage and support implementation and action
Data	Monitoring data
Questions to ask	Is the Action Plan clear to all involved?
	Is there a timeline for implementation of the Action Plan?
	Are all key stakeholders (especially principal and teachers) aware of the plans and prepared for their roles?
	What are we learning from the monitoring data? Are we reaching milestones and achieving outcomes?
	What problems are users having with implementation?
	What next steps are needed to enhance implementation and help us achieve outcomes and the goal?

(Continued)

Task-at-a-Glance (Continued)

Concepts	The monitoring role of the Data Team
	The "4Ps of Change": Practices, People, Policies, and Processes
	Understanding individual change through the Concerns-Based Adoption Model
Activities	Activity 18.1: The Big Picture of Change: Action Planning
	Activity 18.2: Monitoring: Action/Reflection Cycle

WHAT IS TASK 18?

In Task 18, the Data Team uses the Logic Model and Monitoring Plan developed in Tasks 15–17 to prepare a detailed Action Plan. The Action Plan includes the strategies, expected outcomes, and Monitoring Plan identified in Tasks 15–17 as well as actions, a timeline, resources needed, and people responsible for each strategy. The Data Team members may be the ones taking immediate action in their own classrooms, such as changing the types of questions they ask, increasing the amount of reading students do, modifying the approach to inquiry, or instituting more opportunities for students to assess their own learning. The Data Team may also be supporting other teachers to implement new strategies in their classrooms, through coaching, sharing protocols, and providing professional development. Team members may be attending professional development to learn how to implement their chosen strategies. They may be organizing new classroom materials and resources for use in their own classrooms or making sure the materials other teachers need to implement new practices are readily available. Taking action can include everything from small-scale changes being made by individual teachers to whole-school improvement involving multiple teachers and grades.

During implementation, the Data Team will be responsible for playing a major role in ongoing monitoring, including gathering data on results with students, such as from frequent common assessments, and results with teachers, such as measuring teachers' gains in content knowledge. It also includes collecting data on the implementation of the strategies, such as the amount of time spent teaching new units or using new instructional strategies. At this stage, the Data Team can even start to look more like a change-leadership team that uses data to guide an improvement effort in the school. The essential work of Task 18 is to ensure that the Action Plan is developed and communicated clearly to everyone involved and that monitoring data are gathered and analyzed. The product of this task is the completed and shared Action Plan. A sample Action Plan, shown in Table 7.2, is based on work conducted at one of the Using Data Project sites.

Table 7.2   Sample Using Data Action Plan

Student-learning goal	By June of next year, fifth-grade students at our school will improve their performance on nonroutine problem solving, and achievement gaps between White and African American and Hispanic students will narrow as evidenced by • an increase of 15 percentage points in students scoring proficient on the state CRT, • a narrowing of achievement gaps by 10 percentage points, and • an increase of 25 percentage points in proficiency levels on both the MARS assessments and on our monthly problem of the week.						Student-learning results
Strategy 1 (from Logic Model)	Actions	Person(s) responsible/ by when	Resource/ Budget	Expected outcomes (from Logic Model)	Monitoring tools (from Logic Model)	Person(s) responsible/ by when	Outcome results
Implement Bridges to Classroom Mathematics professional development training	Arrange release time for participating teachers	Data Coach, Sept 30	Consulting fee ($1,500)	Teacher knowledge: Develop understanding of content in the curriculum and how curriculum builds across grades K–12	Teacher feedback in meetings and through online survey	Data Team, monthly and biannually	
	Schedule workshop facilitator to lead sessions	Math coordinator, Oct 15					
	Purchase teacher materials	Math coordinator, Oct 15	Materials ($1,250)	Teacher practice: Implement the curriculum with fidelity	Classroom observations	Principal, every month, Dec–May	
	Request substitutes	Principals, Oct 15	12 @ $80/day		Analysis of lesson plans	Data Team, once per month, Dec–May	
	Arrange logistics for sessions	Data Team members, Sept 30	Room, supplies, and catering				
	Develop/ administer teacher feedback survey	Data Coach, Nov 15, Feb 15, May 15	District evaluator, 8 days				
	Review revised lesson plans	Data Coach, Dec–May	Data Team, monthly				

A Data Team in Action: Canton City Middle School Mathematics. Part IV: Monitoring and Sharing Success—Pam Bernabei-Rorrer, Mathematics and Data Coach, Canton City, Ohio (continued from Task 11)

One of the most valuable outcomes from the collaboration between the teachers was the sharing of instructional strategies that had been proven successful by the common assessment. For example, one middle school scored particularly high in probability on the common assessment, while the scores from the other three schools were more consistent with each other. The teachers from the higher-performing school shared that they had developed a supplemental packet based on a college textbook and used it with their students. Their supplemental packet was duplicated and distributed across the district, contributing to increased performance levels in probability the following school year. Other outcomes from the collaborative inquiry have been modifications in the pacing of the curriculum map, the development of different instructional strategies, and the expansion of differentiated learning plans to meet the needs of individual students in the classrooms. (Continued in Task 19.)

BACKGROUND INFORMATION FOR DATA COACHES

What Role Does the Data Team Play at This Point?

Throughout this component of the process, Data Team members will be wearing two hats—as implementers and monitors. As implementers, they will be putting strategies into action in their own classrooms and/or providing the support and training for other teachers to implement in their classrooms. As monitors, they are gathering data that will be used to improve the Action Plan and determine whether outcomes are being met. In essence, the Data Team engages in cycles of taking action, reflecting on the results, making adjustments, and taking new action. As they reach key milestones or benchmarks, they publicly recognize their success. They then reenter the cycle by asking, "Where do we go next? What other actions need to be taken to enhance student learning?"

The monitoring data will play a key role in helping the Data Team make adjustments in the implementation of the Action Plan as well as to know when outcomes have been met. For example, if your Action Plan starts with a teacher professional development program to enhance content knowledge, one set of monitoring data will focus on the quality of the program (e.g., gathered through observations of the sessions) and another on the extent to which teachers enhanced their content knowledge (e.g., gathered through pre– and post–teacher assessments). The analysis of the monitoring data can help the Data Team know if the program that was provided was of the expected quality and whether it contributed to teachers' learning.

The job of the Data Team also includes identifying any obstacles to the plan and working with the leadership to remove them, amplifying success by supporting everyone to share what is working, and carefully monitoring whether the strategies are leading to changes in teacher practice and improvements in student learning.

What Are the Key Areas That the Data Coach Focuses On to Support Implementation of the Action Plan?

At this stage in the process, the Data Coach's role expands from applying data literacy and facilitating the Data Team to sustaining continuous improvement (see Figure 7.1 and the actions in the outer circle, Lead for Sustainability, and refer back to "Select, Prepare, and Empower Data Coaches" in Chapter 2). To carry out this role in leading and sustaining change, it is very important for the Data Coach to have an understanding of research and models for educational change. Data Coaches and Data Teams should pay close attention to the "4Ps of Change" as they implement strategies and monitor their results (Loucks, 1983). The 4Ps of Change are Practices, People, Policies, and Processes.

Practices

Success is likely to increase when the practices you plan to implement are clearly defined, useable for the target audience, and valid for addressing the identified

Figure 7.1   Data Coach's role.

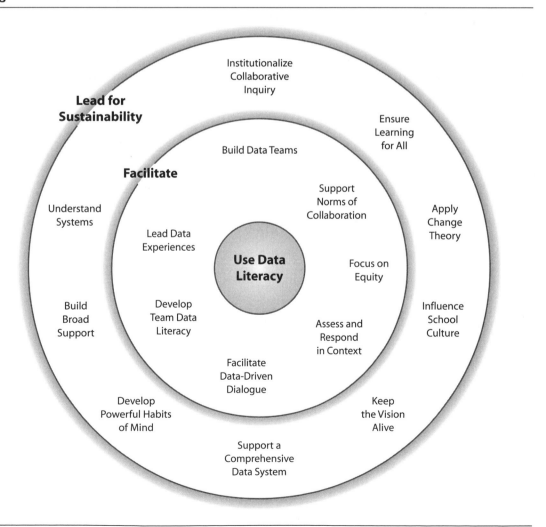

Figure 7.2 Swingset cartoon.

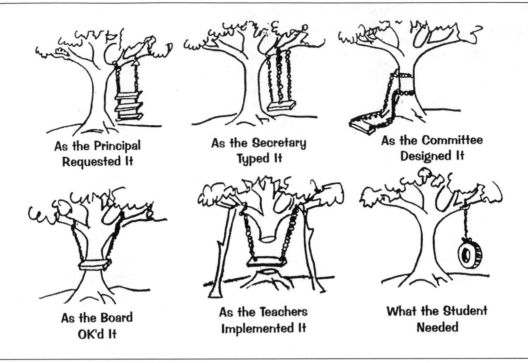

SOURCE Adapted from Alexander, C., Silverstein, M., Angel, S., Ishikawa, S., & Abrams, D. (1975). *The Oregon Experiment*, p. 44. New York: Oxford University Press. Reprinted and adapted with permission of Oxford University Press, Inc.

student-learning problem. Too often teachers are asked to do something without an explicit understanding of what the new practice is, its purpose, or how it should be implemented in the classroom. Such lack of clarity is the enemy of effective implementation. By going through the activities in Tasks 15–17, you chose strategies that have evidence of success in addressing the student-learning problem. It is important to communicate with all users so that they understand why the strategy was chosen and how the practice is intended to be implemented, and then to continue to monitor users to make sure they understand the practice and how it is best used. Figure 7.2 illustrates what can happen when implementers have varied understandings of the intended results!

> *Since change is made by individuals, their personal satisfactions, frustrations, concerns, motivations, and perceptions all contribute to the success or failure of a change initiative.*
>
> —Loucks-Horsley & Stiegelbauer, 1991, p. 18

People

One common adage says, "Change would be easy if it weren't for all the people!" We can't agree more that people must be a major focus of any change effort.

As the Data Coach, your job is to work with your Data Team to address any questions they have about implementing the Action Plan, make sure they understand the practices they will implement and/or support others to implement, and ensure that they receive the training and support to implement effectively. You will engage the Data Team in actively reflecting on what is working and what needs to be adjusted to fully implement the Action Plan.

Be prepared for some people to resist using or to have concerns about using the new practices. Data Coaches are wise to seek out and talk with those people who are reticent about trying new practices. Ask them what they are concerned about and how you can help. As Michael Fullan (1999) says, "problems are our friends," (p. 18) and in this case, you can gain insight about potential pitfalls of your plan by talking with people who are somewhat resistant. For example, they may have valid reservations about using the practices the Data Team chose; find out what these are and address them before others raise the same issues. Check in with everyone who is part of the Action Plan and make sure that all people know what is expected of them, have had an opportunity to express their concerns and gotten help in addressing them, and are accountable for taking action. Pay special attention to principals and other key administrators since they need to have an understanding of the plan and clear expectations about the outcomes, and know the resources needed. Offer suggestions for how they can support the Data Team to implement the Action Plan.

Policies

Clearly communicated policies about what will be done and how it will be supported strengthens implementation. In addition, when principals follow up and monitor the use of new practices, there tends to be a much greater use of the practices (Fullan, 2005; Schmoker, 2004a). New practices that are working well and producing results should be integrated into the standard operating procedures of the school (e.g., in the schedule and budget) so that they are more likely to be sustained. If your Data Team is working to increase engagement in science classes through more investigations, the teachers will need new materials, or, if teachers are trying new instructional strategies to teach mathematics, they may need ongoing coaching and other forms of professional development to learn how to use the techniques. Are there policies to support getting the materials and the professional development? If the team is working on closing achievement gaps and eliminating tracking, a district policy statement against tracking students and with a strong antiracist stance will help to cement this change.

Processes

Change is a process that usually moves from initiation (getting started, developing the action plan, adopting or developing a new program, getting prepared by attending orientation or professional development, and doing the initial try-out) to implementation (using the practice, identifying and solving problems, and gathering data on its effects) to institutionalization (sustaining the practice, setting policy to adopt the practice, and integrating the practice into existing and ongoing school operating procedures). Too often people think of change as more of an event than a process. As Kaser, Mundry, Stiles, and Loucks-Horsley (2006) write:

What is different when people see change as a process? . . . They . . .

- involve the people affected by the change in planning for and leading the change;

- account for the impact of change on the people involved;

- know that any significant change takes time and plan accordingly;

- employ professional development over time to ensure that people acquire the right knowledge and skills to implement the change; and

- set realistic expectations for implementation, build a culture of support for the change that avoids blaming people for past mistakes, and apply a monitoring procedure to track key benchmark events. (pp. 73–74)

Are There Tools and Models to Help the Data Team Guide Implementation?

The Concerns-Based Adoption Model (CBAM; Hall & Hord, 2006) offers tools and background to help Data Coaches and Data Teams pay attention to the 4Ps of Change and monitor as people make changes in their practice. The model is based on three overall principles: (1) Change is a process, not an event; (2) change requires developmental growth; and (3) change happens in individuals first and organizations second. Based on these principles, the CBAM offers three tools that are extremely useful for monitoring implementation of an innovation (see the Toolkit for complete instructions for using two of these tools). The first tool is called the Stages of Concern. It assesses perceptions, feelings, and motivations so that change leaders can know, and even predict, what concerns people have about the change and can respond appropriately. Hall and Hord identified seven predictable stages that people move through as they implement a change. Table 7.3 depicts the Stages of Concern and what people express at each stage. The third column gives examples of what teachers from a school that is instituting formative assessment practices to improve student-learning results might express at the different Stages of Concern.

There is a Stages of Concern questionnaire that you can use to gather this data (see Hall & Hord, 2006), but for more informal assessment, Data Coaches and Data Team members can gather the data through short conversations. In conversations and/or at Data Team meetings ask, "How is the use of [the innovation] going? What are you concerned about as you implement it?" Listen for the concerns the users express. Alternatively, you can gather written reflections on the same question. The Data Coach and team can use the information gathered to assess the concerns and decide how to respond. (For more information on the use of the written reflections and guidelines for how to help people at each stage, see Toolkit: Stages of Concern.)

A second CBAM tool is used to clearly define the practice or innovation being used. Called the Innovation Configuration (IC), this tool lays out the key elements one would see being used and describes what they look like in practice. For example, if the innovation is "use of higher-level questioning in the classroom," the IC would describe what you would expect to see a teacher (and a student) doing when higher-level questioning is being used in the classroom. Each element is described on a continuum from nonuse to highly effective use.

The IC has several uses. It can serve as an effective way to develop a shared understanding of what the innovation entails and to communicate expectations for implementation to users. It can also be used as an observation protocol for classroom visits to assess how well teachers are using all elements of the innovation. If your

Table 7.3   The Concerns-Based Adoption Model (CBAM): Stages of Concern

Stages	Expressions of typical concerns	Using Data Process examples
VI: Refocusing	I have some ideas about something that would work even better.	I heard about a hand-held computer that can do all the student assessment for you. I am interested in using that instead.
V: Collaboration	How can I relate what I am doing to what others are doing?	I have been using the common benchmark assessments, and now I am interested in sharing and discussing the results with the other teachers at my grade level.
IV: Consequence	How is my use affecting learners? How can I refine it to have more impact?	I seem to be getting more in-depth responses and more insight into my students' thinking by using open-response items. I am thinking about using these in my other subjects too.
III: Management	I seem to be spending all my time getting materials ready.	I am trying to do more ongoing student assessment, but developing and scoring open-response items is taking me a long time, and I am not even sure that the ones I have done are on target.
II: Personal	How will using it affect me?	I am already spending most of every night planning lessons. I can't see how I can add hours of scoring student work to my busy life.
I: Informational	I would like to know more about it.	I give tests, but I don't know that much about using formative assessment in the classroom. What's involved?
0: Awareness	I am not concerned about it.	I haven't heard anything about it.

SOURCE Adapted from Hall, G. E., & Hord, S. M., *Implementing Change: Patterns, Principles, and Potholes*, 2e. Published by Allyn & Bacon, Boston, MA. Copyright © 2006 by Pearson Education. Reprinted/adapted by permission of the publisher.

Data Team will be monitoring the same practice in multiple classrooms, it would be useful to spend the time to develop an IC for this purpose. (For more information on using ICs, see Hall & Hord, 2006.)

The third tool, the Levels of Use Scale, is useful for assessing the extent to which an intervention is actually being implemented. Table 7.4 shows the six levels, behaviors associated with them, and examples of how Data Teams can respond. Information on a protocol for conducting a Levels of Use Branching Interview and guidelines for teaching this tool to the Data Team are in the Toolkit: Levels of Use.

Table 7.4 The Concerns-Based Adoption Model (CBAM): Levels of Use and Behavioral Indices

Levels of use		Behavioral indices of level	Examples of what Data Teams do to address each level
VI	Renewal	The user is seeking more effective alternatives to the established use of the innovation.	Discuss the results achieved with the innovation. Check to see that the practice has been implemented as intended. Identify where change is needed and help to enhance use of innovation.
V	Integration	The user is making deliberate efforts to coordinate with others in using the innovation.	Convene teachers within and across grade levels to discuss how to extend the use of the practices.
IVB	Refinement	The user is making changes to increase outcomes.	Modify instruction to better reach all learners.
IVA	Routine	The user is making few or no changes and has an established pattern of use.	Convene teachers and discuss what is working well, what impact they are having, and whether they are satisfied.
III	Mechanical	The user is using the practice in a poorly coordinated manner and is making user-oriented changes.	Provide teachers with coaching, demonstrations, and guidelines to follow.
II	Preparation	The user is preparing to use the innovation.	Provide initial training and materials.
I	Orientation	The user is seeking out information about the innovation.	Establish clear expectations about what the innovation is and its purpose.
0	Nonuse	No action is being taken with respect to the innovation.	Examine and communicate about student results to raise awareness of the need for action.

SOURCE Adapted from Hall, G. E., & Hord, S. M., *Implementing Change: Patterns, Principles, and Potholes*, 2e. Published by Allyn & Bacon, Boston, MA. Copyright © 2006 by Pearson Education. Reprinted/adapted by permission of the publisher.

What Are the Challenges and Pitfalls Inherent in This Task?

This task is where programs and practices are planned and initiated to address the student-learning problem. The biggest pitfalls are that the Data Team may not feel empowered to act on the changes that need to be made, or the changes may be so complex that they lack the resources to put their plan in place. The Data Coach and the Data Team must remember that there are many improvements they can make themselves in their own classrooms. They can start action planning by asking, "What short-cycle improvement actions can we make in our own classrooms?" For the larger-scale changes, such as curriculum revisions and adoptions, the team will need to involve key administrators and others to get their help in planning and implementing such changes to avoid the pitfalls. Some examples of both short- and long-cycle strategies are given in Table 7.5.

Table 7.5 Examples of Strategies Implemented in Using Data Project Sites

Short-cycle strategies	• Use higher-order questions • Implement quarterly benchmark assessments • Implement a problem-of-the-week • Provide extra help for students who need it • Share rubrics and student-learning data with students • Use vocabulary walls • Assess and reteach concepts as needed using a different approach
Long-cycle strategies	• Adopt and implement a new mathematics curriculum • Institute lesson study to design and use model lessons in mathematics • Implement use of graphing calculators or other technology • Implement a standards-based instructional model • Institute a new reading program focused on informational text (nonfiction)

Several other pitfalls may be encountered at this point, including inadequate monitoring, resulting in little follow-through; a lack of clarity of what people should do, resulting in mixed implementation and confusion; and failure to allow enough time for people to learn how to use new practices, resulting in frustration and resistance. Pay attention to these potential pitfalls; keep key administrators and staff up to date, and ask for their help. See Chapter 2 section, "Build Stakeholder Support," for ideas for communicating with key stakeholders.

RESOURCES

Guskey, T. R. (2000). *Evaluating professional development*. Thousand Oaks, CA: Corwin Press. (See Chapters 4–9.)

Hall, G. E., & Hord, S. M. (2006). *Implementing change: Patterns, principles, and potholes* (2nd ed.). Boston: Allyn & Bacon/Longman. (See Chapters 6–9.)

Loucks-Horsley, S., Love, N., Stiles, K. E., Mundry, S., & Hewson, P. W. (2003). *Designing professional development for teachers of science and mathematics* (2nd ed.). Thousand Oaks, CA: Corwin Press. (See Chapter 5.)

Love, N. (2002). *Using data/getting results: A practical guide for school improvement in mathematics and science.* Norwood, MA: Christopher-Gordon. (See pp. 112–115.)

MAJOR ACTIVITIES FOR TASK 18

Activity	Time required	CD-ROM materials: Task 18 link	CD-ROM Toolkit: Relevant tools
Activity 18.1: The Big Picture of Change: Action Planning	2.5 hours (allow more time if you are implementing a schoolwide Action Plan)	Handout H18.1: Action Planning Template	
Activity 18.2: Monitoring: Action/Reflection Cycle	Regular (monthly or bimonthly) check-in meetings of 1.75 hours		Data-Driven Dialogue, Group Roles, Levels of Use, Seven Norms of Collaboration, Stages of Concern, Stoplight Highlighting

PREPARING FOR THE TASK

• Read "Background Information for Data Coaches"; see the CD-ROM: Task 18 for handouts and sample goals and agenda; and review "Standard Procedures for Data Team Meetings" (see the introduction to Chapter 3 in this book and on CD-ROM). You can reference in-depth descriptions of relevant Toolkit entries on the CD-ROM.

• Plan agendas and a schedule for meetings. This task involves an initial 2.5-hour meeting to develop the Action Plan, followed by shorter monthly meetings to analyze monitoring data. The number of these monitoring meetings will vary according to the time period over which you are implementing the Action Plan.

MATERIALS PREPARATION

• Post the Logic Model and Monitoring Plan charts from Tasks 15–17 on the Data Wall.

• Make one copy for each Data Team member of Handout H18.1 and of *Knots* poem in Data Coach Notes.

• Using three pieces of chart paper, label one "Skills," the second "Incentives," and the third "Resources." Post them on the wall.

• On chart paper, create a table using Handout H18.1 as a guide.

DATA PREPARATION

For the initial Task 18 meeting, you will not need to prepare any data. However, at each subsequent meeting, prepare copies of the data gathered from the monitoring tools. The Data Team will use these to analyze and monitor the Action Plan and determine outcomes and progress toward the student-learning goal. See the data examples in the Task 14 CD-ROM link for samples of survey, interview, and classroom observation data that can be used for monitoring purposes.

DATA COACH NOTES

 ### Activity 18.1: The Big Picture of Change: Action Planning

1. Ask Data Team members to read the excerpt from R. D. Laing's *Knots* (see sidebar). Ask for general reactions to the reading, and then ask, "As professionals, how often have you faced the dilemma reflected in this poem?" Discuss some of the following questions: "What would make it safe to speak out about the skills we lack and the knowledge we need? As a Data Team what skills and knowledge do we honestly need to enact the changes we have chosen to implement?" Document comments on the sheet of chart paper labeled "Skills." Note that the Data Team will be revisiting this list regularly since, to paraphrase Laing, we don't yet know what it is we don't know! They will be adding to the list as they implement their plan, identifying new skills and knowledge they will need along the way.

Excerpt from R. D. Laing, *Knots* (1970)

There is something I don't know
   that I am supposed to know.
I don't know what it is I don't know,
   and yet am supposed to know,
And I feel I look stupid
   if I seem both not to know it
   and not know *what* it is I don't know.
Therefore, I pretend I know it.
   This is nerve-wracking since I don't
   Know what I must pretend to know.
Therefore, I pretend to know everything.

SOURCE From *Knots* by R. D. Laing, copyright © 1970 by R. D. Laing. Used by permission of Pantheon Books, a division of Random House, Inc.

2. Acknowledge that taking the actions they have chosen will require Data Team members and other teachers involved to put in extra time and effort. Ask the team to consider what incentives will motivate everyone to do this extra work and keep at it when the going gets tough. Document these ideas on the sheet of chart paper labeled "Incentives." For example, incentives might include recognition for raising student achievement, time to meet with and learn from other teachers trying the same strategies, or funding to attend professional development or professional meetings.

3. Direct the Data Team's attention to the sheet of chart paper labeled "Resources." Ask the team to consider what resources will be needed to enact a plan of school improvement to address the student-learning problem. Document their ideas on the chart paper.

> **Facilitation Note:** As a follow-up to this meeting, plan to communicate with key leaders about the incentives and the resources that the Data Team suggested to negotiate how they can be provided.

4. Let the Data Team know that they will use all of the ideas they have generated about skills, incentives, and resources along with their Logic Model to create the Action Plan. Distribute Handout H18.1, and lead the team through the Planning Template, recording all responses and decisions on chart paper.

- Student-Learning Goal: Fill in your goal from your Logic Model.
- Strategies: List each strategy from the Logic Model. Use additional copies of Handout H18.1 if you have more than two strategies.
- Actions: Brainstorm and list each specific action to take to accomplish the strategy.
- Person(s) Responsible: Identify the people who will carry out these actions and by when.
- Resources/Budget: List the materials, budget, time, and other resources needed to carry out actions.
- Expected Outcomes: List the teacher, student, and school outcomes expected from the actions taken (from Logic Model).
- Monitoring Tools: List the tool(s) that will be used to gather monitoring data for each strategy (from the Logic Model).
- Person(s) Responsible: Identify the people who will facilitate the gathering and organizing of the monitoring data and by when.
- Results: As you implement the plan and monitor the results, you will fill out this column, including Outcome Results and Student-Learning Results.

5. When the Action Plan is complete, post it on the wall. Identify the immediate next steps the team will take to implement the plan, and make sure they are clearly assigned to people and the timeline for completion is clear. Review assignments with the Data Team, and establish a schedule for your monthly monitoring meetings. This is a document you and the Data Team will continually revisit, updating it when strategies have been implemented, documenting that monitoring data have been collected, and, possibly, adding new strategies based on what you learn from the monitoring data. During each Data Team meeting, examine each strategy and document what you know about results so far. Post these on your Data Wall.

Activity 18.2: Monitoring: Action/Reflection Cycle

Convene the Data Team monthly (or at least every two months) to assess the implementation of the Action Plan and analyze the monitoring data using the procedures suggested here:

Check-in (10 minutes). If the Data Team members are the people implementing the strategies, start with a check-in on their progress, asking: "What did you try? How did it go? What problems are you having? How are the students reacting? What help do you think you need?" If the Data Team members are facilitating others to implement strategies in classrooms, ask the same set of questions, as they relate to what the Data Team members are observing as others implement. Record responses.

Review monitoring data (10 minutes). Review what evidence/data the team will be examining during the meeting. Record the information on chart paper, and post the chart on the wall.

Develop criteria for analyzing evidence (10 minutes). Clarify what the Data Team will look for in the data and what questions the data will help them answer about either the implementation of a strategy or the achievement of an outcome. Refer back to the outcomes you established for each strategy.

Data-Driven Dialogue (30 minutes). Engage the Data Team in the four phases of Data-Driven Dialogue to investigate the monitoring data. Apply Stoplight Highlighting criteria to the data during the Observe phase. For example, compare the results with the expected outcomes on your Logic Model and Action Plan. Green criteria might include data that suggest better-than-expected progress, yellow might indicate adequate progress, and red or pink might indicate less-than-expected or -desired progress.

Draw conclusions (30 minutes). Engage the Data Team in using the evidence from the monitoring data to improve the Action Plan. The following questions can help focus the discussion:

- What is the evidence that the strategies are being implemented? What is the quality of the implementation? What problems need to be addressed?
- Do the data indicate that outcomes are being met? Is there any evidence of student impact yet?
- What successes do we have and what is the evidence?
- How can we spread successful practices and amplify the successes we are experiencing?
- What do we do if we are not making progress on an outcome? Did we expect the outcome too soon, or do we need to make adjustments in the strategies? Are we making progress through other strategies that may in fact help us achieve this outcome?

Next steps (15 minutes). Explore next steps, including specific changes to be made in the Action Plan, implementation of the strategies, and/or adjustments in the Monitoring Plan. Fill in results achieved on the last column of the Action Plan (see H18.1). Explore whether there are successes to share and celebrate and with whom they should be shared (see Task 19).

Task 19: Celebrate Success and Renew Collaborative Inquiry

Task-at-a-Glance

Purpose	Celebrate successes in achieving outcomes and student-learning goal; identify next steps for continuing collaborative inquiry and school improvement
Data	Monitoring data
Questions to ask	What changes are being made in practice?
	What are the student-learning results?
	Has the student-learning goal been met?
	How will we celebrate successes?
	What new outcomes and/or student-learning goals need to be established?
	How has our school culture grown? What's needed next?
Concepts	Community celebration
	Sustaining collaborative inquiry
Activities	Activity 19.1: Celebrate and Share Results
	Activity 19.2: Adjust and Renew Collaborative Inquiry
	Activity 19.3: School Culture Review

WHAT IS TASK 19?

At this stage in the collaborative inquiry process, the Data Team is well into the implementation of the Action Plan and making improvements based on the monitoring data. This task focuses on helping the Data Team celebrate their successes and take the next steps in continuous improvement efforts through ongoing collaborative inquiry.

BACKGROUND INFORMATION FOR DATA COACHES

Individuals are more likely to believe their work is significant, to feel a sense of achievement, and to be motivated to give their best efforts to tasks before them when they feel that those efforts will be noted and appreciated.

—DuFour, 1998, p. 57

How Can We Share and Celebrate Our Successes?

As part of the Action/Reflection Cycle the Data Team began in Task 18, you will have started to document results. Every time you meet you are looking at data to learn what is working and what results you have. These might be reports on the numbers of teachers trying new strategies or documentation of new learning among teachers. Later in the implementation of the Action Plan, you may have benchmark assessments that show growth in student learning. On a regular basis, the community can celebrate these successes. Once you begin to identify evidence of impact, schedule a Data Team meeting to develop a plan for celebrating and sharing success.

Celebrations call attention to and help amplify what is working and the results achieved. They are also fun and feel good! Rick DuFour (1998) cites these benefits to schools that use celebrations:

- Recipients of public recognition feel appreciated and motivated to continue their actions.
- Celebrations reinforce shared values and signal what is important.
- They provide real-life examples of the school's values in action and encourage everyone to emulate those actions.
- Celebrations fuel momentum, keep people going, and help sustain changes— success breeds success.
- They are fun!

Here are some guidelines to keep in mind as you plan your celebrations. First, be crystal clear about what you are celebrating, what was accomplished and the evidence the accomplishment was based on, and why it is important. Second, recognize people for the specific things they have done that support the school's values. Some schools choose to highlight the students and what they have accomplished; others like to recognize both what the staff has done to support students and what the students have accomplished. Next, be sure to recognize the little wins ("school dropout rates are down slightly") as well as the big wins ("we have closed the achievement gap between African American and White students substantially"). Finally, avoid having the same people recognized all the time. DuFour (1998) suggests creating opportunities for "lots of winners" (p. 59). (For some examples of celebrations from Using Data Project sites, see sidebar in Activity 19.1.)

Once the initial student-learning problem identified by the Data Team and its corresponding Action Plan have met with success, the Data Team is at a decision point about what to do next. Activity 19.2 provides specific suggestions for next steps, including taking action on other identified student-learning problems, exploring other content areas and/or grade levels in need of improvement, or engaging additional teachers in the inquiry process by establishing new Data Teams. Whichever path the Data Team takes, the overall goal is to sustain collaborative inquiry in the school as a foundational process to guide ongoing improvement of teaching and learning.

MAJOR ACTIVITIES FOR TASK 19

Activity	Time required	CD-ROM materials: Task 19 link	CD-ROM Toolkit: Relevant tools
Activity 19.1: Celebrate and Share Results	Bimonthly Data Team meetings and annual celebrations (60–90 minutes)		
Activity 19.2: Adjust and Renew Collaborative Inquiry	Dependent on decisions for next steps		
Activity 19.3: School Culture Review	30 minutes		Program Elements Matrix (PEM) of a Using Data School Culture

PREPARING FOR THE TASK

Review the Program Elements Matrix (PEM) tool on the CD-ROM.

MATERIALS PREPARATION

- Gather and prepare materials and/or data as needed, such as portfolios or data presentations.

- Make sure the Program Elements Matrix (PEM) of a Using Data School Culture chart is posted on the wall.

Celebrations at Using Data Project Sites

- Presenting Data Team members with stuffed animals representative of their special contributions to the collaborative inquiry process, such as a dolphin for navigating through the murky waters.
- Sharing a PowerPoint slide presentation with the names of each Data Team member and accompanied by inspirational music as each person received a letter of recognition.
- A Data Team presentation of the team's journey and portfolio to a larger audience, including building administrators from other schools.
- Data Team presentations at school board meetings to highlight achievements.
- A presentation to the community by the Data Coach, including quotes from members of the Data Team.

DATA COACH NOTES

 **Activity 19.1: Celebrate and Share Results**

1. Convene the Data Team, and review all the findings the team has documented through their ongoing analysis of the monitoring data and adjustment of the Action Plan. Ask the team: What do we have to celebrate? What are the successes that everyone should know about? What specific strategies have led to our success? How can we spread those strategies to achieve even greater success in the future? Who are the people who should be recognized for what they have done?

2. Ask the Data Team to consider how best to celebrate the accomplishments they have noted. Share some examples, such as hosting an event (e.g., a dinner or special school community event) where the story of

what has been accomplished is told and people are recognized with certificates, plaques, mugs, hats, or other tokens of appreciation and recognition. Consider using both ongoing ways to celebrate, such as notices in newsletters, e-mails, or recognition at staff meetings, as well as larger, year-end events   .

3. Encourage the Data Team to brainstorm additional ways to celebrate, such as the following:

- Be prepared to "brag" about what is working. Prepare a two- or three-minute summary of the results that the Data Team members can share with parents, other teachers, or school board members whom it may be important to inform of the successes. Write up the key points so that team members can hand them out to the individuals or groups they speak with.
- Assemble and display a Data Team portfolio (see "Standard Procedures for Data Team Meetings" in the introduction to Chapter 3 in this book and on CD-ROM). The purpose of the portfolio is twofold: (1) to reflect on your own progress and (2) to share your learning with the larger community. See the sidebar for suggestions of items from your portfolio to share with others and Figure 7.3 for an example of a Data Team portfolio.
- Reflect back on Task 3: Raise Awareness of Cultural Proficiency, and celebrate progress that has been made in attitudes and practices along the Cultural Proficiency Continuum.

- A celebration of significant gains on the state test, at which Data Team members responded to the question "What do you think made the difference?"
- A party for second graders after they achieved the goal for vocabulary improvement set by the Data Team.

Using Data Process Portfolios

Data Teams in the Using Data Project prepared portfolios with the following elements to share their process with a wider audience:

The journey: Evidence that represents (1) a summary of the data analyzed, (2) the student-learning problem statement, (3) Cause-and-Effect Analysis, (4) the Logic Model, and (5) the Action Plan.

The results: Summarize and report monitoring data and results accomplished, and use the Program Elements Matrix (PEM) to show how your culture is shifting.

Reflective questions: Select two or three Data Team tools or processes that were found to be most helpful, and describe how they were helpful.

Facilitation Note: This is also a good time for you to celebrate your progress as a Data Coach. For example, go back and look at the self-assessment you did in Chapter 2, note your own growth, and set new goals for the future.

 ## Activity 19.2: Adjust and Renew Collaborative Inquiry

1. Convene the Data Team after they have achieved significant milestones with their first experience through the collaborative inquiry process, and ask them to start looking to the future. Explain that besides celebrating successes, there is a commitment to continuing to engage in collaborative inquiry to address other areas of school improvement.

2. Consider how the Data Team and the school wish to change and/or expand the use of collaborative inquiry to continue to improve teaching and learning. Most commonly, Data Teams are eager to continue the Using Data Process with new data that become available. But there are many possible ways to renew collaborative

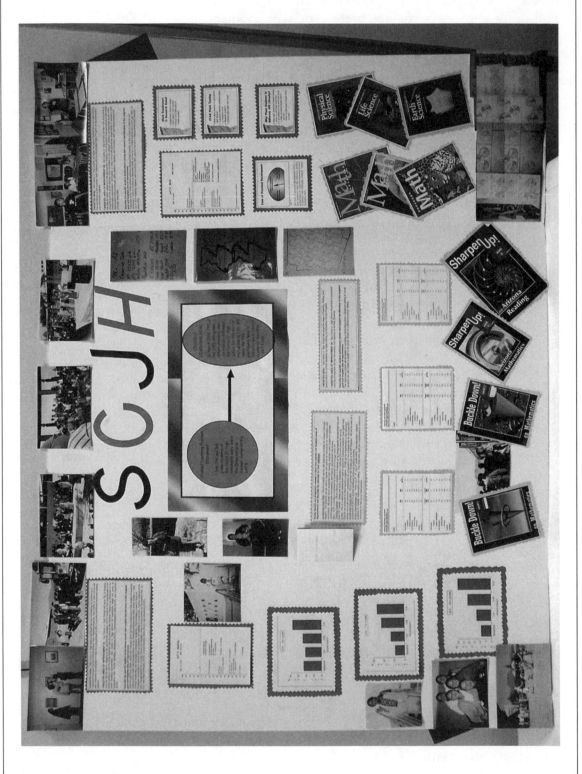

Figure 7.3 A Data Team portfolio.

Table 7.6 Examples of Continuous Use of Data to Improve Learning

What we want to do next	Path
We want to develop more Data Teams to expand the continuous use of data to improve learning.	Select new Data Teams; start back at Task 1 and build the foundation.
We want to tackle other subject areas to plan improvements in student learning.	Ask the Data Team to commit to engaging in another round of data use; start back at Task 6 to analyze another subject area.
We want to implement other strategies to further the student-learning goal we have been working with.	Get commitment from the team to continue; start back at Task 15.
We want to strengthen our foundation and learn more about cultural proficiency.	Go back to Tasks 1–4.
We want to address some of the other problems we saw in the student-learning data we analyzed.	Go back to Task 12.
We want to repeat the process with new data that we have.	Start at Task 6.
We want to learn more about data and statistics.	Choose activities from Task 5.
We just got our common assessments in place and want to make effective use of them.	Start with Task 11.
We want to expand our Data Team to include representatives from each grade level.	Recruit new Data Team members; start at Task 1.

inquiry, some of which are illustrated in Table 7.6. Whatever your needs, the power of collaborative inquiry can continue to help you find and address student-learning problems and build a community of collective accountability for student success.

Activity 19.3: School Culture Review

1. Convene the Data Team and pause to take stock of where you have been and where you are now with respect to the school culture.

2. Using the Program Elements Matrix (PEM) of a Using Data School Culture, rate where you see your school now on each of the elements. As a team, compare the ratings with ones you did earlier. Where do you see the shifts? What additional work is needed?

3. Guide the Data Team to think about next steps for enhancing the school culture by reflecting on any of the following questions most relevant for your context:
   - Have you involved key people and leaders in building the culture to support collaborative inquiry? Who else needs to be involved?

- How well integrated is the use of data within ongoing structures such as faculty meetings, curriculum committees, and other planning and policy-making groups? What else do you need to do to enhance this integration?
- To what extent has the school or district leadership established the use of data as an expectation for all staff? What is the evidence? What else needs to be done?
- What is the focus of faculty conversations about learning? Have conversations shifted away from blame and toward collective responsibility for closing achievement gaps?
- What are your ideas as a Data Team for building on your own work and spreading it to others in the school or district?
- Building on this review and the decisions for next steps, engage the Data Team in moving forward with collaborative inquiry.

A Data Team in Action: Canton City Middle School Mathematics. Part V: Celebrating Success and Reflecting on Our Learning—Pam Bernabei-Rorrer, Mathematics and Data Coach, Canton City, Ohio (continued from Task 18)

Through using the Using Data Process, the Canton City Middle School has achieved dramatic gains in student achievement in mathematics.

Although our path through the educational jungle has been forged, there are vines that still need to be cut down for us to continue on our journey. First, although many teachers on the mathematics Data Team are excited about the information that the data provide, cultivating strong relationships of mutual trust and respect must be an ongoing process in order to maintain teachers' support for the initiative. Building and district data are always shared with administrators so that they can better understand the curriculum in their buildings and support their staff, but individual classroom data are kept among the team in order to ensure that they are in no way used for evaluative purposes. Second, the necessity for meeting in professional learning teams requires that the administration support these meetings through release time for the teachers. After explaining the significance of the teamwork and of providing supporting research, the Canton City Schools administration has provided opportunities for the teachers to participate in the process of collaborative inquiry during late-start days and professional release days.

The increase in student achievement cannot be attributed to any one factor, but to the effective plan of action developed and implemented through collaboration by the mathematics Data Team in the Canton City Schools. There is no one hero who stands alone in the effort to increase student achievement, but an entire team of teachers who hold the belief that people can accomplish more together than in isolation. Reflecting back over our journey, I now realize a hidden result of the professional learning community that has developed: the empowerment of future teacher-leaders. I am confident that the mathematics Data Team will continue down the path toward increasing student achievement through the collaboration of the team and the developed leadership skills of its members.

8

Clark County, Nevada

Collaborative Inquiry in Action

By Lori Fulton, Super Data
Coach and Project Facilitator
for Mathematics, Science, and
Technology, Clark County School
District; Thelma Davis, Coordinator
of K–5 Mathematics and Science, Clark
County School District; Janet Dukes and
Greg Gusmerotti, teachers and Data Coaches; and
Joan Lombard, Principal of Katz Elementary School

This is the story of how collaborative inquiry unfolded in one large urban district, Clark County, Nevada, as told by staff who participated in the Using Data Project. The district collaborated with the Using Data Project as a pilot site. The first part of the chapter describes the overall district context and the design and rationale for implementing the Using Data Project at the district level, including reflections on what has been learned about supporting collaborative inquiry. The second part tells the story of how each stage of the Using Data Process played out in one of the Clark County schools, Katz Elementary School, and includes commentary from the principal and the project facilitator.

CLARK COUNTY ORGANIZES FOR COLLABORATIVE INQUIRY

The Clark County School District, covering nearly 8,000 square miles in and around Las Vegas, Nevada, serves approximately 281,000 students K–12 in urban, suburban, and rural communities. It is the fifth largest school district in the nation and includes one of the country's fastest growing urban areas. The six percent growth rate in the county leads, on average, to the construction of 14 new schools and the hiring of more than 1,500 new teachers annually. The student enrollment includes 35 percent Hispanic, 14 percent African American, 8 percent Asian, 1 percent Native American, and 41 percent White.

Funding from the National Science Foundation's Teacher Enhancement and Local Systemic Change (LSC) Initiatives provided teachers in Clark County School District with professional development support over the past 15 years. Through the Mathematics and Science Enhancement (MASE) and MASE K–5 Using Technology LSC projects, over 8,000 teachers worked to improve student learning as they increased their own content knowledge and implemented reform of mathematics and science teaching in their classrooms. Professional development focused on learning content through engaging in mathematics problem solving and science inquiry in collaborative settings. This collaborative process became a hallmark of the LSC projects, where teachers engaged in learning together through conversations focused on student thinking.

The advent of the standards and accountability movement challenged teachers to learn how to use multiple data sources to determine what students know and can do. This became a critical need in the school district. The Using Data Project, with its emphasis on collaborative inquiry, met this need while at the same time aligning well with the foundation of collaboration that had been built in Clark County School District through the work of the LSC projects. By invitation, Clark County School District, in 2002, became a collaborating site with the Using Data Project to pilot and contribute to the development of a professional development program for Using Data Coaches (formerly called Data Facilitators) over the next three years. Through this partnership, Clark County School District hoped to increase student achievement while developing teams of teachers within each region who were prepared to provide leadership in the Using Data Process within the district.

To facilitate these two goals, the director of K–12 mathematics, science, and instructional technology and the coordinator of K–12 mathematics developed a plan and shared the vision of the project with the school district's five regional superintendents. The plan that emerged was that three schools would participate in each region—two elementary schools and one middle school that they feed into. Each participating school would designate a three- to five-member Data Team of teachers and administrators who would participate in a Using Data Coaches professional development program and implement the Using Data Process in their school.

An important consideration in selecting participating schools was to build upon the existing work of the LSC initiative. This led to inclusion of one MASE LSC project school within each regional team. These schools were strongly immersed in mathematics and science reform and had administrative and teacher leadership in place, teachers involved in decision making, and a culture of collaboration. Each principal enthusiastically requested involvement with the Using Data Project, citing the vision of the work as an important next step in moving their schools toward learning to use data for instructional decision making.

Identifying the middle schools and additional elementary schools that would participate in the project was largely based on the feeder pattern between the middle schools and elementary schools, although the willingness of the administrators within each school to commit to the project also influenced the decision. Major goals of the project were to articulate student achievement and instructional needs across grade levels and to form a knowledgeable team within each region to provide leadership as the district moved forward in the process of using data to inform instruction.

THE ROLE OF THE SUPER DATA COACH

Each school-based Data Team was assigned a project facilitator from the Curriculum Division of the Clark County School District. This role turned out to be critical to the success of the project. Each of five project facilitators, four from the LSC project and one providing middle-school science professional development for the district, was assigned to work with the schools within that one region. Project facilitators attended professional development sessions with the Data Teams, worked with project staff, and provided support for the school teams as they implemented the collaborative inquiry process in their school.

This unique role earned them the designation "Super Data Coach," in part because they had the superhuman challenge to move between their role as learners—new to the Using Data Process—and as Coaches of the Coaches, who were often called upon to bring clarity to steps in the process they had just learned themselves. Even with this challenge, the Super Data Coaches provided just-in-time support that kept the Data Teams motivated, on task, and able to push through some of the obstacles they faced in their work. They brought depth of experience in challenging teachers to think deeply about their practice, as well as knowledge of the district's curriculum and assessment processes.

A secondary role of the Super Data Coaches was to help shape the professional development design of the Using Data Project. The collaborating sites provided a forum for testing the professional development design and for reflecting with the Using Data Project staff. As they learned each step in the collaborative inquiry process, the Super Data Coaches implemented the steps with their school teams, reflecting on the successes and challenges in the process and often tailoring the steps to meet the contextual needs of the schools. The Super Data Coaches provided a bridge between the Using Data Project staff and the school teams, learning with and from each other about the design of the professional development that would ultimately become the basis for this book.

IMPLEMENTING THE USING DATA PROCESS

The Using Data Process was embraced in schools where a strong culture of collaborative inquiry was already in place, and the collaborative culture was enhanced through the strategies the team learned through the project. With the support of the Super Data Coach, each Data Team designed a series of regularly scheduled sessions to implement the various steps in the process. On average, the teams met monthly to work through the Using Data processes and often utilized district professional development days or common grade-level planning periods to introduce the processes to their colleagues. During these sessions, the teachers worked through difficult questions centered on addressing the needs of students. To support the school teams with implementation of this process, extra duty pay or substitute release time was provided through grant funding.

At the same time that these schools were learning the Using Data processes, the district was developing the Instructional Data Management System (IDMS) to provide computer-based data management of local, state, and norm-referenced student assessment data. Through IDMS, the district also administered trimester benchmark assessments, which provided data for Structured Teacher Planning Time (STPT), 55-minute planning periods for grade-level teams of teachers to address instructional needs. The district provided three hours of professional development for representatives of each school to learn the STPT process and share the information so that the grade levels could implement the process. The challenge was how this new data management system would align with the Using Data Process.

Schools where the leadership recognized the value of engaging the teachers in collaborative inquiry and using more than one data source to determine the root causes of student-learning problems welcomed the Using Data Project and looked for ways the two data projects could complement each other. For example, IDMS provided core data for collaborative inquiry by generating the tables and charts of the data for state criterion-referenced tests, the Iowa Test of Basic Skills, and the trimester benchmark assessments. IDMS also color-coded data using Stoplight Highlighting. This saved the Data Teams time in collecting and displaying data, allowing more time for analysis and dialogue. In addition, some Data Teams recognized the value of additional data sources, including performance assessments and student work, to help teachers understand more fully the needs of the students. In these Using Data schools, STPT was enhanced through the use of these data sources.

In short, several Using Data Project schools blended the collaborative inquiry process and the STPT process, adapting both to meet their needs. A few schools, however, elected to solely address the requirements of the district to participate in IDMS and discontinued their participation in the Using Data Project.

LESSONS LEARNED

The collaborative inquiry process is most successful when the following factors are in place:

1. The principal
   - visibly values and embraces the collaborative inquiry process,
   - values the time spent,
   - provides time for Data Teams to meet,
   - allocates sufficient time and resources, and
   - supports the Data Team as they learn to utilize data to improve student learning.

2. The school culture changes to support the collaborative inquiry process by
   - breaking through isolation and shifting toward a culture where teachers meet to discuss hard questions about learning of all students,
   - recognizing that when one group of students is unsuccessful, it is everyone's responsibility to determine the reason and work toward a solution,
   - instituting the use of Data-Driven Dialogue and collaborative norms, and

- providing time to develop the patterns of interaction that will successfully support collaborative inquiry, as these skills are uncommon among groups of teachers.

3. Multiple sources of data become the basis for instructional improvement. Applying Data-Driven Dialogue to multiple and varied data sets determines the "whole story" of student understanding and prevents teachers from making uninformed decisions about student learning. Adequate time to thoroughly analyze multiple data sources is critical to making needed changes in practice.

The Clark County teams found the Using Data Process of Collaborative Inquiry to be extremely valuable to schools interested in utilizing multiple data sources to improve student learning and achievement. Through effective leadership, restructuring of the school culture to include collaborative inquiry, and the dedication of time and resources to the process, teachers began to demystify the use of data to improve student learning and achievement.

KATZ ELEMENTARY SCHOOL: PROBLEM SOLVING ABOUT PROBLEM SOLVING

Building the Foundation

Located in the northwest region of the Clark County School District, Katz Elementary School serves approximately 800 students in Grades K–5. The school staff learned about the Using Data Project in March 2003 and formed a Data Team consisting of four Data Coaches who were trained to use the tools and processes of the Using Data approach. The Coaches included the principal, two fourth-grade teachers, and a district-based project facilitator who provided assistance to the school in the areas of mathematics and science. These four became Katz's original Data Team, functioning as its own entity. The group had a history of collaborating and had begun to work together to build a vision for learning. Therefore, they felt ready to jump right into using and analyzing data.

In December 2003, the Data Team decided to ask all third- and fifth-grade teachers to give their students the practice version of the state's criterion-referenced test for mathematics. The team felt that this assessment would allow them to look at several layers of data and provide them with valuable information about the areas that needed improvement before students were administered the actual assessment. At the same time, the team recognized that they would need help in examining the data because of the short amount of time they had to accomplish the work. They decided to establish a study group that would meet three hours a week for five weeks to analyze the data. They advertised this study group to the entire staff and recruited 15 people who were interested in learning more about data. The data project was moving forward.

Just as the Data Team and the study group of data users were getting started, however, the team suffered a setback. The principal moved to a new school and planned to take the two site-based Data Coaches with him. The next six months became a transition period for the school and the Data Team. From the study group, two new site-based Data Coaches emerged (one primary- and one intermediate-level teacher) to take the place of the two fourth-grade teachers who would be leaving. The work became focused on turning the project over to these individuals and a new principal.

At that point, knowing that three of the four Data Team members would be new, the team recognized the need to expand and engage more staff in the project. They invited the entire school staff to become involved with the Data Team. Along with the invitation, the Data Coaches talked with individuals at each grade level to encourage them to join the work, explaining the potential benefits for the students. Little did the original team know at the time how important this decision was to building a strong foundation for their work. The invitation resulted in increased diversity and depth on the Data Team, which now consisted of 10 people: one representative from each grade level K–5, one primary site-based Data Coach, one intermediate site-based Data Coach, the new principal, and the district-based project facilitator. In addition, the two outgoing site-based Data Coaches agreed to continue in the role of providing support for the group to learn how to use the process. The school's Data Team was now reestablished and was moving forward again.

Both the size and the newness of this team meant that the group did not have experience or norms for working together. The Data Coaches listened to the urging of the new principal to back up a bit and focus on grounding the group in the principles and tools of collaboration. Although the Data Coaches were anxious to jump into the data just as the original team had, they had learned that the Using Data Process is about much more than examining test results. It is also about building a commitment to teacher collaboration focused on promoting student learning.

The principal saw the potential the Data Team had to influence professional development, collaboration, and student learning throughout the school and wanted to capitalize on that potential by preparing the way for a strong, collaborative team. The new Data Team established a schedule to meet after school every other week in the school library for 90 minutes. The principal made these meetings a priority and attended every one as a fellow Data Coach. The other Data Coaches worked as a group to introduce the Data Team members to the collaborative inquiry process. During these initial meetings, they utilized data from the previous year's Iowa Test of Basic Skills to introduce members to the tools from the Using Data Toolkit.

Involving the Whole Faculty

The new team began to take root. Since there was now representation of all grade levels on the Data Team, the team had a mechanism to actively involve the entire faculty. Data Team members met, examined data, and discussed ideas and then took the information back to their individual grade levels, thereby involving the entire school in collaborative inquiry into data. During the Data Team meetings members examined schoolwide data, enabling the team to develop a larger view of school practices and results and discover the importance of understanding how learning develops across the grade levels. Data Team members took responsibility for communicating their observations, findings, and ideas to all faculty members at the monthly grade-level meetings. This created an opportunity to gather input and develop ideas further. Although this was a good start, the Data Coaches soon realized that this structure would fall short of their goals if they did not do something to acknowledge and support the change in school culture that the Using Data process was promoting. They therefore decided to bring all staff members together and to work as a group to establish a culture of collaborative inquiry around data. The Data Team knew that this culture would be key to ensuring that the new grade-level-based structure was successful in involving all staff members in the process.

In March 2004, the team engaged faculty from all grade levels in learning more about data. They explored who their students and teachers were demographically and what they wanted to learn from the data, and, using the tool Body of Our School (see Toolkit), they identified both positive aspects of their school and challenges to be met. Tables 8.1 and 8.2 present some of the data they used to get a better picture of the school's demographics.

Table 8.1 Katz Elementary School Student Population by Race/Ethnicity and Free and Reduced Lunch Status

Race/ethnicity	Percentage of total population
African American	20
Native American	1
Asian	8
Hispanic	23
White	48

Free and reduced lunch status	Percentage of total population
Qualify for free and reduced lunch	42

Table 8.2 Katz Elementary School Student Population by Educational Program Enrollment

Program groups	Percentage of total population
Limited English Proficiency	10
Gifted and Talented	6
Special Education	8
Regular Education	76

The Team also explored data about teachers' years of experience and qualifications, as well as age and race/ethnicity, illustrated in Table 8.3.

Table 8.3 Katz Elementary School Teacher Demographics by Age and Race/Ethnicity, 2003–04

	Age				Sex		Race			
	20–29	30–39	40–49	50+	F	M	Caucasian	Hispanic	African American	Asian
Number of teachers	7	17	7	14	41	4	38	3	2	2

Katz operates on a five-track, year-round schedule. The school year begins in August and ends the following August. There are staggered breaks throughout the year, and one-fifth of the students and staff are on break at all times. Each track contains at least one classroom for each grade level K–5.

At the faculty's meeting with the Data Team in March 2004, each track constructed the Body of Our School (see Toolkit) from its perspective. The five "bodies" were then shared with the entire group and later posted in the teachers' lounge so that everyone had a picture of the data and what the staff members were thinking about critical aspects of the school. This activity also provided the Data Team with an informal assessment of the staff's thinking and orientation toward the school and toward using data and indicated next steps that might be needed to create a culture that utilized data in the decision-making process.

Two months later, the Data Team brought the staff together again to strengthen understanding of the shifts in culture the school hoped to make and to develop a commitment to working collaboratively to improve the school. The Data Team created a fun-filled day that helped to establish unity and a sense of teamwork. The day started with a rousing game of Jenga, which requires players to pull a stick at a time out of a tower of crisscrossed sticks. Teams worked steadily to see how many sticks they could pull out before their towers came crashing down.

As the towers started to tumble, one of the Data Coaches jumped in and asked everyone to consider why some towers remained standing while others had collapsed. Teams observed that the standing towers all seemed to have strong bases and the sticks had been removed in such a way as to avoid leaving big gaps along the way. Another Data Coach pointed out that the same philosophy was important in developing a school. He noted that the fifth graders were not a reflection of the fifth-grade teachers alone, but rather of every teacher in the building. All teachers help build the foundation for these students and their results. If that foundation has holes or inconsistencies in it, the fifth-grade teacher will always be building on a shaky foundation, creating a situation where the students are likely to tumble. From this exercise, the staff concluded that Katz Elementary School needed to focus on building a strong foundation across the entire school and filling any gaps in philosophy and practice. Data and collaboration would provide the foundation for the work they had ahead of them.

The fun continued that day as the teams participated in a scavenger hunt with a twist. The teachers were asked to form groups of five. Three individuals were tethered to one another with a piece of rope and were provided with clues to find puzzle pieces hidden within the building. They navigated through the building to retrieve their group's materials. A fourth person was blindfolded and took direction from the fifth person to put the group's puzzle pieces together. This task was designed to show that a team—or a school—is only as good as its weakest link. With that idea in mind, the teams began to understand the importance of establishing that everyone, not just the Data Team, was a part of the data project and would play a role in the mission to improve the school.

Finally, the staff dug into student data. Members of the Data Team introduced two data tools to the staff that day—Data-Driven Dialogue and Stoplight Highlighting. The Data Team chose data from the mathematics portion of the state's criterion-referenced test to examine together. They broke the staff into grade-level groups, and members of the Data Team led the groups in using Data-Driven Dialogue. They first made predictions of what they thought they would see when they looked at the data. Then, using predetermined cut points based on district and school standards, the grade-level groups color-coded their data using Stoplight Highlighting to paint a picture of student achievement. Next, the groups went on to observe the data, stating just the facts they could see in the data. After that, they finally made inferences from the data. The groups displayed their data for all to see, demonstrating the power of "going visual." The staff looked for and noted trends using this one piece of data. As a next step, the Data Team built on this data analysis as it began to dig deeper into the results from the state criterion-referenced test (CRT) and other data to identify a student-learning problem.

Project Facilitator's Commentary

As an outside member of the Data Team, I think the transition that took place with this school was a healthy one. The new principal's emphasis on collaboration and shared decision making caused the team and, ultimately the school, to back up and reestablish their beliefs about collaboration. While the process was slow and it took the school close to a year to move forward with the Using Data Process, once they started moving they took ownership of the project and incorporated it into all that they did. It is my belief that the commitment displayed by the principal played a key role in the success of the Data Team and the school. She was present at all meetings and served as a side-by-side leader, learning and making decisions with the team rather than on her own. Furthermore, the structure of the team and their dedication to building a strong foundation to work from helped establish a culture of collaborative inquiry within the school.

Principal's Commentary

As a new principal in the building, I wanted to get to know the staff and what they considered to be important. I knew they had gone through quite a bit of change over the past few years and that the last two administrators operated from very different styles. I knew that one of the first tasks we needed to do was rebuild the community within the school. The data gave us a reason to have a discussion and begin to examine who we are as a school. I knew the Data Team could play an important role, and I saw it as more of a steering committee for the entire school rather than a group of isolated people. If this was to be the case, though, I felt very strongly that the Data Team needed to grow to include representation from all grade levels. I was happy to see the Data Team expand and feel that they did a great job of coming together as a group and in bringing the entire school together.

Identifying a Student-Learning Problem

In order to get a clear picture of what was happening in the mathematics curriculum at Katz Elementary School, the Data Team decided to focus on three sources of data: the state criterion-referenced test, given in Grades 3 and 5; the norm-referenced test used by the district, the Iowa Test of Basic Skills (ITBS), given in Grades 3, 4, and 5; and an open-response test utilized by the school/district, the Mathematics Assessment Resource Services (MARS) assessments, given in Grades 3, 4, and 5.

As noted earlier, the original team began with this process in December 2003 with a pretest for the mathematics portion of the state practice test. All third- and fifth-grade teachers gave the assessment to their students. A group of teachers interested in learning about the process then proceeded to analyze the data under the guidance of the Data Coaches. Through this analysis, the teachers determined that students were having difficulty with mathematics problem solving on this particular assessment. However, this assessment did not prove useful for further diagnosing the problem, since the teachers were only able to examine aggregated data to the level of the teacher but were unable to disaggregate the data further. They also felt that looking at the data by teacher seemed to point fingers at people, and this was not the type of collaboration and school focus that was intended. It proved to be a valuable learning experience. It showed the team the need for developing collaboration within and across grade levels to help facilitate difficult discussions. It also reinforced the idea that collaborative inquiry into data is not about quick fixes based on a single source of data, but rather about looking at the big picture. So, with these data in hand and the experience of analyzing it, the team decided it was important to look at other sources of data.

Accordingly, the team decided to examine the Mathematics Assessment Resource Service (MARS) assessments used at their school. Two classes in Grades 3 and 5 had taken their grade-level assessments, and all classes in Grade 4 had taken the fourth-grade assessment during the fall of 2003. These assessments usually consist of four to five tasks, each with either a single problem or a sequence of problems. Together, these tasks allow students to demonstrate their mathematical ability in both content and processes outlined in the National Council of Teachers of Mathematics (NCTM) *Principles and Standards for School Mathematics.*

Katz Elementary School received the results for the MARS assessments in February 2004, and the Data Team, including the principal, decided to bring all third-, fourth-, and fifth-grade teachers together to examine the data through the Using Data Process. Substitutes were provided for the teachers so they could attend the session. The teachers were introduced to three Using Data tools, Data-Driven Dialogue, Go Visual, and Stoplight Highlighting, to use to look at their data. Since the group had a great deal of work to do in a short amount of time, the Data Team decided ahead of time that they would use the district guidelines for student growth as the cut points for the Stoplight Highlighting activity: 69 percent correct and below would be coded as red, 70–89 percent as yellow, and 90–100 percent as green. Guided by a colleague who had participated in the previous data analysis, grade-level groups worked independently to make predictions, create visual charts, make observations, and finally make inferences about the data.

This information was then shared with the other grade-level groups. Once all groups had examined the aggregated data, they began to look at how students performed on each of the five tasks on the assessment. Figure 8.1 illustrates the percentage correct on each of the five third-grade tasks.

Then they drilled down further into the results for each question or item within the multiquestion tasks. Table 8.4 illustrates the results at the item level for one task. (See also Appendix A at the end of this chapter for an example of a MARS task.) Examining these data from Grade 3 to Grade 5 brought about a lively discussion and

Figure 8.1   MARS results, fall 2003: Percentage correct on third-grade tasks.

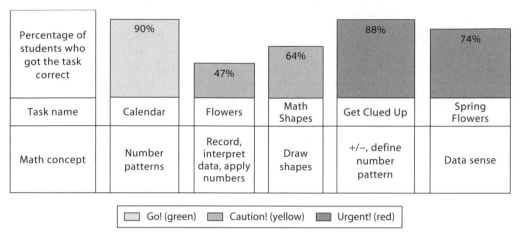

Table 8.4   Third-Grade Item Data From "Spring Flowers" Multi-Question Task: Number of Students Scoring Each of the Possible Points for Each Item

Question 1-Adding and Counting

Points	0	1
# of students	7	36

Question 2-Adding and Counting

Points	0	1
# of students	3	40

Question 3-Adding, Subtracting, Finding Difference

Points	0	1
# of students	10	33

Question 4-Drawing Symbol on Pictograph

Points	0	1
# of students	8	35

Question 5-Adding and Explaining in Words

Points	0	1	2	3
# of students	15	1	3	24

a recognition that student performance declined as they progressed through the years. They formulated inferences about the data, which included

- Test items became more difficult in Grade 5 and were much more reading intensive;
- Students' stamina gave out by the end of the test, resulting in lower scores on later problems; and
- Students were not exposed to these types of problems on a regular basis.

With these data in hand, Data Team members who had participated in the MARS analysis went back to the entire Data Team and shared the thinking that was generated that day. The team decided to look at the ITBS results next. The team predicted what they would see in the third-, fourth-, and fifth-grade data. Using data provided by the district's Instructional Data Management System, each member of the team used the same standards as set above for Stoplight Highlighting to create a visual picture of the strengths and weaknesses of their students' performance in mathematics. Once this was represented, the team made observations based on the data and then discussed inferences and questions about the data. This process was completed for all grade levels as well as across the three grades.

Finally, the Data Team looked at a third source of data, third- and fifth-grade mathematics results from the 2002–03 state CRT. This is the data source the team used when working with the entire staff during a professional development day in May 2004. The entire faculty, in track groups, examined the CRT data. They started with aggregated data and observed that 60 percent of third graders were proficient or above compared to 52 percent of fifth graders, the same pattern of decreasing performance from Grade 3 to Grade 5 observed in the MARS data. Their analysis of disaggregated data revealed that the gap between White students and African American and Hispanic students was wider in Grade 5 than in Grade 3. Then they examined their strand-level data, illustrated in a graph in Figure 8.2.

Figure 8.2   2002–03 CRT mathematics results by strand, Grades 3 and 5, percentage of items correct.

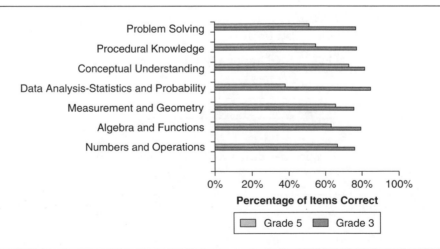

SOURCE From Standards Based Assessment Program, Testing and Evaluation Report, Edith and Lloyd Katz Elementary School, 2002–2003.

Based on all the data examined, the teachers then made a series of observations and inferences, some of which are shown below.

Examples of observations

- Conceptual understanding decreased 8 percent from Grade 3 to Grade 5.
- Problem solving is one of our weakest areas in Grade 5, with 51 percent of students proficient.
- Seventy-seven percent of third graders are proficient in problem solving.
- Fifth graders perform worse than third graders in every strand.
- There is a 47 percent decrease from Grade 3 to Grade 5 in data analysis and statistics and probability.

Examples of inferences

- The data analysis question in Grade 5 dealt with a stem and leaf graph. That might have confused them.
- Students may not have good test-taking strategies.
- Maybe our students lack persistence in mathematics problem solving. They give up too easily.
- The fifth-grade test is more difficult.
- The reading level and vocabulary in the mathematics problems might be a factor in the fifth-grade score.

Now with three complete sets of data, the team was ready to identify a student-learning problem. Examining all the data together, the team noted that problem solving by fifth graders was a common area of concern in all three data sources. Since they had also identified this as an area of concern when looking at the pre-CRT data, they felt that this was the student-learning problem that should be focused on first. They crafted the following problem statement:

Fifth-grade students are below acceptable levels in problem-solving.

- Fifth graders scored below proficiency with an average of 51 percent correct in problem-solving as evidenced by performance on the 2002–03 CRT test.
- Sixty-one percent of fifth graders are below proficiency in problem solving as evidenced by performance on the 2003–04 pre-CRT administered in December 2003.
- Eighty-nine percent of a sample of 56 fifth graders scored below acceptable proficiency on MARS problem-solving assessments administered in December 2003.

Based on previous experiences with data, the teachers were accustomed to looking for the quick fix—examining one piece of data, identifying a problem with it, attempting to fix it, and moving on to the next problem. However, they recognized that this process had done little to fix problems over the long term and that they were always revisiting problems a year or two later and looking for the next quick fix. Data-Driven Dialogue was a powerful tool for the team, as they were accustomed to jumping to inferences without looking carefully at data and comparing it against their own preconceptions of what the data showed. They found that they needed to slow down, look carefully at what was before them, and determine the meaning in the information.

They often noted that the districtwide project facilitator helped keep them objective and on track. By the end, the team was able to say with a great degree of confidence that the main student-learning problem in mathematics was problem solving since it had emerged as an area of low achievement on three different assessments.

Although the Data Team did a great deal of the work throughout this stage, they still recognized the importance of involving the entire staff in the process. They had worked hard to engage the faculty in the beginning and knew that it was important to continue this involvement. The team provided the staff with regular updates in staff meetings and posted charts in the staff lounge for everyone to see. This allowed the entire staff to stay on top of what was happening without requiring that everyone be equally involved, something that would have slowed down the process.

Project Facilitator's Commentary

The process of drilling down into multiple pieces of data takes a great deal of time—something most teachers and administrators don't feel that they have. Throughout the process, it seemed as though I needed to be a cheerleader and remind the group that the work they were doing was important and part of a bigger picture. Since we often get caught up in issues of time and want to fix things right away, we often jump to making inferences based on tiny pieces of data. A major role for me throughout this process was to help clarify the difference between an observation and an inference and to remind people where we were in the stages of Data-Driven Dialogue, reminding them that inferences need to be examined and checked out to help us take the best actions. I think the idea of predictions also played an important part but was sometimes left out. As we make predictions, we are stating our own assumptions and biases. Unless we put them out on the table and then take the time to really observe what we see before us, these biases can influence the decisions we make without our realizing it. As we worked through the dialogue process, I would often hear teachers express amazement at the difference between what they thought they would see and what they actually saw. To me, this was a major learning. It helped us to see beyond what we normally see and bring about change.

Principal's Commentary

We learned so much through this process. First, the visual representation and color-coding using Stoplight Highlighting was quite an eye-opener. Seeing the data displayed visually with so much red and yellow really made us want to dig further for a better understanding. The amount of time it took to drill down was frustrating, yet as we went through the triangulation process with our data sources, we experienced many "aha's." We realized that the data we had available to us did not always allow us to go as far as we wanted. We decided that we needed other assessments put in place that we could use to examine data at the item level, something we were unable to do with the CRTs and the Iowa Test. This caused us to create our own benchmark assessments in mathematics so we would have them as future data resources. Overall, this was an eye-opening experience for us as a school.

Verifying Causes

With the problem statement now firm in everyone's mind, the team needed to determine causes that might be leading to the stated problem. For this they used the Fishbone tool and generated the possible causes shown in Figure 8.3.

Figure 8.3   Fishbone Cause-and-Effect Analysis.

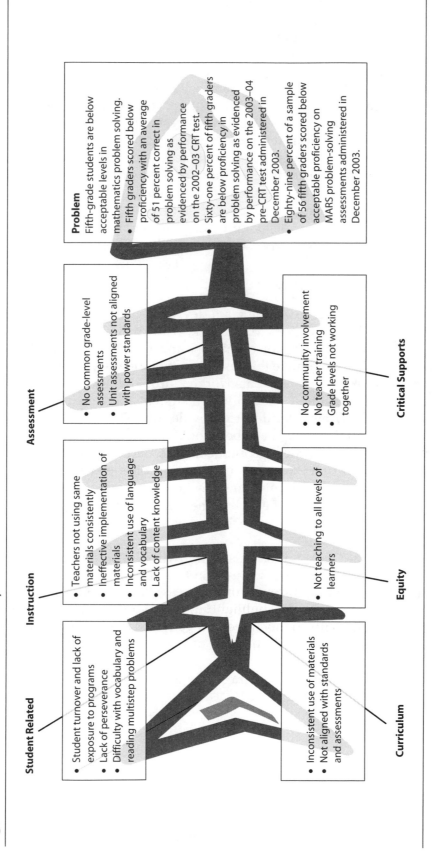

Student Related

- Student turnover and lack of exposure to programs
- Lack of perseverance
- Difficulty with vocabulary and reading multistep problems

Instruction

- Teachers not using same materials consistently
- Ineffective implementation of materials
- Inconsistent use of language and vocabulary
- Lack of content knowledge

Assessment

- No common grade-level assessments
- Unit assessments not aligned with power standards

Problem

Fifth-grade students are below acceptable levels in mathematics problem solving.

- Fifth graders scored below proficiency with an average of 51 percent correct in problem solving as evidenced by performance on the 2002–03 CRT test.
- Sixty-one percent of fifth graders are below proficiency in problem solving as evidenced by performance on the 2003–04 pre-CRT test administered in December 2003.
- Eighty-nine percent of a sample of 56 fifth graders scored below acceptable proficiency on MARS problem-solving assessments administered in December 2003.

Curriculum

- Inconsistent use of materials
- Not aligned with standards and assessments

Equity

- Not teaching to all levels of learners

Critical Supports

- No community involvement
- No teacher training
- Grade levels not working together

Then, applying the Spend-a-Buck strategy, the Data Team used colorful dots to mark areas they felt were contributing most to the student-learning problem. Each member was provided with five dots to "spend" to indicate the causes of the problem. After all members placed their dots, the team tallied the results and considered which cause they would look into further.

The results indicated that the team believed the problem was student related. The possible causes that received the highest votes were lack of strategies, lack of perseverance, and lack of reading skills. Based on the data, the team decided to look further into perseverance as the cause of the problem. They felt that a strong piece of evidence to support this cause came from the MARS data: Students had consistently done worse on problems that occurred later on the test. This led the Data Team to two conclusions. First, they felt that students grew tired as they went through the test and lacked the perseverance to finish it. Second, they thought that students did well on the beginning portion of a problem but were not persisting within the problem, causing them to do poorly overall.

Examining Student Work

To test the possible cause, the team devised a plan to test 40 randomly selected students in Grades 3–5 using a MARS task, "Addworm" (see Appendix A at the end of this chapter for an illustration of this task and a student's work). The team decided to have the students complete this task in an interview-style format, where a teacher watched and took notes as students worked through the problem. This would allow the teachers to assess the extent to which students persevered through the task or gave up early. They also decided to provide multilink cubes as manipulatives for students to use on the task. The cubes would be available on the table, but the facilitating teacher would neither encourage nor discourage their use. All team members agreed to help with the task and interviews, working with students during their preparation periods or administering the task during their track breaks. To ensure that everyone administered the task in the same manner, they created the following script for the teachers to follow, beginning with this instruction to the student:

"While you are working on this task, I will be working on my part of this assignment. On your own, I want you to work on this task and do your best at it. When you are finished, put your pencil down and turn your test over. Let's read page 1 together; follow along as I read." (Read up to question #1. At that point, offer no more explanation. Take notes to describe student behavior/action while working.)

For example, you might note the following:

- Use of fingers
- Head bobbing
- Mouth moving
- Tapping to count
- Some kind of skip counting
- Use of pictures
- Use of cubes
- Jumping through the problem, skipping or leaving out parts
- Other behaviors:

Once the student has finished the test, say: "Now that you are finished with this task, let's talk about your work. I need to remember what you say, so I will be writing down exactly what you say."

Ask the following for each question:

a. Where did you start?
b. What did you do next?
c. What were you thinking?
d. Why? (Clarify observations with this, e.g., Why did you change this from 38 to 40?)

The team agreed to the directions and decided to meet again in one month, after the conclusion of spring break. They felt that this would give them plenty of time to conduct the interviews and return with data for further consideration. Feeling good about the task at hand, the group moved forward to see where students broke down in the problem-solving process. This turned out to be a more arduous task than they had anticipated. Each interview took between 40 and 60 minutes, and the four teachers found themselves struggling to get to all identified students. At the next Data Team meeting, the members shared their frustration with the process and how time intensive it was. They began to question if it was worth continuing or if they had gathered enough data at this point. Those who had completed interviews shared some of their observations, and the team determined that they did not have enough data to draw any firm conclusions. The data they had collected proved to be interesting and raised questions about the cause since the students tested did not seem to be giving up as the team thought they would. (See Appendix B at the end of this chapter for an example of one teacher's observations.) The team decided to continue interviewing students and to meet again in two weeks to revisit the data and determine next steps.

After six weeks of working with students, the team had managed to complete the process with a majority of the identified students, so team members shared the data they had gathered. The team determined that, contrary to their expectations, the students tested had shown perseverance, so much so that the task was taking longer than anyone had expected. At this point, team members shared some of the observations they had made:

• Students were willing to struggle with the problem for an extended period of time and did not give up on the task as had been proposed. The team therefore decided that perseverance was not a problem for the students.

• Students seemed to understand the task, as evidenced by their responses to the interview questions. The team therefore ruled out the idea that reading comprehension difficulties were adding to the problem.

• Students seemed to lack a variety of strategies for solving the problem and attempted to solve the problem in a similar manner. Very few drew pictures to represent their thinking or made use of the manipulatives provided.

• Students who did use the manipulatives or had a variety of strategies tended to come from classrooms that relied heavily on one of the school's mathematics curriculum materials, Investigations in Number, Data, and Space.

The information the team now had before them indicated that the students were capable of completing the work and that the cause of the low scores in problem solving might be more directly tied to the instruction and the types of tasks teachers used with students. The fact that students did not make use of the manipulatives and struggled to come up with strategies for solving the task led the team to believe that students were not being exposed to a variety of strategies on a regular basis in the classroom. A team member also suggested that an upcoming change in staff would present a new challenge, in that several of the incoming staff had probably not received training in full implementation of the school's mathematics curriculum, nor would they have experience with use of the pedagogy the school was attempting to use, including inquiry-based learning and higher-level questioning. The team found research to support the idea that students learn when presented with a coherent curriculum and that the teachers' understanding of pedagogy and content influence student learning. With this information in hand, the team decided to investigate instruction and effective implementation of the school's mathematics curriculum as possible causes to verify with local data.

The next step was to share with the staff where they were in the process. At the next staff meeting, the team presented the data they had collected during the student interviews and the conclusions they had drawn. Next, the team explained the research on curriculum implementation and its relationship to student learning and made the case for now pursuing instruction as a possible cause of the student-learning problem.

Collecting Local Data About Curriculum Implementation

The team felt that it was important to explore further this idea of a coherent curriculum and enlisted the help of the principal to gather data. It was determined that old lesson plans might provide evidence of the type of mathematics instruction taking place in the classrooms. As a next step, the principal agreed to review teachers' lesson plans covering a two-week time span to determine how many lessons were based on the use of the school's curriculum materials. Over the next week, the principal scanned lesson plans for 19 teachers and found that 17 indicated a consistent use of the curriculum over the two-week period. The other two sets of lesson plans did not have any indication that the district's curriculum materials were being used.

During this time period, the principal also conducted classroom "walk-throughs" to see what type of instruction was taking place during the mathematics period. These visits demonstrated that although most teachers had stated in their lesson plans that they intended to use the curriculum materials and strategies, it was not always evident in practice. Moreover, when the principal did see evidence of the curriculum being implemented, she noted that it was being taught in a very mechanical manner and that the questions being posed were often at the lower level of Bloom's taxonomy (Bloom, 1984). The principal also noted that teachers were supplementing with various materials that lacked the higher-level thinking skills the team thought should be in place.

These data along with the research the team studied served to verify two causes of the student-learning problem:

- Teachers do not expose students to higher-level questions on a regular basis.
- Teachers are not implementing the mathematics curriculum in a consistent manner.

Project Facilitator's Commentary

Although this proved to be a frustrating time for the group, I think it was some of the most valuable time spent. The team dug into the "verify cause" process and found that if they had followed their first instincts, they would have ventured down the wrong path. I think the group's first inclination to identify the problem as student related is very natural. It is easier to put the burden on students rather than examine our own practices more closely. Because the team chose to study the issue in more depth, however, they gained valuable information that they were able to use to move forward. The verification process proved to be a valuable learning experience, as it demonstrated the need for ensuring that a problem really exists before throwing money and time at it in order to make it better.

Principal's Commentary

We had ideas of what was leading to students' low problem-solving scores, but the issue of problem solving seemed so big that we did not know where to begin or what type of assessment to use to analyze it further before moving into solutions. When the team came up with the idea of using a common assessment in a one-on-one interview style, I thought that was a good idea. It proved to be very informative, as it steered us down a different path than the one we were on. Even though this task was very time consuming, I think it empowered the teachers because they became so aware of the issues that lay before us. It led us to a more valid conclusion due to the effort that was put forth during this stage of the Using Data Process.

Generating Solutions

Once the team verified a likely cause for the student-learning problem, the team moved on to seek valid solutions to the problem. Working through the Using Data Logic Model to arrive at interventions that would directly address the identified cause of the problem, they listed the causes and then generated strategies to address the causes, specified the outcomes they expected from implementing the strategies, and developed a plan for monitoring the outcomes, shown in Figure 8.4.

While generating solutions, the team drew upon the expertise of the group members and the many years of training they had through the Mathematics and Science Enhancement (MASE) project. Several of the team members had considerable experience in the project, and some had served as teacher-leaders. The team searched for articles on questioning and found resources for the teachers about Bloom's taxonomy (1984), and they provided each teacher with an easy reference card with examples of the different levels of questioning that could be used during planning and lessons.

Like the Verifying Causes phase of the Using Data Process, this final phase was a difficult process for the team. They knew what they hoped to accomplish, but deciding how to implement the plan proved to be difficult. Once the strategies were determined (1984), the team had the difficult task of deciding how to monitor progress along the way. This particular stage seems to have been a bit weaker than others simply because the team wasn't used to thinking about monitoring progress over the long term. They were more accustomed to applying a quick fix to a problem in order to see test scores rise in the next round and then move on to the next crisis. The Using Data Process challenged the team to think and act differently by constructing and implementing a longer-term action plan directly tied to a particular student-learning problem.

Project Facilitator's Commentary

Although I have worked with schools for years to address the needs of professional development, I had a difficult time with this stage and felt unprepared to help the team move forward. The Logic Model made perfect sense and was something I should have been using for years, yet it was new to me and I struggled to make sense of all the parts and pieces. To help with this learning process, I decided to apply the Logic Model to some of my own work. Rather than going it alone with this tool, I enlisted the help of the Using Data Project staff and my colleagues at the Data Team meeting where we planned to put our own Logic Model together. The idea of actually monitoring our progress was novel. For the past few years, we had offered a variety of professional development opportunities to the teachers. The sessions were worthwhile and provided assistance to teachers with what we thought were problems within the school. However, we never actually monitored the impact of the professional development to find out whether we were progressing. I think we learned a great deal about generating solutions during this stage, but the team will need to continue to develop its capacity to monitor implementation and impact in our school.

Figure 8.4 Logic Model.

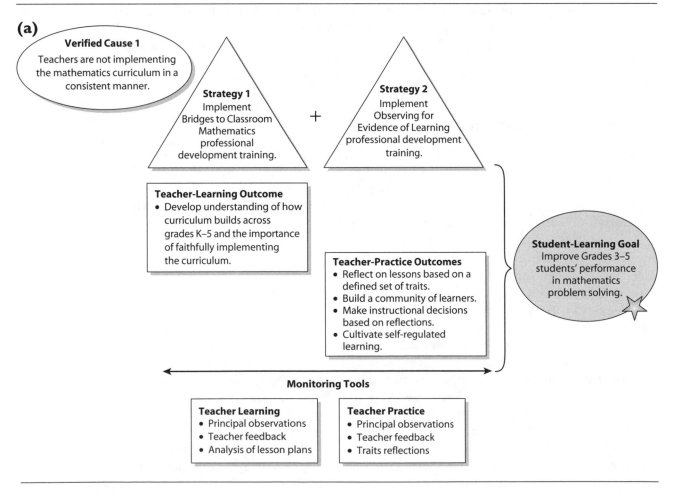

(b)

Verified Cause 2
Teachers do not expose students to higher-level questions on a regular basis.

Strategy 1
Professional development in higher-order questioning strategies

+

Strategy 2
Grade-level teams analyze questions used in math curriculum.

+

Strategy 3
Implement a "Daily Problem" in Grades 3–5

Teacher-Learning Outcomes
- Raise awareness of higher-order thinking skills.
- Analyze the types and levels of questions teachers use in the classroom.

Teacher-Learning Outcomes
- Raise awareness of types of questions presented in the mathematics curriculum.

Teacher-Practice Outcomes
- Increase the use of higher-level questioning strategies.

Teacher-Practice Outcomes
- Construct higher-order questions in grade-level teams.
- Use these questions in instruction.

Teacher-Practice Outcomes
- Students exposed to difficult problems on a daily basis.
- Teachers use a resource bank of problems.

Student-Learning Goal
Improve grades 3–5 students' performance in mathematics problem-solving.

Student-Learning Outcome
- Increased level of response/thinking/discourse from students

Student-Learning Outcome
- Increased level of response/thinking/discourse from students

Student-Learning Outcome
- Increased level of response/thinking/discourse from students

Monitoring Tools

Teacher Learning
- Assess teachers' understanding of different types of questions

Teacher Learning
- Principal observations
- Teacher feedback
- Analysis of lesson plans

Student Learning
- Student work from daily problem
- MARS
- District trimester benchmark assessments
- State CRT

Principal's Commentary

We are still in this stage. We are learning how to use Bloom's taxonomy (1984) in order to bump up our level of questioning. We have examined the questions presented in our math curriculum and found a stronger relationship between the types of questions presented in Investigations in Number, Data, and Space and on the CRT. We did this correlation as an entire staff, and it generated a great deal of dialogue. In doing this, we also found that the types of questions asked in Investigations in Number, Data, and Space are inductive. This most likely presents an issue for those students who are deductive learners and for the teachers in making connections for those students.

Taking Action and Celebrating Results

In the fall of 2004, the team hit the ground running, ready to implement strategies to improve student learning. A team of K–5 teachers was selected to learn about a modified version of the popular lesson study model, Observing for Evidence of Learning (OEL), which would serve as a valuable tool for focusing on lessons and the level of questioning that was involved. This team returned to the school to facilitate grade-level meetings in which teachers worked together to plan a lesson in mathematics, implement the lesson, and then debrief the lesson. Teachers found this to be a useful process for focusing on the essential components of a lesson: the mathematical content, instructional practices, and questioning strategies.

Teachers were scheduled to meet four times during the school year to plan and implement lessons using the OEL process. The first session was scheduled for early November. Grade-level teams worked together to plan and deliver their lesson. Teachers stated that this process brought new insight to the Investigations in Number, Data, and Space curriculum, as new and experienced teachers worked together to craft the lesson, including the new uses of higher-order questioning. Classroom observation afforded teachers the uncommon luxury of being in another teacher's classroom and watching the lesson unfold. The planning and debriefing sessions provided teachers with a venue to share ideas and discuss successes and challenges that were encountered. These sessions seemed to have the potential of raising the level of awareness teachers had for the curriculum and the questioning involved as evidenced by the OEL trait checklist, teacher feedback, and principal observations.

In late November, however, the district suspended the use of substitute teachers for all professional development offerings, which caused a change in plans. In January the teachers arranged to meet after school to plan the lesson, rearranged schedules so they could observe the lesson during their 50-minute prep periods, and then debriefed the lesson after school. Although this arrangement worked, it was difficult, and the teachers finally decided to discontinue the OEL professional development.

Meanwhile, another group of teacher-leaders facilitated professional development on the Bridges to Classroom Mathematics curriculum. All teachers were scheduled to attend five three-hour sessions designed to help them understand how concepts from Investigations in Number, Data, and Space built on one another. Participants were to learn how concepts were developed and practiced within this curriculum and the importance of implementing such components as choice time, games, and 10-minute math. It was hoped that this professional development would help teachers begin to understand the importance of implementing the curriculum fully to allow students time to develop concepts at different levels each year.

Teachers attended their first session in October, and the feedback indicated that it had the potential of being a useful monitoring tool, as teachers expressed amazement at seeing how a concept they introduced in Grade 1 was built upon using a similar but higher-level technique in all the other grades. However, this professional development offering was also cut due to the new policy on the use of substitutes during professional development.

Despite the suspension of both professional development strategies, grade-level groups worked to implement the daily problem in mathematics. During their monthly grade-level meetings, teachers shared difficult problems and what their students had done with them. They brought samples of student work for others to examine and discuss, focusing on the way questions were phrased within the problems. They considered possible revisions that would produce higher-level questions. Along the way teachers were accumulating thought-provoking questions they could use with their students.

Throughout this time, the Data Team continued to meet about twice a month. The tasks before the team shifted to handling problems and monitoring progress within the grade-level groups. During these meetings, team members supported one another's efforts to move the school forward even though some of the strategies had to be adjusted and others eliminated. Since the strategies that had brought the entire school together were no longer in place, the required monthly grade-level meetings became a key component for ensuring that the entire school continued to focus on problem solving and faithful implementation of the mathematics curriculum.

Despite the implementation challenges and the adjustments that were made, the school saw positive results: The school's test scores for 2004–05 in mathematics problem solving improved from 59.9 percent proficient to 67.5 percent proficient (Joan Lombard, personal communication, May 17, 2005). Katz Elementary School joined other Using Data Project schools in celebrating their success at a gala celebration in the spring of 2005. Each Using Data Project school created a visual representation of their journey and their results and shared their story with the whole group. The Using Data Project staff acknowledged each participant in the project with a certificate and a humorous gift and shared the findings from project evaluators that documented positive changes in school culture, collaboration, and data use.

Project Facilitator's Commentary

The implementation did not go quite as planned, but still went forward even though the staff encountered what they deemed to be a major setback with the inability to use substitute teachers during their professional development sessions. The staff proved to be dedicated to the cause and came up with creative ways to find time to work and learn together. Team members strongly supported each other and, ultimately, the school as they continued to push forward with a focus on improving mathematics problem solving. While some monitoring was taking place through dialogue, I think this is one place that the team still needs to focus on more in their future work.

Principal's Commentary

Through this process we learned the importance of monitoring our progress continuously rather than just at the end as well as the importance of having resources to use for monitoring. We learned early on that we had few data sources that would allow us to look at student progress in the area of problem solving throughout the year and the importance of having such data sources. Through the Using Data Process we realized we needed, and therefore we created, benchmark assessments that would allow us to examine student understanding along the way in order to make adjustments in instruction and continue to move forward. We believe these assessment tools will be invaluable as we continue to strive for improvement in learning for all students.

Summary Reflections

The process of learning to engage in collaborative inquiry around data proved to take a bit longer than anyone thought it would, but it was time well spent. The Data Team worked steadily to learn how to use the different tools presented in the Using Data Toolkit and then shared that information with the staff through grade-level meetings or staff meetings.

Although the team spent close to a year learning the process in a hands-on fashion, the time proved to be invaluable. In the fall of 2005, the Data Coaches put together a three-day Data Team retreat in which they worked through the entire process to determine student-learning problems, possible causes, and potential strategies. To help with this process, the Data Team was once again expanded to include two teachers per grade level to ensure that there would always be a grade-level representative at every data meeting regardless of track breaks. The Data Team also changed its name and is now referred to as the School Improvement Team, since their goal is to use data to bring about school improvement.

Finally, the team has expanded its work with data from mathematics to all subject areas. Using the process to examine reading and writing, they have found that students seem to struggle in communicating their understanding of concepts that deal with higher-order thinking skills. It appears as though problem solving is not only an issue for students in mathematics, but a challenge in all areas. With that idea in mind, the team has decided to work on problem solving across the curriculum in the hope that this will bring about long-term benefits for all students at Katz Elementary School.

APPENDIX A: STUDENT WORK ON "ADDWORM" TASK

Name: Date:

The Addworm

This problem gives you the chance to

■ *use simple rules*
■ *complete a chart and look for patterns*
■ *solve problems*

Many unusual animals live on the planet Htam.

Some of them have bodies that are made of cube shapes.

These animals grow by getting new cube shapes on each birthday.

When the Addworm is born it looks like this.
It is 1 cube long and it has 2 legs.

On its first birthday it looks like this.
It is 4 cubes long and has 8 legs.

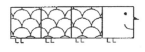

The Addworm continues to grow in this way.

On each birthday it gets 3 more cube shapes and 6 more legs.

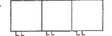   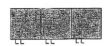   

(Continued)

(Continued)

Name:	Date:

Now try to answer these questions about Addworms.

You may find it helpful to make Addworms using colored cubes.

Use some of the squares provided to draw each Addworm.

1. Draw a picture of an Addworm when it is 2 years old.

How long is it?   _7 cubes long_

How many legs does it have?   _14 legs_

2. Draw a picture of an Addworm when it is 3 years old.

How long is it?   _10 cube long_

How many legs does it have?   _20 legs_

3. How long is an Addworm when it is 6 years old? _19 cubes_

How many legs does it have?   _38 legs_

You may wish to draw it.

Explain how you figured it out. _I filled in the cubes untill I had 3x6 cubes then I counted each leg by 2's._

4. Scientists are studying how Addworms grow. They have collected some in their laboratory. One Addworm is 13 cubes long. How old do you think it is? _4 in a half_

Name: Date:

5. Another Addworm has 32 legs. How old do you think
it is? _5 years old_____

| ≋ | ≋ | ≋ | ≋ | ≋ | ≋ | ≋ | ≋ | ≋ | ≋ | ≋ | | | |

Explain how you figured it out. _I added cubes
so that I could see each cube had
two legs. I counted each of
legs until I got 32. Then I counted
each 3 cubes as 1 year old and got my answer._

6. The scientists who are studying Addworms have begun to
make this chart. Try to help them by filling in the empty
spaces.

Age	Number of cubes long	Number of legs
at birth	1	2
1st birthday	4	8
2nd birthday	7	14
3rd birthday	10	20
4th birthday	13	26
5th birthday	16	32
6th birthday	19	38

7. Describe any number patterns you see in the chart.
_The pattern I see is that in
birthdays the age keeps getting
3 cubes. The leg pattern you x
it with the number of cubes._

(Continued)

(Continued)

Name:	Date:

8. Try to figure out the age of an Addworm when it is 28 cubes long. The number patterns in the chart may help you. Use a calculator if you wish. Explain how you figured it out.

    I went back to the begig of my paper and kept counting until I could get to 28. I didn't and had a cube left. So I counted the cubes again in threes this time and got 9. I thout for a while and tought that made the other cube stood for ½ so its 9½.

9. Try to figure out the age of an Addworm with 50 legs. The number patterns in the chart may help you. Use a calculator if you wish. Explain how you figured it out.

    I drew a body of an addworm and made 3 cubes for each year. I counted each cube by 20 until I got 50. Then I counted each each 3 cubes again and got 8.

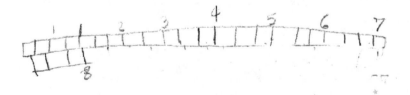

APPENDIX B: TEACHER OBSERVATIONS OF STUDENT WORKING ON "ADDWORM" TASK

Name of Student: _____   Date: 6/10/04

Interviewer: Jones   Grade: 4

Say:

While you are working on this task, I will be working on my part of this assignment. On your own, I want you to work on this task and do your best at it. When you are finished, put your pencil down and turn your test over. Let's read page 1 together, follow along as I read. (Read up to question # 1. At that point, offer no more explanation. Take notes to describe student behavior/action while working.)

Observations:

Now try to answer these questions about Addworms.
You may find it helpful to make Addworms using colored cubes.
Use some of the squares provided to draw each Addworm.

1. Draw a picture of an Addworm when it is 2 years old.

How long is it? _____
How many legs does it have? _____

2. Draw a picture of an Addworm when it is 3 years old.

How long is it? _____
How many legs does it have? _____

3. How long is an Addworm when it is 5 years old? _____
How many legs does it have? _____
You may wish to draw it.

Explain how you figured it out. _____

4. Scientists are studying how Addworms grow. They have collected some in their laboratory. One Addworm is 13 cubes long. How old do you think it is?

5. Another Addworm has 32 legs. How old do you think it is?

Explain how you figured it out. _____

6. The scientists who are studying Addworms have begun to make this chart. Try to help them by filling in the empty spaces.

Age	Number of cubes long	Number of legs
at birth	1	2
1st birthday	4	8
2nd birthday		
3rd birthday		
4th birthday		
5th birthday		
6th birthday		

7. Describe any number patterns you see in the chart.

_____

Asked about drawing pictures with cube
Looked back at beginning
Shaded cubes
Looked back again
answered question
wrote # of legs

began shading in cubes
pointed/counted cubes
answered
pointed/counted cubes
answered # of legs
began shading cubes
pointed/counted cubes
Shaded
pointed/counted cubes
Shaded.. pointed/counted
wrote answer
pointed/counted-recounted
wrote # legs- Looked back at beginning-wrote explanation - recounted
wrote answer- shaded cubes
looked back at the beginning
erased answer - shaded more
cubes - recounted/pointed-
Shaded 1 more- recounted
wrote answer-erased- rewrote
Shaded all of cubes - counted/pointed
cubes -recounted - erased 4 cubes-
recounted - wrote answer-
erased it - wrote answer
wrote explanation -erased part of
it & rewrote. -erased beginning of
explanation - rewrote - erased
ending & rewrote

Filled in 8 cubes-erased
wrote 7... wrote 14 legs
wrote 10 cubes - 13 cubes- 16-19-
wrote 20 legs-- wrote numbers
by 13 - wrote 26 -erased numb.
wrote # by 16 - wrote 32 - erased
#'s - math problem 19/19 -
wrote 38 legs- erased problem
looked over chart again after
writing explanations. Erased
part of explanation -rewrote

---

1. a Drawing it
   b. Went back to 1st page -
      1st- birthday has 4 cubes
   c. Putting 3 more cubes for
      each yr. /birthday.
   d. long pause- I did it this way
      because I thought it was the only
      way of my mind

2. a. Same way (after long pause)
   b. Filled them in until..
      each 3 cubes... until I
      have 3 of the 3 to make
      3 yrs. old.
   c. How could I keep adding 3
      when there was 4 in the 1st year.
   d. When it starts out it has 1
      cube- it gets 3 more-
      its confusing whether to add
      3 more for each year

3. a. Drawing it- I find it easier
      to draw it before doing it.
   b. I counted each 3 again
      for the year. I counted each
      cube having 2 legs,
   c. How to explain it.
   d. Because it's hard to explain
      the way to tell others, you know
      but you can't say it.

4. a. Drawing it again
   b. Then I thought what
      will I do with extra cube-
      left over from each 3.
   c. That maybe the extra
      meant 1/2.
   d. Because there's an extra
      one & its the only thing on my
      mind I think it means.

5. a. Drawing it.
   b. I started to count each cube
      having 2 legs.
   c. How many cubes I would need
      to make 32 legs.
   d. Because that's how I thought
      of doing it.

6. a. Looking how many cubes
      at 1st & 2nd birthday
   b. adding 3 more to 4
   c. How should I try to find the
      number of legs. (TE-How did
      you do it?)
   d. timesing the number
      of cubes- 2 times

(Continued)

8. Try to figure out the age of an Addworm when it is 28 cubes long. This number patterns in the chart may help you. Use a calculator if you wish. Explain how you figured it out.

hesitated
looked back at
beginning –
pointed / counted squares
wrote explanation

8. Try to figure out the age of an Addworm with 50 legs. The number patterns in the chart may help you. Use a calculator if you wish. Explain how you figured it out.

worked problem
off to side
50
50
50
150
wrote
explanation
erased problem
kept answer, wrote
150 ÷ 2

300 = 100 X 3

2 X 50 = 300
wrote explanation
wrote new problem
50 + 50 = 100
erased all problems
+ part of explanation.
erased again + rewrote
Asked if she could draw
on bottom. – Drew squares
 # after every 3 – recounted
squares
drew square underneath
20 23 – 24 • 26 – 28

Once the student has finished the test, say: *Next row.*
28. 29. 30. 40. 50. 60.

Now that you are finished with this task, let's talk about your work. I need to remember what you say, so I will be writing down exactly what you say.

erased 30 – 31 – 33 – 36 – 39 – 4
New row.

Ask the following for each question:
a. **Where did you start?**   *erased all but*
                                      1st row – recounted
b. **What did you do next?**
c. **What were you thinking?**   *add squares to 8*
                                      erased explanation –
d. **Why?**   *rewrote explanation*

8. a. Went to front page –
      I counted 3 – until I
      got to 28 – I didn't
      I had a cube left
   b. I decided it was a half.
   c. How to find out what 20
      cubes showed how old an
      addworm was.
   d. Because that's how I thought
      it.

9. a. Trying to 2 times 50.
   b. Trying to figure out if
      50 + 50 that you needed 100
      cubes to have 50 legs.
   c. I decided to draw the
      body of the addworm.
   d. I thought if I
      drew it it would be
      easier to figure out.

CD-ROM
Toolkit Guide

This CD-ROM Toolkit Guide is a directory to the 29 tools in the Toolkit located on the CD-ROM, including their purposes and the tasks in the Using Data Process in which they are used. An example of one tool, Introducing the Logic Model, is illustrated to show you what will find in the CD-ROM Toolkit. Use this guide to help you select tools from the CD-ROM Toolkit to fit your needs.

Tool	Tasks	Purpose
Best Use of Data Charts and Graphs	Task 5	To help Data Team members understand a variety of data displays and their appropriate use, especially for going visual with data.
Body of Our School	Task 2	To better understand the context and demographics of the school.
Cause Cards	Task 13	To surface and explore a variety of potential causes for the identified student-learning problem(s).
Consensogram	Tasks 2, 5	To gather and display data (e.g., participants' uses of or beliefs about data) from a group of participants for immediate analysis; to introduce participants to the need for data and the Using Data Process; and/or to introduce Data-Driven Dialogue and basic data concepts.
***Cultural Proficiency Continuum**	Task 3 and ongoing	To understand and strengthen a Data Team's and staff's use of culturally proficient language, attitudes, and actions.
***Data-Driven Dialogue**	Tasks 2, 6–11, 14, 19	To provide the Data Team with a process for analyzing data in a respectful, thoughtful manner that creates shared meaning of the data.
Data Wall	Tasks 6–11	To provide a visual focus for the Data Team's collaborative inquiry and display of data.
Final Word Dialogue	Tasks 3, 7	To create a process for structuring a dialogue about difficult issues, such as beliefs and assumptions about race or class that surface during Data Team meetings.

(Continued)

(Continued)

Tool	Tasks	Purpose
Fishbone Cause-and-Effect Analysis	Task 13	To engage the Data Team in brainstorming possible causes for their identified student-learning problem.
***Go Visual**	Task 2 and ongoing	To display the work of the Data Team and make thinking public.
Group Roles	Tasks 6–19	To provide team members the opportunity to experience and practice different facilitative roles that enhance team effectiveness.
Human Bar Graph	Task 5	To provide for a large audience a kinesthetic experience with data literacy (mode, median, and mean).
Human Scatterplot	Task 5	To provide for a large audience a kinesthetic experience with graphing concepts and data literacy.
Impact/Effort Matrix	Task 13	To assist the Data Team in prioritizing and winnowing potential causes for addressing an identified student-learning problem.
Interview Design and Dialogue	Any task in which you want to gather information about a topic or issue from either the Data Team or a larger audience	To gather data from a number of people at one time in response to several questions or prompts.
Introducing the Logic Model	Tasks 15–17	To introduce the idea of a Logic Model using a physical movement activity and a graphic organizer.
Key Concepts/Key Words	Task 1	To help the Data Team create a greater shared understanding of a reading selection.
Levels of Use	Tasks 14, 18–19	To determine the level of implementation of an innovation.
My Culture	Task 3	To help Data Team members think about their own culture and the dominant influence of culture in their lives as a foundation for understanding others' cultures.
***Program Elements Matrix (PEM) of a Using Data School Culture**	Task 2 and ongoing	To help the Data Team or staff identify the elements of a Using Data School Culture, to reflect on the progress toward that vision, and to help determine what steps are needed to reach the vision.
***Seven Norms of Collaboration**	All tasks	To build awareness and use of norms of collaboration as a way for Data Teams to engage in productive dialogue and team work.

Tool	Tasks	Purpose
Spend-a-Buck	Tasks 12, 13, 16	To provide the opportunity for each member of the group to have a voice in making a decision based on majority preference and priorities.
Stages of Concern	Tasks 14, 18–19	To understand the stages of concern of individuals as they undertake use of an innovation and to determine appropriate interventions to enhance use.
Stoplight Highlighting	Tasks 6–9, 11	To focus the Data Team on data that indicate a need for urgent attention.
Student-Learning Problem Statement Template	Task 12	To conclude the "identifying a student-learning problem" tasks by writing a clear summary statement of the problem and the supporting evidence.
Synectics	Task 1	To activate prior knowledge about data and share experiences with and perceptions of using data.
Verify Causes Tree	Tasks 13–14	To engage the Data Team in brainstorming possible causes for their identified student-learning problem and to winnow causes based on verification through research and practice.
Visualizing Data	Task 5	To provide an opportunity for Data Team members to assess their understanding of data terms with a highly interactive activity.
Why? Why? Why?	Tasks 7–11, 13	To provide a structure to help the Data Team probe deeply into their inferences about the data they are observing and to reflect on a variety of possible causes for the student-learning problems found through their data inquiry; also to provide an effective strategy for probing into underlying assumptions.

*Denotes a foundational tool introduced in Chapter 3, "Building the Foundation," and used throughout the Using Data Process.

Sample Tool From CD-ROM Toolkit

INTRODUCING THE LOGIC MODEL

Time

20 minutes

Materials

Handout: TH1—Using Data Process Logic Model
General: paper, marking pens

Purpose

To introduce the idea of a Logic Model using a physical movement activity and a graphic organizer.

Overview

A Logic Model is a theory of action that maps out a logical sequence; in this case the sequence is from the student-learning problem and verified causes to strategies, intended outcomes, and achievement of the student-learning goal. The Data Team uses student-learning data, other local data, and research to generate possible strategies to achieve their goal. The strategies are based on desired outcomes for teachers, students, and the school's programs and/or policies and are monitored for their effectiveness and the extent to which student learning is increased. The Logic Model is introduced below using the Human Chain activity.

Audience

Data Team; staff and community

Use

Primary Task: Tasks 15–17

Advance Preparation

1. Make one copy for each Data Team member of Handout TH1 (Logic Model Example).

2. On two sheets of 8½" × 11" paper, prepare one sign with an identified student-learning problem and a second sign that says "Student Achievement Improves."

Procedure

1. Introduce the concept of a Logic Model by engaging the Data Team in the Human Chain activity (adapted from Killion, 2003, pp. 32–34, with permission of the National Staff Development Council):

   a. Hand the student-learning problem sign to one team member and ask him or her to stand against one wall and hold the sign so that it is visible. Hand the student achievement sign to another team member and ask him or her to stand next to the first person. Then ask the team to discuss what is wrong with this picture. What interventions/strategies might be necessary to make this "line-up" result in increased student achievement?

   b. Have the person who suggests the first intervention/strategy write it on a piece of paper and stand between the person representing the goal and the person representing the problem. As each additional suggestion is made and written down, ask the person to determine where he or she might logically stand in the growing sequence of interventions/strategies between the problem and the goal.

   c. Ask the team members to look at their strategies and organize themselves into any that need to work together. Ask what is missing. Record the responses.

   d. Then ask team members to consider what might happen as a result of each strategy: What will the outcome be? Who will learn or do something differently as a result of this strategy? As team members suggest outcomes/results, ask each person to write the outcome on a piece of paper and stand in front of the strategy resulting in the outcome he or she noted. (If the group is too small, record the outcomes on separate pieces of paper and give them to the person representing the strategy related to that outcome.)

   e. Review the Human Chain by following the logic of moving from the student-learning problem to the increase in student achievement. Point out that the Logic Model helps avoid what too often occurs in education: jumping too quickly from problem to solution. These chains represent the complexity of thought that describes a Logic Model, an articulated plan that addresses an identified problem through a series of strategies; these strategies in turn achieve outcomes, which lead toward the accomplishment of the student-learning goal.

2. Distribute Handout THI (Using Data Process Logic Model). In pairs, have team members discuss the graphic and how it relates to the activity they just did. Have partners share their comments with the whole group. Make the following points in the discussion:

   - Outcomes and strategies are aligned.
   - Outcomes can be teacher, student, or policy/practice based.
   - Outcomes are to be monitored.
   - Changes in strategies are based on the results of carrying out a Monitoring Plan.

Using Data Process Logic Model

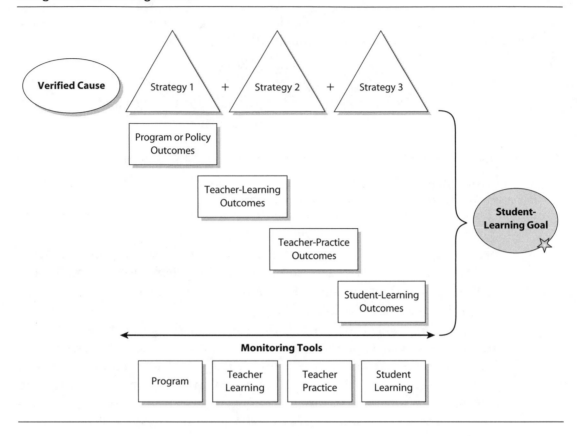

References

Abrams, L. M., & Madaus, G. F. (2003). The lessons of high-stakes testing. *Educational Leadership, 61*(3), 31–35.

Adelman, C. (1999). *Answers in the tool box: Academic intensity, attendance patterns, and bachelor's degree attainment*. Washington, DC: U.S. Department of Education.

Ainsworth, L., & Christinson, J. (1997). *Student-generated rubrics: An assessment model to help all students succeed*. Lebanon, IN: Dale Seymour.

Ainsworth, L. B., & Viegut, D. J. (2006). *Common formative assessments: How to connect standards-based instruction and assessment*. Thousand Oaks, CA: Corwin Press.

Alexander, C., Silverstein, M., Angel, S., Ishikawa, S., & Abrams, D. (1975). *The Oregon Experiment*. New York: Oxford University Press.

American Association for the Advancement of Science. (1993). *Benchmarks for science literacy*. New York: Oxford University Press.

Arizona Department of Education. (2005). *Arizona school report card: San Carlos junior high school*. Retrieved June 13, 2006, from http://www.ade.az.gov/srcs/find_school.asp/

Arter, J., & Chappuis, J. (2006). *Creating and recognizing quality rubrics*. Princeton, NJ: Educational Testing Service.

Arter, J., & McTighe, J. (2001). *Scoring rubrics in the classroom: Using performance criteria for assessing and improving student performance*. Thousand Oaks, CA: Corwin Press.

Atkin, J. M., Coffey, J. E., Moorthy, S., Sato, M., & Thibeault, M. (2005). *Designing everyday assessment in the science classroom*. New York: Teachers College Press.

Baker, W., Costa, A. L., & Shalit, S. (1997). The norms of collaboration: Attaining communicative competence. In A. L. Costa & R. M. Liebmann (Eds.), *The process-centered school: Sustaining a renaissance community* (pp. 119–142). Thousand Oaks, CA: Corwin Press.

Barnes, F. V., & Miller, M. (2001, April). Data analysis by walking around. *The School Administrator,* 20–25.

Barth, R. (2006). Improving relationships within the schoolhouse. *Educational Leadership, 63*(6), 8–13.

Bernhardt, V. L. (1998). *Data analysis for continuous school improvement*. Larchmont, NY: Eye on Education.

Bernhardt, V. L. (2003). *Using data to improve student learning in elementary schools*. Larchmont, NY: Eye on Education.

Bernhardt, V. L. (2003). *Using data to improve student learning in middle schools*. Larchmont, NY: Eye on Education.

Bernhardt, V. L. (2005). *Using data to improve student learning in high schools*. Larchmont, NY: Eye on Education.

Bernhardt, V. L. (2006). *Using data to improve student learning in school districts*. Larchmont, NY: Eye on Education.

Black, P. (2003, April 23). *A successful intervention: Why did it work?* Paper presented at the annual meeting of the American Educational Research Association, Chicago.

Black, P., Harrison, C., Lee, C., Marshall, B., & Wiliam, D. (2003). *Assessment for learning: Putting it into practice*. Maidenhead, Berkshire, England: Open University Press.

Black, P., & Wiliam, D. (1998). Inside the black box: Raising standards through classroom assessment. *Phi Delta Kappan, 80*(2), 139–148.

Bloom, B. S. (1984). The search for methods of group instruction as effective as one-to-one tutoring. *Educational Leadership, 41*(8), 4–17.

Boudett, K. P., City, E. A., & Murnane, R. J. (Eds.). (2006). *Data wise: A step-by-step guide to using assessment results to improve teaching and learning*. Cambridge, MA: Harvard Education Press.

Briars, D., & Resnick, L. B. (2002). *Standards, assessments—and what else? The essential elements of standards-based school improvement* (CSE Technical Report 528). Los Angeles: National Center for Research on Evaluation, Standards, and Student Testing.

Brown, J. H., & Shavelson, R. J. (2001). *Assessing hands-on science: A teacher's guide to performance assessment*. Thousand Oaks, CA: Corwin Press.

CampbellJones, B., & CampbellJones, F. (2002). Educating African American children: Credibility at a crossroads. *Educational Horizons, 80*(3), 133–139.

Carr, J., & Artman, E. M. (2002). *The bottom-up simple approach to school accountability and improvement.* Norwood, MA: Christopher-Gordon.

Collins, J. (1996). Aligning actions and values. *Leader to Leader, 1*(Summer), 19–24.

Collins, J. (2001). *Good to great: Why some companies make the leap . . . and others don't.* New York: HarperBusiness.

Colorado Department of Education. (2005). *2004–2005, 2003–2004, and 2002–2003 school accountability reports for Wildflower Elementary School, Harrison 2, Colorado Springs, Colorado.* Retrieved February 10, 2006, from http://reportcard.cde.state.co.us/reportcard/CommandHandler.jsp

Confrey, J., & Makar, K. M. (2005). Critiquing and improving the use of data from high-stakes tests with the aid of dynamic statistics software. In C. Dede, J. P. Honan, & L. C. Peters (Eds.), *Scaling up success: Lessons from technology-based educational improvement* (pp. 198–226). San Francisco: Jossey-Bass.

Costa, A., & Garmston, R. (1994). *Cognitive coaching: A foundation for renaissance schools.* Norwood, MA: Christopher-Gordon.

Cozemius, A., & O'Neill, J. (1999). *The handbook for SMART school teams.* Bloomington, IN: National Education Service.

Cozemius, A., & O'Neill, J. (2006). *The power of SMART goals: Using goals to improve student learning.* Bloomington, IN: Solution Tree.

Cross, T. L. (1989). *Toward a culturally competent system of care.* Washington, DC: Georgetown University Child Development Program, Child and Adolescent Service System Program.

Cross, T. L., Bazron, B. J., Dennis, K. W., & Isaacs, M. R. (1993). *Toward a culturally competent system of care* (Vol. 2). Washington, DC: Georgetown University Child Development Program, Child and Adolescent Service System Program.

Darling-Hammond, L. (2004). *Collaboration and development.* Retrieved December 20, 2006, from http://www.schoolredesign.net/srn/server/php?idx=228

Darling-Hammond, L., Berry, B., & Thoreson, A. (2001). Does teacher certification matter? Evaluating the evidence. *Educational Evaluation and Policy Analysis, 23*(1), 57–77.

DeCuir, J. T., & Dixson, A. D. (2004). "So when it comes out, they aren't that surprised that it is there": Using critical race theory as a tool of analysis of race and racism in education. *Educational Researcher, 33*(5), 26–31.

Delpit, L. (2006). *Other people's children: Cultural conflict in the classroom* (2nd ed.). New York: New Press.

DiRanna, K., Osmundson, E., Topps, J., Barakos, L., Gearhart, M., Cerwin, K., et al. (2008). *Assessment-centered teaching: A reflective practice.* Thousand Oaks, CA: Corwin Press.

Doran, G. T. (1981, November). There's a S.M.A.R.T. way to write management goals and objectives. *Management Review* (American Management Association), 35–36.

DuFour, R. (1998). Why celebrate? *Journal of Staff Development, 19*(4), 58–59.

DuFour, R. (2004). What is a "professional learning community"? *Educational Leadership, 61*(8), 6–11.

DuFour, R., DuFour, R., Eaker, R., & Karhanek, G. (2004). *Whatever it takes: How professional learning communities respond when kids don't learn.* Bloomington, IN: National Educational Service.

DuFour, R., & Eaker, R. (1998). *Professional learning communities at work: Best practices for enhancing student achievement.* Bloomington, IN: National Educational Service.

DuFour, R., Eaker, R., & DuFour, R. (Eds.). (2005). *On common ground: The power of professional learning communities.* Bloomington, IN: National Educational Service.

Eaker, R., DuFour, R., & DuFour, R. (2002). *Getting started: Reculturing schools to become professional learning communities.* Bloomington, IN: National Educational Service.

Education Trust. (2001). *Achievement in America 2001.* PowerPoint presentation. Washington, DC: Author. Retrieved August 7, 2007, from www2.edtrust.org/NR/rdonlyres/47501795-973A-490A-9345-A03110A9651E/0/AchievementAfricanAmericanveryfinal.ppt

Education Trust. (2003). *Dispelling the myth—online.* Retrieved August 7, 2007, from http://www2.edtrust.org/edtrust/dtm/

Ellis, D. (2002). *Falling awake: Creating the life of your dreams.* Rapid City, SD: Breakthrough Enterprises.

Elmore, R. F. (2002). *Bridging the gap between standards and achievement: The imperative for professional development in education.* Washington, DC: Albert Shanker Institute.

Elmore, R. F. (2003). A plea for strong practice. *Educational Leadership, 61*(3), 6–10.

Fullan, M. (1993). *Change forces: Probing the depths of educational reform.* London: Falmer.

Fullan, M. (1999). *Change forces: The sequel.* Philadelphia, PA: Falmer.

Fullan, M. (2005). *Leadership and sustainability: System thinkers in action.* Thousand Oaks, CA: Corwin Press.

Gamoran, A., & Hannigan, E. C. (2000). Algebra for everyone? Benefits of college-preparatory mathematics for students with diverse abilities in early secondary school. *Educational Evaluation and Policy Analysis, 22*(3), 241–254.

Garmston, R. J., & Wellman, B. M. (1999). *The adaptive school: A sourcebook for developing collaborative groups.* Norwood, MA: Christopher-Gordon.

Garmston, R. J., & Wellman, B. M. (2002). *The adaptive school: Developing collaborative groups syllabus* (Rev. ed.). El Dorado Hills, CA: Four Hats Seminars.

Gordon, W. J. (1961). *Synectics: The development of creative capacity.* New York: Harper and Row.

Grinder, M. (1997). *The science of non-verbal communication.* Battle Ground, WA: Michael Grinder & Associates.

Guskey, T. R. (2000). *Evaluating professional development.* Thousand Oaks, CA: Corwin Press.

Guskey, T. R. (2003). How classroom assessments improve learning. *Educational Leadership, 60*(5), 6–11.

Hall, G. E. (1979). The concerns-based approach to facilitating change. *Educational Horizons, 57*(4), 202–208.

Hall, G. E., & Hord, S. M. (2006). *Implementing change: Patterns, principles, and potholes* (2nd ed.). Boston: Allyn & Bacon.

Haycock, K., Jerald, C., & Huang, S. (2001). Closing the achievement gap: Done in a decade. *Thinking K–16, 5*(2), 3–22.

Hein, G. E., & Price, S. (1994). *Active assessment for active science: A guide for elementary teachers.* Portsmouth, NH: Heinemann.

Herman, J. L., Aschbacher, P. R., & Winters, L. (1992). *A practical guide to alternative assessment.* Alexandria, VA: Association for Supervision and Curriculum Development.

Hilliard, A. (1991). Do we have the will to educate all children? *Educational Leadership, 49*(1), 31–36.

Holtzman, M. (2006). *Public education and black male students: The 2006 state report card.* Cambridge, MA: Schott Foundation for Public Education.

Hord, S. M., Rutherford, W. L., Huling-Austin, L., & Hall, G. (1987). *Taking charge of change.* Alexandria, VA: Association for Supervision and Curriculum Development.

Jerald, C. (2005, April). *Planning that matters: Helping schools engage in collaborative, strategic problem solving* (Policy brief). Washington, DC: Center for Comprehensive School Reform and Improvement.

Johnson, R. (1996). *Setting our sights: Measuring equity in school change.* Los Angeles: The Achievement Council.

Johnson, R. S. (2002). *Using data to close the achievement gap: How to measure equity in our schools.* Thousand Oaks, CA: Corwin Press.

Kagan, S. (1997). *Cooperative learning.* San Clemente, CA: Kagan Publishing.

Kane, T. J., & Staiger, D. O. (2002). Volatility in school test scores: Implications for test-based accountability systems. In D. Ravitch (Ed.), *Brookings papers on education policy, 2002* (pp. 235–283). Washington, DC: Brookings Institution.

Kaser, J., Mundry, S., Stiles, K. E., & Loucks-Horsley, S. (2006). *Leading every day: 124 actions for effective leadership* (2nd ed.). Thousand Oaks, CA: Corwin Press.

Katzenbach, J. R., & Smith, D. K. (1994). *The wisdom of teams: Creating the high-performance organization.* New York: HarperBusiness.

Kaufman, R., Guerra, I., & Platt, W. A. (2006). *Practical evaluation for educators: Finding what works and what doesn't.* Thousand Oaks, CA: Corwin Press.

Keeley, P. (2005). *Science curriculum topic study: Bridging the gap between standards and practice.* Thousand Oaks, CA: Corwin Press.

Keeley, P., Eberle, F., & Farrin, L. (2005). *Uncovering student ideas in science: 25 formative assessment probes* (Vol. 1). Arlington, VA: National Science Teachers Association Press.

Keeley, P., & Rose, C. M. (2006). *Mathematics curriculum topic study: Bridging the gap between standards and practice.* Thousand Oaks, CA: Corwin Press.

Kendall, J., & Marzano, R. (1996a). *Content knowledge: A compendium of standards and benchmarks for K–12 education.* Alexandria, VA: Association for Supervision and Curriculum Development.

Kendall, J., & Marzano, R. (1996b). *Designing standards-based districts, schools, and classrooms.* Alexandria, VA: Association for Supervision and Curriculum Development.

Killion, J. (2002). *Assessing impact: Evaluating staff development.* Oxford, OH: National Staff Development Council.

Killion, J., with Munger, L., Roy, P., & McMullen, P. (2003). *Training manual for assessing impact: Evaluating staff development.* Oxford, OH: National Staff Development Council.

Kober, N. (2002, October). What tests can and cannot tell us. *TestTalk for Leaders, 2,* 1–15.

Landsman, J. (2004). Confronting the racism of low expectations. *Educational Leadership, 62*(3), 28–33.

Lee, C. D. (2002). Interrogating race and ethnicity as constructs in the examination of cultural processes in developmental research. *Human Development, 45*(4), 282–290.

Lindsey, D. B., Martinez, R. S., & Lindsey, R. B. (2006). *Culturally proficient coaching: Supporting educators to create equitable schools.* Thousand Oaks, CA: Corwin Press.

Lindsey, R. B., Nuri Robins, K., & Terrell, R. D. (2003). *Cultural proficiency: A manual for school leaders* (2nd ed.). Thousand Oaks, CA: Corwin Press.

Lindsey, R. B., Nuri Robins, K., & Terrell, R. D. (2005). *Facilitator's guide: Cultural proficiency—A manual for school leaders.* Thousand Oaks, CA: Corwin Press.

Lindsey, R. B., Roberts, L. M., & CampbellJones, F. (2005). *The culturally proficient school: An implementation guide for school leaders.* Thousand Oaks, CA: Corwin Press.

Little, J. W. (1982). Norms of collegiality and experimentation: Workplace conditions of school success. *American Educational Research Journal, 19*(3), 325–340.

Little, J. W. (1990). Teachers as colleagues. In A. Lieberman (Ed.), *Schools as collaborative cultures: Creating the future now* (pp. 165–193). New York: Palmer.

Lortie, D. C. (1975). *Schoolteacher: A sociological study.* Chicago: University of Chicago Press.

Loucks, S. F. (1983). At last: Some good news from a study of school improvement. *Educational Leadership, 41*(3), 4–5.

Loucks, S. F., Newlove, B. W., & Hall, G. E. (1975). *Measuring levels of use of the innovation: A manual for trainers, interviewers, and raters.* Austin: Research and Development Center for Teacher Education, University of Texas at Austin.

Loucks-Horsley, S., Love, N., Stiles, K. E., Mundry, S., & Hewson, P. W. (2003). *Designing professional development for teachers of science and mathematics* (2nd ed.). Thousand Oaks, CA: Corwin Press.

Loucks-Horsley, S., & Stiegelbauer, S. (1991). Using knowledge of change to guide staff development. In A. Lieberman & L. Miller (Eds.), *Staff development for education in the 90s: New demands, new realities, new perspectives* (pp. 15–36). New York: Teachers College Press.

Louis, K. S., Kruse, S., & Marks, H. (1996). Schoolwide professional community. In F. Newmann and Associates (Eds.), *Authentic achievement: Restructuring schools for intellectual quality* (pp. 179–203). San Francisco: Jossey-Bass.

Love, N. (2002). *Using data/getting results: A practical guide for school improvement in mathematics and science.* Norwood, MA: Christopher-Gordon.

Love, N. (2003). Uses and abuses of data. *ENC Focus: Data-Driven Decision Making, 10*(1), 14–17.

Love, N. (2004). Taking data to new depths. *Journal of Staff Development, 25*(4), 22–26.

Ma, L. (1999). *Knowing and teaching elementary mathematics: Teachers' understanding of fundamentals of mathematics in China and the United States.* Mahwah, NJ: Lawrence Erlbaum.

Martin, R. A. (2006). Wake-up call brings a jolt of alignment to the curriculum: Teacher leaders hear the warning and develop common assessments to improve student achievement. *Journal of Staff Development, 27*(1), 53–55.

Marzano, R. J. (1992). *A different kind of classroom: Teaching with dimensions of learning.* Alexandria, VA: Association for Supervision and Curriculum Development.

Marzano, R., Waters, T., & McNulty, B. (2005). *School leadership that works.* Alexandria, VA: Association for Supervision and Curriculum Development; and Aurora, CO: Mid-Continent Research for Education and Learning.

McIntosh, P. (1990, Winter). White privilege: Unpacking the invisible knapsack. *Independent School Journal, 49,* 31–36.

McLaughlin, M. W., & Talbert, J. (2001). *Professional communities and the work of high school teaching.* Chicago: University of Chicago Press.

McTighe, J., & Ferrara, S. (1998). *Assessing learning in the classroom: Student assessment series.* Annapolis Junction, MD: National Education Association.

Meisels, S. J., Atkins-Burnett, S., Xue, Y., Nicholson, J., Bickel, D. D., & Son, S. H. (2003). Creating a system of accountability: The impact of instructional assessment on elementary children's achievement test scores. *Education Policy Analysis Archives, 11*(9). Retrieved June 14, 2006, from http://epaa.asu.edu/epaa/v11n9/

National Council of Teachers of English. (1996). *National standards for the English language arts.* Urbana, IL: Author.

National Council of Teachers of Mathematics. (2000). *Principles and standards for school mathematics.* Reston, VA: Author.

National Research Council. (1996). *National science education standards.* Washington, DC: National Academy Press.

National Research Council. (2001). *Classroom assessment and the national science education standards.* Washington, DC: National Academy Press.

National Research Council. (2005). *How students learn: History, mathematics, and science in the classroom.* Washington, DC: The National Academy Press.

Nevada Department of Education. (2005). *Nevada annual reports of accountability.* Retrieved July 6, 2006, from http://www.nevadareportcard.com/

Nevada Department of Education. (2006). *Adequate yearly progress (AYP).* Retrieved July 6, 2006, from http://www.doe.nv.gov/accountability/ayp.html/

Nunnaley, D. (2004). Test scores: What can they tell us? *Hands On!, 27*(1), 4–7.

Nuri Robins, K., Lindsey, R. B., Lindsey, D. R., & Terrell, R. D. (2005). *Culturally proficient instruction: A guide for people who teach* (2nd ed.). Thousand Oaks, CA: Corwin Press.

Nuri Robins, K., Lindsey, R. B., Lindsey, D. R., & Terrell, R. D. (2006). *Culturally proficient instruction: A multimedia kit for professional development.* Thousand Oaks, CA: Corwin Press.

Oakes, J. (1993). The tracking wars: Is anyone winning? *Harvard Education Letter, 8*(3), 1–4.

Ohio Department of Education. (2003). *Guide to test interpretation for Ohio sixth-grade proficiency tests.* Columbus: Author.

Ohio Department of Education. (2005). Links to *2004–2005 school year report card* for Hartford, Lehman, and Souers middle schools, Canton, Ohio, including data for 2002–2005. Retrieved December 13, 2006, from http://www.ode.state.oh.us/GD/Templates/Pages/ODE/ODEPrimary.aspx?page=2&TopicID=1266&TopicRelationID=1266

Ohio Department of Education. (2006). *Canton City School District: 2005–2006 school year report card.* Retrieved August 6, 2007, from http://www.ode.state.oh.us/reportcardfiles/2005-2006/DIST/043711.pdf

Paley, V. G. (2000). *White teacher.* Cambridge, MA: Harvard University Press.

Pankake, A. M. (1998). *Implementation: Making things happen.* Larchmont, NY: Eye on Education.

Pelligrino, J., Chudowsky, N., & Glaser, R. (Eds.). (2001). *Knowing what students know: The science and design of educational assessment.* Washington, DC: National Academy Press.

Popham, W. J. (2001). *Truth about testing: An educator's call to action.* Alexandria, VA: Association for Supervision and Curriculum Development.

Popham, W. J. (2005). *Classroom assessment: What teachers need to know* (4th ed.). Boston: Allyn & Bacon.

Preuss, P. G. (2003). *Root cause analysis: School leader's guide to using data to dissolve problems.* Larchmont, NY: Eye on Education.

Reeves, D. B. (1998). *Making standards work* (2nd ed.). Denver, CO: Center for Performance Assessment.

Reeves, D. B. (2004). *Accountability in action: A blueprint for learning organizations* (2nd ed.). Denver, CO: Advanced Learning Press.

Research for Better Teaching. (2006). *Observing and analyzing teaching.* Acton, MA: Research for Better Teaching. Unpublished course materials.

Rodriguez, M. C. (2004). The role of classroom assessment in student performance in TIMSS. *Applied Measurement in Education, 17*(1), 1–24.

Rosenholtz, S. J. (1991). *Teachers' workplace: The social organization of schools.* New York: Teachers College Press.

Sanders, J. R., & Sullins, C. D. (2006). *Evaluating school programs: An educator's guide* (3rd ed.). Thousand Oaks, CA: Corwin Press.

Sandham, J. L. (2001). Driven data. *Education Week, 20*(17), 62–63.

Saphier, J. (2005). Masters of motivation. In R. DuFour, R. Eaker, & R. DuFour (Eds.), *On common ground: The power of professional learning communities* (pp. 79–84). Bloomington, IN: National Educational Service.

Saphier, J., & D'Auria, J. (1993). *How to bring vision to school improvement through core outcomes, commitments, and beliefs.* Carlisle, MA: Research for Better Teaching.

Sargent, J. L. (2003). *The data retreat facilitator's notebook, 2003.* (CESA #7). Green Bay, WI: Cooperative Educational Service Agency.

Schachter, J. (2001). Geographical mobility population characteristics, March 1999 to March 2000. In *Current population reports* (pp. 20–538). Washington, DC: U.S. Census Bureau. Retrieved June 23, 2006, from http://www.census.gov/prod/2001pubs/p20-538.pdf

Schlechty, P. C. (2002). *Working on the work: An action plan for teachers, principals, and superintendents.* San Francisco: Jossey-Bass.

Schmoker, M. (1999). *Results: The key to continuous improvement.* Alexandria, VA: Association of Supervision and Curriculum Development.

Schmoker, M. (2004a). Learning communities at the crossroads: Toward the best schools we've ever had. *Phi Delta Kappan, 86*(1), 84–88.

Schmoker, M. (2004b). The tipping point: From feckless reform to substantive instructional improvement. *Phi Delta Kappan, 85*(6), 424–431.

Schoenfeld, A., Burkhardt, H., Schwartz, J., & Wilcox, S. K. (1999). *Elementary grades assessment, package 1* (part of *Balanced assessment for the mathematics curriculum* series). Parsippany, NJ: Pearson Learning Group/Dale Seymour Publications.

Senge, P. (1990). *The fifth discipline: The art and practice of the learning organization.* New York: Doubleday/Currency.

Senge, P., Cambron-McCabe, N., Lucas, T., Smith, B., Dutton, J., & Kleiner, A. (2000). *Schools that learn: A fifth discipline fieldbook for educators, parents, and everyone who cares about education.* New York: Doubleday/Currency.

Shaha, S. H., Lewis, V. K., O'Donnell, T. J., & Brown, D. H. (2004). *Evaluating professional development: An approach to verifying program impact on teachers and students.* Oxford, OH: National Staff Development Council.

Singham, M. (2003). The achievement gap: Myths and realities. *Phi Delta Kappan, 84*(8), 586–591.

Singleton, G. E., & Linton, C. (2006). *Courageous conversations about race: A field guide for achieving equity in schools.* Thousand Oaks, CA: Corwin Press.

Sparks, D. (2004). How to have conversations about race: An interview with Beverly Daniel Tatum. *Journal of Staff Development, 25*(4), 48–52.

Sparks, D. (2005). *Leading for results: Transforming teaching, learning, and relationships in school.* Thousand Oaks, CA: Corwin Press.

Spring, J. (2004). *American education* (11th ed.). New York: McGraw-Hill.

Stiggins, R. J. (2006). *Student-involved classroom assessment* (4th ed.). Upper Saddle River, NJ: Prentice Hall.

Stiggins, R. J., Arter, J. A., Chappuis, J., & Chappuis, S. (2004). *Classroom assessment for student learning: Doing it right—using it well.* Portland, OR: Assessment Training Institute.

Stiggins, R. J., & Chappuis, J. (2006). What a difference a word makes: Assessment FOR learning rather than assessment OF learning helps students succeed. *Journal of Staff Development, 27*(1), 10–14.

Stigler, J. W., & Hiebert, J. (1999). *The teaching gap: Best ideas from the world's teachers for improving education in the classroom.* New York: Free Press.

Stiles, K. E., Mundry, S., & Kaser, J. (2006). *Facilitator's guide to leading every day: 124 actions for effective leadership* (2nd ed.). Thousand Oaks, CA: Corwin Press.

Tennessee Department of Education. (2005). *Report card 2005 for Johnson County.* Retrieved June 18, 2006, from http://www.state.tn.us/education/mdata.shtml

Tennessee Department of Education. (2006). *Report Card 2006 for Johnson County.* Retrieved October 1, 2007, from www.k-12.state.tn.us/rptcrd06/system2.asp?S=460

Tucker, S. (1996). *Benchmarking: A guide for educators.* Thousand Oaks, CA: Corwin Press.

Tufte, E. (1983). *The visual display of quantitative information.* Cheshire, CT: Graphics Press.

Walsh, J. (1992). *Targets for trainers.* Charleston, WV: Appalachia Educational Laboratory and Kentucky LEAD Center.

Weissglass, J. (1997). *Ripples of hope: Building relationships for educational change.* Santa Barbara, CA: Center for Educational Change in Mathematics and Science, University of California, Santa Barbara.

Wellman, B., & Lipton, L. (2004). *Data-driven dialogue: A facilitator's guide to collaborative inquiry.* Sherman, CT: MiraVia.

WestEd. (2000). *Teachers who learn, kids who achieve: A look at schools with model professional development.* San Francisco: Author.

WestEd, & WGBH Educational Foundation. (2003). *Teachers as learners: A multimedia kit for professional development in science and mathematics.* Thousand Oaks, CA: Corwin Press.

Wiggins, G. (1998). *Educative assessment: Designing assessments to inform and improve student performance.* San Francisco: Jossey-Bass.

W. K. Kellogg Foundation. (2001). *Logic model development guide: Using logic models to bring together planning, evaluation, and action.* Battle Creek, MI: Author.

Zuman, J. (2006). *Using data project: Final evaluation report.* Arlington, MA: Intercultural Center for Research in Education. Unpublished report.

Index

CORWIN PRESS

The Corwin Press logo—a raven striding across an open book—represents the union of courage and learning. Corwin Press is committed to improving education for all learners by publishing books and other professional development resources for those serving the field of PreK–12 education. By providing practical, hands-on materials, Corwin Press continues to carry out the promise of its motto: **"Helping Educators Do Their Work Better."**

T E R C

Our Vision and Mission

We imagine a future in which learners from diverse communities engage in creative, rigorous, and reflective inquiry as an integral part of their lives. We see teachers and students alike as members of vibrant communities where questioning, problem solving, and experimentation are commonplace. Such communities focus on actual problems for which there are no simple solutions.

The mission of Research for Better Teaching is to build teacher, leader, and institutional capacity to promote and sustain increased student learning and achievement. This means . . .

Teachers will:

- communicate to all students that they can achieve at high levels
- help students to develop a positive academic identity
- use multiple sources of data to make decisions about teaching
- be reflective about their practice
- provide expert instruction in every classroom

Leaders will cultivate, support, and sustain expert instruction by:

- sharing a common language and concept system about teaching and learning with teachers
- creating professional communities that believe in continual improvement and engage in the study of teaching and learning
- distributing leadership throughout the organization
- developing structural mechanisms and resources that foster organizational effectiveness
- ensuring shared responsibility and accountability for student learning and achievement

RBT will dedicate its resources to rally the courage and commitment of schools and districts to ensure expert teaching in every classroom.

WestEd, a research, development, and service agency,
works with education and other communities to promote excellence,
achieve equity, and improve learning for children, youth, and adults